also by scott eyman

John Wayne: The Life and Legend
Empire of Dreams: The Epic Life of Cecil B. DeMille
Lion of Hollywood: The Life and Legend of Louis B. Mayer
John Ford: The Complete Films, 1894–1973
Print the Legend: The Life and Times of John Ford
The Speed of Sound: Hollywood and the Talkie Revolution, 1926–1930
Mary Pickford: America's Sweetheart
Five American Cinematographers

With Louis Giannetti

Flashback: A Brief History of Film

With Robert Wagner

You Must Remember This: Life and Style in Hollywood's Golden Age
Pieces of My Heart: A Life

simon & schuster paperbacks

new york   london   toronto   sydney   new delhi

ERNS

l a u g h t e

cott eyman

UBITSCH

n paradise

SIMON & SCHUSTER PAPERBACKS
An Imprint of Simon & Schuster, Inc.
1230 Avenue of the Americas
New York, New York 10020

First Simon & Schuster paperback edition April 2015

SIMON & SCHUSTER PAPERBACKS and colophon
are registered trademarks of Simon & Schuster, Inc.

Designed by Nina D'Amario/Levavi & Levavi

Manufactured in the United States of America

1   3   5   7   9   10   8   6   4   2

The Library of Congress has cataloged the hardcover edition as follows:

Eyman, Scott, date.
Ernst Lubitsch: laughter in paradise / Scott Eyman.
p.   cm
Filmography: p.
Includes bibliographical references and index.
1. Lubitsch, Ernst, 1892–1947. 2. Motion picture producers and
directors—United States—Biography. I. Title.
PN1998.3.L83E95   1993
791.43'0233'092—dc20
[B]   93-25608
CIP

ISBN: 0-671-74936-6
ISBN: 978-1-5011-0381-0 (pbk)
ISBN: 978-1-5011-0382-7 (ebook)

in loving memory of
lily latté and fritz lang,
who also came to america

c o n t e n t s

Ernst Lubitsch, rising young director, in an official portrait, circa 1920.

In that Golden Age of Hollywood that everybody's always talking about there were only two directors whose names meant anything to the public and critics: Cecil B. DeMille and Ernst Lubitsch.

— c l a u d e t t e   c o l b e r t

None of us thought we were making anything but entertainment for the moment. Only Ernst Lubitsch knew we were making art.

— j o h n   f o r d

"I'd like to repay you . . ."
"All right, give me a letter of introduction to Lubitsch."
"I might be able to do that too . . . Who's Lubitsch?"

— f r o m   p r e s t o n   s t u r g e s ' s
s u l l i v a n ' s   t r a v e l s

p r o l o g u e

Los Angeles
Thursday, March 13, 1947

The pain was growing worse, much worse, and he believed he was about to die.

The angina had begun just after he walked off the stage of the Shrine Auditorium clutching the surprisingly heavy Academy Award, even as the crowd was applauding.

He knew the pain well by this time, the heavy, wheezing, crunching aggression in the chest that sliced off his breathing. And he knew what it could mean. It might last three minutes, or as long as six or seven, but he could never tell if it would dissipate or escalate. If the latter, it was a heart attack, and he knew that this one would almost certainly kill him. By now, his heart was so fragile, so ragged, that almost any stress or physical exertion, even something so small as hefting the eight-and-a-half-pound Oscar, would deprive his heart of oxygen and sugar and send it into convulsive straining.

He made his way through the backstage area, then the press area, where he managed a tight smile for the photographers. What to do? If he panicked and yelled for help, he might make it worse, might lose consciousness. He arrived at the stage door and decided to sit and wait for Otto to come with the car. He would try to will the pain away.

Later, he would say that the experience was the most terrifying and humiliating of his life. Sitting on the rear steps of the Shrine, with people going back and forth, nobody paying any attention. And Otto? Where was Otto? My God, thought Ernst Lubitsch, I hope I'm not going to die sitting here with an Oscar in my hand.

A few minutes before, Mervyn LeRoy, who exemplified the smooth, anonymous Hollywood machine from which Lubitsch had always quietly distanced himself, had presented him with an honorary Academy Award. LeRoy's speech described the arrival twenty-five years before of "a dark stranger with a rather stern face, a big black cigar, and the merriest pair of eyes under the sun . . .

"He had an adult mind and a hatred of saying things the obvious way. Because of these qualities and a God-given genius he advanced the technique of screen comedy as no one else has ever done.

"Suddenly the pratfall and the double take were left behind and the sources of deep inner laughter were tapped. The housebroken camera learned to stop at a closed door instead of peeking gawkily through a keyhole. A master of innuendo had arrived."

Ten minutes later, Ernst Lubitsch was bargaining with the God he had never particularly believed in not to kill him.

Otto Werner finally made it through the traffic jam that had held him up, and helped his friend and employer into the car. The fast and expert medical attention of Lubitsch's personal physician, Dr. Max Edel, managed to pull him out of yet another cardiac episode.

Ernst Lubitsch was right about one thing; he was indeed dying, but not quite yet. On the night of March 13, 1947, a night set aside to honor his signal contributions to the art of cinema, Ernst Lubitsch had slightly more than eight months to live.

"Who's Lubitsch?"

It's a short question with a long answer.

He directed Garbo in *Ninotchka,* her most radiant performance, her most famous film, and her only successful comedy.

In early, astonishingly fluid talkies like *The Love Parade, Monte Carlo,* and *The Merry Widow* he created the movie musical, and, in the process, the careers of Maurice Chevalier and Jeanette MacDonald.

He made stars of Pola Negri and Emil Jannings, but was particularly valued for his ability to cajole difficult, neurotic performers like Norma Shearer, Jennifer Jones, and Gene Tierney, relax them so they could give their finest performances.

When Marlene Dietrich's career was ebbing because of the rarified vehicles with which Josef von Sternberg had saturated the public, he devised an approach that gave her a new lease on life.

When Paramount Pictures was foundering while trying to escape from bankruptcy, he took over as production head, the only major director in Hollywood history to run a large movie studio.

In a Hollywood career lasting a quarter-century, he was the only studio director whose work was contractually sacrosanct, immune from tampering by studio heads like Jack Warner and Darryl Zanuck.

He crafted entertainments of radiant, rarified sophistication like *Trouble in Paradise* and *Design for Living,* as well as the unsurpassable human warmth and charm that freely flows through *The Shop Around the Corner* and *To Be or Not to Be.*

Years before he made those American films on which his reputation rests, he was the most famous film director in Europe, having evolved from a comedian specializing in rough but appealing slapstick to the creator of the intimate historical epic; his leaving for Hollywood in 1922 created a vacuum in the genres of the epic and the psychological character study that would be filled by Fritz Lang and F. W. Murnau, until they, too, abandoned Germany.

He was a pet hate of Hitler's, who reputedly demanded that a large blowup of his face be mounted in the Berlin train station over the words "The Archetypal Jew."

And, yes, he was the creator of "The Lubitsch Touch," as insultingly superficial a sobriquet as that of calling Hitchcock "The Master of Suspense." But he was so much more besides. For Ernst Lubitsch personified a style and vision that was dying—if, indeed, it ever actually existed outside his imagination—years before he did. Although his directorial career went through at least three separate and distinct phases, with few exceptions Lubitsch's movies take place neither in Europe nor America but in Lubitschland, a place of metaphor, benign grace, rueful wisdom.

What came to preoccupy this anomalous artist was the comedy of manners and the society in which it transpired, a world of delicate *sang-froid,* where a breach of sexual or social propriety and the appropriate response are ritualized, but in unexpected ways, where the basest things are discussed in elegant whispers; of the rapier, never the broadsword. Time itself slows down; a methodical action brings a very slow reaction . . . or nonreaction.

The creative task Ernst Lubitsch set himself was nearly as stylized as restoration comedy, and, like restoration comedy, to succeed it had to function as both metaphor and reality. The Lubitsch tradition of insinuation, of a delicate but intoxicating, self-conscious style would be carried on by Lubitsch's spiritual stepchildren, directors as varied as Keaton and Renoir, McCarey and Wilder, Ophuls and Mankiewicz, d'Arrast and Sturges.

As the critic Michael Wilmington observed, Lubitsch movies "were at once elegant and ribald, sophisticated and earthy, urbane and bemused, frivolous yet profound. They were directed by a man who was amused by sex rather than frightened of it—and who taught a whole culture to be amused by it as well."

For the first fifteen years of his American career, Lubitsch tended to structure his films as conflicts between insensate clods and what Alan Casty called "carriers-of-grace," low humanity mixed with high manners, Molière writing for Laurel and Hardy. Good and evil are almost impossible to find, and no one is ever judged, for the director does not value virtue as much as intelligence. This lucid objectivity is also seen in his camerawork and editing; there is a steady rhythm in even the worst Lubitsch films, but he never tries to build momentum to a frantic third-act climax.

Later, however, Lubitsch's sympathies broadened, his humor gentled, his characters combined both gallantry and goofiness. In the process, Lubitsch created some of the most touchingly complete human beings captured by the cinema.

He invests a good deal of his screen time in objects: canes, swords, handbags, whatever. It is not the objects themselves that are important, but their relationship to the people who claim them. For Lubitsch, objects are totems of character, physical manifestations of feelings . . . and desires.

His was a style based as much on omission as commission—what is unsaid, what is unshown. Partially, this is his way of transforming and subverting conventional movie clichés of storytelling and character, making characters of paper and paste suddenly believable and human, while at the same time rarely relinquishing a gentle cynicism about the world and the people who inhabit it. Perhaps Gerald Mast put it best: "The talent of Lubitsch was to turn the trivial into the significant."

At his very best, from (roughly) 1932 to 1943, Lubitsch takes the basic moral assumptions that fuel the entire apparatus of the American cinema and gently but persistently demolishes them, while creating characters of complete believability and complexity.

To the unsophisticated eye, Lubitsch's work can appear dated, simply because his characters belong to a world of formal sexual protocol. But his approach to film, to comedy, and to life was not so much ahead of its time as it was singular, and totally out of any time.

These remarkable films have been examined and analyzed, but the man who made them has virtually escaped scrutiny, except in obligatory, often erroneous terms. One of the primary components of this fascinating life and what it birthed is how Lubitsch's career is a paradigm of the immigrant experience in Hollywood. Lubitsch was the first established, world-class talent to arrive there; Tourneur arrived earlier, but at a nascent stage of his career, while Lang, Murnau, and Seastrom all followed years later, after Lubitsch had already shown them that the way to succeed in Hollywood was not to replicate what they had already done in Europe, but to make films that fell into well-known American genres with the addition of a European twist, a European eye, a European "take." In short, to be Hollywood's idea of what Europeans were like.

He did all this in an abbreviated life of only fifty-five years. It seemed as if he knew he had to hurry, for, by the time Lubitsch was twenty he was moving in the highest reaches of the European theater; at thirty, he was directing the most popular movie star in the world. He was even in a hurry on the set, keeping up a low, steady hum of genial energy, the director as whimsical dervish.

The man who did all these things, who evolved into the primary exponent of silken sexuality, was the son of a middle-class Berlin tailor. The life of Ernst Lubitsch is fascinating not only because of the intrinsic drama of where he started and where he finished, but for the gap between what he was and what he portrayed.

"As an artist," commented Samson Raphaelson, who wrote nine films with him, "he was sophisticated, as a man almost naive. As an artist shrewd, as a man simple. As an artist economical, precise, exacting; as a man he was always forgetting his reading glasses, his cigars, manuscripts, and half the time it was an effort for him to remember his own telephone number."

Behind the cultured, gleaming surface of the films was a warm, loving human being who never received much love in return; an ambitious man who could completely reinvent himself without hypocrisy, get his way without trampling on the lives of those around him; a director who maintained a level of influence, prestige, and power shared by very few of his peers, in spite of the fact that a great many of his films were commercially unsuccessful.

In the world of Lubitsch films, sex was a given, a game whose rules were invariably understood by both parties, a mutually understood part of the social contract. Yet, in his life, he married two women who could not be said to have his best interests at heart. His first wife had an affair with his best friend, leading to a public brawl at a Hollywood party. His second wife, universally disliked by his friends, considered him personally common but his money attractively elegant, and divorced him after she bore him a child.

Always, he remained shockingly vulnerable, sensitive about his diminutive stature, his lack of physical grace. His personal charm, kindness, and creativity made his coworkers and friends fiercely protective and loyal to him. (After he died, his secretary of some twenty years, Steffie Trondle, spent her life savings so that she could buy a burial plot adjacent to his at Forest Lawn.)

Ultimately, the career of Ernst Lubitsch can be viewed as an artist's attempt to create an alternative fantasy existence, the one that he would have liked to have lived. For this was the secret of Lubitsch's films: they were fantasies of blithe sexuality and emotional noninvolvement, not just for the audience, but for him as well. In this superior world of the imagination, the men are tall and elegant and humorously adept at getting a beautiful lady into bed, and the women are capable of giving as well as receiving love.

Because Ernst Lubitsch put such creative intensity into the creation of this world, he took millions of people into it with him. This is the story of that life, and the work that consumed and defined it.

c h a p t e r o n e

Historians have long theorized that the Lubitsch family emigrated from Hungary, or from the southeastern Austrian empire, perhaps Galicia. But the film historian Michael Hanisch, after analyzing the files of the East Berlin civil magistrate, has confirmed that Ernst Lubitsch's father, Simon, was actually born in Grodno, Russia, probably under the surname Simcha, on August 17, 1852. Today, Grodno is virtually on the Polish/Soviet border; in the mid-nineteenth century, it was deep within the empire of the czars.

Grodno was largely settled by Jews expelled from Lithuania between 1000 and 1500. It was, in turn, the site of several major pogroms in the seventeenth century. By the early nineteenth century, Grodno was part of the Jewish Pale of Settlement, the mandated residence of five million Russian Jews. Yet, for all the tribulations of its people, Grodno was a sophisticated area, possessing its own Hebrew printing press by 1789, nine years before the Jews of Berlin could make an equivalent boast.

Family legend has it that Simon spent a good part of his youth and childhood in Vilna, coming to Berlin only to avoid service in the Russian army. His son Ernst would tell friends a slightly different story: Simon was a military tailor who liked his business a great deal more than he liked living under the czar. Certainly, that would jibe with Simon's arriving in Berlin for the first time in the mid-1880s, when he would have been in his mid-thirties, too old for the draft.

Simon's wife, Anna Lindenstaedt, was born April 27, 1850, in a little town about an hour outside of Berlin called Wriezen-on-the-Oder. Simon's name appears in the Berlin city directory for the first time in 1887, even though he and Anna had been married for some years by that time, and had already started their family. Another factor arguing against a drastically earlier arrival was Simon's lack of a pronounced Berlin accent, except for certain words. He never spoke Yiddish.

Although Simon chose a less glamorous line of work, there was a strong strain of the theatrical in the family. One of Simon's cousins, a man by the name of Morewski, achieved renown playing the Dybbuk for the Vilna troupe, a Jewish theater ensemble. Another relative, Max Ehrlich, was an actor featured in productions such as *The Threepenny Opera.*

Whatever the specific year of Simon's arrival, Berlin had only recently become the center of a unified country. Otto von Bismarck had guided Germany through three wars—against Denmark, Austria, and France—that bore fruit in a new German state in 1871. While Bismarck was a superior tactician, his need to continually arouse the people led him to the short-term tactic of scapegoating, fingering enemies that could only be defeated by a united Germany. The enemies varied. In the 1860s, it was the liberals, in the 1870s the Catholics, in the 1880s the socialists. Bismarck's unvarying refrain of "The Reich is in danger" only emphasized class differences and ideological divisions, and kept Germany a nation of hostile fragments.

But Bismarck's reliance on a war economy had force-fed German industry; in the early 1870s, Britain produced twice as much steel as Germany, but by 1914 German steel production was as great as that of Britain, France, and Russia combined. Between 1861 and 1913, German coal consumption increased thirteen-and-a-half times, whereas Britain's only increased two-and-a-half times. In the space of a generation and a half, Germany became the most formidable industrial and military power in Europe, partially as a result of an astounding population shift: in 1870, Germany's population was two-thirds rural; forty-four years later, the equation was reversed.

Nor was this vast industrialization achieved on the backs of the citizens. In the last two decades before World War I, real per-capita income increased by 30 percent. Incomes of 4,000 marks, the equivalent of $1,000

A very young Lubitsch (far right) on the set of one of the early shorts. With him, from left, are Ernst Mátray, Leo Stein, and Kurt Kolany.

at the time, were taxed at only 4.5 percent; for wealthy people earning 200,000 marks ($50,000), the tax rate rose to a minimal 8 percent. Sales taxes were unknown, and indirect or excise taxes totaled no more than 3 percent. Much of the government was financed through the enormous profits of the state-owned railroads.

Simon Lubitsch had arrived in Berlin at precisely the right historical moment for a smart, ambitious man to make his way. The economist Moritz Bonn wrote about the Berlin of this era as being "new and extremely clean; streets and buildings were spacious, but there was a lot of tinsel meant to look like gold . . . the place was not unlike an oil city of the American West, which had grown up overnight and, feeling its strength, insisted on displaying its wealth."

Berlin displayed its newfound status proudly, elegantly. There was the Unter den Linden, a stately, wide boulevard lined with linden trees and anchored by the world-famous Adlon Hotel; the Kurfürstendamm, with its cafes and beerhalls; the Tauentzienstrasse, site of the Romanische Cafe.

Amid this flowering splendor, Simon founded the tailoring firm of S. Lubitsch and saw it prosper. So did his family. In 1891, after Simon had already started the business, which was located on Schönhäuser Allee, in the northern part of Berlin, the Lubitsch family moved to an apartment a block away, at number 82A Lothringer Strasse. The building still stands, and it was here, in a second-floor apartment, that Simon and Anna's last child would be born.

It was cold and rainy that January; a major strike by typesetters to win a nine-hour workday had recently been suspended without success, and the twenty-seventh of the month marked the thirty-fifth birthday of Kaiser Wilhelm II. It was in this land, amid these events, that Ernst Lubitsch was born, on Friday, January 29, 1892, at seven in the morning. Assisting at the birth was midwife Johanna Francke.

Elsa Lubitsch, Ernst's sister, would remember that when Ernst was born the other children hated him. They were all considerably older (Marga was born in 1884, Elsa in 1885, and Richard, the eldest, in 1882), and, where there had been a tightly knit unit of three, now there was an interloper; the other children were all jealous. Since it was fairly obvious that Ernst's arrival was unplanned—Anna Lubitsch was already past forty when he was born—the other children promptly christened him with a phrase that translates as "leftover vegetables."

In 1896, the family moved to an apartment above the store at 183 Schönhäuser Allee. It was that building that Ernst Lubitsch regarded as his home, one Simon attempted to rule like the autocrat he obviously wished to be. A strict man, just under six feet tall, an elegant dandy—he would never go outside the house unless he was freshly shaved—Simon was something of a curmudgeon and perfectly capable of holding a massive grudge. When still a young man, he had a fight with his younger brother Max and they refused to speak to each other for the rest of their lives.

As might be expected from such a personality, he demanded a high level of compliance from his children. Whenever his two daughters would go out, they had to wear their hair up, "like ladies." As soon as they were around the corner from the Lubitsch apartment, they would take the pins out and let their hair down, but they had to be careful to remember to pin it back up before they returned home.

22

laughter

in paradise

Simon's family would remember him as extremely quiet and reserved, never even giving his grandchildren presents, but with a plaintive air all the more touching for being unexpressed.

"I always felt sorry for my grandfather," remembered his granddaughter Ruth Hall, the daughter of Marga Lubitsch. "He would never do anything like dangle you on his knee. Never. But I would be in my room and he would stick his head in the bedroom and say, 'Do you sleep already?' We would say No, and he would come in. Sometimes he would just sit in a corner while I did my homework. I got the feeling he was such a lonely man."

But not all the time. There was a persistent family legend to the effect that Simon Lubitsch had a taste for the ladies, and that, one time, Ernst even found a brassiere left behind by one of Simon's female friends. Years later, after Ernst's mother had died and he had become a successful director, he told a friend that he was constantly having to send money to Simon for expensive locksmith bills. It seems that Simon's sexual demands caused a heavy turnover in housekeepers. If the housekeeper didn't become his mistress, he fired her; if she did, he would get bored and install a new lock to keep her out of the apartment. If the stories are true, Simon was capable of a harsh sexual calculation his son would never be able to master.

The siblings were a varied lot; Elsa was quiet and placid, while Richard Lubitsch was tall, as good-looking as his father, with a devastating charm. But Ernst took after his mother, as did his beloved sister Marga, whom he alone always called Greta. All three were short, with faces like friendly gargoyles: broad, irrevocably homely, but innately likable. Like her older brother, Marga was immensely charming and outgoing. The family used to say that if Marga was at a bus stop, and it was raining, she would soon have a selection of umbrellas to choose from.

The downside to her personality was a restlessness so extreme she couldn't sit still. There was a German saying that the family applied to both Marga and Ernst; roughly translated, it says that he/she "has a peppercorn in their behind."

In the Lubitsch household and in the Lubitsch business, it was Anna who ran things. Because of her manifold duties, she tended to delegate responsibility for Ernst's care to his older sister Elsa. "Grandmother," remembered Elsa's daughter Evie Bettelheim-Bentley, "was not a good-looking woman, but she was quite a character." At the firm of S. Lubitsch, wholesalers to the trade, the division of labor was simple: Simon, who knew good clothes and dressed accordingly, often in fur coat and derby, bought the fabric; Anna designed the clothes.

Schönhäuser Allee was centrally located, about a twenty-minute walk from the Alexanderplatz, and only a fifteen-minute walk from the Sophien Gymnasium, an excellent liberal arts school. The first floor of the house was given over to the business and was actually two apartments combined. There were seven rooms, with two or three presses in the area that had been the kitchen. The workshop was big, with nearly a half-dozen rooms; one was for storing material, one was a showroom, and so on.

S. Lubitsch employed about eight people, with two cutters working on the premises, preparing the clothes that would be sewn as piecework by seamstresses working at home. Most of the company's business was in women's clothes, suits and coats that would be sold to retailers in Holland, Belgium, Scandinavia, and large department stores in Berlin.

Although eight employees plus jobbers do not sound like a large operation, evidence indicates that it was a fair-sized business for the turn-of-the-century Berlin clothing industry. Overseeing everything was Anna Lubitsch. "Grandmother knew every stitch in every piece of cloth," was the way Evie remembered it. Anna's omnipresence was a partial necessity, for, in spite of his verbal fluency, Simon Lubitsch never learned to read or write German.

Upstairs, in the living quarters, there were fewer than a half-dozen rooms and one of them was for the maid. The boys doubled up, as did the two girls. There was no bath, just a toilet. To bathe, the Lubitschs would attend a nearby bathhouse. Nor was there central heating; stoves did a good job of warming the apartment, except for the bedrooms, which remained unheated because it was thought heat while sleeping was unhealthy.

Like many of their Jewish brethren in Berlin, the Lubitsch family was assimilated and not at all religious. The synagogue was a place for an obligatory visit on the High Holidays and little more. For Richard Lubitsch, it was not even that, for he early on abandoned Judaism and became a dissident, going so far as to christen his son, Hans, a Protestant. (In 1900, there were 92,000 Jews in a total Berlin population of 2,529,000.) Politically, the Lubitsch family was modestly left-wing, usually voting for the Democratic ticket, a more moderate party than either the Communists or the Social Democrats. Overall, the family's specific identity was as Berliners, not Jews.

The only one of his children Simon really loved was his youngest son. His oldest son, Richard, and he didn't get along at all, and his two daughters were . . . girls. But Simon's younger son, recalled his granddaughter Evie, "was his everything, his piece of gold."

"The Lubitsch family was very colorful, maybe a little bit hysterical," she remembered. "Richard blew up very easily; grandfather, the sisters, they all blew up. But Ernst wasn't like that."

Richard was the family rebel; there was usually a fight going on between him and his father, a situation amplified by Anna Lubitsch's habit of spoiling her firstborn. If Richard needed a suit, his mother would order him two. "Richard could spend money like water," remembered his niece Evie. "He was always on the go, highly intelligent, and a little bit bohemian." Anna spoiled her youngest as well; since Ernst had to wear special shoes for gym class, and he didn't want to have to lug an extra pair of shoes around to classes all day, Anna Lubitsch would make a special trip to bring the shoes to him.

The other Lubitsch children were noisy; Ernst was quiet. The other Lubitsch children were carefree about money; Ernst was careful. When they were teenagers, Richard would take a carriage to the theater, while Ernst would take a bus for five cents. Richard would kid Ernst about being cheap, but the frugal young man would counter by saying, "We will see who goes further, you with your carriages or I with my five-penny bus." And, in fact, although Richard completed his education and had considerable gifts both in his chosen profession of medicine and as a linguist, he would often be forced to ask his brother for financial help.

The competition between the two boys extended even to their musical talents. Since Anna Lubitsch had an idea that children should be kept occupied, music lessons were mandatory. Ernst, therefore, learned to play the cello, Richard the violin, but the younger boy would soon grow to be an adoring partisan of the piano, picking out tunes by the time he was five. Indeed, music always called to his soul. He was a particular fan of a bandmaster in a nearby Berlin park. He became so enthralled by the conductor's rhythmic grace that he fashioned a baton of his own and stood back in the shadows, watching and imitating the way the conductor flexed his hands and wrists. "I was still doing it when I came to America," Lubitsch would shyly confess to his friend Grover Jones.

The love of music never left him; there was usually a piano on his movie sets, where he would amuse himself between setups by playing the light classics. People who heard him play considered him modestly proficient but with a heavy left hand. He was not of professional caliber but had a childlike pride in his ability, thinking nothing of competing at parties with renowned composers like Oscar Straus.

Even as a child, Ernst was particular and very punctual; his residual shyness would occasionally be overwhelmed by a mischievousness that would become a principal characteristic. When he was a small child, there was a restaurant near the family apartment run by a man named Steinemann. The diminutive Ernst would burst through the door of the restaurant and begin screaming "Steinemann! Steinemann!!" Since Ernst was shorter than the tables, Herr Steinemann would have a desperate time trying to find the rambunctious child, who was usually headed out the door by the time Steinemann located him.

In the Berlin of that era, boys and girls were educated separately. Upper-class students aged ten or so would enter either a *Gymnasium,* which emphasized Greek, Latin, and the humanities, or a *Realschule,* which emphasized science and modern languages and had less status. (A teacher at a *Gymnasium* would deign to speak to a teacher at a *Realschule* only if absolutely necessary.) Berlin had more than a hundred *Realschules,* compared to only thirty *Gymnasien.* After either eight or nine years, depending on the requirements, a student graduated and was ready for the university . . . or a job.

Sophien Gymnasium was built in 1865–66. Attached was an elementary school that Ernst probably attended from 1899 to 1902. By the time Ernst began studying at the Gymnasium, there were twenty-three senior teachers, sixteen of them with doctorates.

The Sophien offered 550 students (247 of them Jews) eighteen subjects, including instruction in Judaism, Catholicism, and English, the latter a subject that Ernst almost certainly ignored. The most frequented areas of study at the Sophien were law and philosophy. In 1906, Ernst's class had their choice of three essay topics: "Everybody Finds Poverty Bad, Everyone Is Proud of His Fatherland"; "What Is It That Appears Unmodern to Us in Goethe's *Hermann and Dorothea"*; "What Advantage Does One Get from Traveling?"

The Sophien seems to have been the right school for the young boy; Lothar Mendes, who attended the Sophien along with Ernst and would, like his friend, become a film director, would remember that Lubitsch often performed in amateur theatricals, always in old men's roles. Yet the theater was not his first choice. Music was.

Meeting with an unsatisfactory parental reaction to his nascent ambitions, the child made a slight adjustment. He would be an actor! This met with an equally glowering response; Simon Lubitsch decreed that his son must complete his education.

Simon was not being entirely unreasonable; he seems to have wanted a secure life for his favorite child. The life of a musician can be arduous, while Ernst never had the demeanor—or the looks—of a successful actor. By 1900, Simon was advertising his business, with phone number (111-8011), as "An establishment for the making of coats for women," and there is no doubt that he wanted to be able to alter the name of the company to "S. Lubitsch & Son."

Simon's skepticism about his son's physical features could not help but be transmitted to Ernst. With the objective eye of the born outsider, Lubitsch never grew completely accustomed to his looks. Like many short men—his full height at maturity was no more than five feet six inches—he put on weight easily and had a build that tended naturally to stockiness. He would come to grumble that "Although I exercise daily and am little, if any, overweight, I am often described as 'roly poly.' " Years later, when Ben Hecht wrote of him that he had "the dark, mocking leer of a creditor," it struck a nerve; Lubitsch would often bring up the line himself in a self-deprecatory way, under the theory that if you say it first, no one else can say it, which is where the hurt comes from.

In later years, he would gesture at himself and say, "My God, no wonder I look like this; my father sat sewing cross-legged all his life." The implication was that Simon was a half-step out of the *shtetl,* which made Ernst seem that much more admirable for bettering himself so rapidly, but the truth was that Simon and Anna Lubitsch's household was comfortably middle-class.

As Lubitsch remembered later in his life, by the time he was eight he was filled with a thorough hatred of schools because "they tried to mold my way of thinking and compelled me to study subjects that held no interest for me." Indeed, he became so stagestruck that he never graduated from the Sophien Gymnasium, quitting school at the age of sixteen. (Lubitsch's niece Ruth Hall would attend the same school, and even have some of the same teachers as her uncle. For all his punctilious habits, it was clear from the professor's remarks that Ernst had not covered himself in academic glory.) The only certificate Ernst earned was that of a middle-school graduate.

An angry Simon Lubitsch got his son a job as an apprentice at the textile firm of Hoffman Brothers, on Königsstrasse, not far from the Alexanderplatz. Bruno Mendelsohn, the head of the shipping department, attempted to train Ernst as a shop assistant but found that, unless constantly supervised, "he would hide behind the bolts of material and read Schiller or something like that." He was, remembered Mendelsohn, "overcome by the virus of the theater."

Ernst's responsibilities at Hoffman Brothers were to measure, measure, measure and write everything down. But Ernst's bills always had to be carefully checked because the numbers were usually wrong. Simon, who must have feared for his son's future, finally put him to work in his clothing store, but Ernst had no more aptitude for the business under his father's watchful eye than he had had under Bruno Mendelsohn's.

The first week on the job at S. Lubitsch, the obstinate young man enrolled in a drama school that offered courses at night. Clearly, Ernst Lubitsch would not be denied.

The man who would become Ernst Lubitsch's directorial mentor was born Max Goldmann in Baden, near Vienna, on September 9, 1873. Like Lubitsch, Goldmann's early bent toward the theater was frustrated by parental opposition, and he was obliged to apprentice at a trade, first in a factory, then in a bank. Forcing the issue at the age of seventeen, he became involved in a student theater, but, within two years, was engaged by Otto Brahm, manager of the Deutsches Theater in Berlin.

Changing his name to Max Reinhardt, he worked in Brahm's ensemble for eight years. Unlike many directors, he was a very good actor, especially when he played old men. Brahm was one of the first exponents of naturalism, except for the classics, which tended to be declaimed. Reinhardt grew increasingly uncomfortable with these rigid dichotomies. Straight naturalism struck him as gray and dull, while he felt that Shakespeare and other classics should be approached as if no one had ever acted or seen them before. Reinhardt's taste was for a sensuous theater, while the prevailing taste at the Deutsches Theater was for a spiritual, intellectual, more academic approach.

Reinhardt left Brahm in 1903 and opened the Little Theater, where a succession of groundbreaking productions of Gorky, Wilde, Strindberg, and Shakespeare make him the rising young turk of the European stage.

In 1905, he returned in triumph to the Deutsches Theater, this time as the managing director. Reinhardt's first production was Shakespeare's *A Midsummer Night's Dream,* a play about enchantment. It was no accident; to Reinhardt, theater was a bottomless ocean of wonders and magic. His production clearly delineated the style that would make Reinhardt the most vital personality in the European theater until the rise of Bertolt Brecht.

In terms of the physical style of his productions, Reinhardt was a follower of Gordon Craig, especially in his tendency to use indicative light to replace elaborate, naturalistic sets. But Reinhardt went beyond Craig by using the entire controlled space of the proscenium as a visual frame for the author's drama. For Reinhardt, the setting was every bit as important as the music, the actors, or the words they spoke. "The theater," he said, "is neither a moral nor a literary institution," and he set out to put at the center of every Reinhardt production either spectacle or an intense, mysterious magic.

Reinhardt's method of working was to insert a blank sheet of paper between each page of the script. On that blank sheet would be written a complete breakdown of everything that would happen onstage while that page was acted. "Every gesture, every eye-blink, every inflection of the performance was there, not just the attitudes and physical line, but the internal life of the play also," remembered Norman Lloyd, who worked with Reinhardt in 1939.

Under this concept, actors were chosen for their inherent emotional coloring or physical presence, rather than for anything they could mine from the text. At rehearsals, Reinhardt would give a series of running instructions as the actors worked, quietly transmitting his personality to the performer, molding but never imposing. The specifics were usually naturalistic, but they were often rather arbitrary. There was never any declaiming in a Reinhardt production of Shakespeare, never any reciting. Rather, there was resolute underplaying, taut silences and subtleties. On those occasions when an actor wasn't cutting it, Reinhardt would work with him once, work with him twice, then quietly replace him.

There was little room for any invention on the part of actors—even the length of a turn was dictated—but that was one way to maintain unity of style and theme. He imposed, but indirectly, and he never raised his voice. In essence, this was not direction as American actors and directors have come to know it, it was choreography, with Reinhardt the kindly but exacting Balanchine.

Mainly, he loved actors. "He was a gentle man," recalled Hedy Lamarr. "I remember one sentence. I had been talking about my idea of luxury, to travel unimpeded but to wake up with the clothes and food and belongings of whatever country I happened to be in. And Reinhardt said,

'Why don't you try acting?' And that led me to Hollywood, which was only another illusion."

When Reinhardt's method of production worked, the play was the star; when it didn't, Reinhardt was the star, one eminently worth watching. Either way, Reinhardt made the theater matter by sheer force of will and talent; as long as they lived, people who saw Reinhardt productions would speak of them in hushed tones, as candles that shed a glowing, lambent light on the theatrical art. The novelist and playwright Bruno Frank was typical, rhapsodizing over a Reinhardt production of a Galsworthy play: "It was like chamber music. The theater was small and exquisite. You sat in armchairs. The performance was flawless. You sat there, in thrall to the world Reinhardt had created."

Reinhardt's passion carried the implicit message that the theater, that art, *mattered,* a view that all of Berlin agreed with. "A new Hamlet would be discussed at breakfast tables all over Berlin," remembered Rabbi Joachim Prinz. "And the biting reviews of Alfred Kerr—they made a *difference* to people." Soon, Reinhardt was ruling over several theaters. In addition to the "official" Deutsches Theater, there was the Kammerspiel, a small, experimental theater used for intimate dramas, and the Volksbühne (People's Theater), holding nearly five thousand people, where he would produce spectacles like his famed version of *A Midsummer Night's Dream.*

Ernst Lubitsch would spend more than six years with this genius and he would watch very closely. Reinhardt's procedures of casting, of painstaking preparation, of gentle control, were the same methods Lubitsch would follow all his directorial life.

All German actors wanted to work for Reinhardt, which meant that just getting an audition was extraordinarily difficult. For a young man whose only stage experience was in school plays, it was impossible. Lubitsch realized that something besides a direct approach was called for. Despite his father's doubts, despite his sloppy academics, Lubitsch's self-confidence—or his desperation—was such that, late in 1910, he called upon Victor Arnold, one of the primary stage comedians of the era and a man who had been working with Max Reinhardt since the latter's cabaret days. Arnold was a short, round man famed for his portrayals of eccentric characters like Polonius or Thisbe. He also appeared regularly in cabarets and founded a loose association of comic artists known as "The Scandalmongers."

"[Arnold] was a versatile fellow," Lubitsch would remember. "[He] could play a part from Molière or Shakespeare one night and broad slapstick the next. I liked him best in the lighter roles." Ernst would sit in the balcony as often as his allowance would permit and watch Arnold.

Arnold was more than a comedian; he was a brilliant character actor who, remembered Max Reinhardt's son Gottfried, "mined his comedy from the deep shafts connecting his own tragic soul to the eternal one of humanity."

Lubitsch begged Arnold to take him as a pupil. As an audition piece, he played Shylock "as it was never played before—nor since, I hope—and I think he was a little frightened. He admitted, however, that I had possibilities . . ."

The sympathetic Arnold agreed to help Lubitsch acquire the rudiments of his craft—the *real* craft, not the one taught by those teachers whose contact with the professional stage was peripheral at best—and for the next year Lubitsch apprenticed under Arnold while working for his father. Ernst was later to refer to this period as his "double life."*

Ernst's commitment to Arnold and the theater was only increased by the development of what appears to have been a psychosomatic allergy to wool, which made his services at S. Lubitsch, or, for that matter, anywhere else in the clothing trade, improbable. Clearly, his future was not with S. Lubitsch but with V. Arnold.

At length, Arnold felt he showed sufficient promise to take him to see Max Reinhardt. "My short stature, black hair, and that 'dark mocking leer' must have impressed him for he put me to work," Lubitsch would remember over twenty years later. The announcement of his apprentice-

---

*Although Lubitsch and Max Reinhardt both gave the credit for Lubitsch's discovery to Victor Arnold, in later years the eccentric comedian and dancer Ernst Mátray took the credit. According to Mátray's version, Lubitsch was a wardrobe helper at the Deutsches Theater who was burning to be an actor. Mátray supposedly shepherded Lubitsch into small parts and a year's contract with Reinhardt, after which Reinhardt declined to renew and a pitying Mátray took Lubitsch on as an assistant. The problem with Mátray's story is that, first, Lubitsch had no reason to lie. Second, Mátray was in no position, then or afterwards, to impose protégés on Reinhardt, while Arnold, whom Reinhardt regarded as a genius, most certainly was. In later years, Mátray became a choreographer at RKO and MGM, where his reputation was that of a deeply contrary man, as is evidenced by the penciled note in his copy of Josef von Sternberg's autobiography: "If this man thinks he knows anything about Hollywood, he's crazy!"

ship was placed in the Berlin papers on August 9, 1911. It was far more of a watershed than Ernst's dismissive crack would indicate, for Lubitsch was not working on some provincial or second-rate stage; rather, he was where all German actors aspired to be: with Max Reinhardt, at the Deutsches Theater on Schumannstrasse. He was only nineteen years old.

c h a p t e r   t w o

Berlin: an island in Germany which produces the Berlin sense of humor: a sharp, dry, matter-of-fact wit mixed with gallows and laugh-at-yourself humor . . . devoid of reverence or self-pity.

— m a r l e n e   d i e t r i c h

By 1910, Berlin was building toward its apotheosis in the twenties. The landed Junkers that lived on the periphery and the nouveau riche that lived near the center all depended on the city for their amusement, and Berlin never failed them.

"Berlin grew metropolitan overnight," said one observer, "skipping all intermediary phases and catching up in less than no time with the other urban centers of the world. In this headlong plunge . . . it was hypnotized by its own aggrandizement and never had enough leisure to integrate, as its venerable sister capitals had done over long spans of time. The Berliners lived *next* to each other, not *with* each other."

In the years before the psychological devastation wrought by World War I, Berlin was a cosmopolitan city with a very specific mentality: fast, funny, sly, skeptical, worldly, with a touch of insolence—as Marlene Dietrich, also a native, would put it, "snotty." Berlin's Jews were akin to Vienna's—educated people who loved culture and whose Jewish identity was not in the forefront of their consciousness.

It was a city and culture in ferment, and much of the discourse centered on sex. There were the plays of Frank Wedekind, the art of Gustav Klimt, the music of Richard Strauss. "Better a whore than a bore," said Wede-kind. Whatever their sexual persuasion, many of Berlin's citizens took the admonition to heart. By 1914, Berlin had about forty homosexual bars and, according to police figures, between 1,000 and 2,000 male prosti-tutes.

Obviously, Germany was changing; the 1912 elections gave liberals, Catholics, and Socialists two-thirds of the vote. One out of every three Germans voted Socialist. For the first time, it seemed that Germany was looking toward the future rather than the past, a trait shared by a young apprentice in the Max Reinhardt company.

Ernst Lubitsch made his first appearance with Reinhardt in the 1910–11 season, in Felix Hollander's *The Fat Caesar,* which opened August 26. Also in the cast was another future luminary of German cinema, Paul Wegener. On October 5, Ernst opened in *Souls Exchanged,* doubling in two parts. In the 1911-12 season, Reinhardt cast Ernst in, among others, Molière's *George Dandin* (April 13), Shakespeare's *King Henry IV, Part I* (October 18) starring Paul Wegener in the title role with Lubitsch playing Peto, and Maeterlinck's *The Blue Bird* opening on December 23.

On February 29, 1912, Reinhardt began rehearsing Molière's *The Ashamed Husband* with Victor Arnold in the title role and Lubitsch as his boy Colin. It was the first time teacher and student officially worked together. The production, as per Reinhardt's usual methods, entailed six long weeks of rehearsal, and was considered a triumph, but no critic noticed the young man at Arnold's side. The pattern of small, mostly thankless parts and critical oblivion was to be consistently repeated over the years with Reinhardt.

Things picked up with the 1913-14 season, when Lubitsch appeared in five Shakespeare productions in five months, among them *Hamlet, Romeo and Juliet,* and *King Henry IV* parts 1 and 2, all directed by Reinhardt. (All these productions ran for between five and forty-seven performances apiece.) In most of these plays, Lubitsch was billed at or near the bottom, and no wonder; in *A Midsummer Night's Dream,* Lubitsch played Snout; in *Hamlet,* he played the second gravedigger, while Victor Arnold played Polonius.

Another small-part actor in *King Henry IV* would also do better for himself and his audiences as a director. As a performer, Wilhelm Plumpe was hampered by his height (nearly six-and-a-half feet) and his red hair, but he was a nascent genius. As F. W. Murnau, his moody, unified, emotionally devastating film masterpieces such as *The Last*

The more-or-less authentic Tudor art direction of Lubitsch's Anne Boleyn, *released in America as* Deception.

Laugh, Sunrise, and *Tabu* would mark him as the other true inheritor of the Reinhardt mantle; it was Murnau who would fully translate the master's style into screen drama, just as Lubitsch would do the honors for screen comedy.

While Ernst worked, he watched . . . and learned. "When I was a young man in Max Reinhardt's company," he remembered in 1940, "I was Shakespearean straight man to one of the greatest Shakespearean clowns [Arnold]. If so much as one snicker still could be heard in the balcony, I had to keep my mouth shut. 'Ride the laugh!' he would yell when we came off the stage. 'Say nothing until the house is ready to listen again.' He would kill me every time I forgot."

Ernst discovered that Reinhardt's techniques were eminently transferable, for Reinhardt's productions were successful everywhere, from the intimate Kammerspiel adjacent to the Deutsches Theater to the ballroom of Vienna's Imperial Palace, from *A Midsummer Night's Dream* at the

Hollywood Bowl to *The Merchant of Venice* in Venice. Reinhardt's lack of didacticism, his creation of a sympathetic alliance between an author and an audience, would become hallmarks of his disciple's art.

"Reinhardt's theater," remembered one of his pupils, the actor Leon Askin, "[was] geared to entertain, not to teach nor to preach.

"It was an ensemble art. Be it a cast of five or a hundred and fifty. But the smaller casts, that was where the genius lay. I saw his *King Lear*, and he did it small, *Kammerspiel*. The same with *The Merchant of Venice*, with Fritz Kortner as Shylock. What he wanted was a mixture of realism and impressionism."

Personally, the older man was immensely charming and seductive, with an ego that rarely intruded, although once, when Reinhardt was directing a production of *Love and Intrigue*, he walked up to Askin and moved—touched!—a hat Askin was wearing so it would be off-center. "Remember this all your life," said Reinhardt as he walked away. Of course, Askin did.

The theater, as represented by Reinhardt, was an accepted component of the lofty German civilization. Cinema, which would elevate many of Reinhardt's disciples to an international fame he would never have believed possible, was little more than an out-of-the-way alcove in the cathedral of German *Kultur*.

In the earliest years of German cinema, exhibitors were mobile, moving from fairground to fairground. But by late 1904, exhibitors began opening the equivalents of nickelodeons in empty shops; between 1906 and 1914 German cinema gradually developed a firm foundation. Companies such as Bioscop and Projektion-A.G. Union were firmly established. In 1908 alone, three hundred new cinemas opened in Berlin, compared to thirty-four preexisting music halls.

The shining light of this period of the German cinema was the astonishingly vivid actress Asta Nielsen, a Danish émigré who was something of a cross between Eleanor Duse and Lillian Gish, a deeply emotional actress incapable of an untrue moment. In films like the Ibsenesque 1911 *Die Arme Jenny* or 1912's *Das Mädchen ohne Vaterland,* Nielsen staked out the high ground with portrayals that encompassed total psychological desolation and death. At the same time, just for a change of pace, she could toss off a performance of flamboyant, hoydenish, ingenious fun of the sort that was being done in America by the gifted Mabel Normand.

The low ground was occupied by action stars like Harry Piel, whose wildly popular adventure films like his 1915 *Der Bär von Baskerville* now seem flat and ludicrous, showing why most European action stars were put out of business by Americans like Douglas Fairbanks when their films flooded Europe after World War I. (An exception is a 1913 film entitled *Das Recht auf Das Dasein,* directed by Joseph Delmont, which features stuntwork and chase scenes that Fairbanks himself could not have bettered.)

When not distracted by a particularly adult plot or brilliant performance, the German cinema of the prewar period lacks the technical expertise that was even then common in the equivalent American films, with spectacularly overstuffed art direction that makes the Victorians look stark by comparison. A film like the 1917 *Lulu* is virtually derailed by the absurd decor and clothes; at one point, the female lead wears what seems to be the hat of an English coachman, topped off by a peacock feather. Later, she displays a particularly unfortunate tam o' shanter, clothing choices that rather undermine a character who is supposed to be a sexual sociopath.

Gauche displays like this are sometimes compensated for by a penchant for location shooting, where a sense of natural geography often related to the character's emotional states. It was a sophistication usually present only in the work of the best directors working in America, such as D. W. Griffith and Maurice Tourneur.

The nature of the films made in Germany were determined by the fact that film distribution was a monopoly, at this stage headed by Paul Davidson, whose Frankfurt-based PAGU (Projektion-A.G. Union) company had evolved out of a chain of cinemas, and whose primary star was Asta Nielsen. It was Davidson who helped create the idea of making a film a highly specialized event, complete with a ceremonial premiere, all structured around the presence of a preeminent star. It was a strategy that would pay enormous dividends for Lubitsch in just a few years. By carefully spacing out the release pattern of his films, by creating what a later generation of marketing executives would call "want-to-see," Davidson could release a smash hit using no more than twenty prints of the film.

One advantage of working with the Reinhardt ensemble, even in small parts, was the prestige that the position conferred. Movie studios would make notations regarding the home theaters of actors who inquired about film work. In the cloakrooms and rehearsal halls of the Deutsches Theater, movies had to have been discussed a great deal. Among others, Paul

Wegener was very impressed by the money to be made in movies, and he also had concrete ideas about their artistic potential. As, apparently, did his boss.

In 1913, with much fanfare, Max Reinhardt made two pictures back to back for Paul Davidson. For Davidson, the signing was enormously prestigious; he took out ads in the trade papers advertising the "Professor Max Reinhardt Cycle." For Reinhardt, it was a chance to experiment with a new form of entertainment he adored and to be paid 50,000 marks. Unfortunately, according to his son Gottfried, "He didn't take the two silent movies seriously at all; they were a vacation. He was taking his holidays in Italy at this time and the films were done on the side."

The first, *Veneziane Nacht (Venetian Nights),* opens with brooding shots of Reinhardt and author Karl Vollmoller, but the material is a semi-silly bedroom farce that unsuccessfully copes with an unhappy ending. The story involves a professor who falls in love with the bride-to-be of a heavily caricatured German burgher. Reinhardt does bring off a rather nice dream sequence, in which spirits come through the door, cavort around the bed in which Alfred Abel (the professor) lies sleeping, get on the bed, and go out the window, after which Abel's own spirit rises up and follows them.

Venetian Nights offers some lovely views of an essentially nineteenth-century Venice, which is, of course, identical with late twentieth-century Venice. But the film feels like a throwaway, with a slapdash aura about it; at one point, the camera, mounted in a gondola, pans left and picks up the gondolier, who quickly ducks out of the frame. It's a sloppiness Reinhardt would never have countenanced onstage.

Interestingly, Reinhardt casts the film with one or two Lubitsch look-alikes, short, dark, swarthy, Jewish types that he uses for comic relief, but the film is only notable for the odd, graceful movements of Ernst Mátray as "The Bat."

Reinhardt's second film for Davidson, *Die Insel der Seligen (Isle of the Blessed)* is an insufferable combination of *Twelfth Night* and *A Midsummer Night's Dream.* Shot in the summer along the Italian coast south of La Spezia, it's even worse than *Venetian Nights.* Both films prove that Reinhardt, for all his theatrical genius, had no sense of film form, of framing, pace, or how to tell a story using a camera. Worse, his films have no sense of the formal control evidenced by his stage work; except for the ambitiousness of the material, they look as if anybody could have shot them; just set up the camera and run off a few takes.

Davidson decided to open *Isle of the Blessed* first and gave it an enormous premiere on October 3, 1913, to a largely negative press and public reaction. Davidson snuck *Venetian Nights* out much later, and the other two films called for under Reinhardt's contract were never made. Reinhardt's prestige was so great that the egregious failure of his foray into film didn't hurt him in the least; rather, it seemed to the cultural intelligentsia that Reinhardt's inability to wrest anything interesting out of the movies was positive proof of this parlor amusement's innate inferiority.

Ernst's starting salary with Reinhardt seems to have been in the vicinity of nineteen marks a month, about ninety dollars. Lubitsch's niece Evie Bettelheim-Bentley thinks that he was also receiving financial help from his parents, but Lubitsch's fierce expenditure of energy implied that starvation was a mere day away. In addition to apprenticing for Reinhardt, he also began working in cabaret, singing, dancing, climbing all over this fascinating business of theater with insatiable, avid curiosity. "Nothing was too much for him," remembered Evie. "Something always interested him."

One of the theaters where Lubitsch worked getting his daily quota of laughs was in Gardelegen, where he met a young actor named Emil Jannings. Jannings told him that he had run away from home at the age of sixteen, working in barns, tents, or shabby theaters. Jannings was a portly bear of a man possessing a marginally greater equation of genius than of ham. On what was one of Jannings' first days' work in the movies, an at-liberty Lubitsch went along for the ride. Director Robert Wiene, who would later make *The Cabinet of Dr. Caligari,* directed Jannings to jump off a bridge.

Jannings began to walk away, insulted that a great artist, even an unknown great artist, was being asked to collaborate in his own humiliation. Lubitsch ran after him and convinced him to go through with the scene. Jannings relented, and another career made it past the birthing stage.

"Jannings considered this two-dollar-a-day bit work cheap and undignified," remembered Lubitsch in 1938, "but he needed the money." Jannings' childlike ardor in pursuing the essence of a character offscreen as well as on drove many directors up the wall, but Lubitsch tended to be more amused than angry. "When he played Nero he ate so much he gained fifteen pounds," Lubitsch commented. "When he played the old doorman in *The Last Laugh,* his wife was ashamed to be seen on the street with him for she said he shuffled along with his head hanging."

Jannings' physiognomy led him to be cast in heavy, tragic roles even when he was virtually hallucinating from hunger. That kind of desperate need was something Lubitsch could not easily relate to, for Simon Lubitsch was a middle-class bourgeois, and Ernst would always value the accoutrements of a comfortable life. Nevertheless, Lubitsch and Jannings shared a mutual compulsion to succeed in the theater, and became fast friends.

The low point of Ernst's theatrical career, the moment that every successful actor enjoys reminiscing about, if only to point up how far he has come, probably came in London, where Lubitsch was playing in Reinhardt's *Sumurun*. There was no money—Ernst had probably underestimated what he would need for the trip and was too proud to ask Simon or his fellow actors for money—and Lubitsch was further isolated by his inability to speak English. He was staying in the cheapest lodging house he could find and was so broke he couldn't afford a fire. Still, for an energetic young man with an undoubted comic talent, things were bound to get better, and soon.

Although Otto von Bismarck had played off one nationality, one ethnic group, against another with a merciless cold-bloodedness, he never had a particularly expansionist mind; to him, Germany's geographical position and small size made a large empire a needless luxury. Yet, after Kaiser Wilhelm II dismissed Bismarck from office in March 1890, a new and very different sensibility began to define Germany's identity.

Now, there was only Wilhelm, a verbally rambunctious, deeply insecure character with a soul to match his withered arm. One of Wilhelm's primary obsessions was a pervasive love-hate relationship with England, which led him to a determination to unite all the peoples of Europe against the English, psychologically more than militarily. He did not want to conquer them, only to impress them with his imperial might.

When Austria's Archduke Franz Ferdinand was assassinated at Sarajevo, virtually the only country with whom Wilhelm was on good terms was Austria-Hungary. Wilhelm stood by his sole ally as an insane miasma of factionalism made World War I inevitable and gave an increasingly paranoid Kaiser the opportunity to show the world, especially the English and their allies France and Russia, the superlative caliber of German steel.

According to the propaganda that filled the German newspapers, the French were degenerates, the English sniveling shopkeepers, and the Russians animalistic swine. For Wilhelm and his people, this war was a spiritual quest for self-definition through the exercise of a German power that had at last arrived. For the Germans, war was not merely a test of spirit, but of vitality, of life, of the culture being represented in battle.

Even Magnus Hirschfeld, the leader of Germany's homosexuals, said that the war was for the sake of "honesty and sincerity" as opposed to "the smoking-jacket culture" of England and France. In the words of historian Modris Ecksteins, this was a war fought "in an existential rather than a physical sense."

In the Lubitsch household and in thousands of others across Germany, it was obvious that the German high command was planning to go to war long before they actually did. Richard Lubitsch had already earned his medical degree but was required to sign an agreement stating that if and when war broke out, he would enter the army immediately.

At some point in 1913, Ernst began his first tentative forays into movies. There are fragmentary mentions in the trade press of that year of him being under contract to the Bioscop company, at the same time Paul Wegener and Asta Nielsen were working for it. But no films featuring Lubitsch appear to have been reviewed in the trade press.

Lubitsch himself remembered that his film debut was in a two-reeler in which he played an old man. The producer requested personal appearances by the actors at the film's premiere. When Lubitsch found himself before the footlights, wearing a fake beard, he panicked, jumped over the footlights, ran up the aisle and out of the theater. Members of the audience, who thought this was part of the show, started chasing him, which in turn brought the police.

The story sounds apocryphal—Lubitsch was already an experienced stage actor, not to mention an inherent ham, so why would appearing in old-age makeup upset him? Not only that, but his first recorded films, dating from 1913 and 1914, both featured him as a go-getting clerk.

But the fact that he stages a very similar scene in 1919's *Meyer aus Berlin* (*Meyer from Berlin*) that could easily have derived from the earlier experience gives the story less of an imaginary air. (It is, of course, equally possible that Lubitsch was replacing the prosaic, hard-working reality common to struggling actors with a sharper, funnier scene he had invented for a film.)

The first definitive appearance that Lubitsch made was in a film called *The Firm Marries,* released in January 1914. Not coincidentally, Victor Arnold played the boss of a clothing firm, while—also probably not coincidentally—Lubitsch plays Moritz Abramowsky, a clothiers apprentice. The film was a smash ("quite chic, the hit of the season" read one review), playing at nine theaters for two weeks and popping up on Berlin marquees for the next several years.

The film was such a success that it quickly threw off a sequel, *The Pride of the Firm,* shot in the early summer of 1914, but not released until January 1915. But where *The Firm Marries* had essentially starred Victor Arnold, with Lubitsch in a supporting role, *The Pride of the Firm* was indisputably a Lubitsch vehicle—the title refers to Siegmund Lachmann, the first of Ernst's lovable schlemiel characters. It is the first of Lubitsch's films to survive, even though it's not much of a movie—not serious enough for a drama, not funny enough for a comedy.

Nevertheless, the public was immediately enchanted; Ernst's portrait appeared in the advertising of Union Film, the producers of *The Pride of the Firm.* Underneath, the copy read "Ernst Lubitsch's unlimited humor as hero of the famous comedy *The Pride of the Firm* daily causes the audience to break out in laughter." Even before he had been thus encouraged by both critics and public, Ernst made his first tentative steps into direction with a film entitled *Fräulein Seifenschaum (Miss Soapsuds),* shot in the summer of 1914.

Ernst's part of a rough-and-ready hustler in *The Pride of the Firm* was not as singular a characterization as might be supposed. Comedians like Guido Herzfeld and Ernst Mátray were also working off a rough-and-ready sensibility derived from the working-class districts of East Berlin. Certainly, Ernst's new-found success did not tempt him away from the theater; all through 1914 and 1915, he was making frequent appearances, the most notable of which was probably in *The Merchant of Venice,* starring the great Rudolph Schildkraut, which opened on September 15, 1915. Lubitsch played Lancelot, the disloyal servant, to an unimpressive response. "Ernst Lubitsch as Lancelot," wrote the critic for the *Berliner Tageblatt,* "was too much of a good thing."

World War I was to devastate the Lubitsch family as surely as it would devastate their homeland. Among its first victims was Victor Arnold. According to the theater director Felix Hollander, "Like most great comics, Arnold was melancholy and a bit of a hypochondriac." Arnold had made investments in Russian stocks, investments that disappeared soon after the start of the war. Shortly after that, the comedian developed two fixations: that he could not learn another role, let alone play it, and that he would starve to death. Arnold wrote Asta Nielsen a letter asking her to find him a job in films that would get him out of Berlin, where he was assaulted daily by newspaper reports of death and destruction.

In the fall of 1914, during a rehearsal with Reinhardt, Arnold had a complete nervous breakdown. Arnold begged the director to release him from his part, but to give him some kind of office job so he wouldn't starve. Felix Hollander accompanied Arnold to a neurologist, who prescribed rest at a sanitarium in Dresden. Shortly after he arrived there, in October 1914, Arnold committed suicide by slashing his throat with broken glass. Lubitsch, deeply distraught by his mentor's death, was even more disturbed by the perilous circumstances of Arnold's wife. "He gave her all the money he could," remembered Lubitsch's niece Evie. "Nobody who knocked at his door went away empty-handed."

Only a few weeks later, on December 10, 1914, Anna Lubitsch died at the age of sixty-four. She was buried at Weissensee Cemetery in plot number 2135. Anna's comparatively early death established an ominous pattern that would be repeated in that branch of the family. Richard Lubitsch would die at the age of fifty-six, while Ernst's two sisters would both die at sixty. Despite her imperious ways, Anna Lubitsch had been adored by her younger son, and he was devastated by her death. The task of running S. Lubitsch fell to Marga's husband, Max Friedlander, who had married into the family in 1909.

Shortly after the time of Anna Lubitsch's death, the war shortages hit. Soon, there was no food, no clothing, no heat in the schools and, often, no heat at home. Even if Simon and his son-in-law had been able to find anybody to design the clothes as well as Anna had, there was no fabric and no help.

Because of wartime housing restrictions, many families, including the Lubitschs, were forced to move in together. Simon Lubitsch slept on a cot in the sitting room. All this upheaval only increased Ernst's desperate pace, for he willingly accepted the responsibility of supporting his rather large, extended family. Because of his efforts, the family was able to hold on to certain niceties, such as a maid, that were highly unusual during the war.

With a whole crew of mercurial Lubitschs living under one roof, there was bound to be friction. Elsa and Marga would often have sisterly fights, which would force the naturally conciliatory Ernst to leave the room . . . or the house. "I want a nice family," he would say, "with no fights. I don't want to hear that." His nieces, who both lived with him during this period, recalled him as a fantastic family man who somehow never lost his temper despite considerable provocation.

The same could not be said of Simon, who had a temper and did not make much of an effort to control it. In particular, he took delight in tormenting the family maid, who never seemed to get up as early as he wanted her to. If breakfast was not ready when Simon thought it should be, he would be furious and make a great deal of noise. One Sunday morning, after having come in quite late the night before, Ernst was awakened by Simon's loud voice. Fuming, Ernst got every shoe tree in the house and lined them up next to his bed.

The next morning, Simon once again went into his dance. Ernst took one shoe tree after another and hurled them against the door, making a ferocious, long-lasting racket that stunned Simon into silence. Ernst then yelled out that if his father ever again awakened him so rudely he would leave the house the next day. Everybody held their breath, waiting to see just how angry Simon would get, but the old man quietly acquiesced. "The only one who could be excused all the time was Ernst," remembered his niece Evie. "Ernst could do whatever he wanted." More than anything else, Ernst seemed amused by his father, although not if it cost him a night's sleep.

The pace must have been frantic. Mornings, Ernst might be rehearsing at the Deutsches Theater, and playing in the evening at the Volksbühne. After a performance, or when he wasn't cast in a show, he was working at one cabaret or another. When he wasn't rehearsing, or planning one of the practical jokes for which he became renowned within the Reinhardt company, he was filming. If he didn't have time for lunch, Evie, accompanied by the maid, would troop backstage carrying a sandwich and a thermos full of coffee or chocolate for her uncle. While the young girl gaped at the glamour and bustle of backstage, Ernst, in between gulps of food, would tease her about her problematic relationship with one of her teachers. "I saw Miss Brunermann today," he would say. "I think you are not a good girl."

He was a man in incessant motion. "In those days," he would remember, "any actor who had the chance did pictures in the daytime and plays at night . . . if he had the stamina. I did." He even came up with a blackface cabaret character called Black Moritz. Lubitsch would blacken his face at home, then take the bus to the cabaret.

Eventually, Simon Lubitsch had to close his firm because there was no material with which to make clothes. Evie Bettelheim's father, a soldier, even had to bring a coat home on furlough and have his wife alter it to serve as a coat for Evie. For a while, Simon Lubitsch still had money to buy meat for his family on the black market. He told his children and grandchildren that it was horse meat, but they knew better; it was really cat.

The war was becoming a devastating ordeal for Germany, and the citizens reacted accordingly. One day, the radical playwright Ernst Toller, on leave from the army, was wandering in Munich when he saw a raging mob. Someone had heard two women speaking French, and they had immediately been surrounded and beaten. The women had protested that they were good Germans, but they had still been beaten and might have been killed if the police had not arrived to take them away.

Ernst Lubitsch managed to avoid being drafted because, in the Germany of that period, children carried their father's nationality; Simon was Russian, therefore Ernst was Russian, and Russians could not serve in the German armed forces. For that matter, neither could they be doctors, but Richard Lubitsch, who had already made his career choice, had a powerful friend who pulled some strings and got his citizenship changed.

Lubitsch's screen character was seemingly formed instantaneously; short films that he made in 1914 like *The Pride of the Firm* and *Miss Piccolo* show him breezing through with complete assurance, indulging in breezy slapstick leavened with occasional winks at the camera. At first, he appeared in and directed only comedies, because, as he sardonically explained, "the dramatic pictures of that time were so silly, it was much more honest to make comedies."

The archetypal Lubitsch performance can be observed in *Schuhpalast Pinkus (Shoe Salon Pinkus)*, a 1916 release which he directed as well as starred in (on the basis of the surviving films, Lubitsch was always a better actor for himself than for any other director). Incongruously, Lubitsch begins the film by playing Sally Pinkus as a schoolboy. Sally the youth is the matrix for Sally the man: lecherous, no more honest than he has to be, and totally indifferent to the world's expectations. When he tickles girls under the chin, his tongue darts out lasciviously and, apparently, involuntarily. When he buys an ice-cream sandwich, he licks all the way around the sides. Lubitsch, at the age of twenty-four, looks far too old to convincingly play a high school student, which adds a further touch of the grotesque to the proceedings.

Sally is expelled from school for cheating on a test, and goes to work as a shoe store clerk, but is fired for making advances to the owner's daughter. Hired at a fashionable salon, he is again fired, this time for tickling the foot of an attractive customer.

Clearly, Sally is a horny cartoon, but he is a smart horny cartoon. When a vain customer rejects all the shoes the boss shows her because they are too large, Sally writes the number of a smaller size over the correct size. The customer's ego assuaged, she buys the shoes and Sally is reinstated. He's a German Duddy Kravitz, full of irrepressible chutzpah. When the owner of the shoe salon hires him, Pinkus smiles and says "I can only congratulate you." The pluck and assurance of the Jewish character are fairly typical of pre-Fascist Berlin, but the actor's speed and gaiety are surprising.

Sally and the customer, a successful dancer, begin seeing each other, and she volunteers to finance him in his own store. Faced with a genuine opportunity, Sally turns Shoe Salon Pinkus into a success. (Sally is a dictatorial, domineering boss, and one of the people he harasses is a young screenwriter/actor named Hans Kräly, who would become his closest collaborator for the next fourteen years.) Sally ends up succeeding in business and in love, winning the hand of his benefactress, all on his own terms.

Sally Pinkus is just one of several names applied to the character Ernst had played, with one exception, in all his films since 1914. Whether his name was Moritz or Sally, he is World War I Berlin's answer to the presumptuous, unethical, overtly Jewish Sammy Glick, and, like Sammy Glick, Lubitsch's performances have made a lot of people very uneasy ever since. Certainly, Nazi critics salivated with glee; a Dr. Kalbus claimed that the congenital effrontery displayed by Lubitsch in these early comedies was "extraneous to the German race." But even later generations would be bothered by Ernst's exuberance, as if by inhabiting a stock character he had somehow called down the fires of heaven on German Jews.

Andrew Sarris's appraisal is typical: "His performances are broad, abrasive and, by today's standards, virtually anti-Semitic. The Jew is shown to be cunning, grasping, shrewd and lecherous as he lumbers through life with maniacal ambitions . . . there is an overbearing presumption in the eyes and an insinuating sensuality in the lips, combined with an overall lack of charm and grace."

These issues came up at the time as well; in a 1916 interview, Ernst defended his use of Jewish humor by saying "Jewish humor wherever it appears is sympathetic and artistic, and it plays such a large role everywhere that it would be ridiculous not to include it in cinema."

Certainly, there's more to Lubitsch's comic character than his critics are prepared to acknowledge. It should not be overlooked that Sally owes a great deal to beloved stock characters from Berlin's cabaret culture. True, he has a killer's instinct for the main chance, but there is something heartening about his calculated insolence, his refusal to acknowledge the fact that many of his coworkers laugh at him, his persistent unwillingness to be at the servile beck and call of every customer who walks in; clearly, he's a comic exaggeration of Ernst's own impatience at the firm of S. Lubitsch.*

Absent all these contexts, all we can see is a grinning comic gargoyle of negative comic character traits, traits that quickly brought Ernst the recognition that had eluded him at the Deutsches Theater.

By 1915, Lubitsch had attained sufficient renown to make the equivalent of special guest appearances in the films of others, such as Max Mack's *Robert und Bertram,* a dire, alleged comedy featuring the low-comedy Bavarian equivalents of Abbott and Costello. Although Lubitsch gets third billing, he has what amounts to a cameo that spins off his already established aggressive sexuality. He makes his entrance staggering out of a door in an evident postcoital daze, followed by an adoring young girl. When she is spirited off by the remarkably unfunny title characters, he plots his comic revenge.

It's a typical Lubitsch performance: cocky, directly establishing his empathetic presence despite the surrounding desolation. Although he had already directed himself and others quite well, Lubitsch was here working for a filmmaker of demonstrably shallower gifts, a mistake probably attributable to his compulsive work habits.

Shortly after *Robert und Bertram,* Ernst grew restless with the rut he felt he was digging for himself. "Like every comedian, I longed to play a straight leading man, a sort of 'bon vivant' role," he would write in 1947. The result was a film he remembered as carrying the unpromising title of *Als Ich Tot War (When I Was Dead)* which is probably the film released as *Wie Ich Ermordet Wurde (How I Was Murdered).* Under any title, the film is lost, as are most of Lubitsch's early acting appearances. As Lubitsch would

47

*Sally was also the name of one of Lubitsch's uncles, his mother's only brother, a man who occupied the unenviable but inarguable position of family failure. Uncle Sally was a hustler, a gambler, and not a very good one; most of the time he was supported by his sisters. It's entirely possible that Sally Pinkus and his spiritual successors are the equivalent of in-jokes, but with happier endings than real life usually has.

ruefully remember, the film's failure was predictible. "Had I looked in my mirror, I could have realized all that in advance," he would say in 1921.

"This picture," he wrote the critic Herman Weinberg, "was a complete failure as the audiences were unwilling to accept me as a straight leading man. I decided to switch back again to the kind of parts which had brought me my first success . . ." The pragmatic willingness to follow the audience's reaction is instructive. Clearly, he felt that at this stage of his career, he had to sublimate his own instincts to those of his audience; in later years, he would be considerably more independent, persisting in making the kinds of films he liked in spite of an often indifferent commercial reception.

All right; it would be back to comedy, to recoup the ground he had lost. On May 15, 1915, a film trade paper noted that "well-known film actor Ernst Lubitsch, about whom we have good memories . . . has signed a new contract with [Union] film . . . We all await his films with a very lively interest." A month later, an advertisement told theater owners to be "sure that you have the series of films in one act with Ernst Lubitsch, the indestructible humorist of the screen . . . the amount of laughter is colossal." Lurking in his fertile brain was a comic theory that seemed to have possibilities. The central idea would be, as he put it, to "develop something big out of something not so big."

Although by 1915 Ernst had attained a certain status in the world of film, Reinhardt was not jealous. In fact Lubitsch's mentor was giving him bigger parts. Lubitsch was fifth-billed in Goethe's *The Fair at Plundersweilern* (May 21); in Reinhardt's 1916 production of *The Green Flute* (April 26) he was billed third, while he played Kostylew in a new production of Gorky's *The Lower Depths* (October 7).

Shoe Salon Pinkus jump-started Ernst's stalled career. It opened in the early summer of 1916 at two Berlin theaters. After eight days, it had been seen by 10,872 people; a week after that, it opened in six more theaters. In Ernst's interview in *Kinematograph* in 1916, his first with the trade press, he is characterized as a "small, lively, still-youthful man." The article reports that he never has any free time, and is always embarking on new plans, thoughts, and works. Lubitsch refused to discuss the art of the film, because, he said, he already had enough earnestness in his first name.

A month after *Shoe Salon Pinkus* opened, Ernst was playing in a combination film and stage show at the Tauentzien Palast. The show was called *Der Schwarze Moritz (Black Moritz)*, with Ernst starring as his blackface character. For the next year, he turned out a series of one- and two-reel comedies, but he also took the opportunity to play a plum part for another director.

In Edmund Edel's *Doktor Satansohn* (1916) Lubitsch plays the devil, complete with a gray-flecked goatee. Lubitsch's devil is a true imp of the perverse, with lots of eyebrow-waggling and handrubbing, malevolent and mischievous. While undeniably "busy"—the stock Jewish gestures by which he defines the character, complete with head-tilting and hand-wringing, mark him as the kind of actor that the mature director Lubitsch would never have hired—Ernst provides the only spark of life in the otherwise stodgy film. While he was never a versatile actor, Lubitsch, when correctly cast, was highly effective, and here he plays the devil with the same glint in his eye that he directed Laird Cregar to display in *Heaven Can Wait,* his last masterpiece, more than twenty-five years later.

While Ernst was assuming control of his film career, his stage career suffered a setback. His opening in *The Lower Depths* on October 7, 1916, ended any ambitions that Ernst might have had to be regarded as a successor to Victor Arnold. Ernst was playing the same part that Victor Arnold had drawn raves for, but Fritz Engel, the critic for the *Berliner Tageblatt,* wrote that "Ernst Lubitsch . . . is not quite a replacement for Victor Arnold."

It must have seemed a propitious time to walk away, with movies obviously offering more opportunity and money, if not prestige. Besides, Lubitsch must have known for a long time that Reinhardt's talent was essentially dramatic and his own talent was essentially comic. After two more productions for Reinhardt (*The Miser,* opening on April 16, 1917, and Tolstoy's *The Living Corpse,* opening five months later, on September 25), Lubitsch left the Deutsches Theater.

A careful man like Lubitsch would not have cut himself loose from his foundations unless he was sure that his film career would extend past haphazard comic one-reelers. It was a big move for an actor, even if he was being extolled in advertisements for Union film as exemplifying "Exuberance, wit, and humor. Who could better embody these qualities than Ernst Lubitsch, the never-tiring creator and actor of comical quid pro quos."

He had gotten all there was to get from Max Reinhardt. It was time to strike out on his own, and it could not have been entirely accidental that he chose to concentrate on the field where Reinhardt had his only conspicuous failure.

· · ·

An event of primary importance to both German film and Lubitsch occurred in November, 1917, with the founding of the Universum Film Aktien Gesellschaft, or UFA, a successor to an educational and propaganda service that the German army began in the early part of 1917. UFA's capital of 20 million marks—the rough equivalent of a million pounds sterling—was in part (8 million marks) supplied by the Reich, with the rest being raised by investors as varied as the Hamburg-America Line, the Bank of Dresden, and, representing Silesian heavy industry, Prince Henkel von Donnersmarck. Leading German companies like Projektion-A.G. Union and Messter were absorbed into UFA, which also took over the German assets of Nordisk, and controlled the largest German chain of cinemas.

With the companies came their contract artists; Davidson's company brought Lubitsch, Hans Kräly, and a young actress named Pola Negri to UFA. Of the important companies, only Deulig, which was affiliated with the brilliant producer Erich Pommer, remained outside the UFA umbrella, but it too would be absorbed by the early 1920s.

In addition to studios at Tempelhof and Neubabelsberg, UFA controlled a hundred regional theaters and ten of the best theaters in Berlin. They acquired cinemas in Spain, Holland, Switzerland, and Scandinavia, and the company's acquisition of the assets of Nordisk Film and Sascha Film gave them a serious competitive edge in Denmark and Austria as well. The deeply fragmented German film industry was on its way to being centralized. UFA immediately began construction on a flagship theater, the UFA-Palast am Zoo, opening in October 1919, "towering like a beacon in the busy traffic of the Potsdamer Platz."

Competition was essentially passé; with production centralized, those films and filmmakers deemed worthy of support had access to far greater resources than they ever could have had before. "The founding of UFA," wrote a German journalist, "marks the first step in the creation of a young and flourishing film industry. It signals the gathering of forces and the forging of weapons in the struggle for the world market." It all came down, he added ominously, if slightly incoherently, to "one word: the will to power."

Serendipitously, while all this was going on, Ernst began to tentatively move toward his artistic maturity with the November 1917 release of *Wenn Vier dasselbe tun (When Four Do the Same)*. It's a key transitional work, away from caricatured situations and toward genuine, complicated emotions in a real, painstakingly sketched-in environment. Lubitsch even indicates his own pleasure with the film by offering a shot of himself smiling benevolently in his directorial credit.

The story (written by Lubitsch and Erich Schonfelder) posits Emil Jannings as a widower whose daughter (Ossi Oswalda) is in love with a clerk (Lubitsch) in a bookshop owned by Jannings' girlfriend. Part of the film's strength derives from the unusually strong cast. Jannings' pompous middle-aged (at the time, he was only thirty-five) burgher is a dry run for his schoolmaster in *The Blue Angel,* and the actor seized on the character's underlying reality. "I can't describe how I tortured myself with this role," the actor recalled in his autobiography. "I wanted him to maintain his human characteristics after he wandered from the path. Because this kind of motivation was unknown in films at this point, my role was received with great accolades."

When Four Do the Same offers much more simple humanity than Ernst's previous films. Except for the technical stolidity—there was, after all, a war on—the film is sufficiently sophisticated emotionally to have been made ten years later. Take, for instance, a ball sequence, in which each of the principals discovers their love. Afterward, Lubitsch shows us each of the four people alone in their room, each dancing with joy, each in their own way—Jannings with a stiff little waltz, Ossi with flamboyant exhilaration, and so on.

Lubitsch unerringly creates a picture of the life of the *petit-bourgeoisie,* their insistence on the primacy of their pride, their emphasis on their dignity, their essential *Höflichkeit* (courteousness). It all looks forward to *The Shop Around the Corner,* not in specific plot, but in milieu, the general feeling of affection the picture generates for its characters.

Maturity of theme was still accompanied by a requisite playfulness. *Ich Mochte kein Mann Sein (I Wouldn't Want to Be a Man),* released in October 1918, is a brisk trip through the world of sexual role-reversal á la *Victor/ Victoria.* Ossi (Oswalda) enjoys the pleasures of life—playing cards, smoking, and drinking, all, according to her uncle and governess, traits unbecoming a lady. She is therefore forbidden from doing all the things men do in public and women do in private. Ossi decides to try life as a man and gets dressed up in drag for a night on the town.

It turns out there are drawbacks; she can't knot a tie to save her life, she has to give up her streetcar seat to women, men are far less respectful of each other's person than women are, and females prove to be nearly as crude in their attentions as men. At a ball, she sees her guardian, Dr. Kersten, who is promptly jilted by his date. Ossi and Kersten end up getting drunk together and, on the way home, they kiss—and not in a particularly comradely way—several times.

Getting their destinations crossed, each ends up at the other's house and in the other's bed. Once her true identity is revealed, and Kersten realizes why he was so drawn to this young man during the cab ride the night before, they meet halfway . . . on a bed. As they embrace, she tells him "I'll cut you down to size" and, finally, "I wouldn't want to be a man!"

Lubitsch's direction plays all the gender confusion for merry farce, although he would seem to have missed a few laughs by not having Kersten show more confusion over his slightly lingering kisses with what he believes to be a young man. Still, *I Wouldn't Want to Be a Man* is one of Lubitsch's most notable early achievements, not just because it indicates the director's native exuberance, but because of the pungent, teasingly sexual premise, and all without Lubitsch having to maintain a presence as an actor. The director's communicative skills were expanding just as surely as his success.

Unhappily, *I Wouldn't Want to Be a Man* was promptly followed by one of his least notable early achievements. *The Eyes of the Mummy Ma (Die Augen der Mummie Ma)* is a very rough rewrite of Rider Haggard's *She* combined with *Svengali,* emphasis on the latter. It was Ernst's most lavish picture to date. "Actors were hired regardless of cost," asserted Emil Jannings. "The script called for expensive props, among them palm trees and limestone mountains."

The Eyes of the Mummy Ma is Lubitsch's stab at the Far Eastern exotica that would pay rich dividends for Fritz Lang and Joe May, but it lacks their hysterical panache; Ernst plays the silly plot for romance rather than thrills. There are some good touches—a lantern that careens wildly during a fight, fitfully illuminating the struggle; a subtle tracking shot as Emil Jannings exerts his hypnotic power over Pola Negri—but there are just as many odd absurdities: Negri awkwardly struggling to haul herself on to a horse, Harry Liedtke struggling to lift Negri and almost failing. Ernst's staging and blocking lack the fluidity of the comedies that had been animated by his own vigorous sense of humor or the presence of Ossi Oswalda.

The Eyes of the Mummy Ma was an experiment with inappropriate material that would rarely recur. Ernst wanted to be more than a comedy director, just as he had wanted to be more than a comedian, and he was working his way through other genres to better define his talents. Clearly, exotic melodrama was out. But that left many other tantalizing possibilities.

After Reinhardt, there was still one more stage appearance. Lubitsch opened on October 1, 1918, in a review at the Apollo Theater promisingly entitled *The Decline of the World*. The second act finale involved the entire company assembling on the stage and singing a patriotic ode climaxing in "Germany must win, Germany can win, Germany *will* win."

One night in November, Lubitsch did his show, went home, and woke up to find that Germany had not won; Germany had lost. Everybody was bewildered, especially the revue's producer, who had to come up with a new ending. After what Lubitsch remembered as an emergency rehearsal, the hortatory anthem was replaced by a comedy sketch which Ernst played in front of a monkey cage.

On November 8, Lubitsch and Negri attended a press preview of their new picture, *Carmen*. "There was applause at my first appearance," remembered Negri. "Over it and lingering for just a moment after, I heard a faint sound in the distance . . . gunfire." But the audience, apparently deeply engrossed in the picture, didn't seem to hear anything. Negri began to think she was hallucinating. She turned to Lubitsch and asked if he heard what she heard. "Yes, shhh," he snapped. "There's nothing anybody can do. Watch the picture."

The Kaiser abdicated the next day. That night and for the next several nights, all movie, cabaret, and burlesque performances were canceled. More than 1,773,000 Germans had been killed in the war that claimed at least 8.5 million dead. Four million more Germans were wounded. The armistice that was hammered out tried to encompass the idealism of Woodrow Wilson, the revenge mandated by Clemenceau, and the cool political pragmatism of David Lloyd George. It pleased no one, least of all the Germans, who were obliged to shoulder a moral guilt they didn't feel.

The government was handed to the Social Democrats, who had been advocating revolutionary change for the last fifty years. Confronted with power instead of rhetorical dreams, the Social Democrats lost their nerve and decided to cooperate with the monarchistic military and social bureaucracies. A new constitution was drafted that minimized any meaningful political or economic change. Thus, the right wing still had access to power, while the left wing was alienated.

The fiasco of the war drove German intellectuals from their study tables. Suddenly, to leave unquestioned the tenets of yesterday, today, and tomorrow seemed both intellectually and socially irresponsible. Some found themselves drawn to radical politics, one absolute, incorruptible truth which relegated all other factors to a subservient position; others believed that the time was ripe for a new German spirit, based in religion. Returning German soldiers were startled by the changes in Berlin, especially in its popular culture as represented by "Jewish" films like Victor Janson's *The Yellow Ticket.*

Of course, there was no money. As late as the spring of 1919, the British maintained their blockade of Germany, where 750,000 deaths were attributable to malnutrition. Maids in hotels were happy to receive their tips in chocolate; taxi drivers took bread in lieu of money. Potatoes were rationed at four pounds a week, and meat was doled out at the rate of a half a pound per week per person. Clothing was impossible to obtain and the purchase of something as minor as a pair of socks required a permit.

Ernst was absolutely supporting the family. The loss of Simon's wife and business had caused Simon to recede to a level of only nominal significance. Until his death on February 15, 1924, Simon became Ernst's responsibility, even living with him most of the time at Ernst's apartment at Kufsteinnerstrasse 13 in western Berlin, where he moved in 1919.

With the war over, some of the Lubitsch family began to piece their lives together. Lubitsch took to charging into his sister Greta's apartment every Sunday afternoon. He would march through the apartment "like a tiger" remembered his niece, play the piano with his immutably heavy rhythm, and drop cigar ashes everywhere. Greta, who was a careful housekeeper, tried to stave off apoplexy as ashes fell into her beloved piano. "He was very impatient," remembered his niece Evie. "All Lubitsch people are impatient. But it was always fun when he came."

Lubitsch began edging toward the films that would give him directorial fame far outstripping his comedic reputation, when he made his version of *Carmen,* released in December 1918. Lubitsch retained Prosper Mérimée's flashback structure in which a campfire storyteller tells "the tale of a man bewitched."

The sets are up to the Hollywood standards of the period (for the Spanish sierras, Ernst used the chalk pits of Rudersdorf), but there is a roughness in the technique—extras sneak looks at the camera—that gets in the way. In addition, Lubitsch has not yet finessed his way past the standard presentational costume-picture style. Although there are some good angled horizon shots, Lubitsch seems uncomfortable whenever the material makes demands on him. In particular, the climactic duel is disappointing because of its indifferent staging.

As Carmen, Pola Negri is tigerishly sexy and believable, animated but never hammy, and Lubitsch gives her one piece of business that is both funny and sensual. As Don José is smoking, Carmen yanks his head back and hungrily kisses him before he's exhaled the smoke. She's a far more imposing figure than Harry Liedtke, who plays Don José almost entirely with his shoulders and eyeballs.

(Oddly, Carmen is never called Carmen but "La Carmencita," although this may be a result of the editing and retitling the film underwent for American release a full two-and-a-half years later, when it was called *Gypsy Blood*.)

By this time, Lubitsch's increasing celebrity was reflected both in public and in private. In February 1919, while bitter street fights broke out around the Sophien Gymnasium and Schönhäuser Allee, the Union cinemas were offering Lubitsch retrospectives. Newspapers, especially what the Berliners called the boulevard newspapers, often featured sarcastic cartoons that Ernst would draw or witty, sardonic sayings he coined. He was finding that it was a good idea to keep your name in front of the public.

Success meant that he could begin his lifelong love affair with the culture and theater of Hungary. "When Ernst went on vacation, it was always to Budapest," said Evie Bettelheim-Bentley. Ernst found that Budapest was lively and very exciting, with a profusion of light, inconsequential, but tickling theatricals. Ernst found himself attuned to the typically Hungarian matter-of-fact attitude about sex. Although it lacked the elegance of, say, the French, it also lacked hypocrisy. The flip side of the Hungarian character was a faint air of vulgar, if charming, coarseness.

For years, one of Ernst's favorite jokes revolved around an actor in a Hungarian road company with a slightly older, famous leading lady. The actor passionately pestered the star; every time they embraced during the play, he would whisper in her upstage ear, "When? When?!" Finally, she succumbed, but before she could even sit up in bed, he was putting his clothes back on.

"Where are you going?" she asked.

"To the tavern," the actor replied.

"Why?"

"To tell."

Then there was the food; for anyone who loved to eat as much as Ernst did, Budapest was gastronomic ecstasy. A young, single man could have a lot of fun in Budapest.

Not that Ernst was a ferocious lady's man. There were women, but they tended to be for when he wasn't working. When he was busy, remembered his niece Evie, "he didn't want to know about anything. Just leave him alone."

A new addition to the Lubitsch ménage was Pola Negri, who would become his primary object of female contemplation for the next four years. Aggressive where Ossi Oswalda was passive, ferociously sexual where Oswalda was girlish, Negri's mere presence changed the chemistry of Ernst's films, and of his surroundings. A naturally imperious personality, born in Poland sometime between 1899 (her date) and 1894 (the likely date), Negri would become virtually the only person who ever referred to Lubitsch as "Ernie."

Like Jannings, Lubitsch chose to be amused by Negri's turbulent temperament. "I believe she was one of the most vital persons I have ever known," he would say of her in 1938, "combining those two most important requisites—natural color (the art of being talked and written about) and a highly developed and sensitive artistic instinct."

Negri's own sense of passionate commitment to craft was transferred to her director; as Lubitsch would later write, "after making my first dramatic film with Pola Negri and Jannings, I completely lost interest in being an actor."

"What was impressive was the agility with which he expressed his often brilliant thoughts," wrote Negri in her memoirs, "and the witty manner in which he indicated that he was two steps ahead of anybody else in any intellectual gambit. A steady stream of eloquence flowed out around the cigar eternally planted between his lips . . . He was so funny that I even laughed when the jokes were on me."

Like her director, Negri had a good eye for the weak spots of others, and correctly assessed Lubitsch as "the complete cosmopolite. Any town with a population of less than a million was beneath his consideration."

As much as he enjoyed directing, Ernst still had some small itch to act. His increasing sophistication in form and character was once more evident in the delightful *Meyer aus Berlin (Meyer from Berlin)* released in January 1919. Meyer—another name for Sally Pinkus or Moritz Abramowski—wants to get away for a fun weekend without his wife, so he fakes an illness for which his doctor prescribes fresh air and a country environment.

As soon as he gets out of town, he gets duded up in what he thinks country villagers wear, a hilarious Tyrolean mountaineer's outfit, complete with plumed hat and a rope for climbing. Passers-by stare, children chase him. The bulk of the film explores the enormous, unbridgeable comic gap between an urban Jew and the natural environment.

By this time, Meyer, aka Sally, aka Pinkus, has become a complex comic character, something of a cross between Woody Allen (the utter helplessness in any environment but concrete) and Groucho Marx (the sexual aggressiveness, the insulting one-liners). Upbeat, effervescent, for all of his efforts at fomenting extramarital episodes, Meyer remains adamantly unconcerned if his passes don't get him anywhere.

"This is the women's compartment," he's told when he gets on the train.

"That's why I'm here," he says with an amiable leer.

When his wife discovers him in a mountain shelter with another woman, she says, with rather too much wounded dignity, "I'd hoped I wouldn't have to see you like this." (One can almost hear the fluty tones of Margaret Dumont.)

"Well, turn your head," he snaps.

Rigorously unsentimental, *Meyer from Berlin* clearly shows why Lubitsch was a comic star. His timing is sharp, the characters are caricatured but believable in the manner of Bob Hope's vehicles of the 1940s, and his increasing directorial sophistication is indicated by the fact that he enlivens the basically static camera by consistently cutting on action. *Meyer from Berlin* makes you regret the fact that Lubitsch was slowly weaning himself away from acting. In fact, he would appear in only one more film.

Between 1919 and 1923, the German economy plummeted into chaos. Inflation—made worse by the government's printing of increasing amounts of currency backed by little but good wishes—unemployment, and huge reparations payments meant that even the basic needs of most German citizens went unmet. Children victimized by the chronic food shortages resembled Käthe Kollwitz drawings.

"The city [of Berlin] seemed to me like a stone-gray corpse," wrote the artist George Grosz. "The streets seethed with unemployed. To pacify them, they were given chess games instead of work . . . Many of the younger elements who had never been regularly employed . . . formed small bands that played some kind of imitation jazz for the few pennies dropped into their hats . . . real and fake cripples sat around on corners and turned their heads to one side when anyone passed by, quivering, quaking, pretending war injuries . . . The people . . . had long since become inured to the strange, unusual and repulsive . . . We wanted something more, but what the 'more' was we could not exactly say."

The impressions of Ilya Ehrenburg were similarly grim. "The Germans were living as though they were at a railway station, no one knowing what would happen the next day . . . shopkeepers changed their price-tickets every day: the mark was falling. Herds of foreigners wandered along the Kurfürstendamm: they were buying up the remnants of former luxury for a song. In the poorer quarters several bakeries were looted. It seemed as though everything was bound to collapse . . . I remember two popular songs: 'Yes, We Have No Bananas' and 'Tomorrow's the End of the World.' However, the end of the world was postponed from one day to the next."

The desperation, the unrest, were reflected in the music of Schoenberg, Berg, and Webern, the art of Feininger, Kandinsky, and Klee, and in the angry conversations that filled the Romanische Cafe, the agreed-upon gathering place for Brecht and favored actors such as Fritz Kortner and Alexander Granach.

The old days of blood and iron, of authoritarian rule, began to seem a Golden Age. Ironically, it was in these same years that the German film industry attained the smooth melding of style and content that the American cinema was to acquire in just a few years. Despite the fact that, according to Siegfried Kracauer, the German audience yielded only 10 percent of production costs, the German film industry did rather well economically.

The surplus of labor meant that films of comparatively large scale could be made quite inexpensively, be sold cheaply abroad, and still return a profit. And, because German films began to accumulate foreign currencies that were far stronger than the mark, the movie business gradually found itself with a firmer financial base than industries that had to rely exclusively on the German market.

Unlike Negri, Ernst's relationship with Ossi Oswalda seems to have extended beyond the studio lot. While they were in production on their next collaboration, *Die Austernprinzessin (The Oyster Princess),* Ossie would pick Ernst up from Schönhäuser Allee every morning in her open car. Ernst's family could not help noticing that she adored him and seemed to assume that they would be married. Yet, if Ernst was attracted to Ossi, it was as a friend rather than lover.

The Oyster Princess opens with a series of curtain calls, each actor and technician bowing at the camera as his name appears on the screen. Lubitsch himself does not bow, but contents himself with an enigmatic half-smile. In content, *The Oyster Princess* is a rough precursor of situation comedy, crossed with aspects of screwball comedy but with a distinctly Bavarian twist. A boorish, vulgar tycoon lives in a house of spectacular hideousness, complete with recumbent lions lining a stairway and patterned marble floors. The tycoon (Victor Janson) is waited on by secretaries who take down his every word, while platoons of black servants hold his coffee cup and wipe his mouth every time he takes a sip. Mainly, he wants to marry off his daughter (Ossi Oswalda).

Tossed into the mixture is an impoverished aristocrat named Prince Nucki (Harry Liedtke, reminiscent of Maurice Chevalier, especially in a drunk scene), who is reduced to washing out his own socks in his one-room apartment. There is also a homely, knowing little kid who's a direct precursor of the precociously sophisticated Pepi in *The Shop Around the Corner* and drawn, one strongly suspects, from a little boy who hated working in his father's clothing shop and loved upsetting the owner of Steinemann's cafe.

Lubitsch's sense of social satire is vigorous but rough; he's still essentially the Berlin comedian, using titles that say "Meschugga!" Yet, the film is clearly a transitional work, with the component parts of the singularly observant Lubitsch sensibility in nascent form.

A poor man is waiting in the millionaire's entrance hall. He has been waiting a long time. He observes the complicated design of the parquet floor and, to while away some time, begins walking along the outlines of the intricate pattern, the tracing movement relieving his frustrations as well as deftly revealing his gentle, methodical character. It is in the delicate human reactions of Lubitsch's characters, not their motives or environments, that their creator is already beginning to distinguish himself.

At film's end, Prince Nucki and Ossi steal away from the dinner table to their room. Her father, the tycoon, follows them and looks through the keyhole to see them in bed nuzzling. The light goes out and the tycoon turns to the camera to say "Das imponiert mir" ("This excites me!").

Even in a half-formed picture like *The Oyster Princess,* Lubitsch's personality comes through clearly: antic, playful, and, at this stage, a bit vulgar. Films like *The Oyster Princess* seem oppressively busy compared to the calm clarity of his later movies, when he was after a sense of emotional reality and simplicity. With *The Oyster Princess,* which comments on reality without actually reflecting it, Lubitsch was evolving into the kind of director Americans love.

Outside the theaters, the streets of Berlin saw bloody riots; the drawings of George Grosz replaced satire's mockery with brutal savagery, and Kafka wrote "In the Penal Colony." The devastation of World War I was followed by social desolation and a despair so profound that only the apparently redemptive power of a rampant nationalism seemed to offer a way out.

Inside the theaters, Lubitsch was sliding past all that *tsimmis,* all that controversy, and with one exception *(To Be or Not to Be)* always would. Astonishingly, he would get away with it. Because of his essential good nature, his sardonic jokes amused but didn't wound; the cruel edge of satire would always be tempered by gaiety. Ernst Lubitsch, whether the man who made *The Oyster Princess* or the man who made *To Be or Not to Be,* always wanted to be liked. More importantly, he genuinely wanted to give pleasure.

By this time, Lubitsch's occasionally touchy relationship with his father had been smoothed over, and a Simon Lubitsch awash in paternal pride enjoyed visiting theaters and requesting Lubitsch pictures, without ever telling anybody who he was. In addition, he refused to acknowledge the existence of any star who had failed to work with his son, and used his paternal connection with the glamorous world of show business as a way of getting dates.

The relationship between father and son was cemented when *Madame DuBarry* was the opening attraction at the UFA-Palast in Berlin on September 18, 1919. There was an invited audience of 4,000, and Ernst, Emil Jannings, and Pola Negri were in a special box decorated with flowers. The audience greeted the film with rapturous, thundering applause. Afterward, Max Reinhardt walked up to Simon and said, "Mr. Lubitsch, the student has surpassed the master."

Madame DuBarry, a free-form fantasia about the mistress of Louis XV, was the film that would have the greatest influence on Lubitsch's career. Sensing the picture's importance, Negri had thrown herself into research, reading books, studying portraits, trying to extract the essence of the character.

Emil Jannings was fascinated by Louis XV, and believed that the character embodied passion, humor, trickery, the tragic and the comic. But Lubitsch saw the character as a far more courtly construct, charming and diplomatic. Jannings and Lubitsch had what the actor recalled as "endless conversations" about the part, but the two men could never come close to an agreement about the nature of the character. Finally, a desperate Jannings pleaded with Lubitsch to "let me try it, let me play just one single scene. If you don't like me, you can always get someone else for the part.

"Lubitsch gave in to my constant urgings. I played a scene in which I showed both the self-composed Louis and the demons underneath. My Louis had depth and magnitude . . . I got the role."

Standing in for Versailles was Frederick the Great's Sans Souci, in Potsdam. When the company arrived to do their location work, the weather was cold and Negri was wearing flannel underwear under the thin silks of her costumes. Noticing the slight bulkiness, Lubitsch lifted her dress and snapped, "Get into some silk panties. Can you imagine DuBarry wearing those?" Negri obeyed, and froze for the rest of the location shoot.

Madame DuBarry is not as sumptuous as Hollywood epics of the period, but the comparative starkness works to its benefit, giving the film a more realistic, lived-in appearance. After Jeanne Vaubernier attracts her first admirer, she is invited to his apartment. A servant shows her in to a drawing room in front of a velvet curtain. The curtain slowly opens to reveal a sumptuous setting and a beautifully set table. The display, the contrast between the rich man's apartment and Jeanne's mean life, is as much for the audience as it is for Jeanne.

Overall, *Madame DuBarry* makes it clear that Lubitsch was learning much from Griffith. Some of it was camera style: there are startling experiments with frame size, matteing images into the modern screen rectangle, or deeply angular up-and-down frame sizes. (Lubitsch also emulates Griffith in the unfortunate custom of using white actors in blackface.)

Other stylistic matters are entirely Lubitsch's own. He displays a very singular tic that involves opening a scene with a close-up, then dissolving to a medium shot. Mostly though, the lesson learned from the great American director is the importance of behavioral details in making a scene or characterization come alive.

In a scene at the Paris Opera, Lubitsch opens on a shot of Jeanne's swinging feet, then raises the matte to reveal the rest of the frame. It is an impressive set, with lots of extras, but what makes the scene real is Jeanne, swinging her legs like a little girl with a fishing pole.

Which, in a sense, is what she is, fishing for men. At first, she is attracted to power and rank, but later Lubitsch manipulates history so she's doing it all to protect Armand, her true love.

At the beginning, Negri is girlish, almost Mary Pickfordish, full of exuberant high spirits. While Emil Jannings' Louis XV mulls over his preferred method of seduction, Negri simply plops herself down beside him, and a revealing close-up shows Jannings thinking that this isn't going to be so hard after all. If it's possible for an actress to believably play a character who sleeps her way to the top and still remains innocent, Negri manages to pull it off.

Later, she marries, gains the name DuBarry, and grows imperious and willful, which Negri communicates through body language. Lubitsch ventures into territory von Sternberg would later make his own when he shows Jannings kissing her feet and quietly doing her nails. Negri's quiet, cat-that-ate-the-cream satisfaction is perfect; because she is sexy, she doesn't have to play it sexy.

After six reels of ladder-climbing assignations, Lubitsch begins to tighten the screws as Madame DuBarry pays the price for aligning herself with dissolute tyrants. The surprising thing about the vaunted crowd scenes of the French Revolution that caused such pleasured astonishment at the time is that Lubitsch doesn't linger over them, doesn't milk them for effect, but uses them with dispatch to make his necessary narrative points. Nor is he afraid to show the ugliness of violence. When Jeanne's old love is shot for trying to help her escape, blood streams down his face and on to his shirt.

DuBarry is carried to the guillotine on a tumbril, then tied to the guillotine. Lubitsch cuts to a long shot of the impressive scene. The guillotine blade comes down; the crowd exults and the film fades to black. No rides to the rescue, no happy endings.

While *Madame DuBarry* is a good film, it's also slightly anonymous, and offers less of a sense of the director's personality than the comedies Ernst had been making just a year or two before. No matter; it was the right film at the right time. Lubitsch's handling of the mob scenes in *Madame DuBarry* galvanized critics and audiences. The revolutionary masses around the guillotine ritualistically pump their right arms in rage, a formal movement that probably derives from Reinhardt's 1910 production of *Oedipus Rex*. Yet Ernst gives the crowds a pulsing mobility that would have been impossible to attain or sustain on a stage.

Unlike the crowd scenes of directors such as DeMille, who sought to particularize each member with a specific bits of business or, in the sound era, dialogue, Lubitsch turns his extras into a unified mass—Lang would do the same thing in *Metropolis*—making the crowd scenes an expansive, almost expressionist counterpoint to the whispers and internecine intimacies of the rest of the film.

Madame DuBarry would serve as the matrix for Lubitsch's first wave of influence; for the next fifty years, historical films posited a world in which changes and upheavals were the result of individual action by the ruling and upper classes, usually motivated by sex. Indeed, Alexander Korda's scampish 1933 *The Private Life of Henry VIII* was a careful replication for sound of what Lubitsch had been doing fifteen years before.

The response of succeeding generations of German critics to this new twist on an old genre has always been considerably less favorable than that of American critics. Lotte Eisner, for one, carped at the fact that Lubitsch ignored the sweeping radical commentary of contemporary plays like Büchner's *Danton's Death* and based his film on a "trite" love story. "It was typical of him," she wrote, "to portray events only as seen from the curtains of an alcove . . . for Lubitsch history is only a pretext to make films in period costume: silks and velvets attract the former draper's assistant and delight his connoisseur's eye at the same time as he seeks out the occasion to mingle melodrama and a love affair."

In her influential book *The Haunted Screen*, Eisner would go on to elaborate on her negative feelings, analyzing Berliners as "realistic and even materialistic . . . To perfect his famous 'touch,' Lubitsch had merely to develop his Germanness: his Berliner's presence of mind, his taste for realistic detail, and his Jewish liking for the suggestive implication leading quite naturally to images with a double meaning."

Nor was Eisner the only one. Siegfried Kracauer in his book *From Caligari to Hitler* wrote that "Considering the speed with which Lubitsch exchanged murders and tortures for dancing and joking, it is highly probable that his comedies sprang from the same nihilism as his historical dramas . . . The vogue [Lubitsch] helped to create originated in a blend of cynicism and melodramatic sentimentality . . . they characterized history as meaningless . . . an arena reserved for blind and ferocious instincts, a product of devilish machinations forever frustrating our hopes for freedom and happiness."

Aside from the overweening importance attached to oppressive sociology, the too-sweeping generalizations, and some unfortunate stereotyping, Kracauer's analysis verges on National Socialist rhetoric, while Eisner seems infected by something of a regional prejudice. Looming over everything else is the authors' allegiance to classical German "High Culture," with a resulting intolerance for anyone who chose to work a different side of the street.

Such criticisms ignore a consistent theme in Lubitsch's German period, in both comic and dramatic films—that of an aggressive, bumptious outsider who refuses to abide by the constraints of social conventions or even nominal politeness. This describes *I Wouldn't Want to Be a Man* as well as *Madame DuBarry, When Four Do the Same* as well as *Schuhpalast Pinkus.* When Ossi Oswalda displays these traits, she is considered to be a charming hoyden, even a harbinger of the woman's movement; when Lubitsch inhabits the character, he is a negative Jewish stereotype. The subjective judgment of an actor's personality and the Berlin character has far more to do with these late-blooming criticisms than the films themselves.

Besides, if the qualities that combined to form Lubitsch's point of view were such common currency in the Berlin zeitgeist, why was he such a singular, unimitatable, one-of-a-kind talent?

These sort of attacks were to dog Lubitsch throughout his life. Why, these people wanted to know, would such an obviously gifted man waste his time making such impeccably crafted movies based on trivial material?

While Ernst was directing *Madame DuBarry* at UFA's Tempelhof studios, the film's dramatic core, that of a collapsing monarchy trooping to the guillotine, was being mirrored in the headlines. What replaced Germany's emperor was a very nervous democracy, accompanied by enormous economic uncertainty and revolutionary cultural change.

The young republic banished nearly every form of censorship, but the film industry just as promptly adopted the Reich Film Act. Passed on May 29, 1920, it avoided any hint of political censorship per se, but mandated that each picture had to be passed by one of two boards, in either Munich or Berlin, before it could be shown to the public. An appeal could be lodged with the Supreme Censorship Board. No children under the age of twelve were allowed into movies at all, and, between the ages of twelve and eighteen, they were only allowed to see movies that had a special certificate.

In 1921, the German cinema produced 646 films, a figure that the increasing monopolization of the country's film industry during the twenties would reduce to slightly more than 200, still a far greater total than any other European country. (In 1927, Germany produced 241 films compared with 74 for France and 44 for England; in America, the industrial base that World War I had only strengthened was reflected by a production total of 743 films.)

Perhaps as a result of all the ferment, Ernst's next directorial effort was a calculated retreat from reality. *Die Puppe (The Doll),* which premiered just three months after *Madame DuBarry,* is a consistently delightful, inventive film containing an astonishing opening sequence. Lubitsch, busy, bustling, never acknowledging the camera, assembles a miniature set out of a box. He lays out a lawn, a house, some trees. He lifts the roof off the house and drops two small wooden figures inside, then puts the roof back on. The scene dissolves to a full-sized set, an exact re-creation of the set we have just seen him build. The movie proper begins. Ernst's pride in authorship and in his own creativity would never again be so explicitly stated.

The plot of *The Doll* is an airy thing about a master dollmaker who constructs a mechanical doll to take the place of a real girl who doesn't want to marry the man to whom she has been betrothed.

It's an enchanting little fairy tale, adapted from themes by E. T. A. Hoffmann and a resulting operetta. The finished picture could be a collaboration between Hans Christian Andersen, the Brothers Grimm, and George Méliès, but with a typical Lubitsch satirical sprightliness. A shot of one fat priest eating opens up to reveal three fat priests eating. (The film has some good if unstressed fun at the expense of Catholicism; one of the priests gorging himself on a slab of pork notices a hungry man. Ever helpful, he immediately cuts him a piece of dry bread.) A character falls into the water and pleads for some sun. The sun immediately comes out and steam begins to rise.

The sets are mostly in forced perspective, and props like kitchen utensils are drawn on the walls, while two men in horse costumes pull carriages. The film is nimble, light on its feet, as is Ossi Oswalda, who is charming, effervescent, and delightful in her syncopated little mechanical dance.

Most important, however, is the way that the film reveals characteristic Lubitsch themes and characters in an embryonic state. Again Lubitsch introduces a bumptious, worldly-wise apprentice, who regularly breaks the fourth wall to address the audience, á la Chevalier in the later musicals.

Ernst knew he had brought off something remarkable. In 1921, after he and his films had conquered America as well as Europe, he was asked about his favorites among his pictures. "Possibly I like a little fantastic film of mine, *The Doll,* best of all," he said, and, at the very end of his life, he would point with pride to what he believed to be the three best comedies he made in Germany: *The Oyster Princess, The Doll,* and *Kohlhiesel's Daughter.* Unfortunately, *The Doll* would play only a few American engagements, and then only in 1928.

In films like *The Doll,* the German cinema was acquiring a sense of visual style and sophistication desperately needed to balance its often startling thematic maturity.*

With much of German cinema engaged in mournful expressions of inner agony, Lubitsch, whether in his spectaculars, his sex comedies, or his playful fantasies, was filling a vacuum, making comedies of social transposition that pointed up middle-class manners and life—or offered escape from it—in a way that nobody else in Germany was doing.

---

*1916's *Das Tagebuch des Dr. Hart,* the first film directed by the brilliant Paul Leni, who would become a good friend of Lubitsch's (Ernst served as the executor of his estate), is clearly neorealist in style. In its portrayal of a common man who goes off to war for the fatherland without any particular political agenda and with a notable lack of polemics, concentrating instead on the specifics of what happens to him and how much he misses his wife, the film is a clear precursor of *The Big Parade* and *All Quiet on the Western Front.* Although Leni would earn a place in film history for the delirious expressionism of *The Cat and the Canary* and *The Man Who Laughs,* it's obvious that he also had a considerable gift for the quieter delineations of objective reality.

Richard Oswald's 1919 film *Anders als die Andern (Different from the Others)* told a story of a well-off homosexual (played by a particularly cadaverous Conrad Veidt) and his young lover, complete with a scene in a drag bar. Oswald dramatizes their homosexuality by characterizing Veidt and his lover as a pair of opera queens, with their passion for music spilling over into impromptu musicales at home: Veidt playing the piano and the boyfriend accompanying him, complete with soulful glances that come to an end when Veidt meets another man at a gay bar.

He takes his trick home and begins to fondle him, only to have the man slowly hold out his hand for money, and threaten Veidt with exposure under Statute 175, the German law that made fellatio a felony. The blackmailing causes Veidt to go into a fast downhill spiral, ending in the requisite tragic death.

This was subject matter that wouldn't be touched by American movies for fifty years. But what the German films gained in themes they sometimes lost in treatment, with stolid acting and an essential humorlessness, as well as flat, ugly lighting and art direction that seems to anticipate neorealism but was probably just a response to the exigencies of World War I.

Pictures like *When Four Do the Same* and *Meyer from Berlin* were the precursors of a format that would become a staple of the American cinema in all eras, beginning with Mr. and Mrs. Sidney Drew and continuing on through Reginald Denny, Tracy and Hepburn, and so on. It is doubtful that Lubitsch consciously saw the idea of portraying the middle class to itself as a need waiting to be filled, but he was doing it nonetheless.

Equally as important was the psychological shift that was taking place within the films. So long as Lubitsch was acting, his films were predominantly presentational, and his directorial skills nominal. A camera was to provide a frame for the comic performance and little more. Absent his own presence as an actor, Lubitsch's concentration began to be focused on the settings, the camera, the ensemble. As the critic and archivist Enno Patalas has written, "The milieu grew from a mere background to a comic and dramatic force."

Shortly after the production of *The Oyster Princess*, Ernst finally moved out of the apartment at 183 Schönhäuser Allee. The neighborhood had changed and was now prey to street fights and the civil unrest that was to become pandemic in Berlin. The western part of Berlin was becoming the in place, so he moved to an apartment on Kufsteinerstrasse. Ernst remained very close with his father; when Ernst would go out of town on the weekends to an artists' retreat by a lake, he would often take Simon with him, to the old man's delight.

Somehow, he managed to find time for one of his first serious relationships—a tall, attractive blonde named Hedy. Although Hedy took up residence at Kufsteinerstrasse, with his directorial career burgeoning Ernst had little time to spend with her. He asked a lawyer friend to take care of her and make sure that she wasn't ever bored. The friend took such good care of Hedy, they ended up getting married. There were no hard feelings.

"If my uncle had a weakness, it was blond women," said his niece Evie. "And he could be taken advantage of; he could be influenced by persons he trusted, who weren't really trustworthy. But when his cronies would take advantage of him, he didn't seem to care."

In the latter part of 1921, there was a strike at the UFA studio. Henry Blanke, a twenty-year-old assistant to director Paul Stein, refused to report to work out of sympathy with the workmen. For his solidarity with the working class, Blanke was fired. Soon afterward, he read about the formation of EFA (European Film Alliance), an offshoot of the Famous Players–Lasky company that was the precursor of Paramount Pictures. EFA involved Paul Stein as well as Lubitsch, Jannings, and the producer Paul Davidson.

Blanke called Davidson, who had heard about the stand the young assistant had taken. Davidson took him onto the back lot, where he called Lubitsch up to a balcony. "This is the man I want to work with you, here and always," Davidson said. That was good enough for Lubitsch, who took the young man by the hand and led him down to the set of *Loves of Pharaoh*. Lubitsch grew to rely on the young man, and valued his judgment so highly that he would check with Blanke after a particularly good take to see if Blanke agreed that that was the keeper. Blanke remained Lubitsch's assistant for the next five years, until the young man's manifest abilities led him to become one of Hollywood's finest producers, with films like *The Treasure of the Sierra Madre* and *The Nun's Story* to his credit.

The twenty-seven-year-old Lubitsch was now working at top speed, completing seven pictures in 1919, and slowing down only slightly to make five the following year. In all of these movies, there is a palpable sense of a man savoring his prestige, his freedom; there is a sense that he is exultantly sampling all kinds of material, trying on stories and actors to see what fits most comfortably.

Ernst embarked on two back-to-back Shakespeare adaptations, or, rather, transmutations. *Kohlhiesel's Töchter (Kohlhiesel's Daughter)* is a variation on *The Taming of the Shrew*, a negligible bit of rustic roughhouse that's sole distinction is the opportunity it gives Henny Porten to play the dual roles of Gretel (Bianca, more or less) and the vile-tempered Liesel (Kate). Liesel has a homely face to go with her homely soul, and Porten manages to create two believable characterizations without resorting to the easy alternative of extreme character makeup, although Lubitsch helps her out with some very fine split-screen work. Despite its failings, *Kohlhiesel's Daughter* was an enormous commercial hit, the most popular of all of Ernst's early comedies. In later years, Lubitsch seemed slightly embarrassed by it, calling it "typical German."

In a romp like *Romeo und Julia im Schnee (Romeo and Juliet in the Snow)*, Lubitsch reverts to the boisterous comedies of four and five years before. Montague and Capulet are transformed into Montekugerls and Capulethofers, congenitally crude, snarling Bavarian burghers, forever wiping their hands on whatever's handy. Even the magistrate is prone to bad manners, wiping his mouth on a crumpled legal document, then uncrumpling it in case he needs it for a case. In their bustling contention, if not their vulgar manners, the Capulethofers and Montekugerls are undoubtedly Lubitsch's projection of the boisterous, voluble Lubitsch family times ten.

Lubitsch manages to create some laughter, as when the elder Montekugerl dresses up for a ball as a Wagnerian knight, complete with an enormous, unwieldy sword that is put to use as a bread slicer. Other elements are simply overplayed, such as the role of a rival for the affections of Juliet, who has an inbred moron's face eminently suitable for a Tod Browning horror movie.

Romeo and Juliet in the Snow might have worked better if it was played for gentle satire rather than sprawling slapstick, but it has the feel of a throwaway, something Lubitsch was not fully engaged by. Even with comparative failures like these two pictures, however, Lubitsch is incapable of wasting his time completely. In *Kohlhiesel's Daughter,* he puts ceilings on many of the interior sets to give them a dark, smokily realistic look, and he also experiments with using languorous dissolves as transitions to different angles rather than direct cuts. So far, so good.

Then, in September 1920, came *Sumurun,* based on a classic Max Reinhardt pantomime in which Ernst had appeared, although exactly when is open to dispute. Alfred Hitchcock recalled seeing Lubitsch in a February 1911 production at the London Coliseum, but a program for the same production lists Ernst Mátray in the role of the hunchback clown. In 1969, Mátray said that Lubitsch took on the part when Reinhardt had lost interest in the production. "I took it over and set it to rhythm," said Mátray, "and then put Lubitsch in it." *Sumurun* (retitled *One Arabian Night* for its American release in October 1921) was the last film in which Ernst would appear.

Pola Negri remembered its production as "a very easy and happy chore. Except for a few Lubitsch innovations, it was essentially a photographed stage play." And evidently a bad one. "Evidently" because Lubitsch made the picture in twelve reels, but First National, who released the film in America, cut it to eight reels, which may be the reason for its irritating, arhythmic jumble.

Lubitsch, who is credited on the American release prints as "Ernest Lubitsch," was always an emphatic actor, but here, doing a Lon Chaney as a pathetic hunchback clown in love with a faithless Pola Negri, he gives a performance so overwrought it makes Emil Jannings look like a minimalist.

Only Negri—very beautiful—and the majestic Paul Wegener, with his riveting Tartar features, manage to make any impression at all. As with the fling with Egyptiania represented by *The Eyes of the Mummy Ma,* an Arabian Nights setting is simply not Lubitsch material. Except for a few moments—eunuchs sitting in a geometrically perfect row formation—the film is bereft of the director's typical playfulness; at this still-developing stage of his career, he lacks the flair needed to integrate a dramatic narrative with such a frankly fanciful, fairy-tale environment.

By this time, it was obvious that Reinhardt's use of chiaroscuro, of the expressionistic style that had been one of the hallmarks of his historical and costume productions, was not a style Lubitsch had much sympathy for or interest in. Lighting, for Lubitsch, took a distinct back seat to composition and performance. Lotte Eisner would ascribe this lack of interest in avant-garde style to a lack of intuition resulting from Lubitsch's Berlin background; "as such," she wrote, "[he] was without illusions, without a taste for the mysterious."

While there is an element of truth in Eisner's comment, it is also likely that Ernst's solipsism made it impossible for him to give his allegiance to any artistic movement but his own.

Ernst's next film was a return to the historical epic, with a generous budget of 8.5 million marks. *Anne Boleyn* begins as the title character (Henny Porten) bobs into the frame in the cabin of a violently rolling ship on the open ocean. The film is made on a large scale; massive gates open to reveal an immaculately designed seaside dock, complete with masts in the background. The art direction is, for the most part, surprisingly convincing—although the Tower of London in the film looks nothing like the actual Tower—and the film captures a realistic sense of the hurly-burly of Elizabethan life.

The film belongs to Emil Jannings, whose Henry VIII is introduced to us as he grossly jams food into the mouth of a jester. Jannings lacks the patina of childish willfulness that Charles Laughton would give the character. His Henry has a certain immature charm, but it is that of a manipulative bad seed; Jannings gives the character a selfishness verging on the homicidal.

When Anne bears Henry a daughter instead of the son he demanded, Lubitsch has him express his frustration by breaking into tears rather than a fit of temper. Soon, he is on the trail of another woman, callously putting his crying daughter into a chair so he can make love to her nurse.

Even though the film is called *Anne Boleyn,* the title character is too passive to sustain interest; at the end, when she goes off to the scaffold and the headsman's ax, it seems as though there should be a coda with Henry, who creates every movement of the plot. But Lubitsch chooses to fade out on Anne's stoic acceptance of her fate in a scene echoed in John Ford's dreary *Mary of Scotland.*

Since the story is fairly well-known and cannot, in any case, endure much juggling, Lubitsch again plays with frame sizes, following the lead of Abel Gance, who had begun similar experiments as early as 1916. Sometimes the image is matted into an arch or a diagonal slash, other times into a ratio approximating CinemaScope. If a scene ends with a wipe from the top down, the next opens with a wipe from the bottom up. If a scene is not inherently interesting, Lubitsch feels compelled to find a way to make it interesting.

More important, Lubitsch already clearly has one eye on the American market, for the spectacle and psychological realism of *Anne Boleyn* derive far more from DeMille's historical melodramas such as *Joan the Woman* than from Griffith's spectacles, whose tendentious moralizing nearly obscured their elemental emotions and spectacular technique.

It was at this point that Lubitsch began to be called "The Griffith of Europe," a considerable compliment but a misleading one, referring as it did almost exclusively to a skill with large-scale epic form. Certainly, Griffith's simplicity was leagues removed from Lubitsch's sly, knowing jibes at his characters' foibles and sexual drives.

Yet, for the benefit of the press, Lubitsch acknowledged his appreciation of the older man. "Griffith," he said, "is the man to whom we all owe an unpayable debt of obligation. Griffith was the pioneer in so much that the movies in their present form may be said to owe most to him. He was a great argonaut, and only time will tell how much the movies owe him."

But Lubitsch was already using the past tense in paying homage to Griffith; in truth, the era that Lubitsch was about to usher in would make it impossible for Griffith's magnificent naïveté to survive, let alone flourish.

In any case, the critics took the "Griffith of Europe" sobriquet far more seriously than Lubitsch did, for immediately after *Anne Boleyn,* he returned to the playful, phantasmagorical world of *The Doll. Die Bergkatze (The*

Mountain Cat) is, in plot, a comic opera—the daughter (Pola Negri) of the leader of a band of mountain brigands falls in love with the leader of the military command charged with arresting her father.

In style, it is like nothing else committed to film, as overtly stylized as a late von Sternberg/Dietrich film. The decor—by Ernst Stern and Max Gronert—is gingerbread candybox, something out of rococo German fairy-tales. (Lubitsch and Stern had one disagreement: Stern, believing that nature cannot be caricatured except in a studio, didn't think the film should have any location footage at all, but Lubitsch asserted his preroga-tive.)

The statues and decorations of Fort Tossenstein—built on location in the Bavarian Alps, in and around Garmisch-Partenkirchen—look as if they're made out of cake icing, all scrumptiously rounded out of spun sugar. In other films, Lubitsch experimented with different mattes to alter the frame size at the beginning or ending of a scene. Here, virtually every shot is framed into some baroquely decorated diagonal or oval. The overall effect is as energetic and infectious as the characters; at one point, the brigand band attempts to storm the fort, but they hear an orchestra playing and are so overcome by the melody they stop to dance.

In the midst of all this are a thousand or so extras, a tempestuous Pola Negri, one character who rather enjoys being whipped across the but-tocks, and a plot that culminates in Rischka, the title character, marrying one of the brigands. To symbolize that fact, the bride and the groom are handcuffed together.

Done straight, *The Mountain Cat* would have been of minor interest; done in the Lubitsch manner, it's an exercise in riotous artifice, as much pure fun as anything in Lubitsch's canon. Unfortunately, this extravagant, wonderful film was a total financial failure in Germany and was never distributed in America. Lubitsch remained stubbornly proud of it; as he wrote in 1947, "this picture had more inventiveness and satirical pictorial wit than many of my other pictures . . . [but] I found the German audiences in no mood to accept a picture which satirized militarism and war."

Because of the vagaries of film distribution, American critics were unaware of movies like *The Doll* or *The Mountain Cat* and thus continued to judge Ernst solely by the far more sober historical spectacles that were imported, giving them a distorted idea of the nature of his talents, and making his later, satirical domestic comedies seem like far more of a radical change than the evolutionary refinement they actually were.

In a remarkably prescient May 1920 interview with *Moving Picture World,* Erich von Stroheim said that "American producers had better look out for foreign picture makers . . . Just as foreign literature is different from American literature, so are foreign plays different from American plays. Foreign writers go more into the deeper relationships of mankind than do American authors. They depict more emotion and less of the frivolities of life. This is reflected in the European screen."

Tentatively at first, word of the quality of postwar German films began to appear in the world press, and the world couldn't help noticing, often with backhanded tributes laced with strong amounts of xenophobia left over from World War I. *DuBarry,* although a hit in Germany, found no takers for American distribution for a year, until, in the early fall of 1920, the film was finally purchased by Associated First National, who paid between $30,000 and $60,000 for the American rights and promptly retitled it *Passion.* But, as far as First National was concerned, revealing the film's country of origin was something to be avoided at all costs.

The New York Times, undoubtedly working off information supplied by First National, first said that the picture was of Italian origin, then corrected itself a week later. First National announced that the film had been shot in "Northern Germany with an international cast," leaving the reader with the distinct impression that Germany was merely a location site rather than the country of origin.

The film was originally scheduled to open on October 4, 1920, but that date came and went without a screening. There is some evidence to suggest that the company in fact gave *Passion* its American premiere in late November or early December in Paterson and Passaic, New Jersey, out-of-town tryouts calculated to see if the film or its distributor would be torched by enraged audiences.

The reason for all this paranoia? The Strand Theater, First National's usual New York showcase house, had refused to run the picture. While they searched for another major New York theater, First National opened the picture in Atlantic City and Philadelphia, to critical and public acclaim.

Finally, First National struck a deal with S. L. Rothapfel's Capitol Theater, on Broadway at 51st Street. Rothapfel felt that the film's titles needed punching up and hired Katherine Hilliker to do the rewriting, then commissioned a new musical score. The film itself was left virtually untouched except for the interpolation near the end of a rather effectively theatrical series of shots of a candelabra, whose flames were progressively extinguished as DuBarry's lovers died. The opening night ad in the December 12, 1920, *New York Times* called *Passion* "the most important film event of the year."

That same edition of the *Times* mentioned that "The origin of *Passion* is to be excused because its star is a Pole, and its subject matter is French." All this fumbling over national origins was swept aside the next day, as the *Times* review proclaimed *Passion* "One of the pre-eminent motion pictures of the present cinematographic age." *Variety* chimed in by calling it "100 percent good market stuff," and used Lubitsch as a club with which to beat Griffith. Its critic wrote that "If Griffith had done it his mannerisms would have been everywhere in it. [Lubitsch] . . . made the story his first consideration, subordinating everything else. This is great direction."

An enraged Griffith responded by booking a reissue of *The Birth of a Nation* into the Capitol early in 1921 for the express purpose of outgrossing *Passion*. Although it played for three weeks, one week more than *Passion, Variety* unhelpfully pointed out that *The Birth of a Nation* had only been playing two shows a day, and that *Passion* had played more performances and attracted larger audiences. Griffith promptly canceled his subscription to the paper.

Passion was a smash hit, earning $10,000 a day at the 5,500-seat Capitol, with a total attendance for the first week of 106,000, earning more in that one week than First National paid for the picture. *Passion* was held over for an unprecedented second week, and *Variety* heralded the picture's success in a front-page story under the headline "Picture Sensational Draw." The film that nobody had wanted, whose distributors were so unsure of it that they virtually abdicated responsibility for its presentation to the exhibitor, had conquered New York.

A month later, on January 30, the *Times* opined that the "apparently Teutonic Lubitsch" must have worked in Paris, or been under French influence, because the picture was not "heavy." At least they got his name right; in *Variety*'s review of *Passion,* the director was "Emil Subitch," in the December 13 *Times* he had been "Ernst Lubitch," while the *Morning Telegraph* printed spellings as variable as "Lebitsch" and "Libitsch."

The firestorm success of *Passion* naturally impelled similar importations; *Anne Boleyn* was quickly retitled *Deception,* billed as "the Masterpiece of Ernest Lubitsch, creator of *Passion,*" and premiered at the Rivoli Theater, on Broadway and 49th Street, on April 17, 1921. While *Deception* was in its fourth week, the Strand, which had been afraid to play *Passion,* opened *Gypsy Blood,* the retitled *Carmen,* as "another great triumph by Ernest Lubitsch, creator of *Passion.*"

Within five months, two other Lubitsch spectacles opened in New York; five months later, in October 1921, *Sumurun* (retitled *One Arabian Night*) opened, and five months after that, Ernst's new film, *The Loves of Pharaoh,* opened virtually simultaneously in both New York and Germany. *One Arabian Night* was credited to "Ernest Lubitsch, the creator of *Passion,*" and a parenthetical note was included in the ads: "Mr. Lubitsch appears in this production in the role of the hunchback."

In less than a year, Lubitsch had become an American brand name; at one time or another in this period, *Variety* would write that Lubitsch was either directing or preparing *Richard III, Lucrezia Borgia, The Golem,* and a serial entitled *The Mistress of the World* that was actually being directed by Joe May. When Asta Nielsen's *Hamlet* was released in New York in the fall of 1921, the posters prominently displayed a blurb from Lubitsch proclaiming that Nielsen's performance was "art itself."

By late 1921/early 1922, New York intellectuals could talk of little else besides German movies, and of the New Wave of German directors. Of *The New York Times'* fifteen most important movies of 1921, eight were German and three were directed by Lubitsch. Benjamin De Casseres conferred the official imprimatur of cultural arrival when he wrote a story about the German invasion for the *Times* Book Review.

"That they have caused a tremendous mental and emotional commotion in the greatest of American entertainment enterprises one can feel by being present at any place where motion picture people congregate. Conversation has not progressed for ten minutes when the latest German film becomes the crux of the talk. What do you think of Pola Negri? Of Mia May? Of Ernst Lubitsch? ... Does Lubitsch achieve better mob effects than Griffith? Camera work, lighting, architecture, sets—all these are overhauled and dissected for the thousandth time."

The protectionist trade press wasn't nearly as enthusiastic. As early as mid-April 1921, *Variety* was complaining about the "dumping" of German films on American screens. On April 22, the paper reported that Actor's Equity, First National, Famous Players, and the American Legion were all calling for a ban on foreign films, particularly German ones, on the grounds that they were causing unemployment in Hollywood.

W. Stephen Bush, writing in an October 1921 *Moving Picture World,* said that "the great majority of [Germany's] dramatic features are tainted by morbid sexual themes, slow in action and shriekingly Teutonic in matter of casts . . . the offense as committed in so many of the German films is rank and smells to heaven. American public opinion would never tolerate things of this sort, even if they escaped the censors."

Behind the rhetoric, American studios were trying to have it both ways; buying up and distributing the German-made movies, deploring the fact that Hollywood could not hope to equal their quality at a like price, and then hiding behind smug I-told-you-so's when the films failed to attract large audiences in the provinces. By November 25, *Variety* was sniffing that "*The Golem* . . . has followed in the trail of its predecessors. A hit in New York, it has flopped in out-of-town territory. This was true also of *Passion, Deception* and *Caligari,* all sponsored by different companies."

The backlash continued in James Quirk's *Photoplay,* normally a reasoned, critically reliable publication. In June 1922, it published an article claiming that, out of seven years of intense production, "the entire German industry has produced so far as America is concerned, one 100 percent financially successful picture—*Passion*—three or four mediocrely successful pictures—*The Golem, Gypsy Blood, One Arabian Night*—and several failures, such as *Hamlet* and *Deception.*"

The reasons, according to Quirk? The Germans enjoy "horror and suffering on the screen," enjoy "eating, drinking and ordering people—especially your women—about." Moreover, they revel in watching "other people's emotions put in a test tube . . . with a residue of nastiness left in the bottom."

Americans, on the other hand, believe in "the eternal destiny of splendid youth, in the glory of motherhood, in the square deal, in the equality of sexes, in equal opportunities for all."

Robert Kane, who "prepared," i.e. edited, all of the German films that Famous Players would release, said his job was not an easy one. "The German mind cannot condense. It is prolix. It must put every detail of the story as originally written in novel form on the screen. Editing seems to be an unknown art in the film studios of Germany. It is as though a newspaper should print every word in all the Associated Press stuff that comes in over the wire at night—just slap it in." Kane regularly sliced as many as five to nine reels out of the German pictures that were handled by Famous Players–Lasky, and none of Lubitsch's German films played in America entirely unscathed.

The xenophobia was not total; writing in the September 1921 *Motion Picture Classic,* Frederick James Smith listed five German films *(Passion, The Cabinet of Dr. Caligari, Deception, The Golem, Gypsy Blood)* among his ten best of the year.

The irony of all this point/counterpoint is that, while *Madame DuBarry/Passion* is a good film, it is certainly not a great film, and not as good as contemporary American films like *Broken Blossoms, The Kid,* or *Four Horsemen of the Apocalypse.* Why the critical and commercial raptures?

Scholar Russell Merritt has theorized that America's passion for *Passion* was one of the first manifestations of that distinctly American habit of colonizing and enveloping new cultural trends from other countries, especially countries that have been militarily defeated. But Kevin Brownlow may be closer to the mark with his comment that "after reels and reels of stiff, dignified costume dramas, here was suddenly a film in which the people behaved like human beings. The sexual aspect must have been eye-opening because it was so *different.*" Lubitsch had, for the first time, dared to place sexual game-playing in the foreground of a large historical pageant. That, and perhaps just a touch of cultural snobbery, won the day, and made Lubitsch his American reputation.

With German films drawing so much attention, canny businessmen like Adolph Zukor decided to get involved . . . quietly. "This 'German Invasion' fright is the oldest and silliest of alarms," Zukor told *Photoplay* in July 1921. "One would think that the Germans had some magical recipe for making great pictures. A European might just as sensibly, after seeing *Birth of a Nation, Miracle Man,* or *Four Horsemen,* fall into a panic and believe that every American film was of equal caliber." At almost precisely the same time he was saying this, Zukor was leaving for Europe to negotiate for the services of Pola Negri.

The American money that was beginning to flow into Germany couldn't help but have its effect, both within the industry and without. Lubitsch's next film, *Das Weib des Pharao (The Loves of Pharaoh),* showed the effects of a larger-than-usual budget, as well as being the first film for which he would form his own company: Ernst Lubitsch–Film.

The sets are vast and impressive, fully the equal of the best work of directors of spectacle like DeMille and Griffith. Not only that, but Emil Jannings plays a bald pharaoh nearly forty years before Yul Brynner, as well as getting yet another dry run for his performances in *The Last Command* and *The Blue Angel.* Just as in the von Sternberg movies, his prideful, commanding character is robbed of his lofty position and roundly humiliated by the people that once feared him. Mortified, he falls dead. (In the original German version, the death of Pharaoh was complemented by the deaths of the young lovers, who are stoned to death by a mob; when the film was released in America, the lovers survived their tormentor.)

But the actors fail to give any sense of antiquity, of times past; they act in a barnstorming manner that attempts to match the outsized dimensions of the sets, possibly because they were attempting to compensate for a script that designer Ernst Stern characterized as "preternaturally feeble." *The Loves of Pharaoh* is of interest today because it shows Lubitsch employing Max Reinhardt's methods in ways Reinhardt could never have dreamed of. For example, during a slave riot, a man clambers over the edge of a cliff in the foreground while, in the valley hundreds of feet below, rioting slaves rush around like so many ants.

With as many as 2,000 extras in some scenes, Ernst Stern hit on an idea to make the organization of the extras as easy as possible. Each type of costume—warrior, slave, priests, whoever—was photographed and placed in an album. For each day's shooting, Lubitsch would go through the album and announce what he wanted for the day's shooting: "Five hundred number four's, twenty number fives, sixteen number twenty-threes," and so on.

The system worked, but however impressive the diagonal torrents of the masses, however formally beautiful the looks and movement of the film, the unmodulated melodramatics of the acting diminish the film's effectiveness.

Americans visiting Berlin in this period were struck by the city's bustling resemblance to Chicago; the lobby of the Hotel Adlon was as busy at 5 A.M. as at cocktail hour, and hungry-looking Bolsheviks, whose business in the city usually centered on women, were the equivalent of Chicago's gangsters. "When not childishly pretentious," wrote Anita Loos, "the night life was pretty decadent. Any Berlin lady of the evening might turn out to be a man; the prettiest girl on the street was Konrad [sic] Veidt . . ."

But the forces of reaction were already asserting their own particular view of Germany. In 1922, UFA, prodded by the industrialist/military money behind the company, produced *Fridericus Rex,* about the Prussian monarch Friedrich II, here portrayed as a brilliant, kind military genius and hero who might have succeeded in the Seven Years War if only his supporters had not abandoned him. The parallels to Kaiser Wilhelm II were obvious; the leader was correct, the policy was correct. The fault was in the hands of others. Weaklings. Traitors. Bankers. Jews.

In the midst of all this decadence and danger, Ernst managed to keep his head down and concentrate on his work. The locations for *The Loves of Pharaoh* were about three hours outside of Berlin, and the extras were recruited from unemployment agencies. It was not hard to keep the extras stirred up, for the 200 to 300 marks a day that Lubitsch was paying was barely sufficient to put food on the table.

Lubitsch utilized current political animosities in directing the crowds. "Here, you!" he would scream to a group of extras. "Run as though the Spartacans were turning machine guns on you!" Another group would be told that "The price of bread has gone up. Over there is a rich baker's shop. Go for him!" He humored them, cajoled them, paid attention to them. And he was careful to handpick the twenty or so extras that would be placed closest to the camera.

Lubitsch had already arrived independently at the same realization that had come to DeMille and Griffith: everyone in a movie was an actor, no matter how small their part. After Lubitsch instructed extras in what the spirit of a scene was to be, he would climb off his camera platform, take up the spear or sword, and show them what they were to do. "I wave my arms, I scowl, I rage, I do everything that is needed," he explained. "I am a mob in myself."

For the principal actors, he was equally exhaustive, giving them the entire story of the film, then asking them to lose themselves within it. "Don't bother about your own part or interpretation. Wait until you have heard mine as director. Yours may be better, or worse, as part of the picture, but . . . we must make every part harmonize with the whole."

Midway through shooting of a battle scene, one side of the army suddenly went on a work strike, demanding "more money—like the Americans get." They were paid off, causing the competing army of extras to demand the same. Labor was so cheap in Europe that Ernst was able to make a spectacular like *The Loves of Pharaoh* for about a fifth of what a comparable picture would have cost in America; Theodore Huff put the budget at $75,000.

While the critics, then and now, have pointed to the Reinhardt-influenced groupings, Ernst was also spending time studying classical composition, especially Velasquez. "Look at the battlefields," he would enthusiastically point out to a young assistant. "See how they're designed, how the painter used a hill to set up a battalion better than if it were in the valley."

Ernst told the writer Heinrich Fraenkel that the true inspiration for his crowd scenes had been Mauritz Stiller's 1919 Swedish film *Mr. Arne's Treasure.* At the same time, Stiller's 1920 *Erotikon* stimulated Lubitsch to give serious thought to ways to adapt *Kammerspiel,* intimate dramas of psychological nuance—and, perhaps, sex—to the movies.

· · ·

When Anita Loos was invited to visit the UFA studio, Lubitsch had made a point of seeking out her husband and, "torn with anxiety," asked him what kind of reception an enemy alien like himself could expect in America. John Emerson told him that Americans, while as vulnerable to xenophobia as anybody, don't hold grudges. Emerson assured him that there shouldn't be any problems. Ernst seemed to think that was too good to be true. He was right.

Lubitsch arrived in America for the first time on Christmas Eve 1921. He had just completed the editing of *The Loves of Pharaoh* and was planning a trip that would encompass a visit to Hollywood and attendance at the American premiere of his new film on February 21, 1922. He admired the American movie palaces ("They are very beautiful," he said through an interpreter, "much more pretentious than anything we have in Berlin") and told Louella Parsons that he did his own editing and believed no director should ever entrust that particular job to anyone else.

On December 27, he gave an interview to a reporter from *Moving Picture World,* and expounded on his production methods and his favorite films and filmmakers from America.

"The titles are all written before the shooting begins," he said. "As I shoot, I plan how I'll cut the picture and carefully keep a record of intended cuts, so that it usually only takes me ten days for the editing work.

"I have not had the opportunity to see most of your great pictures, but I consider that, among those I have seen, *Broken Blossoms* is incomparable and I doubt if you have any to equal it. The German people went wild over it. This is the picture which decided me to visit your country and study your methods."

He was particularly struck by the vast differences between the American and German systems of production. The latter struck him as "limited," as apparently, did the acting talent. "All of the German stars, with the exception of the dynamic Pola Negri, are actors who have proved themselves on the legitimate stage." To a writer from *The Nation,* he freely admitted that "most German films . . . are what we call 'kitsch' . . ."

While in New York he attended the premieres of von Stroheim's *Foolish Wives* and Griffith's *Orphans of the Storm,* and was even given a guided tour of Sing-Sing, where he received a button signifying three years' good behavior. He was asked about his favorites among his own films, and replied that "the last is always my favorite. I rush into them with such high spirits, and live so close to my work, that my mind always grasps my last work as its favorite."

He went to his first Broadway shows, and was particularly enthralled by the *Music Box Revue*. The power of metaphor was further impressed on a mind that had little sympathy for literalism or expressionism. "I found a Spanish environment and atmosphere projected by a few simple but exquisite things—a shawl, a fan," he exclaimed. "That is a charming use of the symbolical, the suggestive.

"I can assure you that the scenes, dances, choruses, decorations of your musical comedies and revues are unrivaled. They are superior to anything in either Berlin or Paris . . . American dancing is the best and most beautiful in the world. The dancers that I have seen don't dance as though they were paid to do it, but as though they were artists practicing a necessary expression of themselves."

Although Ernst had intended to go on to Hollywood to attend the American premiere of *The Loves of Pharaoh,* he abruptly cut his visit short after little more than three weeks, because of what *Variety* reported as unpleasant phone calls and letters and the "belief that he was regarded here as an unfriendly person and an enemy of the American actor." Ernst sailed for Germany on January 17.

Even though his visit was limited to the East Coast, Lubitsch could see that the facilities and equipment in America were vastly superior to anything he had access to in Germany. While there were some 1,600 film companies in Germany by the early 1920s, half of them in Berlin, all supplying 3,700 theaters, they were ants at a sparse picnic, beset by insufficient material, both physical and spiritual.

Ernst had discovered that in America, the art director was less important than the cameraman. "The American cameramen are the best in the world," he would comment in 1929. "How we used to envy them in [Germany]. They knew one thing that we would have given anything to know: they could photograph their people so that the makeup didn't show! They made pictures of *human beings* rather than *actors.*"

Two years later, having made a few American movies, Ernst would write an article praising American cameramen like Charles Rosher and Charles Van Enger.

"They take care and train their cameras as a dog fancier would his pets. Every cinematographer has his particular technique—his peculiar tricks . . . when the day's shooting is done, the cinematographer goes to the laboratory and experiments—he tries out what he can do with his camera—he, himself, will invent some technical novelty—he will tell the director the next day: 'See what I can do with my camera,' or, 'Do you want that certain effect? I can give it to you, my camera can do it!' This

. . . ambition of the cinematographer is the mainspring of his progress and success."

To a director used to having to cope with an omnipresent coal shortage, which restricted production by limiting both lighting effects and the hours of work, just the specter of unlimited electricity seemed enormously seductive. "When we made *Gypsy Blood,*" he said, ". . . I don't think we had more than eight lights for the whole picture!"

Arriving back in Germany, Lubitsch found that things were continuing to turn ugly; in June 1922, Foreign Minister Walter Rathenau was assassinated by fanatic nationalists, which began the terrible era of inflation that paralyzed Germany economically. That summer, the value of the mark declined to 400 per dollar. By January 1923, it would sink to 7,000 to the dollar; by July, 160,000 to the dollar; by August, a million to the dollar. Germany was going insane.

"I have a pretty thorough knowledge of history," wrote novelist Stefan Zweig, "but never, to my recollection, has it produced such madness in such gigantic proportions." Mathias Erzenberger, a civilian who had been stuck with the unenviable task of signing the Armistice ending World War I, was assassinated by right-wingers. One government fell in a dispute over the proper colors for Germany's *naval* flag. Fritz Lang, already considered one of Germany's major directors, reported seeing a poster that summed up the entire era: *Berlin, sein Tanzer is der Tod* (Berlin, your dancing partner is Death).

By the end of 1924, Bertolt Brecht would suggest a vicious switch on the conventional phrase Germans used to describe themselves: a nation of Denker und Dichter (thinkers and poets). Brecht's suggestion was Denkes und Dichter, Denke being a mass murderer who had sold sausages made of human flesh to customers used to eating roast dog and cat during the war shortages. "I contend," said Brecht, "that the best people of Germany . . . failed to recognize the qualities of true German genius which the fellow displayed, namely: method, conscientiousness, cold-bloodedness, and the ability to base one's every act on a firm philosophical foundation."

In Munich in 1923, a man named Hitler gathered around him a crew of ex-officers, anti-Semites, and political cranks. Collectively, they attempted to break up a meeting of a Bavarian political party. For his temerity, not to mention his lack of success, Hitler was sentenced to five years imprisonment, but served only a few months, during which time he wrote a book and enjoyed the tea and flowers that sympathetic women would bring to the prison.

It was Hitler's belief that Jews and Marxists had formed a fifth column that had stabbed Germany in the back during the war, resulting in her humiliation before the entire world. Anointed by Germany's Aryan soul to weed out the Jews and Communists infecting the otherwise superior body politic, Hitler believed that the answer to any and all problems bedeviling Germany was fanatical nationalism.

For anybody raised in the liberal traditions of the Berlin Jewish bourgeoisie, indeed, for all German intellectuals, Hitler's message was anathema, but it was also absurd, not to be taken seriously. It wasn't merely the fact that he looked like Charlie Chaplin; there was the matter of his accent. "He spoke a terrible German," remembered the playwright/producer Felix Jackson. "A deep, deep, slang Austrian/German; it sounded very funny." Hitler was a joke, no more a serious political threat than Al Capone.

Inflation, however, was serious. It wiped out the savings of the entire Lubitsch family. Anna Lubitsch had three sisters, Ida, Flora, and Francie, as well as her ne'er-do-well brother Sally. The sisters had always banded together to take care of Sally on those frequent occasions when the cards turned against him, but now they were poor, too. Ernst undertook to support them all.

For a man who disliked uproar or neurosis of any kind, a man who wanted "a nice family," Germany in 1922 was no place to live. Ernst knew that in America there was a good deal of latent anti-German hysteria left over from the war, but it was not enough to dissuade him from fixating on this land of milk and honey. "Next time we meet," Ernst had told Louella Parsons in New York, "I shall try and learn English." The next time they met, Lubitsch would indeed be speaking English, although not very well. But that was the least important of the changes that ten months would bring.

On his return to Germany, Lubitsch solemnized a relationship that had begun some time earlier. Helene (Leni) Sonnet was born in 1898 in a small town near Frankfurt. She married a German soldier who died of influenza during World War I and left her with two small children, Edmund, born in February 1917, and Heinz, born in July 1915.

Leaving her children with her parents, Leni moved to Berlin, then began working onstage and as an extra in the movies. One day she was invited to attend a birthday party at the UFA studio to which Lubitsch had also been invited. That night, she went home with him and never left.

Leni Sonnet was an attractive, very sensual woman, just the sort to bring a hidebound, lonely man suddenly roaring out of his workaholic's closet. She was also another in a long line of non-Jewish blondes that Lubitsch would be attracted to. A typical man of his time, Lubitsch would tell Leni that he would never be able to marry a Jewish woman. "It would be like marrying my sister," he claimed. On August 23, 1922, at eleven in the morning, Ernst Lubitsch married Leni Sonnet Kraus, after which they honeymooned in his beloved Budapest.

He prepared and shot *Die Flamme (The Flame),* his last film in Germany, released in America in 1924 as *Montmartre.* Production was difficult, for Pola Negri's displays of temperament had grown insupportable. She had always been difficult, but it was getting worse. Most days, she wouldn't appear on the set until noon.

Lubitsch was probably thinking of Negri when he wrote in 1932 that "The relation between a director and an actress is like the relation between a man and his mistress. They are bound together by contract, but there is no sentimental attachment."

When an American reporter visiting the set of *The Flame* told Lubitsch that he had heard Lubitsch and Negri were married, the director, "brimming over with glee" hurried off to tell Negri. Negri tossed back her head and laughed, then affectionately patted Lubitsch on the cheek.

For public consumption, Ernst paid tribute to his leading lady's fiery talents, calling her "a wonderful, wonderful woman." Privately, Lubitsch later told the cameraman Charles Van Enger that on *The Flame* he had to prepare two scripts, one for Negri and one for everybody else. Her scenes were shot in a compressed period, then Lubitsch would give her time off while he did the rest, free from her interference.

"He left Germany before she saw *The Flame* and they were very bitter about one another," remembered Van Enger. It didn't show. From the only surviving fragment of the film, at the Munich Stadtmuseum, it is obvious that Lubitsch felt considerably more at ease with La Boheme Paris than ancient Egypt or fairy-tale Persia. The film bears witness to the calmer, more focused dramatic style that Ernst was gravitating toward. A portion of the film that is now lost bore witness to the inferential style that critics would believe was only brought to fruition by the influence of Chaplin's *A Woman of Paris.*

In *The Flame,* Negri is contemplating whether to leave her husband. She sits at her dressing table nervously fingering her wedding ring. She takes it off, weighs it in her palm. She puts it in a drawer. She takes an empty box, puts the ring in it, then puts the box back in the drawer. As she shuts the drawer, a framed photo of her husband falls over. The full implications of her act become obvious. She suddenly grows frightened, her body stiffening. She sets the photo back up, takes the box out of the drawer, takes the ring out, puts it back on her finger, gets up, and runs into the next room to embrace her husband.

As Heinrich Fraenkel noted, "Told in words, this is tedious. [But] in half a minute of action on the screen, its detail and symbolism combine to make, for its period, a revelation of what the film could achieve in the hands of an inventive filmmaker."

The underplayed subtlety of *The Flame,* its sudden modulation of style in both acting and direction, could be perceived as a conscious attempt at playing to the American market, but it wasn't. According to Lubitsch, "As an antidote against the great big historical canvasses, I felt the necessity of making . . . small, intimate *Kammerspiel."*

Indeed, with few exceptions, for the rest of his career Ernst would use Max Reinhardt's unified blending of script, setting, and performance, even on material generally thought too insubstantial to warrant such painstaking care. The result would be a foundation of grave, methodical intent supporting a blithe, carefree, beautifully textured surface structure. In time, this construct would come to be known as "The Lubitsch Touch."

When *The Flame* was released in America in 1924, Paramount inserted an alternate ending and made other cuts, resulting in a film that, said Lubitsch, "did not give the slightest idea of the dramatic value and impact of the original version."

In the latter part of 1922, Famous Players bailed out of their experiment with EFA. Despite the profusion of press attention, the majority of German films released in America had not been successful. Adolph Zukor decided to recoup his investment by importing the most likely of the German talent to America. Pola Negri left for America in 1922, and Zukor also offered Ernst a job.

While *The Flame* was being made, Ernst had begun construction of a house on the edge of Schöneberg Park. It was a house that would never be lived in by its owner, for, by the time it was ready to be occupied, Lubitsch would be on his way to Hollywood, with a contract to direct the biggest female star in the world.

c h a p t e r   t h r e e

I loved Lubitsch, mainly for his tremendous desire to make something funny with class . . . It was strange—he really should have been a Frenchman.

— e d g a r   g .   u l m e r

Although she always claimed to have been born Gladys Marie Smith in 1893, Mary Pickford was actually born Gladys Louise Smith in 1892, a small but not untypical evasion of reality. Entering movies with the Biograph Company in April 1909, Pickford's ease, natural charm, and innate star quality propelled her to the top of her profession by 1915. Although an extremely gifted, versatile actress, Pickford's early poverty had indelibly marked her, and she was afraid to stray far from the tight vise of public expectations, which, in the heavily indicative scorecard of the box office, meant playing winsome adolescents. This in spite of the fact that by 1923 Pickford was over thirty, the only female movie mogul, and had a background of considerable color that included two marriages and numerous lovers.

It was at this point that she decided she wanted to do an adult role, a *real* adult role, with no fantasy sequences or dual roles as a sop to her public. At the same time, she had been looking at some of the German films that had reached America in the wake of the critical success of *The Cabinet of Dr. Caligari*. It seemed to her and her husband, Douglas Fairbanks, an inveterate enthusiast about virtually everything, that the best of them were directed by Ernst Lubitsch. After some fairly simple negotia-

Lubitsch signs the contract with Mary Pickford (right) for his first American picture, while Mary's mother, Charlotte, displays her Irish charm.

tions, Mary signed Lubitsch to a contract, the announcement of which prompted a sizable wave of anti-German sentiment left over from World War I. The film was to be an adaptation of *Faust*.

Accompanied by his wife, Leni, and Henry Blanke, Lubitsch left Germany on December 2, 1922, from the port of Bremerhaven. (Leni's boys were left with her parents; they would follow their mother and stepfather to America a year later, when it became clear that Ernst's career mandated that the family stay in America.) The Lubitsch family was there to see their boy off; according to a story related by Hans Kräly, the seventy-year-old Simon was "close to tears at the idea that his son was traveling to California, to a world full of Indians, mountain lions, rattlesnakes, and any number of other wild animals." When the time came to say good-bye, Ernst's sister Marga broke down in heavy sobs. "Don't cry, Greta," Ernst said. "We Lubitschs are not sentimental." He would return to his homeland only twice more, in 1927 and 1932.

As it turned out, Ernst left Germany at a good time. In January 1923 the German government hesitated with their reparations payments for World War I and the French promptly occupied the Ruhr Valley. From January to August of 1923, the exchange rate for one American dollar rose from 10,000 marks to 4.6 million.

By 1926, UFA was forced to accept a partnership with Universal, Paramount, and MGM. In return for a large infusion of capital, UFA had to form a releasing organization with the three American companies, with the resulting combine (Parafamet) distributing ten films from each of the partners. Paramount and MGM could each choose ten UFA films of their choice for American distribution, and UFA had to fill 75 percent of its theaters with Parafamet product. All this led even the liberal German film journal *Lichthild-Bühne* to sound a xenophobic note with a headline reading "Americanization of UFA?" As the first German to emigrate to Hollywood after World War I, Ernst was the point man in a brain drain that, over the next ten years, would decimate German film.

Nathan Burkan, the attorney for Charlie Chaplin, Pickford's partner in United Artists, quietly met Ernst in New York in an effort to defuse any bad press. Lubitsch's appearance did not jibe with the image of a director who had "humanized history." He wore egg-top trousers and banana yellow boots, and had several gold teeth in the front of his mouth. He looked like a middle-class Jewish burgher.

After considerable struggle, Burkan outfitted him with a new wardrobe and had his own dentist replace the gold teeth with porcelain ones. Lubitsch, his wife, and Blanke took a train to Chicago, where they were met by Douglas Fairbanks' brother Robert, who accompanied them on the train to California. Another passenger on the train was Western star William S. Hart, whose singular, endearingly horse-faced presence must have made Lubitsch feel like a Berlin version of Frank Baum's Dorothy; he was definitely not in Germany anymore.

Robert Florey, later a director, then doing foreign publicity for Pickford and Fairbanks, met Ernst at the train. "It happened to be the most disagreeable night I have seen in California," Lubitsch remembered. "It was cold and foggy and dark . . . I was cold in body and spirit. I was homesick and miserable in every way." Florey took Lubitsch and Blanke to the Ambassador Hotel where they were met by relays of protesting American veterans of World War I.

"They didn't start anything," remembered Henry Blanke in 1976, "they just demonstrated and protested on the street, outside, against

Lubitsch working in America. We didn't go near it. What a welcome." According to Florey, Lubitsch talked of nothing but the sets for *Faust,* and was anxious to get to the studio so he could begin work with Sven Gade, the art director.

By daylight, the town seemed not merely hospitable but enticing. What particularly impressed Lubitsch were the houses; some Tudor, some Moorish, some in the Mission style. All of them struck him as simultaneously quaint and artistic. Then there was the quality of the California light, white and clear, lending a brilliant phosphorescent brightness to the blue bowl of sky. It seemed to Ernst as though he could reach out and touch the mountains that divided Hollywood from the San Fernando Valley.

Louella Parsons called, wanting to know if Lubitsch "had been in the trenches during the war." When it was explained that he had been a civilian noncombatant, suspicion lessened, but there was no question that they were not about to be welcomed with open arms. By late December—Henry Blanke celebrated his twenty-first birthday that month—Lubitsch was ensconced at the Pickford-Fairbanks studio fighting for his life. As Mary Pickford remembered, "poor Ernst Lubitsch arrived not knowing what kind of demon I was."

Pickford and Ernst were officially introduced by Edward Knoblock, a successful playwright and friend of the Fairbankses who was working on their scripts and who also spoke fluent German. Lubitsch took Pickford's hand, then threw it away as if it was a dead thing. "My God," he told Knoblock in German, "she is cold. Yeah, she is cold. How can she be an actress and be so cold?"

Pickford rather tactlessly informed Lubitsch that *Faust* was being canceled because of an explosively negative reaction from her mother, Charlotte, who absolutely forbade her daughter playing the part of Marguerite, an unwed mother who kills her baby. Instead, she was substituting *Dorothy Vernon of Haddon Hall,* an adaptation of a hoary novel from 1898. Lubitsch was aghast. Two days after the change was announced, Pickford noticed Lubitsch walking through the wheatfield where Douglas Fairbanks had built his enormous castle set for *Robin Hood.* He was talking to himself and gesticulating. "There goes trouble," she told her mother.

Later that day, Lubitsch told Pickford he didn't want to direct *Dorothy Vernon of Haddon Hall.* "Der are too many qveens and not enough qveens," he said by way of explanation, meaning that the story, which involved Elizabeth I and Mary, Queen of Scots, was so grand that there was no room for Dorothy Vernon. According to her own recollections, Pickford was disappointed ("It was [like] a blow to the face . . .") but she could understand his point of view and suggested that they try to find another story. Lubitsch went out and button-holed Knoblock. "My God, now I know she is cold. She took it standing up. She is cold. She can't act."

"Well," said Knoblock, "wait until you get her before the cameras and then you'll see."

Despite some disagreement within the Pickford unit, everyone finally settled on a script tentatively titled *The Street Singer,* adapted by Knoblock from a minor French play called *Don César de Bazan.* Just before production began, there was an argument when Lubitsch found out that Mary, not he, would have the final authority in any disagreement. "I told him that I would never interfere with him on the set, never gainsay him," said Pickford. "But if it comes to an issue, I have to put the money up. I will be glad to arbitrate it, bring in a person we both respect, but you are not the person of last appeal."

For Lubitsch, this was a nightmare, worse than dealing with Pola Negri. However temperamental she might have been, Negri was only a hired hand, and hired hands can always be finessed. Now Lubitsch was the hired hand. Despite Edward Knoblock's assurances that Pickford would not be unreasonable, that Lubitsch was being foolish to make such an issue out of something that would probably never even happen, Ernst lost his temper and tore all the buttons off his clothing, then pounced on Knoblock's papers, throwing them in the air.

Most of this atypical behavior was nothing more than displaced nerves, for Lubitsch later confessed to a newly arrived Victor Seastrom that he was continually on edge during his first few months in Hollywood. Seastrom, whose career in Hollywood had been made possible by enthusiastic testimonials from Lubitsch and Chaplin, found Ernst to be "small, typically Jewish, very lively and very interesting."

Despite these obvious intimations of a fatal misalliance, shooting of *The Street Singer* (as it was known during production) began on March 5, 1923, and lurched on until May 31. Pickford would claim that the battles became so pitched that the only way the film was finished was by her acquiescing to Lubitsch's authority.

Simple things like Lubitsch's thick German accent seemed to offend Pickford's decorousness. Preparing a setup, Lubitsch would turn to cameraman Charles Rosher and say, "All right, upset your camera," which was good for a few giggles. In a scene involving Holbrook Blinn and a dagger, Lubitsch gave Blinn the line reading "You should say to her, 'Rosita, ver is da dagger mit da yools.' " Blinn promptly turned to Mary with the cameras running and said, "Rosita, ver is da dagger mit da yools?" resulting in helpless laughter from the actors and confusion from Lubitsch.

At one point, Ernst rushed up to Edward Knoblock and shouted "Vere iss dem dajer mid vass he iss geshtickt?" Knoblock worked the sentence over in his mind and realized that Lubitsch was asking about a prop dagger with which the hero was to be stabbed. "Another time," Knoblock wrote, "when Lubitsch and I had a difference about the interpretation of a scene, he lost his temper and started rushing off the set, but turned to face me and by way of annihilating farewell exclaimed, 'How do you do?' "

There is humor in these stories, but there is also an ugly edge, of actors and writers who should know better having sport with a stranger in a strange land. As far as Pickford was concerned, Lubitsch was personally vulgar—"He ate German fried potatoes three times a day," a habit which was probably what led to an incident where Lubitsch left greasy fingerprints all over Mary's newly painted dove-gray dressing room—and he was a director of props, not actresses.

For his part, Lubitsch believed that he was simply trying to cure Mary of her reliance on "the Pickford tricks," and bring her into his (screen) world of alternating bursts of lighthearted sexual cajolery and dramatic intensity, the coin of the Lubitsch realm. If he seemed more overbearing than absolutely necessary, it might have been because he spoke almost no English and something was being lost in translation.

Despite the misalliance between director and star, Lubitsch did not have to alter his carefully thought-out methods of production. By this time, he prided himself on delineating character and plot through action that would obviate the need for many titles. To Germans like Lubitsch and Blanke, used to the inferential in theater as well as cinema, many American pictures were wildly over-titled. Taking screen time to say "The wedding took place in the cool shadow of the cathedral" struck them as redundant, since the establishing shot would show the audience that the wedding was in a cathedral.

"A photoplay today often is nothing else but the narration of a story told in subtitles and interrupted by a series of moving pictures," Ernst would write in a 1924 book entitled *The Truth About the Movies*. "In some cases this goes so far that not only the telling of the plot but also the characterization is done almost totally by means of subtitles and the motion pictures serve merely as illustrations."

This pedantic laziness, whereby the movie was not so much watched as read, struck Lubitsch as an abomination. "What we must strive for as the ideal to be attained is the title-less motion picture . . . It is the task of the scenarist to invent little pieces of business that are so characteristic and give so deep an insight into his creatures, that their personalities clearly and organically unfold before the eyes of the audience so that the latter feel that the actions of these people are contingent upon their characters, that there exists some kind of a logical fate, and that nothing is left to mere accident, or coincidence of irrelative [sic] happenings. A good scenario should contain the smallest details of business and leave nothing to chance direction or the whim of the moment."

It was as succinct a statement of Lubitsch's theory of filmmaking as he would ever make. Nor was it idle puffery, as he would prove very shortly.

Besides making his films more of a visual and less of a reading experience, Lubitsch imposed his distinctive, methodical sense of rhythm on the filmmaking process itself, setting a brisk but not hurried pace.

"I think over my medium shot when I am making my long shot," he explained, "and I am ready for what I want when it comes to a close-up. I don't want to get the actors fatigued, and only when it appears absolutely necessary do I insist upon going over the scene three or four times. A player may have just the expression you want, but on the fourth or fifth attempt he is too sure of himself." (Lubitsch would find multiple takes "absolutely necessary" a good deal of the time.)

Despite the emotional unease of working in a totally alien environment, the Pickford studio was not entirely a negative adjustment; Ernst adored the bounty of equipment, sets, and even electricity. "They loaded the guns," he would report with delight. "I fired them. I felt as though someone had supplied me with an entire collection of Aladdin's lamps."

Despite the troubled production, Pickford felt that the results were worth it. Her correspondence at the time reveals her to be quite enamored of Lubitsch and their collaboration, so much so that she tried to arrange a production deal for him at United Artists. On June 12, 1923, she, Chaplin, and Fairbanks had a meeting in which they discussed cofinancing a series of Lubitsch pictures for United Artists. After some conversation, Fairbanks and Chaplin backed out because of the heavy expenses for which they were already obligated.

On June 13, two full weeks after *The Street Singer* had been completed, Pickford wrote Cap O'Brien, her attorney, that "Lubitsch would be a great asset to our company if he could do spectacles. Personally, I still believe he is the greatest director in the world and would be willing to back him if I could afford it." Six days later, after O'Brien had gently urged her to title the film *Rosita* ("it is soft and sweet, and if it typifies the character, it ought to be a valuable title"), she reiterated to O'Brien that "I am very pleased with *Rosita* and think it will be well received."

Although United Artists president Hiram Abrams had offered to raise half the money for the proposed Lubitsch unit from eastern banks, Pickford ruled that out because it would give Abrams more of a rooting interest in Lubitsch's productions than in those of the original partners. Lubitsch also wanted to continue with United Artists, and direct Mary in another picture in the early part of 1924, followed by one or two pictures for U.A. without Pickford. But Lubitsch wanted guarantees of financing.

"He wants to know if it is possible to get the money," continued Pickford, "as he has several very fine offers out here, but all of them for very long-term contracts . . . he is like a little boy and always anxious to get things settled." Pickford closed by telling O'Brien that a proposed salary for Lubitsch of $3,500 a week was "exorbitant," that $2,500 to $3,000 was more like it.

As always with United Artists, the company's refusal to cosign loans or guarantee outside financing doomed the venture. Since, technically, Lubitsch had directed *Rosita* on loan-out from Famous Players–Lasky, he began angling for his release so he could accept more lucrative terms elsewhere.

(Jesse Lasky insisted that Lubitsch had never been on the Famous Players–Lasky payroll, but rather on the roster of the Hamilton Theatrical Corporation, a subsidiary that had been formed to make pictures for Famous Players release in Germany, using German talent. It was an odd distinction to make; it is possible that Lasky was none too certain of how American audiences would take to a German director on their shores, and was constructing an out, just in case.)

The industry buzz on *Rosita* was obviously excellent, but Lubitsch was not happy. According to Henry Blanke, Lubitsch was fully prepared to go back to Germany. "After *Rosita,* he went to see Jesse Lasky at the old Vine Street studio," remembered Blanke. According to this version, Lubitsch told Lasky that he wanted to go back to Germany, where his contract gave him complete control over virtually every aspect of his films. "He didn't want to work in the factory system anymore," said Blanke. But Lasky was no longer interested in importing films from Germany and wasn't about to commit himself to letting a still-untested Lubitsch handle their contract stars. The two men agreed to disagree; in mid-June 1923, Lasky settled Lubitsch's contract.

Rosita premiered September 14, 1923, at New York's Lyric Theater and was received with excellent reviews; *The New York Times* called it "exquisite," *Vanity Fair* referred to it as "that distinguished and lovely film," and *Photoplay* said that "there is no actress today who could portray the gay, graceful, coquettish little street singer of Seville . . . as she does," while Lubitsch again showed "why [he] holds his place among the leading directors of the world." The invariably hard-nosed *Variety* said that Ernst had brought out "a Mary Pickford different and greater than at any time in her screen career," and *Moving Picture World* said that Lubitsch "fully lives up to his reputation as being one of the world's leading directors."

The physical production of *Rosita* is stunning: huge, vaulted sets, lavish outdoor constructions of old Seville, populated by thousands of extras. As with the first American films of Murnau and Lang, Lubitsch turned a basically intimate story into something of a visual opera.

Although *Rosita* is a fairly weighty nine reels long, it moves at a far steadier pace than the Pickford films that bookend it. In addition, Lubitsch endows the film with a texture derived largely from a procession of carefully chosen, jaggedly baroque faces, giving *Rosita* a more specific sense of realistic humanity than most other Pickford films. The compositions are precise, formal—there is only one tracking shot and one pan right in the entire picture—without being academic. It is among the most physically beautiful of all silent films.

The premise of the film is simplicity itself: Rosita is a street singer, the idol of the mobs. The king sees her and wishes to make her his mistress, in spite of his wife's disapproval, in spite of Rosita's love for the penniless nobleman Don Diego (George Walsh), in spite of the fact that she sings satirical songs about royalty.

While *Rosita* is a recognizable halfway point between Lubitsch's historical spectaculars and the later, sly sexual comedies, he does not entirely neglect the familiar Pickford turf. There's a delightful scene when a hungry Rosita, a poor girl in a palace, is trying to fight off hunger pangs while alone in a room with a large bowl of fruit. The camera holds on a static shot of the fruit on top of a table, while Pickford passes in back of it, giving it surreptitious glances. After a few practice cruises, her arm darts out and grabs an apple; another pass, and a banana.

But all of Lubitsch's skill can't hide the fact that Pickford's performance is external and obviously unfelt, with the actress uncomfortable with the Mediterranean gestures and displays of temperament. When Rosita believes her lover to be dead and plans to kill the king in revenge, instead of playing the scene for cold fury Pickford flares her eyes and contorts her mouth with the evil avidity of a vampire. Negri could have gotten away with the moment; Pickford, never.

Rosita is a very good film but it is a very good film in spite of its star performance rather than because of it. It was an experiment Pickford would never repeat. Years later, mired in alcoholism and casting about for reasons for the simultaneous departures of her career and her marriage to Fairbanks, Pickford began to develop something of an *idée fixe* about *Rosita*. She would say of Lubitsch that "He tried to be as moral as possible, and I tried to be slightly naughty. I've always felt the results were pretty terrible. I didn't like myself as Rosita. I think it was my fault, not Lubitsch's. We just didn't seem to get together, but I was very proud of the fact that I was able to bring him to the country with no bad effects."

Despite the good reviews and the picture's own self-evident quality, Pickford's memories hardened, and she became convinced that *Rosita* was a terrible film ("It's the worst picture I ever did, it's the worst picture I ever saw") and a failure to boot. Both Mitchell Leisen and Henry Blanke agreed with her. Yet, it grossed $940,872 in the United States, Canada, and South America alone, $35,000 more than the following year's *Dorothy Vernon of Haddon Hall,* which she preferred to think of as a successful recovery from the Lubitsch debacle.

Lubitsch had a more benevolent view of *Rosita.* "I have made better, more significant pictures than *Rosita,*" he told Hedda Hopper in 1943, "but never one that I have loved more. Because with that I associate the finest thing that ever happened to me—the opportunity to come to America, to become a citizen. Besides that good fortune, all else pales."

Publicly, he would never have anything but praise for Mary Pickford ("the most practical artist I have ever met. She can dictate policies, handle finances, bargain with supporting players, attend to booking problems, and still keep her mind on acting. It is no wonder that she held her place at the top longer than any personality in motion pictures"). In private, he would roll his eyes and humorously point out the vast, unbridgeable gap between what the woman was and what she played.

The Los Angeles that Lubitsch had arrived in was undergoing one of the most remarkable transformations in American history. Only ten years before, the population had been a modest 319,198, but during the 1920s the population would surge past a million. By 1930, the residential base was 1,470,516. Between 1920 and 1930, 2 million Americans migrated to California, 1.5 million of them settling in Southern California. The four most prosperous residential districts of the city then were West Adams Heights, Wilshire, Hollywood, and Beverly Hills. Los Angeles was conspicuously proud of its two symphony orchestras, its art museums, public library, three universities, and a good community theater.

From the firmly contained outlines of Berlin, Lubitsch had arrived in a city where twenty-two major office buildings would be erected in 1924 alone, with $87 million committed for high-rise construction the following year. The gridlock of the next half-century was already in evidence; by the end of 1924, 310,000 automobiles, more than the total registered in the state of New York, were entering Los Angeles every day.

The people in these cars were predominantly white. A 1926 census revealed 45,000 Hispanics, 33,000 blacks, and 30,000 Asians. Everyone else, more than 90 percent of the population, were whites of European descent, including a vigorous Jewish population of less than 100,000.

"This steady speedy growth," observed Bruce Bliven in the *New Republic* of July 1927, "creates an easy optimism, a lazy prosperity which dominates people's lives. Anything seems possible; the future is yours, and the past?—there isn't any."

The industries that were fueling this firestorm growth were oil, maritime trade, agriculture, banking, and movies, the biggest of them all. The film industry had made Hollywood, in the words of historian Kevin Starr, "a place energized by dreams." By 1926, the movies had become, according to their own, probably overly effusive estimate, the fourth largest industry in the world—35,000 people were earning $1.25 million working in films. In 1927, the Hollywood studios would spend the heroic figure of $103 million to make movies, a 25 percent increase over the previous year.

Among the least regarded of these studios was Warner Bros.

Warner Bros. had been founded in 1904 as the Duquesne Amusement & Supply Company. The brothers had arrived in Hollywood in 1915, but had not officially incorporated until 1923. The company was ruled by an uneasy triumvirate of siblings: Jack and Sam Warner ran the production end of the business in Hollywood, while Harry ran the New York office. As surely as scissors cut paper, in the movie business, New York rules Hollywood. Although they were brothers, ceding final authority to Harry was always particularly galling to Jack Warner.

"My father had a great commercial sense," remembered Jack Warner, Jr., who was born in 1916 and whose earliest memory of the studio is of Mal St. Clair directing a Rin Tin Tin picture. "But Harry was a little out of his time. He saw movies as a great medium of education, a spreading of the doctrine of brotherhood. They had been making two-reelers with Al St. John and Monte Banks, and in just a few years Harry got enough money together to make good pictures. Since Harry wanted to make classics, they called the series 'Classics of the Screen.' "

It seemed like a perfect marriage; Warners was a studio hungry for prestige, while Lubitsch was an obviously prestigious director with, apparently, a commercial sense as well. According to both Henry Blanke and Hal Wallis, Warners enticed the very available Lubitsch by sending Irene Rich, a beautiful actress then having an affair with Jack Warner, to the front door of Lubitsch's rented house.

She rang the bell. When Lubitsch came to the door, she said "Harry Warner is coming in a few minutes to talk to you about an offer," whereupon she turned and left. Harry had his full attention, for Ernst was enchanted at such unorthodox business methods. The deal, as outlined in a rather laboriously written twenty-page contract, mandated six pictures spread over three years. Lubitsch was to be paid $60,000 per film, plus one-third of the net profits "so long as Warner derives any income, profits or other compensation, directly or indirectly, during the life of each of said photoplays."

But the contract's most remarkable provisions were front-loaded in clause number two, to wit: "Lubitsch shall have the sole, complete and absolute charge of the production of each such photoplay, except . . . in matters involving money . . . and that the story shall be selected by Warner and approved of by Lubitsch . . . Such sole charge shall include . . . the sole direction, control and supervision, as well as the hire and discharge of the scenario writer, the cast . . . the assistant directors, cameraman, working staff and force, sole charge of all properties, costumes, accessories, settings and equipment necessary for such production, sole charge of the picturization of the scenario from the editing of the scenario to the assemblage and completion of the sample positive print, sole charge and control of the assembling, titling and cutting of each such photoplay . . . and the absolute right of selection of locations where the same shall be filmed . . ."

"Warner agrees that . . . there shall be no interference of any kind whatsoever from any source, with Lubitsch, with respect to any matter or thing connected with the production, cutting and final completion of such photoplays."

Should any changes in a film be deemed necessary because of censorship, Lubitsch would make them himself. The deal was exclusive, with the proviso that Lubitsch could direct one picture per year for Mary Pickford so long as the loan-out did not interfere with his productions for Warner Bros.

It was a remarkable contract; in essence, he was given his own production unit. Once the story and budget were agreed to, Lubitsch had final cut, a largely unheard of right for a filmmaker working with somebody else's money then or now. He had earned all this before the industry had a chance to see if his European reputation would transfer. On August 7, five weeks before *Rosita* opened, Lubitsch signed with Warner Bros.

The brothers Warner divided the labor equitably; Jack was mostly in charge of the pictures themselves, Sam ("a very warm, friendly man," according to his nephew) was mostly in charge of the technological end—the cameras, the personnel, the back lot. Harry was mostly in charge of the finances. As long as everything stayed that way, the management of the Warner studio ran smoothly, but Harry eventually left New York to go to California and the friction began. "When bankers start putting on sport jackets, watch out," said Jack Warner, Jr. wryly.

"Jack was more in the public eye," remembered Patsy Ruth Miller, a Warners star of the mid-1920s. "Harry was the businessman in the background. Jack was not a terribly polished man; their background was not high society. He was rather bawdy at times, but he decided what was made."

It was Harry Warner who was responsible for signing Lubitsch, for he had a predisposition toward European talent. "Harry went to Europe a lot," remembered Jack Warner, Jr., "and he would see people over there. Actors, directors, or art directors. He'd sign them up and send them to the studio. William Dieterle was signed that way, as was Michael Curtiz. The last of that group was Errol Flynn.

"When Harry went after Lubitsch, Warner Brothers was a new studio and he wanted to give it some class. Lubitsch was the first real class that my father's company had; until then, they weren't far removed from Poverty Row."

Not far at all. Although the Warner Bros. financial ledgers indicate a well-run company that was consistently grossing nearly twice its outlay, the brothers were interested in expanding as rapidly as possible. Byron Haskin, a cameraman at the studio, remembered production stopping fairly frequently in order to impress potential investors.

"We would get every camera out of the vaults, set it up on a phony set, and grab a few of the extra people around. Anybody was the director, anybody was the cameraman . . . nothing was actually happening; no film in the cameras or anything. Then [Harry] would take them walking through and Jack would tell them, 'Well, here's Monte Blue, and here's Marie Prevost.' "

As the final stop on the tour, John Barrymore would be pressed into service to take the eager marks into the office. There, they would meet Freddie the office boy, who was renowned for the heroic proportions of his male organ, and for his willingness to display it. "We used to lay nineteen nickles on top of it," remembered Haskin. "That would generally be the convincer."

Once Ernst, along with Henry Blanke and Hans Kräly, moved onto the lot, his main tormenter seems to have been Darryl Zanuck, at the time a lowly writer of Rin Tin Tin pictures. Zanuck shared an office with director Roy Del Ruth, and when they weren't drilling holes in the wall to peer at their neighbor, writer Bess Meredyth, they were installing fake phones in Lubitsch's office. The phones would ring, but were otherwise props.

Lubitsch and Blanke were still quite insecure about their English, and Zanuck would get an odd, adolescent charge out of ringing Lubitsch's fake phone every few minutes. When Lubitsch or Blanke finally got up the nerve to answer the phone, there would be nothing on the other end. Result: strangled hilarity from the Zanuck/Del Ruth quarters. Taken all in all, Warners offered a slightly different ambiance than the decorous Pickford lot.

Since Harry had signed Lubitsch, something had to be done with him, but Jack didn't have to like it. Jack liked movies to move, have plenty of snap-crackle-pop, and everybody knew that foreign directors were arty and slow. Jack figured all directors wanted to do was spend his money, always a bad sign. Even if a director was snappy and fast, it didn't mean that Jack would like him, only that he would dislike him less.

Beyond hard practicalities, Warner Bros. was a psychological mine-field. Without knowing it, Lubitsch had walked into the middle of a long-simmering sibling rivalry. All the Warner brothers had great respect for their father, Benjamin Warner, the family patriarch. Jack especially wanted to retain his respect. But Jack was a man whose habits were far more of Hollywood than of Krasnashiltz, Poland, where his father had been born. Inevitably, one of Jack's girlfriends got under his skin and coerced him into divorcing his wife, something his generation of Jewish

scott   eyman

men rarely did, unless they were movie moguls, in which case they all did.

"Harry became a kind of representation of my grandfather after he died," said Jack Warner, Jr. "He was the elder statesman. My father would open up to me about his feelings for Harry, which were absolutely wrong. Jack had a basic desire to be the top boss and he resented the New York office, that is to say Harry."

While Harry was essentially quiet, Jack was social, although not with those that might be thought to constitute his peer group. He never socialized with other Warner executives, or other moguls like Louis B. Mayer or Harry Cohn. "For the most part, his friends were people who weren't even in the industry," remembered his son. "He loved being with people like the Aga Khan, or King Farouk. His greatest thrill was to be with the Duke of Windsor in the South of France. Once the two of them were walking in a rose garden when they both had to go to the bathroom. So my father and the Duke of Windsor watered the roses at the same time. That was the highlight of his social existence."

Although Jack Warner was enormously seductive when he wanted to be ("He could be the most charming, delightful, warm, happy, interesting man in the world," said his son), more often his personality was, according to Douglas Fairbanks, Jr., that of "a sinister clown." He was capable of an astonishing cruelty.

"Years later," remembered Jack Warner, Jr., "there was a man named Steve Trilling, who devoted his life to my father. One day he came to work to find he had been fired. Just like that. And he went home and soon he had a heart attack and died. My father did things like that. There was a lack of humanity in him."

The newly struck partnership between director and producer could never have been successful, for, more than anything else, Jack Warner loved the very thing that Ernst Lubitsch could not abide: conflict.

The first project that Warners floated for Lubitsch to direct was certainly more in keeping with his European past than Warners' American present: *Deburau*, taken from a David Belasco play written by Sacha Guitry. While the famous French pantomimist was certainly a good idea for a movie, the story's realization would have to wait for Marcel Carné's immortal *Children of Paradise*.

Jack's estimation of Lubitsch as Harry's folly, as a dangerous highbrow, only began to be modified when Lubitsch made the acquaintance of their father. Ben Warner lived around the corner from the Warner Bros. studio in a modest bungalow on Bronson. He would come to the Sunset Boulevard lot every day to schmooze, except there wasn't really anybody to schmooze with, for Ben Warner was only fluent in Polish and Yiddish. "None of the brothers spoke Yiddish," remembered Jack Warner, Jr. "For one thing, they weren't religious; they could forget they were Jewish."

Lubitsch and Ben Warner struck up a friendship, based, at least in part, on the fact that each spoke only broken English. Jack Warner, glad that his father had somebody to talk to, began to think that maybe this Lubitsch fellow wasn't so highbrow after all. Maybe he was even a *Landsmann,* a compatriot.

On January 1, 1924, Lubitsch and Nathan Burkan, who had become his attorney as well as Chaplin's, formed Boulevard Pictures, a holding company to which he assigned his contract with Warners, presumably for tax reasons. Ernst was now free to remedy the mistakes he felt he had made with *Rosita.* "In my first picture I had to make all kinds of concessions to what they told me the American people wanted," he told Harry Carr of *Motion Picture Classic.* "This one I am going to make to please Lubitsch."

On the Warner lot, Lubitsch quickly began gathering a nucleus of family around him. As before, Henry Blanke was his assistant, or, as Blanke's widow preferred to remember it, "his dog. My husband worked for him for a dollar a week and a pack of cigarettes." Actually, Blanke remembered his salary as $50 a week, not bad for the period. (According to an affadavit filed with immigration authorities, Blanke was earning at least $100 a week, even better.)

Whatever he was being paid, there is no question that Blanke was earning his money. At night, he would work translating various memos and correspondence into German, so Lubitsch could deal with the minutia of his job. Harry Warner, who also worked nights and on weekends, saw Blanke habitually hunched over his desk long after quitting time and personally authorized a $25 a week raise. "The stingiest man in the world gave me a raise out of his own pocket," remembered Blanke. "I was very proud."

Lubitsch had brought Kräly and Blanke with him, but he had not brought a cameraman. As production neared on his first picture for Warner Bros., an adaptation of Lothar Schmidt's play *Only a Dream* that had been retitled *The Marriage Circle,* the studio assigned him contract cinematographer Charles Van Enger. The cameraman walked on the set his first day on the picture to find that the set had been built too wide and too low, so a long shot was impossible. "This set is all wet," he muttered, which led a puzzled Lubitsch to say, "Sharley, I don't see any water."

Van Enger suggested moving one side wall closer to the center of the set, so it could be properly photographed. After that display of simple competence, Lubitsch and Van Enger developed a good working relationship throughout the length of production, September and October of 1923.

"He would come in the morning," Van Enger told historian Richard Koszarski, "no script, he knew exactly where everybody was going to be, he knew exactly what camera angle he wanted, and not once did he ever look through the camera, as long as I was with him."

Van Enger developed the habit of photographing Lubitsch directing the actors, acting out the scene the way he wanted them to play it. "I would have them print it and the next day after the rushes I would run it for him. He thought that was so funny and if I didn't do it, he'd raise hell. He'd say, 'Sharley, where's my scenes?' "

It didn't take long for Lubitsch to clash with his new boss. A few days before production got under way, Lubitsch asked for real marble on the steps of a set.

"He gets marble paper," snapped Jack Warner.

It had probably been a bluff on Lubitsch's part to see just how much bounty the studio could supply. In Germany, a film company had almost no prop department it could turn to; most furniture for a movie had to be rented. But in Hollywood, "a completely different world," according to Henry Blanke, the well-supplied studios had everything a director could possibly need to make a picture . . . except, possibly, marble.

For the actors of *The Marriage Circle,* used to the hurry-up-and-print-it regimen favored by Jack Warner, Lubitsch was something entirely different; the director found that he had to work his actors harder to get the results he needed. "He made me do simple scenes," complained Marie Prevost, "just coming in and out of rooms fifteen or twenty times. At first it seemed as though there wasn't any sense to it at all. Then it began to dawn upon me what the art of acting was all about, and it seemed intolerably and impossibly difficult. Then I began to see it as he saw it . . . He deals in subtleties that I never dreamed of before."

Shooting locations in Beverly Hills one day, Lubitsch came face to face with Pola Negri, from whom he had been estranged since *Die Flamme.* "I saw what was coming," remembered Charles Van Enger, "so I started the camera and they looked at each other, then they ran and put their arms around one another and they kissed . . . and they started to talk."

The next day, Lubitsch and Van Enger watched the scene of the reunion in silence. "Sharley, would you get me that print?" he asked. Van Enger went into the projection room and cut the scene out. "Now get me the negative," Lubitsch said.

"He took them out and put them on the ground and put a match to it and stood there until that film was all burned up. He was afraid his wife would see it."

To hear them tell it, even though they were partners in United Artists, Charlie Chaplin and Mary Pickford had little in common besides their mutual adoration of Douglas Fairbanks. Actually, they were psychological twins, sharing, besides their diminutive stature, a passion for the dollar caused by identical backgrounds of youthful poverty and deprivation, followed by incessant theatrical touring, culminating in enormous, unforeseen success in motion pictures that they both sought to consolidate by compulsive addiction to work. Finally, both Chaplin and Pickford chafed at the public's complete identification—and confusion—of them with the characters they played.

So it was that in the fall of 1922, Charlie Chaplin decided to scratch a long-standing itch and direct a movie in which he would not appear. Moreover, to firmly establish his credentials as an independent creative artist, it would be a drama.

That summer, Chaplin had had a brief affair with Peggy Hopkins Joyce, a flamboyant party girl who had sliced through five wealthy husbands like a sexual scythe. According to Chaplin's biographer David Robinson, the term "gold digger" was coined just for her. Joyce regaled Chaplin with tales of her past conquests, including a liaison with a wealthy Parisian publisher who was an acquaintance of Chaplin's. At the same time, she would disingenuously claim that she was just a simple country girl at heart, that all she really wanted was a home with a white picket fence and a passel of chubby babies.

Stimulated by such an obvious confusion of identity, Chaplin wrote a story about Marie, a placid country girl who becomes the mistress of a wealthy Parisian man-about-town. Torn between the life of luxury he represents and the emotional commitment she feels for a struggling artist, Marie's decision is made for her when the artist commits suicide. Chastened, humbled, she returns to the country and the simple life.

Despite the relatively conventional melodramatics of the plot, Chaplin determined that, in acting and direction, the keynote of the film he would call *A Woman of Paris* would be a quiet, unindicative irony.

For the leading roles, Chaplin chose Edna Purviance, his leading lady and longtime mistress, and Adolphe Menjou, whom Peggy Hopkins Joyce had once pointed out in a restaurant as having much of the style of her Parisian publisher.

Production began in November 1922, and continued for seven months, with Chaplin repeating one line over and over to his actors: "Don't sell it! Remember, they're peeking at you." Despite the distraction of Chaplin's concurrent affair with Pola Negri, the film turned out to be a deserved critical smash, with Chaplin's storytelling skills being compared to those of Hardy, de Maupassant, and Ibsen. Although it was not a financial disaster (it grossed $634,000 domestically against a cost of $351,000), Chaplin, used to the multimillion-dollar grosses of the Tramp films, pretended it was.

Lubitsch shared in the critical enthusiasm for *A Woman of Paris,* telling a reporter for *The New York Times* that "I like it because I feel that an intelligent man speaks to me and nobody's intelligence is insulted in the picture."

For Hollywood's creative community, *A Woman of Paris* tied in perfectly with what they were thinking and feeling. What the Russian theorist Vladimir Mayakovsky called the film's "organization of simple little facts" leading to the "greatest emotional saturation" signaled a new storytelling and cultural sophistication that was being echoed in the stories of Scott Fitzgerald, and the unindicative stoicism of Hemingway.

All this was a function of the new affluence of the 1920s, and the sense of liberation that came with that affluence. At long last, the Victorian era seemed to be dead. In London, there was Noël Coward; in Paris, Sacha Guitry. And in Hollywood, there was Chaplin . . . and Lubitsch.

They had become good friends, and Chaplin had shown Ernst a rough cut of *A Woman of Paris* before it was released. Henry Blanke, in retrospect, would say that viewing the film "influenced Lubitsch's entire life from then on . . . from being very spectacular [with] big crowds . . . he became very simple, and discovered wonderful American actors that he picked himself."

But that seems a gross overstatement. Sexuality and playfulness had been present in Lubitsch's films for years. Chaplin's film is surprisingly serious—he subtitled it *A Drama of Fate,* and he's not kidding—and the film's only insouciance derives from the incomparably ironic and sly Adolphe Menjou. Moreover, Chaplin's dramatic construction was always direct to the point of bluntness, while Lubitsch was a master of the oblique storytelling that Howard Hawks would later term "three-cushion."

While it is *A Woman of Paris* that has always been taken as the primary inspiration for Lubitsch's American comedies, if Lubitsch was borrowing from anybody in *The Marriage Circle* and the films that followed, it was Cecil B. DeMille and the astonishingly nimble series of marital comedies he made beginning in 1918.

The DeMille films are playfully sardonic about the implicit boredom of marriage, as well as virtually everything else. Humor, a sense of life's innate absurdity, lightens each and every character. DeMille, creating a genre that might be termed the comedy of divorce before he journeyed to his particular promised land of grandiloquent spectacles, passed the torch to Lubitsch, who was just springing himself from the prison in which DeMille was to be so content.

In DeMille's *Don't Change Your Husband* (1919), the screen image dissolves from the spit-shined shoes of a lover to the scuffed, untied shoes of the husband, from the lover's immaculate necktie and jawline to the open neck and flabby jowls of the husband. It's a sequence that could be dropped intact into any of the quiet, pointed comedies Lubitsch began making in 1924. Maliciously witty moments like this make these films the deftest work of DeMille's career.

Nor is DeMille being unnecessarily dragged down by his Victorian heritage; true, most of the women in DeMille's marital comedies are passive, decorative objects. But in *Old Wives for New,* Florence Vidor's character runs a fashionable dress shop. Moreover, DeMille suggests that a pallid lack of fire is a good part of the reason men and women get bored with each other.

This is not to say that DeMille takes it the extra step that Lubitsch delighted in. With the exception of Kay Francis in *Trouble in Paradise,* Lubitsch's women are never captains of industry, but they're smart, they're knowing; they usually understand exactly what to do and why.

DeMille's tendency toward paternalism is amplified in a movie like *Why Change Your Wife?,* where Gloria Swanson and Bebe Daniels fight over the inert Thomas Meighan. For DeMille's patriarchal sensibility, men are the priapic suns around which women worshipfully cluster.

Primarily, Chaplin's film gave Lubitsch an all-important attitude: dry, sardonic, emotionally cool, with the actors invariably giving quiet, uninflected performances. To some degree, the composed tone of *A Woman of Paris* would be present in the rest of the pictures Lubitsch would make.

Also contributing to Ernst's swerve into intimacy was the comparative ease and subtlety of that kind of filmmaking, at least compared to the arduous bread-and-circuses that had been occupying him for the last three or four years. As Henry Blanke said, "How many more thousand people can you show?"

"We are groping slowly on the screen for some definite form of screen art," Lubitsch told an interviewer in December 1923, shortly after he had seen the film and become friends with Chaplin. "Something that will mean to the movies what the technical school of Ibsen meant to the drama—and we are groping slowly . . .

"Chaplin's *Woman of Paris* is a great step forward . . . It did not, like many plays I see, insult my intelligence. So often in pictures one is not allowed to think by the director. But—ah!—in *A Woman of Paris* we had a picture that, as you Americans say, left something to the imagination."

Ernst and Chaplin remained good friends; when Chaplin suffered a nervous breakdown during his divorce proceedings from Lita Grey, Lubitsch, probably at the suggestion of Nathan Burkan, went to his hotel to try to calm him down. Lubitsch's stepson Eddie, who accompanied him, remembered a harried, white-faced Chaplin pacing endlessly back and forth in his hotel room.

The Marriage Circle, adapted by Lubitsch and Paul Bern from *Only a Dream,* a play by Lothar Schmidt that dated from 1909, endured a false start when production began in September 1923. For the part of Doctor Braun, Lubitsch had originally cast the dutiful but inescapably bland Warner Baxter. After eight days of production, Lubitsch turned to Henry Blanke and said, "He looks like a detective." Baxter was dismissed and Lubitsch chose Warner's contract player Monte Blue to replace him. The picture was completed in October and released the following February.

Lubitsch wastes no time in creating the proper, saucy rhythm for *The Marriage Circle,* effortlessly setting up the duality of one perfectly happy marriage contrasted with another couple in a perpetual state of steely indifference salted with loathing.

"The day starts late but gloriously in the home of Professor Josef Stock," announces a title that precedes a desultory Adolphe Menjou getting dressed, only to discover that there are holes in his socks. Menjou reacts with what even then was his trademarked frozen *sang-froid,* a dead nonexpression, but without the customary lightness in the eyes and around the mouth.

His wife, Mizzi Stock, is a slovenly housekeeper, among many other things. When Stock ignores her, the irritating jazz baby responds with an outraged "Keep up with your cruelty and someday I'll leave you." Mizzi convinces herself that she's in love with the husband of an old friend, Dr. Braun, who is actually very much in love with his wife, but can't very well resist when a beautiful little piece of fluff like Mizzi launches herself into his lap. Professor Stock, nobody's fool, hires a detective to follow his wife and gather incriminating evidence so he can obtain the divorce for which he devoutly wishes.

Then come the complications: Dr. Braun's partner is secretly in love with Braun's wife, Charlotte (the stately, impersonal Florence Vidor). She, in turn, suspects her husband of having an affair, but with the wrong woman. Charlotte begins an affair of her own while simultaneously seeking comfort from the woman who is in fact trying her level best to seduce her husband: Mizzi. The Marriage Circle indeed.

The complications are rigorously worked out, and a garden party sequence, where Mizzi lures Dr. Braun into the garden and tosses away her scarf, carries with it the perceptible thrill of a forbidden affair. Lubitsch had discovered that in an atmosphere of hushed whispers and discretion, a mere kiss carries as much erotic charge as penetration.

Ultimately, everyone gets what they think they want. Professor Stock gets his freedom—an admiring appraisal of Dr. Braun's servant girl as Stock makes his exit implies that it will be put to wide-ranging use—his ex-wife gets somebody new to wrap around her little finger, and Dr. Braun gets his wife back.

The casting of Adolphe Menjou is an obvious nod to *A Woman of Paris*, although the actor much preferred Chaplin as a director. "All I had to do to make Lubitsch happy was to step before the camera and mimic every gesture he gave me," Menjou grumbled in his memoirs. Also deriving from the Chaplin picture is the reflexively Continental setting, in this case Vienna, although there is no particular attempt to convincingly replicate a European milieu. Indeed, Lubitsch derives much of the comic tension in the film from the contrast between Menjou's innate elegance and the comparative coarseness of other actors like Marie Prevost and Monte Blue, who gets by because his character is essentially defined by his continually flustered state.

The subject matter of *The Marriage Circle* is only a slight extension of the marital comedies Ernst had made in Germany years before. What is clearly different is the pace. Before, he had charged up the actors to maintain the energy level of farce, but here he takes his time, holding reaction shots for several beats. The editing takes its cue from Menjou's cold stares, and the stylistic alteration from only three years before is startling.

The Marriage Circle is full of scenes with a sense of unspoken formality, of a mutually antagonistic marital Mexican standoff that has been going on for years. In this move-counter-move rhythm, Lubitsch is anticipating the tit-for-tat routines of Laurel and Hardy, but, instead of escalating physical destruction, Lubitsch freezes the emotional temperature. Unlike real people, these characters never lose their control, which is the essence of their absurdity, the center of their wit.

Photoplay marveled at the film's aesthetic economy. "The picture starts, the characters themselves reveal the story, which runs smoothly along to its logical ending. There is no straining for effects . . . it's all very simple, very human and immensely entertaining."

Before, the audience could only see Lubitsch's characters move; beginning with *The Marriage Circle,* we can see them think. Before, there were large sets and hundreds of extras, and, when there weren't, there was much brisk hurly-burly. Now, Lubitsch strips everything down to the essentials: a few actors, a car, a garden, a dining room, a staircase. Lubitsch's German films, even the fine ones, tend to be brass bands, compelling, funny, but unavoidably loud; beginning with *The Marriage Circle,* Ernst became the composer of the cinema's finest, most quietly elegant chamber music.

In 1927, the trade paper *Film Daily* asked the ten men who had been voted the Best Directors of the past year to choose their favorite of their own films. Lubitsch chose *The Marriage Circle* because, as he explained, "In this production I was experimenting . . . My desire was to create a story that would reflect life as it is lived by thousands of married couples—just everyday people that we meet all around us.

"In back of the idea was a desire to create a new form—a different technique . . . I mean the processes employed in developing a story along natural, human lines, with the characters all flesh and blood people who were just a little bit bad and not too good . . . Our heroes and heroines in pictures are so often too good . . . Nothing particularly thrilling happened. But there was suspense—interest—comedy—human beings reacting to given situations as they do in life.

"I call it my picture of no regrets. If I had to do it all over again, of course, there are many little places where I could improve it. Just touches here and there. But I doubt if I would change the story structure. And the cast. Well, there is not one single change I would make if I had to do it again."

Lubitsch acclimated himself to Hollywood very quickly. After renting on Alpine Drive in Beverly Hills for nearly a year, he felt sufficiently secure in his new country to build a house, located at 616 Beverly Drive and costing nearly $40,000. Lubitsch's only show business neighbor was Pola Negri, who lived two doors to the south. (A few years later, Jack Benny would buy the house catty-corner across the street.)

Although an impressive, mini-Tara-like structure from the outside, 616 Beverly Drive was actually comparatively modest inside. The entry way to the house was on the side, which led to a big family room with a fireplace. A few years later, Lubitsch would add a room on top of the family room to serve as his office/study.

Technically, it was only a three-bedroom house, but it had a very deep lot with a large swimming pool in the back yard. There were six servants—a downstairs maid, an upstairs maid, a personal maid for Leni, a chauffeur, and two gardeners. Attached to the garage was a two-bedroom bungalow that was used as a home for the two main servants. Behind the far end of the pool were two bathhouses.

Ernst's contented existence was marred only by the death of his father on February 15, 1924, the day before the release of *The Marriage Circle*. Simon Lubitsch was buried beside his wife at Weissensee Cemetery, not far from a memorial to the Jewish soldiers who fought and died in World War I. Busy with his new life in his new country, and unable to return in time for the funeral, Lubitsch chose to stay in America.

By the end of 1924, Ernst Lubitsch had a life that included virtually all the plush stylings that would be increasingly evident in his movies. All that was missing was the veiled hostility and the infidelity. They would come later.

Between April and June 1924, Lubitsch shot *Three Women,* from a script he wrote with Hans Kräly based on a novel entitled *Lilli's Marriage* by one Iolanthe Marees. Although the setting is explicitly American, there is much open recourse to alcohol, this in spite of Prohibition.

Pauline Frederick is Mabel, a worried woman of a certain age who gets on a scale, finds she weighs 135, and is greatly dismayed. Planning a tryst with an attractive man, she carefully cuts out the daylight in the room and turns on artificial, indirect lights, while Charles Van Enger's camera switches to a subtle soft focus to replicate the effect Mabel is seeking.

Lubitsch's sense of character is revealingly deadly. Lew Cody's Edmund is idly plinking the piano and notices a figurine. He immediately turns it over to check the mark, establishing the acquisitiveness and vulgarity beneath the sophisticated surface.

Mabel's daughter, Jeanne (the indistinct May McAvoy), is attending college at Berkeley and feeling neglected. Eager to see her mother, she arrives home just in time to interrupt the planned mutual seduction. Mabel would rather not spend time with her, so on Jeanne's way out of the house, Jeanne meets Edmund and goes out with him. One thing, as it often does, leads to another and they end up getting married.

Behind his new wife's back, Edmund is having an affair with Harriet (Marie Prevost); we know that because he keeps a separate set of clothes at her apartment. Mabel finds out and demands that he divorce her daughter. He suggests it would be much more appropriate if he blackmails Mabel for having an affair with him first, as her letters prove. His manner is quiet, suave; why be so upset? They can still be "friends." They tussle over a gun, she shoots him. At the trial, she admits her guilt and the affair. She is acquitted and Jeanne is reunited with her college sweetheart. Everybody's happy.

Three Women begins as a textured, highly unconventional domestic drama, acutely but lovingly observed, then gradually loses its edge until it becomes a predictable society drama in which a self-absorbed parent redeems herself through self-sacrifice. Since Marie Prevost has little screen time and exists mainly as a plot function rather than as a character, it might have been better to title the film *Two Women*.

In mid-July Ernst went on loan-out to Paramount to work on *Forbidden Paradise*, a reunion with Pola Negri, whose American career had gotten off to a rocky start. An adaptation of a Lajos Biro/Melchior Lengyel play loosely based on the legendary Catherine the Great, *Forbidden Paradise* was slightly hampered by Negri's insistence on casting her current lover, the dashing but inexpressive Rod La Rocque, as her leading man.

The actress's displays of temperament continued unabated. During a scene in which Negri was to run down a winding stairway, she began to protest, saying that her dress, a brocaded negligee with a sable train, was unwieldy and dangerous.

"Nonsense," Lubitsch soothed her. "You'll manage perfectly."

"If it catches on the railing I'll break my neck."

"What's wrong with you? We did much more dangerous stunts in Berlin."

"I was younger then."

"Three years younger." Furious, Lubitsch marched her into a dressing room, snatched the negligee off her, and stepped into it. Dressed in the negligee, puffing on his cigar, Lubitsch dashed down the stairs and back again, conclusively proving that the costume was not dangerous and that it looked better on Negri.

For Negri, this was just like old times, "fighting on a set again and both enjoying it enormously." But Lubitsch's tolerance for temperament had decreased as his own importance had increased; he would never work with Negri again.

In spite of the uproar on the set, *Forbidden Paradise* is a consistent delight. Although the architecture subtly indicates Russia, and Negri's character is referred to as "The Czarina," Lubitsch updates the setting to encompass a mythical country complete with automobiles.

Lubitsch creates a triangle of a sexually voracious queen, her blasé chancellor (Adolphe Menjou, of course), and an ardent, jejune young officer worried about a rebellion (Rod La Rocque). Both the Czarina and her Chancellor are in on the joke, and think even discussing revolution is a waste of energy, but La Rocque's Alexei is a big, clumsy puppy, a straight arrow who doesn't get it. The Czarina has to work very hard to seduce him; at one point, she brings a footstool over to stand on because Alexei is both too tall and too dim to realize it would help if he'd bend a little.

After the Czarina and Alexei become lovers, Lubitsch stages a banquet, with a long table full of officers, all wearing precisely the same medal that the Czarina has just presented to Alexei.

Lubitsch's taste for aphoristic counterpoint was never sharper. The Chancellor, the ultimate fixer, goes to rebel headquarters. The leader confronts the hated minion of the Czarina. A close-up of his burly hand grabbing his sword pommel is matched by a cut of Menjou reaching into his pocket and pulling out . . . his checkbook. The soldier's hand relaxes, and his fingers begin idly drumming as he awaits his payoff. So much for revolution.

Negri is atypically quiet and sly, but her luxurious, beddy quality is intact and, in keeping with the tone of his leading actors, Lubitsch underplays his set pieces. There is a brilliant sequence when Negri, mistakenly believing the revolution has begun, rushes through the abandoned palace, and Lubitsch unleashes a series of stunning sets by the great Hans Dreier that are vaguely reminiscent of the baroque designs of *The Mountain Cat*.

In a love scene, Alexei and the lady-in-waiting (Pauline Starke) who is his true love, embrace by a lily pond. Lubitsch cuts to a shot looking up at them through the water. A fish darts through the frame and the ripples of the water disrupt the pastoral composition as, simultaneously, the lovers are interrupted.

In the end, the Czarina is confronted with the problem of what to do with Alexei. Since she can't corrupt him, and she likes him too much to kill him, she decides to let him live. He and his lady-in-waiting go off together, and the Chancellor helpfully shows in a French Ambassador. Some time later, he comes out wearing the very familiar medal. As the Chancellor congratulates the Ambassador on his speed and proficiency, the film fades out.

Clara Bow's obvious star quality had been languishing in a series of quickies being produced by B. P. Schulberg. Ernst met her on the Warners lot, where she was making something called *Eve's Lover,* and invited her to test for his next picture, *Kiss Me Again*. During the test, the always insecure Bow noticed Ernst smacking his lips, thought he was making fun of her, and smacked right back at him. Lubitsch turned red, called her "a damned fresh kid," but gave her the job anyway.

The film began shooting in January 1925, finished in late March, and was released in August. Lubitsch and Bow became friends; Clara later referred to Lubitsch, who would lend her a hand during a particularly traumatic time at Paramount, as a "godsend." Unfortunately, no prints of *Kiss Me Again* are known to survive, making the delectable combination of Lubitsch and Clara Bow apparently lost to the ages.

After the false start of *Rosita,* Lubitsch had definitely found his rhythm. When he began production on *Lady Windermere's Fan* in September 1925, it was the fifth picture he had made since leaving Pickford two years before. A gifted young talent named Harold Grieve was chosen to handle the all-important art direction.

"Lubitsch was a very good person," recalled Grieve. "If he trusted you, and if he liked you, he'd let you do your job. I would bring him my sketches, he'd approve them, and that was that." Grieve's serene, uncluttered designs lent the source material welcome undertones of dramatic gravity; he and Lubitsch would collaborate again on *So This Is Paris.*

After a few days of working with Clive Brook in the role of Darlington, Lubitsch realized that he had repeated the same mistake he had made with Warner Baxter. Lubitsch instructed Brook to click his heels and snap his head. Brook refused, explaining that was never done in England. Neither man would budge. "Lubitsch being German, Clive English, and the war pretty recent didn't help the situation," remembered Irene Rich.

Brook left the picture; to replace him, Ronald Colman was quickly borrowed from Sam Goldwyn. In addition to money, Goldwyn demanded a credit line: "Ronald Colman through the courtesy of Samuel Goldwyn." This caused Lubitsch no end of irritation; for most of the shoot, he would give Colman directions such as "Mr. Colman, you walk across the room, courtesy of Samuel Goldwyn, you stop by the table, you pick up the book, courtesy of Samuel Goldwyn, and then you look into the eyes of Miss McAvoy . . . by courtesy of Samuel Goldwyn." Since there is no point in the finished picture wherein Ronald Colman clicks his heels and snaps his head, it's entirely possible that Lubitsch was trying to antagonize Clive Brook into leaving on his own.

Lubitsch wanted to use Warners contract star May McAvoy in the film, but the actress hated the part as written, and promptly headed for Catalina Island with her mother. After a few days, Warners tracked her down and Lubitsch called. "McAwoy" ("He always pronounced it McAwoy," remembered the actress), "what are you doing over there?"

"I don't want to do it," she reiterated. "It isn't me."

"If you don't come over here now, I'm coming over to get you. Nobody else can play the part but you." (What Lubitsch undoubtedly meant was that nobody at Warners could play the part but her, for McAvoy was a pleasant but bland actress.)

At any rate, the timeworn flattery worked. "I didn't want any trouble with Lubitsch because he was a doll and I loved him, so I did it," said McAvoy. Because the actress was just under five feet in height, whenever McAvoy was in a scene with Colman or Bert Lytell, she was photographed standing on a built-up runway.

Except for a brief flare-up of hostilities brought about by Irene Rich's scene-stealing, the shoot for *Lady Windermere's Fan* went smoothly. Lubitsch insisted that the actors speak the dialogue written in the script, so that the emotion and expression would come naturally from the scene's content. He also had Irene Rich dye her hair red; although the film was in black and white, he theorized that it would make her *feel* more sophisticated and mature, perhaps even wicked.

To shoot the racetrack scenes correctly (in England, the race horses run in the opposite direction from those in America), Lubitsch took his wife and a second unit for a few days of filming in Toronto. Then he and Leni went to New York for ten days, socializing with Blanche Sweet and her husband, Marshall Neilan, and visiting Texas Guinan's nightclub when they weren't seeing the shows on Broadway.

While in New York, he did some retakes of Irene Rich's close-ups at the old Vitagraph studio. One observer noticed that most directors would have directed Rich through her close-ups by saying something like "You are watching the races—you turn and watch the people—smile. Good heavens! It's your own daughter—turn away."

But Lubitsch talked Rich through the scene up to the point where she was to see her daughter. "Now!" he said, and snapped his fingers, causing Rich to stiffen her body. The close-up took nine takes before Lubitsch was satisfied.

After New York, the Lubitschs stopped off in Washington, D.C., where he spent a half-hour with that noted movie fan, Calvin Coolidge. Truly, Simon Lubitsch's son had arrived. When they returned to Los Angeles after being gone for five weeks, Lubitsch announced that he considered Washington "the most beautiful city, architecturally, of any city in the United States."

For *Lady Windermere's Fan,* Lubitsch early on decided that none of Oscar Wilde's witty epigrams would be used as titles; in fact, only two lines of the play's dialogue were directly transposed. "Playing with words is fascinating to the writer and afterward to the reader, but on the screen it is impossible," Ernst told *The New York Times.* "Would much charm remain to long excerpts from Wilde's play if the audience had to ponder laboriously over the scintillating sentences on the screen?" Rather, the director chose to find visual counterparts for Wilde's dialogue.

By denuding the material of its verbal wit, Lubitsch strips it to its narrative base—a mother with a scandalous past and the daughter who thinks she's dead, both coming to an understanding through the stirrings of maternal feeling and selfless love. It's well-directed, but it's also nominal silent film material amounting to little more than well-dressed tailor's dummies exchanging significant glances over teacups.

There are flashes, just not enough of them. Lubitsch brings off another stunningly designed, furtive meeting in a formal garden; at another point in the story, May McAvoy is considering jimmying her husband's desk drawer. She thinks better of it and exits frame left. The camera holds on the desk for several seconds. Suddenly, McAvoy darts in from frame right to carry on her investigations.

Lubitsch's gamble almost worked, but the film seems more serious than the play because it isn't punctuated by Wilde's frivolous bon mots cuing the audience that this is a stylized comedy.

What distinction the film has relates to Lubitsch's use of scenery and space. The decor is remarkably simple. Shining floors, a few columns, some draperies, a great staircase, and large doors are really all that is used to indicate a manorial house. The comparatively simple, inferential sets produce a sense of depth and uncluttered spaciousness, clean playing areas for the action.

The critics were not all that impressed; *Photoplay* called the film "smart" but the influential English film reviewer Iris Barry didn't care for it, and *The New York Times* said that the film "shrinks in importance beside the original effort."

Lubitsch's Warner Bros. films were made quickly, efficiently, and on budget, but not quickly, efficiently, or cheaply enough for Jack Warner. The pay structure was decent for the period. On *Three Women,* character actress Mary Carr got $1,000 for a week's work, while Lew Cody received $1,562.50 a week and May McAvoy $1,750 a week. The ubiquitous Hans Kräly got $7,500 for work on that script (for which he was credited) as well as for some quiet work on *The Marriage Circle* (for which Paul Bern was credited), all drawn at the rate of $250 a week. The highest-priced player was Pauline Frederick, who was pulling $2,000 a week. As was common in the period, the free-lancing Frederick had to furnish her own wardrobe while May McAvoy, a Warners contract player, did not. Other, less specific actors had to struggle. Pierre Gendron was only paid $200 a week for working in the same film and had to supply his own wardrobe on top of that.

Jack Warner's expressions of disappointment with the returns on Lubitsch's pictures finally caused Ernst to lose his temper. In January 1926, he offered to buy out his contract after completing *Reveillon,* which would soon be retitled *So This Is Paris.* The conciliatory Harry Warner tried to smooth the matter over. "NOT INTERESTED SEPARATING UNTIL EXPIRATION CONTRACT DON'T ACT HASTY . . . WILL DISCUSS SAME WHEN I RETURN . . ." Harry wired Lubitsch from Europe.

In a concurrent wire to Jack, Harry laid out their strategy: "LUBITSCH MUST MAKE MORE THRILLING PICTURE AND NOT WORRY SO MUCH ABOUT STORY

HIS PICTURES ARE OVER PEOPLE'S HEADS HERE KISS ME AGAIN TAKEN OFF WHER- EVER PLAYED AFTER THREE DAYS SHOW HIM THIS SCHLESINGER REPORTS SAME STORY WEAKNESS GERMANY AND CENTRAL EUROPE STOP DON'T LET HIM KILL HIMSELF BEFORE MAKING BIG PICTURE . . ."

A later cable amplified on Harry's feelings: "DON'T DISCUSS PARTING WITH HIM HE'S LOOKING FOR OUT . . . DON'T START BIG PICTURE WITH HIM UNTIL I RETURN WILL THEN HANDLE HIM PERSONALLY JUST LET HIM MAKE PICTURE TO FINISH THIS YEAR . . ."

Harry wired Lubitsch that "UNNECESSARY GET EXCITED BECAUSE SOMEONE INTERESTED MUTUALLY WITH YOU CALLS YOUR ATTENTION TO WHAT THEY OBSERVE . . . YOU HAVE PICKED YOUR OWN STORIES AND MADE YOUR OWN PICTURES WITHOUT INTERFERENCE BUT MADE THEM TOO SUBTLE THE WORLD WANTS THRILL AND EXCITEMENT STOP AS DISCUSSED WITH YOU WE WANT YOU TO MAKE STILL BIGGER PICTURE HEREAFTER BUT YOU SHOULD LISTEN TO WHAT THE WORLD WANTS TO PROTECT YOUR OWN REPUTATION STOP WE ARE THOR- OUGHLY SATISFIED WITH YOU AND PICTURES AND WHEN I RETURN WILL EN- DEAVOUR TO MAKE VERY LONG TERM CONTRACT WITH YOU TO START AT EXPIRATION OF PRESENT CONTRACT . . ."

On January 27, Lubitsch replied to Harry that "AGREE WITH YOU THAT EUROPEAN MARKET EXPECTS ONLY BIG PICTURES FROM ME STOP IT IS VERY UNFORTUNATE FOR ME THAT FOR PAST THREE YEARS I HAD NEITHER MEANS NOR CHANCE TO MAKE BIG PICTURES AND YOU HAVE NO ONE BUT YOURSELF TO BLAME THAT MY TALENTS ARE WASTED THUSLY STOP SITUATION HAS REACHED POINT WHERE BOTH OF US ARE EQUALLY DISSATISFIED AND I TAKE THIS OPPORTUNITY TO SUGGEST THAT FOR OUR MUTUAL BENEFIT WE SEPARATE AFTER NEXT PICTURE . . ."

Harry decided not to get in a trans-Atlantic argument, and told Jack to "TELL LUBITSCH NOT TO ACT LIKE BABY CAN'T ONE CALL HIS ATTENTION HIS PICTURES GREAT BUT SUBTLE HE HAS PICKED STORIES NEVER WANTED MAKE WHAT WE ASKED HIM . . ."

But Lubitsch was antagonized and had no intention of either being placated or of going back to the more commercially obvious spectaculars that were clearly what Harry and Jack wanted. "YOU ARE MISTAKEN WHEN YOU THINK MY PROPOSAL CAUSED BY EXCITEMENT," he wired Harry on Janu- ary 29. "IT WAS RESULT OF CAREFUL DELIBERATION STOP YOU HAVE ALWAYS BEEN COMPLAINING OF BEING UNABLE TO MAKE MONEY WITH MY PICTURES AND MY OWN EARNINGS CERTAINLY FAR BELOW AMOUNT I COULD GET EVERYWHERE ELSE STOP AM VERY SKEPTICAL REGARDING YOUR PLANS OF BIGGER PICTURES BECAUSE THEY REQUIRE DIFFERENT FACILITIES AND ACTING MATERIAL FROM WHAT YOU HAVE STOP FULLY REALIZE WHAT WORLD EXPECT FROM ME AND THEREFORE REPEAT PROPOSAL OF SEPARATING AFTER NEXT PICTURE BEST REGARDS . . ."

Lubitsch would never have been acting so aggressively had he not had other offers; United Artists' Joe Schenck had offered him a contract with a large salary plus a percentage. While Lubitsch's contract with Warners allowed him to make one loan-out picture at U.A., it had to star Mary Pickford. Before Ernst could accept Schenck's lucrative offer, he had to cut himself loose from Harry and Jack.

An obviously worried Jack Warner wired his brother that "LUBITSCH INCENSED MADE VERY LITTLE MONEY THIS YEAR STATES MUST MAKE BIG PICTURE AFTER NEXT . . ." Jack asked Harry to authorize a payment that would reimburse Lubitsch for the percentages he wasn't getting. "TOLD HIM HE WOULD MAKE MONEY . . . THIS SERIOUS HIS REASON SMALL DIRECTORS MAKING TWICE MONEY HE MAKING AND HE GREAT LUBITSCH . . ."

Lubitsch had effectively rattled Warners' cage; although they had been protesting about the returns from his films, they were clearly not anxious to lose him. After consulting with the company lawyers, Jack decided not to permit any alterations of their original contract or to purchase Lubitsch's percentages. He also began to think that Lubitsch might be playing both ends against the middle. "UNDER NO CONDITION CABLE LUBITSCH HANDLE EVERYTHING THROUGH ME," he wired Harry on February 12. "DID YOU EVER DISCUSS WITH [attorney Nathan] BURKAN OR LUBITSCH THAT HE COULD DIRECT OTHER THAN PICTURE WITH PICKFORD PERSONALLY APPEARING THIS IMPORTANT . . ."

Jack went back to the lawyers to find out what exactly Lubitsch's obligations were under his contract. The answer came back that, because of his loan-out to Paramount for *Forbidden Paradise,* he owed them three pictures for 1926 alone, with an option for a picture in 1927 as well.

Lubitsch's desperation was growing, so he played his final card. "WILLING PURCHASE CONTRACT MYSELF," he wired Harry on February 23. "WILL TRADE IN MY INTEREST IN ALL MY WARNER PRODUCTIONS WIRE YOUR TERMS . . ."

How much truth was on either side in this battle between bruised ego and strong wills? Lubitsch's series of pictures for Warner Bros. had been profitable, but not by much. Records for *The Marriage Circle* specify a negative cost of $212,000, a world gross of $427,000; *Three Women* had cost $329,000 and grossed $438,000; *Kiss Me Again* cost $224,000 and grossed $394,000; *Lady Windermere's Fan* had cost $320,000 and grossed $398,000; *So This Is Paris,* his last picture for the studio, would cost $253,000 and gross $310,000. Warner's distribution fee was only 7.5 percent in America and 15 percent in Europe, but the math was incontrovertible. Warner Bros. didn't need to cook the books; there wasn't a whole lot of net to go around. Besides that, the grosses were in a steady decline. As film editor Rudi Fehr, a close associate of Jack Warner, would recall, "Lubitsch had a following, but they weren't coal-miners, they weren't steelworkers." In short, the mass audience was not interested.

Jack and Harry Warner had undoubtedly assumed that Lubitsch would pull a much larger audience in Europe than he had, but the European returns on his Warner productions were never more than $90,000 apiece; the knowing attitudes about the heavy chains of matrimony that struck Americans as so delicious probably struck many Europeans as business as usual. While Lubitsch's pictures outdrew other Warner productions in Europe, they also cost more.

Lubitsch's complaints about the impossibility of doing a big spectacle because of the unprepossessing Warners actors and facilities were more than a bit disingenuous. The brothers were already making costume pictures with John Barrymore—some of them good ones—that were the costliest items on the Warners production roster (*Beau Brummel* cost $343,000, *The Sea Beast* $503,000, and *Don Juan* $546,000). If Lubitsch's movies were different than they had been in Europe, it was because Lubitsch wanted them that way.

The underlying disgruntlement exhibited by the Warner brothers was spreading throughout Hollywood, for the fact of the matter was that few of the imported European directors and stars were adding much to the net profits of their employers. Even *The Cabinet of Dr. Caligari,* which had received more press attention than any of its contemporary American competition, had failed to attract audiences outside of New York City.

As early as February 1923, *The New York Times* was noting that the European invasion had produced films that "didn't go as they should—according to box-office standards. It seemed apparent that the Continental stories and methods of story-telling were not acceptable to American movie fans."

Of course, the moguls were conveniently overlooking the fact that the émigrés had been intended for prestige as much as anything else. The rave reviews were nice, but after a few years, the thrill of employing "The Griffith of Europe" had clearly worn off.

In the midst of all the contractual sniping, *So This Is Paris* was shot from March 25 to mid-May 1926. Lubitsch was paid an additional $10,000 for the script, with Warners stipulating that if he wished to use any other writers he'd have to pay for them himself. Obviously, Warners had developed a dislike for Kräly's work, but it was to no avail. Kräly duly received credit for the script; Lubitsch simply took the studio's money and signed it over to Kräly.

Warners did their best to make Lubitsch happy, probably against their better judgment. When no likely candidates were found on the lot for the part of Georgette, the script's Other Woman, they got Lilyan Tashman on loan-out for $750 a week, with a four-week minimum. They again hired Harold Grieve as art director, buying his services from Marshall Neilan for $475 a week with a five-week minimum, and hired free-lance writer, editor, and gadfly Rob Wagner to title the picture for a lump sum of $1,500.

"There was no kidding on the set," remembered costar Patsy Ruth Miller. In those days at Warner Brothers, the average picture would take four weeks to shoot, but a Lubitsch production would run between six and eight. He did not shoot a lot of takes, and tried to edit the film in the camera as much as possible. After rehearsals were done to his satisfaction, Lubitsch would announce to cast and crew alike, "This is the picture," meaning that the camera was about to roll.

"If he got what he wanted, he didn't try to cover himself with another take," remembered Patsy Ruth Miller. "Some directors aren't all that sure of themselves.

"The whole film was visualized in his head, so he wasn't very flexible. He didn't want you going off the beaten track with a gesture if it wasn't what he had in mind." Miller noted that the crew liked and respected him, and Lubitsch never raised his voice. "What particularly endeared him to me was the fact that he loved America. Some of the foreign directors, like Victor Seastrom, were so scornful. Not a warm personality. But Ernst loved America, loved the American people."

Lubitsch felt comfortable with Miller and let down his guard of impersonal geniality when he told her that "You must take care of your money. You must save your money. You must always have enough money."

Confused, the young actress asked why.

"Because then you don't have to be nice to anybody you don't like."

Despite the growing acrimony with Jack and Harry Warner, Ernst didn't let his dissatisfaction tempt him toward carelessness; when Myrna Loy, playing a maid, knocked on a door in the conventional overhand way, Lubitsch sprang from his chair. "No, no, this way," he said, turning his palm upward to demonstrate. "Turn your hand over and rap lightly with your knuckles. It is more *gentle* waking her up that way."

While Lubitsch and the brothers Warner were jousting over money and the kinds of pictures that Ernst should be making, the machinery of production ground on and Warners continued to purchase material designated for the increasingly unhappy director.

Case in point: Samson Raphaelson's play *The Jazz Singer*. According to Charles Van Enger, he brought the show to the attention of the Warners and Lubitsch, despite the indifferent reviews the play had received when it opened in September 1925 ("a shrewd and well-planned excursion into the theatre . . . so written that even the slowest of wits can understand it"–*The New York Times*). Harry, Jack, and Lubitsch, had gone to see it, but only Lubitsch agreed with Van Enger that it was good screen material.

Back on the West Coast, Lubitsch, having finished *So This Is Paris*, was fretting about not having a story. Indeed, worry about finding material would become a continual refrain for the rest of his life. Van Enger again mentioned *The Jazz Singer,* and Lubitsch decided to take advantage of the clause in his contract that said Warner Brothers had to buy any story he desired.

On May 20, 1926, Ernst cabled the Author's League in New York about two plays: *The Jazz Singer* and *Garden of Eden*. He had been unable to find out who owned the first and he didn't have the address of Avery Hopwood, who owned the latter. He asked to be wired collect if the rights were available and for how much.

A livid Jack Warner called Van Enger into his office and told him story selection was "none of your goddamn business." As Van Enger's contract was nearly up, and he had been receiving overtures from First National for far more money than the $350 a week he was drawing from Warners, he could afford to be equally belligerent. He promptly quit. The deal for *The Jazz Singer* came together very quickly; on June 4, Warners bought the play for $50,000 and made plans to hire George Jessel, who had made it a hit on Broadway, to star in the film. (*The Garden of Eden* was turned into a charming, *echt*-Lubitsch movie by Lewis Milestone in 1928, but for United Artists.)

Jack Warner's sour intransigence had gotten on Lubitsch's nerves, and it is probable that the contretemps over *The Jazz Singer* was the last straw. By the time the picture went into production in June 1927, Lubitsch was no longer at Warner Brothers. Like his cameraman, Lubitsch too had been getting good offers; like his cameraman, he determined to take one of them.

During the latter part of June 1926, when he was supposed to be working on the script for his next film, Lubitsch was in St. Vincent's Hospital for some minor surgery when he sent his assistant Eric Locke to collect $5,000 due him under his contract. Warners responded by saying that he was not contractually entitled to any compensation whatever when he was incapacitated and unable to work.

At the same time, Warners took Locke off the payroll, and Jack forbade his presence on the lot. If all that wasn't enough to get Lubitsch's attention, Jack then told him Warners was planning on using one of their staff scenarists for the next film rather than hiring an expensive free-lancer like Hans Kräly. When Lubitsch emerged from the hospital in the first week in July, he demanded that Warners rehire Locke, as they were obligated to under his contract. Furthermore, failure to rehire Kräly, he charged, would not only cause a delay in his next picture, tentatively titled *Husbands for Rent,* but would be considered a contractual violation.

On July 6, Lubitsch informed Jack Warner that he wanted to talk, and it was during this conversation that both men realized no reconciliation was possible. All that was left was to negotiate the terms of the divorce.

While in production with *So This Is Paris,* Lubitsch took time out to answer a call for help from Mary Pickford, who was betwixt and between about her production of *Sparrows,* which everyone agreed was running far overlength. "Thanks a thousand times for your prompt and generous co-operation in cutting *Sparrows,*" she wrote Lubitsch on May 29 from her hotel in Lucerne, Switzerland. "As you undoubtedly know they wanted to cut the barrel sequence which to my way of thinking would have been a serious mistake. Evidently you agreed with me as you have made other cuts. I can't tell you how very much I appreciate your kindness."

Pickford went on to tell Lubitsch of her and Douglas Fairbanks' plan to meet Max Reinhardt in Venice in a few weeks. Reinhardt, she said, had expressed an interest in making his motion picture debut with them (Obviously, Pickford had never heard of *Venetian Nights* and *Isle of the Blessed,* which was lucky for Reinhardt.) Pickford told Lubitsch that she was willing to postpone Lubitsch's commitment to her until October or November. "Douglas, you and I should do something fine together–*nicht wahr?*"

When she and Fairbanks returned from their European sojourn in the first week in September, Lubitsch sent a large basket of flowers to welcome them home, and Pickford responded with a dinner invitation and a thank-you note, once again thanking him profusely for his editing help.

Perhaps the wrangling with Warners over contracts and suitable actors was demoralizing to Lubitsch. Certainly, *So This Is Paris* is the least of his films for the studio. When it was released on July 31, 1926, even the censors couldn't get too worked up over it. The always rabid Pennsylvania Board of Censors made only minor changes; the title "After seeing you as a sheik—I have gained back my lost confidence" was altered to "After seeing you as a sheik—well—" Another title ("Mme. Suzanne Girard was 'simply crazy' over those hot Arabian romances—the books our wives read when we are away") had the last nine words cut, while two other titles ("Here's to love and liberty" and "If your husband gets suspicious, tell him it was the iceman") were eliminated entirely. That was all.

Most of the fun to be had from the film derives from André Beranger's portrayal of the neurotic fop dancer Maurice, whose hilarious apache number ("Dance of the Forbidden Fruit") derives from Nijinsky by way of Ruth St. Denis; Delsarte gestures and outstretched arms at the top of which perch absurdly wiggling hands.

For the rest, it's another go-round with Monte Blue as a doctor married to a congenitally foolish woman both of them being afflicted by a wandering eye.

There is some dexterous farcical byplay involving Blue's cane, which implicates him in an affair, and a hilarious, Freudian moment when he dreams that the incriminating cane is being shoved down his throat.

It's a comedy of genial marital deceit, slightly hampered by a second-string cast unable to suggest any emotional reserves deeper than their characters, who, as written, are virtually silhouettes. Since neither the actors nor the characters have anything at risk, there is little corresponding sense of audience involvement. At one point, the mechanics that Lubitsch resorted to in order to get a semblance of panache become transparent, as Monte Blue replicates one of Lubitsch's own acting mannerisms, a barking laugh with the head sliding in increments off to the side and down.*

Again, there is no particular reason for the picture to be set in Paris other than the veneer of Continental sophistication that the setting implies—censors would be noticeably more lenient if a movie was set in Paris than they would if it took place in Grand Rapids. Harold Grieve's sets are

*Interestingly, though, the film, which seems slightly flat on the TV screen, improves noticeably when projected on a large screen, a common occurrence with Lubitsch's work. What seems pinched and small when scaled down seems absolutely appropriate when seen as originally intended, completely vindicating Lubitsch's unerring sense of gestural and psychological proportion.

so subtle you have to see the film several times to notice how perfectly they set off the characters and mood of the film. At the same time, Lubitsch is more than capable of undercutting the quiet authenticity. When Monte Blue runs afoul of a policeman, Lubitsch has in place an actor who seems the simulacrum of the movie cliché of a tough Irish cop.

For the climax, Lubitsch executes an elaborate ballroom sequence done with the impressionistic, multiple superimpositions that would later be virtually patented by Slavko Vorkapich. The scene reasserts Lubitsch's mastery of large sets and multitudes of extras, and amounts to one of the silent cinema's most audacious leaps toward the musical. But the sequence, grand though it may be, feels suspiciously like a contrived, tour-de-force set piece; indeed, it may have been Lubitsch's sole reason to make the picture.

The reviewers noticed. "The ultra touch of the German director seems to wear pretty thin here," said *Photoplay*. "*So This Is Paris* turns out to be the weakest of Lubitsch efforts to date . . . the cast is weaker than usual."

With the completion of *So This Is Paris,* contract negotiations quickly moved from cat and mouse to hardball. Harry Warner notified Lubitsch that Warner Bros. was exercising their option for an extra Lubitsch picture (the one he had agreed to make in return for being loaned out for *Forbidden Paradise*), to start no later than March 1, 1927. It was a transparent negotiating ploy; Warners knew that Lubitsch was never going to make another picture for them, but the option upped the ante; if Lubitsch was going elsewhere, somebody was damn well going to have to compensate Warners for the loss of that final picture.

Negotiations between Harry Warner (for Warner Bros.), Nicholas Schenck (for Metro-Goldwyn-Mayer), and B. P. Schulberg (for Paramount) stretched on until very late at night on August 18, 1926. Finally, the deal was arranged. MGM and Paramount would pay Warners $150,000 for Lubitsch's contract. In addition, Lubitsch would return $30,000 that Warners had already advanced him for his next, unmade picture. Lubitsch would also give up all his percentages in the pictures he had made for Warners. For each picture he would make under the new contract, Lubitsch would receive $125,000, more than doubling his take from Warners.

In 1923, Harry and Jack Warner had needed Ernst to give their shoe-string operation some credibility. But, by the end of 1926, the premiere of John Barrymore's *Don Juan,* accompanied by a Vitaphone sound track, had driven the price of Warners stock from $8 a share to $65. Lubitsch had served his purpose and gotten them the critical attention Harry wanted, albeit without the profits Jack lusted after.

On August 18, Warners issued a statement saying that "the reason for disposing of the Lubitsch unit is solely due to the fact of the success that the Vitaphone attained at the opening 10 days ago in New York City of the production *Don Juan.* Warner Bros. in the future will concentrate their efforts exclusively on motion picture productions which will lend themselves to the synchronization method of the Vitaphone."

Ernst asked Henry Blanke if he wanted to accompany him to Paramount, but Harry Warner had already made it clear that Blanke was welcome to stay at Warners. Blanke explained to his friend and mentor that if he continued to tag along after Lubitsch he would never be able to mount a career of his own. Lubitsch agreed; Blanke would work for Lubitsch only once more, early in 1928 on *The Patriot,* but the two men remained close for as long as Lubitsch lived.

Now that they were out from a situation they regarded as a painful burden, Harry Warner wrote a letter to his brother Abe in New York about the buyout of Lubitsch's contract. "It is a lucky star that this is off our hands," he wrote, "because I think it is the worst lemon we have on our hands, so thank the Lord this is over."*

In three short years, Lubitsch had attained a level of critical prestige shared only by the premiere directors in Hollywood. "Speaking of great directors . . ." wrote Herbert Howe in *Photoplay* magazine in June 1926, "King Vidor stands unchallenged in the lists today, save possibly by Lubitsch." Iris Barry, writing in the London *Spectator,* named Lubitsch one

The Jazz Singer would be directed by Alan Crosland, with Sam Warner ramrodding the difficult production of the first part-talkie feature, which irrevocably altered the motion picture industry. But on October 5, 1927, the day before the premiere, a mastoid infection that had been spreading through his system killed Sam. Jack and Harry Warner settled down to a duel of wits and wills that would last thirty more years.

Finally, in May 1956, Jack orchestrated the sale of the brothers' 800,000 shares of Warner Bros. to Boston banker Serge Semenenko, ostensibly sending both Jack and his brother into prosperous retirement. He then promptly bought back his own shares for what he had been paid. The sweetheart deal locked Harry and Abe out of the company and left Jack in sole charge. On July 25, 1958, Harry Warner died at his home in Bel Air. At last, Jack had what he had always wanted; not only had he outwitted his brother, he had outlived him.

of seven "producers of genius" (the others were Lang, Grune, Wiene, Chaplin, Griffith, and Seastrom).

With Lubitsch's suggestive, inferential style at its height, other directors struggled to attain the same level of subtlety; some succeeded. When Clarence Brown made *Smouldering Fires,* a beautifully directed, psychologically penetrating drama about a marriage between a young man and an older woman that is considerably better than Ernst's similar *Three Women,* producer John Considine, who arrived at the theater after the credits had rolled, simply assumed that Lubitsch had made it. When Considine stayed through to the beginning of the next show and saw who the director actually was, Brown was promptly signed to a contract that jumped his pay from $12,500 a picture to $3,000 a week.

For his part, Ernst had become fully acclimated to America, and the specific demands of its audiences. Yet he refused to play reciprocal pattycake. "The people of Europe are more serious fundamentally than those in America," Lubitsch told *The New York Times* in September 1927. "Americans go to a theatre solely to be entertained; the European, subconsciously perhaps, expects a little lesson with his entertainment . . . A story must be complete and logical to achieve success in Europe, while here the story can be perfectly illogical so long as it amuses."

Lubitsch was describing a double-edged blade of differing sensibilities, but one that particularly suited his effervescent, albeit rigorously logical temperament. He was not the only one. "In America," Emil Jannings was explaining to a reporter, "I have found the art of the motion picture at its best. Producers go to any limit to make fine pictures. Salaries are better here for both extras and stars. Living conditions are better. People really live in the United States. In Europe . . . the men who make pictures . . . are either artistic and unbusinesslike or they are too businesslike and forsake the artistic side. Here, these two characteristics are combined to advantage.

"I have learned American ways. I have learned filming schedules must be lived up to. I have learned that authors, directors and American actors are artists."

Not all of the new arrivals in Hollywood were in search of fame and fortune. Some just wanted to get away from their parents. Walter Laemmle, a nephew of Carl Laemmle, abandoned his father's Munich antiques business and arrived in America in January 1924 at the ripe age of twenty-one, eager to see America and the world of movies.

"I wanted to get away from home, see a little bit of the world," he remembered. "In Germany at that time, it was so controlled. Now, if a child wants to move out and get an apartment, he just does it. But then, a son could not move out of his father's house. It was very rigid."

Laemmle's first impression of America was immutably formed when he was driven down Broadway and saw the huge display set up for DeMille's *The Ten Commandments* at the Cohan Theater. The displays were entire stories high, with neon lighting that made midnight as bright as three in the afternoon. There was nothing like this in Munich.

Laemmle arrived in Hollywood and was given a job as a second assistant director at Uncle Carl's Universal, often working with Edward Sloman. Since Walter's brother Ernst had already embarked on an indifferent career as a director of Westerns, they lived together in Hollywood. Walter's salary of $25 a week wasn't enough to afford a car, so he learned to stand on the corner of Hollywood and Cahuenga every morning and hitch a ride over the hills to Universal in the San Fernando Valley. "Anybody would pick you up," he explained. "there were no holdups, no murders, no robberies."

Carl Laemmle ran Universal as if it was a warm, benign, slightly eccentric extended family. His nickname of "Uncle Carl" was as much metaphor as it was literal description. There was a billboard by the studio entrance, and every Monday Uncle Carl would have a new inspirational bromide put up for display: "Be Kind to Others—[signed,] Carl Laemmle."

Uncle Carl was widely known as the softest touch in the business, as was proved by his habit of employing a wide selection of relatives, spawning the line "Uncle Carl Laemmle has a very large faemmle." Within that circle, though, he expected—and usually got—respect. Once, when Ernst Laemmle got into an argument with his uncle and wrote him an insolent letter, Carl responded with a curt telegram: "You may wire your resignation collect." But Ernst Laemmle never did, and Uncle Carl never insisted.

At Universal, Walter Laemmle quickly fell in with Paul Kohner, an aspiring producer, who introduced him to Lubitsch. "We spent fifty-two Sundays a year at Lubitsch's, including Christmas and New Year's. We usually came in the afternoon. Kohner, my brother, myself, maybe [Henry] Blanke, would have lunch together, then go to Lubitsch's about three or four o'clock in the afternoon until after dark. It was automatic."

Although the guest list at these gatherings ranged from major stars and directors to bit actors and assistant directors, Lubitsch was utterly unconcerned with the caste system that was even then forming in Hollywood. "The atmosphere was very easygoing," recalled Walter Laemmle. "Lubitsch and his wife never pretended to be something they were not. You could talk to him anytime about anything. You were not in awe of him. Not once can I say that I had the feeling that he was pulling rank, and we were all younger than he was. They were very good friends to us and that's all that counted."

Soon, the group of émigrés seized on a name for themselves: "The Foreign Legion." It was an ironic admission of their isolation, with a touch of satirical masochism about their supposedly horrid surroundings, which they all knew were idyllic. The feeling of manning a lonely outpost in hostile territory was confirmed by even so doughty a presence as Fritz Lang; when he visited Hollywood for the first time in November 1924, he said that seeing Lubitsch again "was like greeting a brother." Although Lang was never the most social of men, he was glad to spend his Sundays while he was in town at Lubitsch's house.

If Lubitsch and the rest of the Foreign Legion were crazy about America, then America was returning the favor. In Hollywood, a group of young directors were overtly copying the Lubitsch manner. Among the Lubitsch acolytes were Monta Bell, Harry d'Arrast, Mal St. Clair, and the ill-fated Paul Bern, who graduated from cowriting *The Marriage Circle* to directing a pleasant Adolphe Menjou/Raymond Griffith comedy called *Open All Night*. Stills of Lubitsch visiting Bern's set show the actors and Bern gazing at the German director with open admiration. The talent was beginning to give birth to the legend, and the legend was defined by the fragrant but imprecise phrase "The Lubitsch Touch."

In time, the phrase became a convenient but misleading hook, as if that said all there was to say, a highly insufficient means of approaching the vast differences in style and meaning between the Lubitsch films of the mid-1920s and Lubitsch films of the early 1940s. As Andrew Sarris observed, "To speak of Lubitsch in terms of his 'touch' is to reduce feelings to flourishes."

Lubitsch himself tried to slip away from the phrase. "If there is such a thing, I do not know what it is," he would say. "It exists only in people's minds. If I were conscious of it, I would be afraid I might lose it."

To a large extent, the fabled touch was a byproduct of Ernst's method of production as much as it was his particular sensibility. Lubitsch would freely admit that the picture was worked out in his mind to such an extent that, once the script was done, "I've finished the picture. All I have to do is photograph it . . . As you write the script, you cut the film, you build the sets, you light your players, you design their wardrobe, you set the tempo, you delineate the characters . . . For me, it is virtually all done in the script."

By the time a script was finished, Ernst almost never referred to it, having long since committed it to memory. Shooting a film rarely took more than eight weeks. "When you shoot scene number 150 today and scene number 149 two weeks from now, you must know exactly what emotion each player is to register."

It was a method that would be carried on by Hitchcock, whose precise *mise-en-scène* would also be forced to labor under a misleading, shallow sobriquet, "The Master of Suspense." Unlike Hitchcock, however, for whom actual production was a drab necessity after the creative work of the writing and storyboarding, Lubitsch exuded vitality on the set. Harry Carr, a journalist and screenwriter, compared Ernst on the set to "a bullterrier trying to break loose to run after a tomcat."

Between shots, while the lights were being rearranged, Ernst would pace back and forth, anxious, nervous. Sometimes he'd let off steam by going over to a piano and banging out some jazz. During close-ups, he would sit in his director's chair with his face expressing the same emotions as the actors. "In his intensity," wrote Carr, "he leans forward from his chair, often with his hands gripped on the arms. The more intense the scene, the more pronounced his 'lean.' "

And, always, there was the perfectionism that only his humor and *joie de vivre* kept from becoming onerous. During the making of *The Marriage Circle,* Lubitsch made Florence Vidor unlock a bureau sixteen times before he was satisfied, and he shot more than thirty takes of a kiss between Vidor and Creighton Hale. In the cutting room, he worked quickly. "You would imagine that he was mad at the film," wrote Herbert Howe. "He tears at it until you can almost hear him growl."

What he was after was action that spoke, that communicated the meaning of the dramatic or comic moment to the viewer in a way that rendered titles superfluous.

Lubitsch once fabricated a metaphor for the effect he tried to create. There was, it seems, a girl on the ground and a cat on a roof. The girl, Lubitsch said, should merely hold out her hand and coo "I've got some catnip," rather than yelling and screaming for the cat to come down. "The former," explained Lubitsch, "would catch the attention . . .

whereas the latter would drive him away." Always, Lubitsch meant to entice, tantalize.

To break it down into its component parts, the Lubitsch touch involved sex as frivolous pastime, with the female often being the aggressor. Josef von Sternberg would acidly characterize the Lubitsch style's "often amusing contrivance . . . No matter what happened, one would always have a twinkle in the eye . . . if the wife was caught in bed with a neighbor, his hat would be brushed off, and when escorted to the door, he would be asked to call again."

Added to these behavioral reversals was metaphor and symbolism; objects would be detailed and used as counterpoints to the emotional developments of the characters that used them: Monte Blue's cane in *So This Is Paris,* the shuffling of place cards in *One Hour With You,* the hat in *Ninotchka,* closed doors in any number of films. Mainly, the Lubitsch touch had to be sensed, not just seen. It was a whiff of perfume, a teasing glance of interest from a woman who is supposed to be happily married.

All this couldn't help but appeal to a generation of critics and audiences who came of age after World War I, and were eager to bury the embalmed public pieties of Edwardian artists who, by and large, still controlled the artistic vocabulary of the first twenty years of the twentieth century. Lubitsch's films were like his characters: erotic but well-mannered, enticing but never rude.

Yet, Ernst was also careful to hedge his bets ever so slightly; the films usually take place in conveniently Continental environments, so an American audience would not be threatened and could, if they wished, ascribe the character's actions to very different European mores. Not only that, but he usually structured his scripts of this period to include two couples; one woman is willing to initiate sex while the other might seriously think about it but ultimately decides to settle for the security of monogamy.

In spite of this careful construction, not everybody was buying. In 1927, F. W. Murnau, once a cohort of Lubitsch's during the Reinhardt days, now a director whose legend was approaching Lubitsch's, said that Lubitsch had only been playing, "flirting with his great gifts."

Far more concerted and damaging was the attack launched by Jim Tully, the hobo novelist who wrote *Beggars of Life.* Tully had a brief vogue during which he pretended to despise the Hollywood that bought his books, gave him lucrative magazine assignments and even acting jobs. In December 1926, he published a scathing article about Lubitsch in *Vanity Fair.* To begin with, he said that Mary Pickford certainly didn't need a director like Lubitsch, and that "one of her most successful directors is possessed of a mentality little above a child's" (an obvious slam at the playful Marshall Neilan).

"Lubitsch [seems] content to become a director of frothy films for sophisticated chambermaids and cinema critics," Tully wrote. He reported a conversation he had with Lubitsch in which he had inquired why the director was satisfied to direct comedy when he could have made another *Passion*.

"Molière was content to do comedy," replied Lubitsch. "Chaplin is a genius—he does comedy."

"Chaplin is merely a clever mimic," replied Tully, "hardly to be compared with Molière."

Lubitsch pointed to *A Woman of Paris*, which Tully slammed as a very ordinary story. "But the treatment, the treatment," Lubitsch said. Tully continued his attack. "Leaving Chaplin out of it . . . you remind me of a man who is capable of writing a great novel and is content to idle away his time with clever short stories."

Lubitsch finally responded by crying "Oh, let me alone!"

"Instead of being a great artist," Tully wrote, "he is merely a merchant like his father. But with this difference . . . his father did not deal in second-hand goods."

Tully's attack crudely predated the Marxist film criticism of the 1930s, in which the most important issue was social correctness, weighty themes supposedly being synonomous with weighty aesthetic success. By these standards, Maxwell Anderson was the greatest of all American playwrights, Sergei Eisenstein the greatest of all directors, and King Vidor's greatest achievement was *Our Daily Bread*.

In an article written for *American Cinematographer* in November 1929, Lubitsch defended himself from these theories when he defined his conception of art as "great yet not obviously great. For when art begins to be apparent, to show itself as a definite, studied effort to be artistic, it ceases to be art, for true art needs no label . . . That is the key to my objection to [Carl] Dreyer's *Passion of Joan of Arc*. That picture had brilliant moments, but it was so studied, so obviously calculated to make people gasp and to say, 'See, that is art,' that it overreached itself."

The question of who got first crack at Lubitsch under the MGM-Paramount deal seems to have been determined by who could come up with a suitable property first. As usual, MGM's Irving Thalberg had the edge.

In the wake of the success of Erich von Stroheim's 1925 film *The Merry Widow* (a clear profit of $758,000), Thalberg had offered von Stroheim another operetta, Sigmund Romberg's *The Student Prince*. But Von Stroheim had felt constrained working under Thalberg's close supervision and instead signed a deal with independent producer Pat Powers to make *The Wedding March,* from an original Von Stroheim story similar to the Romberg property.

Thalberg's second choice was Lubitsch, who called in Hans Kräly to work out a script. Although the picture might have worked equally well for MGM's reigning star John Gilbert, Ramon Novarro was just coming off a considerable success in *Ben-Hur,* and the Romberg operetta seemed appropriate for his more boyish, less sexual charm. Opposite Novarro, Thalberg cast his own girlfriend, Norma Shearer.

Lubitsch enlisted the services of Ali Hubert to design the costumes. With an eye for authentic detail worthy of von Stroheim, Lubitsch cabled Hubert his specific requirements: "Buy priests' caps, ribbons and caps in many colors. You need these for 250 students who would be in school in Heidelberg. Need 20 uniforms of officers of various levels, others who are armored soldiers. Parade uniforms, helmets with feathers, six artillery soldiers and one officer. Parade uniforms for military band, six ministers of state, chamberlains, six lackeys, six footmen, three officers of a small town, a sergeant, a customs inspector, three policemen of Heidelberg, 300 hats in the old high hat style, 100 hats of students of various classes, sabres or swords of the students, equipment for duels of the students, 400 beer mugs and accessories for the students' rooms. Advertisement signs, restaurant signs, albums of pictures of Heidelberg."

Then, almost as an afterthought, Lubitsch added, "Tell me what it will cost before you buy." Hubert arrived in Hollywood with thirty-two trunks of clothes and accessories.

Studio production work began in December 1926. With Henry Blanke staying behind at Warners, Ernst had need of a new assistant. As combination assistant/film editor he hired Andrew Marton, a friend of Lubitsch's confidant Charles Puffy. Marton would go on to a long and successful career, mostly as a second-unit director.

Norma Shearer, a nervous actress at the best of times, grew increasingly uneasy at Ernst's habit of acting out a scene as a matrix for the actor's performance. At times, Lubitsch would feign anger while directing, then, walking back to his chair, he would wink at Andrew Marton. After a week of production, Shearer threw a tantrum and sent out a call for help to Thalberg, her soon-to-be fiancé. Thalberg listened to Lubitsch, then

Shearer, then calmly told his girlfriend that "everyone has a lot to learn from Mr. Lubitsch."

For location shots of Heidelberg that Lubitsch initially planned to use, he decided to make it a working vacation, with the emphasis on the latter. He packed Leni and the boys up, grabbed a cameraman to shoot some exteriors, and sailed to Germany. To wish them bon voyage, a group of friends gathered and presented them with an autograph album. Sidney Franklin wished them a splendid trip, while "Conrad" (Veidt? Nagel?) suggested that they "bring your butler a black tie!" Others, like Pola Negri, Maurice Tourneur, Lew Cody, Carey Wilson, Ramon Novarro, Eleanor Glyn, and Paul Bern contented themselves with signatures.

In Berlin, Ernst's return was greeted with much press fanfare and even an honorary retrospective screening of *Madame DuBarry* on May 25 at the UFA-Palast, with Ernst in attendance. In his room on the second floor of the Adlon Hotel, Lubitsch entertained a small army of newspapermen, photographers, and newsreel cameramen. "It's almost as crazy here as it is in America," he commented. "I would never have believed that you could almost outdo the American press here."

Ernst was overjoyed at returning to his native soil, and seeing so many old friends, but he also admitted to a feeling of displacement. "I'm almost out of place here in this hotel," he told one reporter. "I'm like a stranger, and yet my entire existence is rooted in this city. All I need now is for the porter to tell me which tourist attractions I should visit."

To questions regarding the evolution of the German film industry, Lubitsch begged off, saying that he simply wasn't sufficiently familiar with recent German movies, with the exception of Murnau's *The Last Laugh* and Dupont's *Variety*, which he singled out for praise.

Just before he left for Heidelberg, Lubitsch took a sentimental journey to the house at 82 Lothringer Strasse where he had been born, and the house at 183 Schönhäuser Allee. "I want to see if the iron fence that I played in front of is still there," he said nostalgically. Then it was off to Heidelberg.

Walter Laemmle had returned to Munich from Hollywood, and was surprised to get a call from Lubitsch inviting him to come to Heidelberg as Lubitsch's guest. Laemmle and his sister spent a week in Heidelberg, eating lunch and dinner with Lubitsch every day, all on MGM's tab.

Lubitsch found that the trip to Europe was pleasant, but slightly disorienting. It seemed to him now that he was of America far more than of Germany, a mysterious but immutable alteration that had taken place in less than five years. He felt perceptibly out of place in his own native land,

laughter

in   paradise

a feeling intensified on his next and final return to Europe in 1932, when he attended a party in Paris. He was talking in German with the host, when an American woman came up and asked "Who's the funny little Dutchman?" Lubitsch spoke German the rest of the night, so as not to embarrass her.

On July 15, the group began their voyage back to America on the SS *Hamburg*. It had been a pleasurable but pointless trip; Andrew Marton remembered that none of the material shot in Heidelberg was used in the final print and that the only locations that were used were a few scenes shot in Laurel Canyon. The film opened in New York on September 21.

The Student Prince in Old Heidelberg (surviving prints usually carry the simplified main title *In Old Heidelberg*) makes full use of Lubitschean irony from the very beginning, as the principality of Karlsburg prepares to welcome back its crown prince with much imperial hullaballoo. Thousands gather to pay tribute, the railroad car majestically slows down with much attendant steam, the car doors open, uniformed flunkeys step out and stand on either side of the door. There is a beat, another beat, and out troops the child prince in a sailor suit, his mouth stuporously agape.

This is Karl Heinrich, a totally isolated anchorite who wants only to be normal, to roughhouse with the other boys. Instead, he has to settle for aged factotums who gingerly toss a beach ball back and forth so as not to aggravate their arthritis.

Even after he grows up and is magically transformed from Phillipe de Lacey to Ramon Novarro, he is a passive onlooker in a palace drowning in manners and stultifying formality. Squeaking through his college boards, he is sent with his beloved tutor, Dr. Jüttner, to Heidelberg. "Do you know what it means to go to Heidelberg?" inquires the doctor. He leans over and whispers into Karl Heinrich's ear. The prince's quizzical look changes to awe, then delight, then glee.

The rest of the script is familiar; Karl Heinrich's arrival in Heidelberg; his romance with Kathi, the beautiful barmaid; his acceptance by the other students, and the attendant flowering in the wonderful world of convivial, vibrant youth; his return to Karlsburg to fulfill his royal destiny, leaving Kathi—and happiness—irrevocably behind.

Out of this Lubitsch spins a convincing, moving, distinguished picture. He skillfully photographs Norma Shearer's oddly aquiline, pinched features, and she gives a relaxed, animated, and charming performance, particularly when she unself-consciously demonstrates the softness of the mattress in the prince's room.

Lubitsch allows the romanticism to come through untrammeled by cynicism, using his visual epigrams to make character rather than narrative points, as in a beautiful dissolve from the cold, austere tomb of the old king to the country cemetery and the flower-bedecked grave of Dr. Jütt-ner.

The film's centerpiece is the first love scene. Karl is pursuing Kathi through the beer garden. She is trying to escape, but not too hard, and Lubitsch moves with them in a lengthy lateral tracking shot. Finally, behind a tree, Karl catches her, but the camera continues on ahead to observe an empty space animated, after a few seconds, by a barking dachshund. In a few moments, Kathi bursts into the frame, closely fol-lowed by Karl Heinrich, wanting more.

They move to a hillside covered with flowers under twinkling stars. As they lay upon the grass and gaze into each other's eyes, the wind starts up, and the hill comes alive as the flowers pulsate in the breeze. They kiss, the wind dies down, and she runs off. As he lays back on the hill, deeply satisfied, a shooting star creases the night sky.

It's a heady, undeniably effective, metaphorically erotic sequence that is a clear precursor to the much-maligned scene of Rosie's deflowering in David Lean's *Ryan's Daughter* (1970). Rumor has always had it that Thalberg was unsatisfied with Lubitsch's version of the scene and had it reshot by John M. Stahl, but Andrew Marton asserted that Stahl had nothing to do with the film and that it's entirely Lubitsch's. As it hap-pened, Lubitsch was also unsatisfied with the first version of the love scene and reshot it himself.

"The set was already struck," remembered Andrew Marton, "so the meadow had to be rebuilt, and we ended up with a completely different set." Despite the scene's luscious romanticism, Marton remembered that "It was a scene that Lubitsch still hated after he re-did it. There were other problems with the meadow scene besides the set—the chemistry was not the way Lubitsch imagined it. He never thought that Ramon Novarro or Norma Shearer was the right casting for the film, but the studio insisted and he was stuck with them. Lubitsch did marvelously with them, actu-ally, but not to his exacting standards."

At the film's end, with the twin burdens of an arranged marriage and kingship on the horizon, Karl Heinrich returns to Heidelberg to revisit the rapture that might keep him warm in the long, empty years ahead. But the reality is not his *Gemütlichkeit* fantasy, of exuberant old friends wel-coming him home, of Kathi's arms opened wide.

Now the beer garden is bedraggled, scraggly, and abandoned. His old drinking companions are as stiffly inhibited as the acolytes at the castle, and the hillside where he and Kathi first made love is covered only with grass and a dormant tree. And Kathi? Kathi tells him that "You'll marry and I'll marry—and we'll both be very happy." As they embrace for the final time, they both know her words to be wishful thinking.

Back home in Karlsburg, it is Karl Heinrich's wedding day. He rides in the ceremonial coach with his new bride, whom we never see. An old couple looking on agrees that "It must be wonderful to be a king." Lubitsch, as he fades out on Karl Heinrich's empty, contemplative face, thinks otherwise.

The Student Prince in Old Heidelberg is one of Lubitsch's most purely romantic films; perhaps because of the nudgings of Thalberg, perhaps because of an emotional response to the story, Lubitsch doesn't bend the material to his wishes, but, rather, gives himself to it wholeheartedly. As a result, John Mescall's camera, while capturing a particularly glistening light, is also slightly more anonymous than usual, less attuned to the individual visual *bon mot*. As a corollary to the Romberg melodies with which pit orchestras accompanied the film, Lubitsch orchestrates a melli-fluously moving camera to accompany lovers embracing on a hillside under cascading stars.

When the film was released in September 1927, Mordaunt Hall in *The New York Times* said that "In this new offering, Mr. Lubitsch lives up to all that has been written about him. He may be a stylist, but he . . . does not choose to repeat on any of his past bright camera ideas," while Welford Beaton in *The Film Spectator* wrote that the film was "A monu-ment to the versatility of Ernst Lubitsch. *Old Heidelberg* reveals a Lubitsch who is deeply human. I have chuckled with the other Lubitsch, but with this new one I felt something at my throat that gave him a place in my heart that he never had before."

The film opened in London in February 1928 at the Tivoli Strand, where the program announced with palpable surprise that "Lubitsch has adhered faithfully to the original story of the play, and made no attempt to graft on to it an artificial and inappropriate happy ending."

Despite the good reviews, the high cost ($1.2 million) of *The Student Prince* mitigated against financial success. The film lost $307,000.

While Lubitsch had been seduced by the sensual physical environment of Southern California and the technical expertise of the Hollywood studios, he quickly developed an attitude implying that, while he worked in Hollywood, he was not of Hollywood.

Lubitsch realized that America was not for all tastes. When he saw *The*

Crowd, King Vidor's masterpiece of impotence and alienation, he told a German friend that "Americans will not understand this film. Europeans will not understand this film. Only Europeans who have lived in America will understand this film."

The essential problem of Hollywood was the little things, and the symbolic relationship they had to much bigger things. A successful writer in New York might satisfy himself with suits bought off the rack at Saks. But in the social circles of Hollywood, that writer would admire the way someone was dressed and ask who their tailor was. They'd tell him, and the difference would usually be about fifty dollars a suit. To accompany the more expensive suit, they would need new shirts, maybe ten-dollar shirts instead of five-dollar shirts. But what difference did it make? They were making $1,000 a week and paying virtually no taxes.

Then came the rest: cashmere socks, a half-dozen pairs, then the house with the pool, purchased instead of merely rented. Before they knew it they were all living fully up to their income, if not beyond, and looking slightly overdressed in the bargain.

Lubitsch was not immune to these dangers, but he was conscious of the irony. At one point, he even bought a couple of horses and enjoyed riding through the Hollywood foothills before breakfast, often accompanied by John Loder, the newly arrived English actor. "In spite of his short legs [he rode a gray with a back as broad as a big drum] he got along famously," remembered Loder, "and would gallop fearlessly over the roughest country."

But, once they were off the back lot, Lubitsch and his confreres quickly realized that Los Angeles was, and would remain for years, an intellectual Gobi Desert, at least compared to New York, London, or Berlin. It would take talkies and the importation of writers like Hammett, Hellman, and Faulkner, and actors like Edward G. Robinson and Charles Boyer, before Hollywood responded with small gathering places like the bookstores of Louis Epstein and Stanley Rose on Hollywood Boulevard.

There was certainly no equivalent of the cafe set that was such a permanent part of life in European capitals. For a convivial personality like Lubitsch's, the loss was considerable. So, he formed his own. All over Hollywood, émigrés were doing the same thing. The Scandinavian colony—Victor Seastrom, Karl Dane, Lars Hanson, Nils Asther, Greta Garbo, Mauritz Stiller, Sven Gade, and Benjamin Christiansen—tended to congregate at Seastrom's house at 425 Palisade Avenue in Santa Monica. And the

German colony, the Foreign Legion, was headquartered at Lubitsch's, 616 Beverly Drive, Beverly Hills.

With the Foreign Legion, the preferred language was that of their native country, which could occasionally cause amusement. When Conrad Veidt arrived in Hollywood to make *The Beloved Rogue,* Lubitsch took him to a boxing match. The fighters were lackadaisical and the crowd got restless. "Fight, fight!" they began screaming, which caused a flattered Veidt to stand up and make a gracious bow to his adoring fans. "See, you're famous here already," cracked Lubitsch.

Likewise, the preferred cuisine at Ernst's house would always remain German. Steak tartare was a favorite, but Ernst also loved classic German dishes like sausages, sauerbraten, potato dumplings, Wiener schnitzel, cabbage, Hungarian goulash, and kidney stew. Although the American custom for holidays like Thanksgiving and Christmas has always been turkey, Lubitsch would substitute goose.

Some of the customs he observed were purely American. Lubitsch was particularly fond of fireworks and every July 4 had a large display in front of his house, much of which he would light himself. One year, a palm tree in front of the house caught fire, and the fire department had to be called. Ernst ran into the house for his wallet to give the firemen some money.

Ernst always made time for his stepsons, Edmund and Heinz, assiduously attending the PTA meetings at their school. When the circus was in town, he would invariably take them; if he and Leni were going away to Catalina Island or Santa Barbara for any length of time, the boys would accompany them. Once, when the two boys were at a camp on Catalina, Ernst and Leni chartered a 110-foot-long converted minesweeper and made a surprise visit. The splendor of their parents' transportation greatly increased the boys' status among their peers.

Sunday mornings were a special time, for Ernst would rise early, collect the newspaper from the front door, and come into the boys' bedroom to read them the comics, taking a lot of time over their favorite, The Katzenjammer Kids.

Eddie took the comic strip very much to heart. Once, he planted a stink bomb under a massage table that went off just as Ernst was getting his rubdown. A furious Lubitsch careened all over the house looking for the culprit. Eddie, frightened by his stepfather's rare display of anger, climbed out of his bedroom window and onto the roof of the house. When Lubitsch saw the boy clinging to the roof, his anger immediately dissipated. "Come on back, Eddie," he pleaded. "You won't be scolded; you

scott eyman

won't be harmed." The boy came down and Lubitsch was true to his word.

In fact, Lubitsch never laid any but an affectionate hand on either of the boys. One of the few things with which he was impatient were breaches of decorum, as when Eddie, invited to accompany his parents to a party at Adolphe Menjou's house, threw up all over the dinner table. Lubitsch was greatly embarrassed and perturbed, but Menjou, as nonchalant and gracious offscreen as on, calmed Ernst down and comforted the mortified child.

Sunday afternoons were for brunch and swimming parties, all of it fine with the boys, except for the fact that Paul Kohner and the actress Mary Philbin, who were very much in love at the time, would sit in Eddie's swing holding hands for hours at a time. This meant the swing was off-limits to the children, which tickled Ernst no end.

He took his sons on the set of Douglas Fairbanks' *Don Q, Son of Zorro,* and Fairbanks put on a demonstration for the boys by taking his bullwhip and lashing out at Eddie. So expert was Fairbanks with the whip that there was no discomfort whatever as the whip wrapped around him; he could barely feel it. Once, Ernst invited Eddie and his friends to the Paramount lot where he arranged a screening of *The White Hell of Pitz Palu;* another time he took them to the Warner Bros. lot where radio station KFWB was broadcasting and the announcer put the boys on the air live.

Ernst was particularly concerned about the boys because they rode their bikes to the public schools they attended: El Rodeo grammar school followed by Beverly Hills High, with a year at Culver Military Academy in between. "My mother liked the uniforms," remembered Edmund Lewis glumly. "I guess it was the German in her."

Ernst gave them strict, fatherly instructions not to get into any strangers' cars. His own disinterest in religion was reflected in a distinct lack of household ecumenical spirit; once in a while Leni would take the boys to the local Presbyterian church on Santa Monica Boulevard.

When he was in production on a film, the usually jovial Lubitsch might become quiet and far more reserved at home than he normally was. One of the few times his stepson ever saw him upset was at the Brown Derby. Lubitsch had ordered one of his favorite dishes, steak with bearnaise sauce, but the steak arrived sans sauce. Lubitsch berated the waiter by yelling, "Where is my sauce bearnaise, I have no sauce bearnaise." (He seems to have been particularly sensitive in culinary matters; another event that aroused his ire occurred at home when he decided to have some leftovers for dinner, then went into the kitchen to find the help eating filet mignon.)

Although he was, as Edmund Lewis remembered, "a wonderful father," he preferred it if the intimacy went in only one direction. His stepsons never knew, for instance, that Ernst had a brother of his own because he never spoke of his family.

"He was crazy about those boys," concluded Joan Marsh Morrill, the daughter of cameraman Charles Rosher and a frequent playmate of the Lubitsch children in those years. "As far as he was concerned, they were his boys, even though he hadn't sired them. Ernst gave great love."

In the homey living room of the expansive Bel Air house with an orchard in the back yard, where she has lived since 1936, Lupita Tovar Kohner, the widow of Paul Kohner, remembered Sunday afternoons at 616 Beverly Drive with a girlish excitement. "I met my husband at the end of 1928, and at the beginning of 1929, he took me on a Sunday afternoon to the house on Beverly Drive for a swim and coffee. I remember how excited I was when Garbo came in. She was very animated, talking. Then, suddenly, she would be gone. She came alone, always. Joe May would usually be there, Oscar Straus. There was very little shoptalk. They talked about everything. I remember they talked a lot about music; they all went to the Hollywood Bowl."

Lupita Kohner remembered Lubitsch's dancing eyes; the naive young girl from Mexico City found herself in awe of Lubitsch. Throughout the next eighteen years of their friendship, she could never bring herself to call him "Ernst," as the others did. To her, he was always "Mr. Lubitsch."

"He was a teaser," she remembered. "He would go up to somebody and say, 'Everything all right between you and your wife?'

" 'Of course. Why?'

" 'Oh, just asked. Just wondering.' He'd make them a little worried, you know?"

Many of Lubitsch's friends felt that Lubitsch developed both professionally and personally in America in a way he never would have in Europe. "He was an artist," said his niece, Evie Bettelheim-Bentley, "and in Hollywood he could do what he wanted and make a lot of money besides. Not that money was the important thing to him; he was never poor, so if you're never poor, money doesn't have that fascination. But I think everything was too small in Europe for him. In Hollywood, he had so much more of a free hand to do what he wanted to do. He could never have gone back to Europe."

"Partly," said Gottfried Reinhardt, "[his happiness] was because of his collaborators. The atmosphere of creative Hollywood was infinitely more sophisticated than the atmosphere of films in Germany. Films in Germany were déclassé. Today, people unearth the old pictures of Lang and Pabst and Dupont, but in those days it was like pop literature. The actors were basically doing it for the money."

Lubitsch became increasingly social. To celebrate the New Year, Ernst and Leni would begin on New Year's Eve with a buffet for about fifty guests. On New Year's Day, it was open house, with friends dropping in for a drink, lunch, or dinner as they preferred. Regular social gatherings were eclectic; at some parties, there were far more Hungarians (including Vilma Banky, Charles Puffy, Lya de Putti, and Victor Varconi) than there were Germans.

And he grew adept at the game-playing aspects of life in the movie colony. When he and Leni would go to a party and be early or on time, Lubitsch would instruct his chauffeur to drive around for ten minutes so they would arrive late . . . but not too late.

Most of Lubitsch's friends liked Leni. "Lubitsch's wife was a charming young woman," remembered the actress Camilla Horn. "Ernst was very generous with her and was happy when she flirted like hell with other men. She understood how to do that." Like most men, Andrew Marton noticed her sensuality. "Leni . . . was a very, very pretty woman, and very sexy. As a matter of fact, when I was just getting to know them I felt vibrations, and I felt her looks."

Charles Rosher's daughter Joan was invited to the house nearly every weekend she was in town. "Leni was a very nice, lovely woman who really loved her children," she remembered. On Sundays, the chauffeur would drop Joan off at the Lubitsch house around noon, where she and the boys would have lunch. After that, the children would play in and around the pool; sometimes they'd play catch on the front lawn. In the afternoon, the adult guests would arrive, but Leni always made sure to send out to a bakery farther down Beverly Drive for some apricot tarts that were the children's favorite.

But others weren't as easily enthralled by Leni. Henry Blanke couldn't stand her, and told friends that she once tried to back him into a closet for a necking session. There were rumors that she was a kleptomaniac.

"Once," remembered Lupita Tovar Kohner, "I went swimming at Beverly Drive. I had five dollars in my purse. When I was in the pool, I saw her going into the cabana and coming out. I wondered why.

"Anyway, we were staying for dinner. I went to get dressed, and when I got my lipstick out of my purse my five dollars was gone. And I *knew* I had had it. It bothered me. When Paul took me home and I told him what had happened, he said that I had imagined having had it. I said 'Five dollars is a big amount of money; I didn't imagine it.'

"Little things would happen at dinner parties where Leni was. Things disappeared. People would talk, but they couldn't say she had done it. She didn't need the things. She just liked to take."

Leni could be extremely temperamental, even in front of reporters, although Lubitsch never seemed to mind. His nickname for her was "Baby." "In a wave of perfume, a blonde and lovely woman entered," wrote Eleanor Green in the January 1926 *Motion Picture*. "[She] spoke coldly and indifferently to Mr. Lubitsch and went into another room . . . all of a sudden the atmosphere changed. Mr. Lubitsch became sparkling, he became gay, he radiated animation . . . Mr. Lubitsch greeted her not as a wife, but as a prima donna, a queen, a movie star. And she in turn acted like a prima donna, a queen and a movie star."

Leni liked Hollywood, liked being the wife of Ernst Lubitsch and receiving wires from the likes of Norma Shearer ("Very best wishes to you both. Bon Voyage") and anniversary congratulations from Fairbanks and Pickford ("May you celebrate a hundred more"), or having the Los Angeles papers print the guest list for the Lubitsch Sunday afternoons. (One Sunday the invitees included the Fred Niblos, the Clarence Browns, the Sidney Franklins, the Conrad Nagels, the Rob Wagners, the Charles Rays, the Edwin Schallerts, Florence Lawrence and her daughter, John Considine, Marjorie Bennett, Carmel Myers, John Barrymore, Josef von Sternberg, Paul Bern, Hans Kräly, Pola Negri, Prince Troubetskoy, the Charles Puffys, the Joseph Schencks, Walter Laemmle, Mary Philbin, Paul Kohner, Jack Warner, Harry Warner, Constance Talmadge, William Collier, Carol Moos, the Motley Flints, Carey Wilson, Eric Locke, Mae Murray, Hope Loring, B. Leighton, Minna Wallis, Charles Rosher, the Charles Eytons, and someone named Mary Hibben.)

Leni gave interviews to the Los Angeles press in which she claimed to have been "well known on the German opera stage" before her marriage, and she was regularly featured on women's pages sportingly modeling the latest in fashion, or posed in front of the Montmartre restaurant with friends like Florence Vidor, Bessie Love, and Corinne Griffith. Some of the photos were picked up and published by newspapers in Berlin, providing a surprise for those who remembered Leni, and not from the opera. She was a member in good standing of the 1920s version of the Ladies Who Lunch.

At one point, the papers began printing items saying that Warner Brothers had given Leni an acting contract, and there are stills showing Leni being given a screen test on the set of *The Marriage Circle*. Whether there was actually film in the camera or not, the last thing Ernst Lubitsch wanted was an actress for a wife. Leni's "contract" and screen test were solely designed to attract some publicity and assuage her ego; the only screen exposure Leni would ever get was a brief shot of her legs in *Eternal Love*.

Despite the misgivings of some of his friends, Leni and Ernst seemed to have a successful, thriving marriage. They developed a joke between themselves about Hollywood. When they had first arrived in Hollywood, Leni had told Ernst, "I don't think we will meet anyone here from Köpenick" (a small German town). It was the rough equivalent of coming to New York and saying, "Well, we're not going to meet anyone from Peoria."

But the first day on the Pickford lot, a boy had rushed up to Lubitsch and introduced himself. It seemed they had worked together before. "Don't you remember me?" he asked. "I'm from Köpenick." It became a private joke, as well as a metaphor for the entire immigrant experience in Hollywood. Here, they were from all over the world . . . even Köpenick.

After finishing up *So This Is Paris,* Lubitsch entrained for New York, where he went to dinner at a Russian restaurant with a friend. There, the friend told him about the proprietor, one General Lodijenski, who had fought in World War I, but lost an important battle and fled west shortly afterwards, opening a restaurant called the Double Eagle on Sunset Boulevard, which was successful until it was bombed.

Several months later, Lubitsch was at MGM working on *The Student Prince in Old Heidelberg* when he noticed an extra in the costume of a Russian general. "I know you from somewhere," said Lubitsch. "I met you in New York," the extra replied. "I am General Lodijenski." His restaurant's closing had forced Lodijenski into extra work. "Funny, isn't it," he said, "that I should be playing a walk-on bit as a Russian general."

Mulling the encounter over, Lubitsch began to see it as a perfect scenario for Emil Jannings, whose gift for portraying tragic, masochistic characters had long since been established. Lubitsch worked up a story whereby a Russian general who has lost a decisive battle is reduced to working in movies. Hired to portray the commanding officer of the battle he actually lost, he goes berserk. Demented, believing that this time he will win the battle, he gives the command to fight but dies of a stroke on the set.

Lubitsch told the story to Jannings, who expressed interest. A few weeks later, Lubitsch ran into the writer Lajos Biró, who mentioned that Jannings was not only a brilliant actor but had good story ideas as well. Biro then proceeded to tell Lubitsch about the script he was working on, at that point entitled *The General.* It was the same story Lubitsch had told Jannings.

The script was written and given to Josef von Sternberg to direct. Sternberg made some brilliant changes, perhaps the most important being to frame the main story as a flashback, giving the narrative a quality of retrospection, with implications of loss from the beginning. But the general drift of the story, now called *The Last Command,* was the same. (Lodijenski was given a part in the film and can be observed as a thick-set, middle-aged man with short hair.)

Shortly after *The Last Command* was released, Paramount found itself being sued for plagiarism. The story, the claimant said, had been stolen from him. Paramount's lawyers summoned Biró and Jannings. Biró passed the buck to Jannings, Jannings passed the buck to Lubitsch; Lubitsch told the lawyers that since everybody had claimed the story as their own and ignored him, he was not about to take credit for it now. Not being able to offer a counter-claimant as the author of *The General,* né *The Last Command,* Paramount swallowed their pride and settled.

Lubitsch must still have been brooding about the lost opportunity of *The Jazz Singer,* because as soon as he showed up on the Paramount lot, virtually the first property the studio tossed at him was *Abie's Irish Rose,* another to-assimilate-or-not-to-assimilate comedy-drama that had run for years on Broadway in spite of the critics' best efforts at assassination.

As it turned out, the property ended up being filmed by the dutiful Victor Fleming; Lubitsch would have to wait another fifteen years before confronting the comedy and drama of Jewishness, and then only obliquely, in *To Be or Not to Be.* Instead, Lubitsch and Kräly turned their attentions to *The Patriot,* a 1927 play by Alfred Neumann. It was a return to the large-scale spectaculars of Lubitsch's late German period, and a massive, lavish production that was a calculated swipe at the penny-pinching of Jack Warner.

The Patriot is now a lost film, but it centered on Czar Paul I (Emil Jannings), the son of Catherine the Great, a pathetic, oddly childlike monster, a Russian Caligula. Ernst, of course, was well aware of Jannings' penchant for thundering bravado and knew just how to handle him.

Janning's introductory shot as Paul was staged in a vast palace hall filled with pomp and courtiers. On the first take, Lubitsch let Jannings play the scene as Jannings wanted, crouching and shambling á la Quasimodo.

"Very effective," he said. "But I've got an idea. Let's try it once more and maybe this time you shouldn't crouch so much."

"You think so?" asked Jannings.

On the second take, Jannings stooped a little less, played it a little more naturalistically. "How did you like it, Ernst?"

"You know, I think it's better."

"You think so?"

"Let's try it again. We don't have to use it, but this time, come in more majestically." This time Jannings didn't tip the character's hand and came in imperially, ramrod-straight, just what Ernst had wanted all along.

Ernst had to be equally diplomatic with his cameraman, the great but argumentative Bert Glennon. One day on the set, Glennon snapped at Lubitsch, "Ernst, I don't think you know what you want." Lubitsch simply looked at him and said, "Bert, you're right; I don't."

"That's all there was to that," recalled William Clothier, an assistant cameraman on the picture. "Glennon would fight with anybody and Lubitsch just wasn't going to have any."

In his memoirs, Jannings said that he considered *The Patriot* to have featured his "greatest artistic performance in Hollywood" and the film to be "the most European film ever to have been made in America." Although Jannings was writing in 1951, long after his seduction by the Nazis and the *Götterdämmerung* that followed, he was not shy about his residual National Socialist sympathies; contempt for the English and, by extension, Americans, seeped through his memories: "This Czar, half wild animal, half timid despot, could only be made believable by the most detailed art of characterization . . . this type of psychological experiment was not one that was native to the Anglo Saxon character. The English have an expression for this type of experiment; they call it highbrow, by which they mean both arrogant as well as around the bend. Highbrow is everything that doesn't fit into the normal conversation of 5 o'clock tea."

Neil Hamilton, playing the male ingenue opposite Florence Vidor, compared Lubitsch to Griffith and preferred Lubitsch. "Both achieve the results differently. Griffith through an exact mapping out of each move and the submergence of the player's personality in a mathematical effect, and Lubitsch through a bringing out of the 'drama' peculiar to each personality. Lubitsch is much more the actor's director."

For one of the few times in his professional life, Lubitsch was intrigued by a brunette, the beautiful, serene Florence Vidor. "She is the essence of refinement," he raved, characterizing her in a way that defines and encapsulates the Lubitsch world view: "Under the right circumstances, her type might defy the rules of chastity, but never the rules of decorum." He then proceeded to pay her the highest compliment in his vocabulary by calling her "a brunette with a blonde soul."

Stills from *The Patriot* indicate the production's immense scale and make one all the more desperate to see what was obviously intended as a return to the great historical epics of eight and ten years before. Some random shots of huge crowds and revolutions were cannibalized six years later in von Sternberg's *The Scarlet Empress*. When Lubitsch, then running Paramount, chided von Sternberg about his lavishness, von Sternberg pointed out that the lavishness was Lubitsch's, not his.

The Patriot was sufficiently popular and well-reviewed ("hardly a flaw to be found in the entire picture" wrote the critic for *The New York Times*) to earn Lubitsch a nod in *Film Daily*'s annual poll of the ten best directors of 1928–29 (the others were George Fitzmaurice, Frank Borzage, Cecil B. DeMille, F. W. Murnau, William Wellman, Clarence Brown, Raoul Walsh, Lloyd Bacon, and Frank Lloyd).

Ernst finally got around to his commitment to Joe Schenck at United Artists. In the five years since taking over as chairman of the board, Schenck had revitalized the top-heavy, product-short (only eight pictures in 1926) company by the simple expedient of forming the Art Cinema Corporation, getting outside financing (the four principal owners of the company were adamantly opposed to financing any pictures but their own), and stepping up production. Art Cinema would supply the last few pictures starring Valentino, triumphs for Norma Talmadge and Buster Keaton, as well as cofinancing *The Iron Mask* and *The Gaucho* for Douglas Fairbanks.

Ernst and Hans Kräly went to work preparing a script for *The Last of Mrs. Cheyney,* to star John Barrymore. Shortly before production was to begin, Joe Schenck sold the property to MGM as a vehicle for Norma Shearer. A disgruntled Lubitsch quickly took up a property entitled *Avalanche,* which during production was changed to *King of the Mountain,* and finally limped into film history as *Eternal Love.* "The picture was made only to honor commitments," recalled Andrew Marton. "Nobody entered into it with any enthusiasm—Lubitsch didn't, Barrymore didn't, and Camilla Horn didn't."

During production, Barrymore—normally an amusing, extremely intelligent man, albeit a thorough alcoholic—was in a vile mood, obsessed by the thought that his fiancée Dolores Costello was flirting with other men. On location in Canada's Banff National Park and Lake Louise, Barrymore used a double for a hazardous scene in which he crossed a glacier, while costar Camilla Horn played it herself. "They couldn't care less," Barrymore said to Horn about his lack of team spirit. "As long as they get their shot in the camera, we can go and drop dead!"

When she and the double nearly walked into an abyss, Camilla Horn was terrified. Afterward, she was shaking from residual fear. "Lubitsch puffed on his cigar," she remembered. "He and his cameraman had wrapped the scene; they were totally satisfied. Lubitsch winked at me and said, 'Fear becomes you, Camilla. I'll make a note of that.'"

Although he was an experienced rider, the icy mountainous terrain seems to have spooked Lubitsch, and he exhibited a disinclination to get involved with horses and burros. But that method of transportation was the only way to get to some of the locations. Soon, in a long line of horses crossing a glacier or mountain, Lubitsch could always be spotted by following the trail of cigar smoke to its source.

The locations were probably more trouble than they were worth. It took two hours to travel to the locations every morning and two hours to come home every night; figuring an hour for lunch meant that Lubitsch and company had working days of only three to four hours.

During the four weeks of location work, Barrymore managed to stay sober, but once they returned to the studio, his eyes grew irritated at the gypsum that was used to simulate snow and his mood grew ever more restive. "It was not always easy to work with him," remembered Camilla Horn, "particularly when he had been drinking. He stumbled around, forgot his lines, and crossed his beautiful eyes. He often fell asleep in his dressing room and . . . occasionally didn't appear on the set."

Anxious to be off on his honeymoon, ignoring the $150,000 (plus a percentage) he was being paid, Barrymore insisted on a forced-march regimen that impelled the cast and crew to work overtime for three weeks to finish the picture ahead of schedule.

"I wouldn't characterize [Barrymore] as difficult," said Andrew Marton. "You just had to get him in between total inebriation and total soberness . . . When he was sober, he was fine—but unfortunately he was dull when he hadn't had anything to drink. When he was a little tipsy, his eyes became sparkling, and he began to look like a Mephistopheles."

"Barrymore had an odd relationship with soap and water," remembered his leading lady. "Once when he was supposed to stroke my cheek, I looked at the dirt under his fingernails and became quite distressed. Lubitsch, the dear man, noticed this, took a closer look at his male lead and interrupted the shooting for some reason or another. He took Barrymore aside and pointed out his *faux pas* [Lubitsch's favorite word]. Barrymore disappeared without a word, then reappeared grinning broadly on the set, and showed Lubitsch his clean hands, as a servant would show his master."

Since Barrymore was in no mood for frivolity, Lubitsch reserved his best practical jokes for Camilla Horn. Once, Lubitsch suggested that Horn seemed a little heavy, and a good massage might tighten up her body. She thought that sounded like a good idea.

The next morning, the masseur arrived, a stunning male paragon who almost took the actress's breath away. After the rubdown began, the masseur began stroking and kneading Horn's breasts. "I didn't do a thing, but thought 'Someone has put him up to this; Lubitsch is behind this.' In the meantime, he was massaging me in another quite sensitive area and I responded. In the end, he took me in his arms and kissed me. I found it wonderful and I was ready."

The next day, Lubitsch teasingly inquired as to the shine in her eyes and asked if she was satisfied with the skills of the masseur. "He was excellent, a real expert," she replied. "But it's too bad that your wife has raised his price so high. He told me that your Leni has paid him more than I was prepared to give." Lubitsch twisted his cigar in his mouth, took a drag, then murmured in Berlin dialect, "What a bum," leaving Horn to wonder if he was referring to her or the masseur.

Production dragged on. "[Barrymore] never did walk like a mountaineer," remembered Andrew Marton. "He couldn't hold the rifle right. And he insisted on this Peter Pan horror of a hat. Lubitsch trimmed as much as he could from Barrymore's head when he framed the shots . . . It didn't jell, and Lubitsch knew it. We all knew it, but we just had to get through it. And you can feel it when you watch the film. It was as they say in Germany, 'ohne Liebe gemacht'—made without love. It was a child not conceived in love."

Eternal Love is one of those misbegotten efforts that blight even the most distinguished careers. Set in 1806 Switzerland, it involves a mountaineer (Barrymore) who refuses to disarm ("My gun is my life. Who dares to take it from me?"), even though that primary characteristic turns out to have nothing to do with the plot.

Lubitsch seems helplessly unable to give the material any inflection. It's a conventional romantic melodrama that he could have knocked off easily ten years before, but Lubitsch had matured as an artist since then, and seems to realize that the material is unworkable. He concentrates on the locations, the verisimilitude gained by shooting in the Canadian Rockies, and indulges in a great deal of elaborate moving camera work—typical of the late 1920s, when Hollywood went dolly-happy in the wake of Murnau's *Sunrise,* but atypical for Lubitsch, who here tried to conceal the banality of the story through visual splendor.

The film runs barely eighty minutes, and the ending is noticeably hurried and confusing, possibly a result of Barrymore's rush to pull the plug. Had it been made three years earlier, at the height of the silent era, *Eternal Love* would still have been an embarrassment; released as late as May 1929, after sound had already started to displace talkies, Lubitsch at least had the small consolation of knowing that few would see what in fact was his worst film.

When *Eternal Love* was released it did a fast fade. The domestic gross was a mere $525,000, little more than such famous contemporary U.A. flops as *The Rescue* (a gross of $650,000 against a cost of $800,000), *DuBarry,* and *One Romantic Night,* pictures that damaged the starring careers of Norma Talmadge and Lillian Gish by grossing, again respectively, only $435,000 and $400,000.

All those other pictures were talkies, and their failures were instructive. Clearly, making a talkie demanded something more than taking the exotic love stories or adventures that were the staples of silent movies, casting actors that had also been staples, adding dialogue, and expecting the public to line up. The prestigious director Rex Ingram had proved that by making *Three Passions,* a part-talkie, but thematically another one of his emotionally florid melodramas, only to see it limp to a pathetic gross of $249,000, against a cost of $540,000.

The rules of the game had suddenly changed. Lubitsch chose to deal with the situation by avoiding the problem entirely. Rather than solve knotty questions of tone, context, or the level of realism demanded by sound, he resolved to use the new technology to explore alternatives that would dodge the question of reality altogether. He decided to turn to the kind of movie that silent films had dealt with only in passing, his very own beloved Mittel-Europa staple, the operetta. In so doing, he invented a new kind of movie altogether: the musical.

chapter four

Hollywood was a wonderful place when I first went there . . . it was a bright dream about a beautiful democracy in a world under the shadow of tyranny. I suppose there were fakes and phonies, but I can't help thinking there was an innocence which has now vanished. Once Hollywood forgot the dreams and got down to reality it failed.

— d i m i t r i   t i o m k i n

Nineteen twenty-nine was not the best time to run a movie studio. By the end of the year, 8,700 theaters had been wired for sound, an enormous capital investment. Even more important, performers, technicians, and movie technique itself were all being called into question by the advent of sound.

The studio heads were not fools. They correctly sensed that they were entering uncharted waters. True, most silent stars made the transition to sound, but the *new* stars, the ones who were created by talkies, would never have been as successful in silent films. Actors like Cagney, Gable, Tracy, actresses like Lombard, Hepburn, Davis, were of the people and for the people. No more could stars be worshipped as semi-deities because of their ethereal removal from everyday life. Dialogue made actors *real,* and the kind of dialogue that audiences fell in love with was tough, slangy, colloquial.

Aside from the obvious changes in style, talkies demanded more from the technicians. While talkies didn't require as many setups—in the beginning the camera was enclosed in a soundproof booth, to prevent the sound of the mechanism from being audible on the sound track—there was no mobility for the microphone, which meant there was no mobility for the camera.

Kay Francis, Herbert Marshall, and Miriam Hopkins—the hushed, erotic eternal triangle of Trouble in Paradise.

The only way to get a a sense of movement into a film was to use three cameras (long shot, medium shot, and close-up) for most scenes. It was a system that prefigured the methods used to film TV sitcoms. Although Lubitsch would resort to it, using three cameras demanded a broad, flat, sterile lighting that disturbed him.

"On silent pictures we only used to use one camera and that kept the cameraman busy," he wrote while in production on his first talkie. "Now, on the talkies, we have to use three or four cameras always, and sometimes more. It is entirely the wrong system. They tell us that by using so many cameras we are saving the company time and money. Well, if we are, those of us who have been making silent pictures the other way these last twenty years ought to be in jail. Just think of the money we must have wasted by concentrating on one angle of a scene at a time—and making it good!"

Sound also complicated inferences and metaphors, the virtual building blocks of Lubitsch's art. "There are incidents that can be introduced into a silent film which with words in a talking picture would be extremely delicate. You can't talk about a chair and mean a woman. It all gives one a great headache. You can't have the man say, to help the story pass the censor, 'Gee, I'm glad I'm going to marry you after a while.' "

In short, sound affected both content and style, and in ways that imperiled what Ernst Lubitsch did, what Ernst Lubitsch was.

"It is much more difficult . . . to find a leading lady," he complained to New York reporters in April 1929, his first visit to New York in two years. "Those who are attractive often have poor voices and those who can act and have good voices are not so pleasing in their appearance. The screen now demands a girl who looks well, can act well, and speak well."

Yet, there was much about sound that represented pure opportunity as well. Lubitsch had always felt that much of his directorial success came from his sensitivity to music. Music, he believed, was the art upon which the other arts depended. His own pictures had often been structured in musical terms: allegretto, diminuendo, and largo, up to a dramatic or comic crescendo. Sound was a chance to overtly use music to set the rhythm of a scene, of an entire film; to put an entirely new spin on familiar thematic material.

It was also a chance to bring the audience in on the joke; with sound, Ernst would become, explicitly, a magician. Like any good magician, he would first announce that he was about to do something patently impossible, then, smoothly, casually, gracefully, do it.

While in New York, Lubitsch stopped at the Little Carnegie Theater to see Carl Dreyer's *The Passion of Joan of Arc*. A young film enthusiast named Herman Weinberg recognized Ernst and began praising the film. They went next door to the Russian Tea Room and Weinberg went into effusions over the film. "Who will ever surpass it?" exclaimed Weinberg.

"Are you through?" asked Lubitsch.

"You didn't like it?"

"I don't like it? *I don't like it?* Of course I don't like it. It's a wonderful tour de force but it'll get the cinema nowhere. One can't learn from it—it's too individual a style of expression. It has pathological interest as a study of hysteria."

When Weinberg brought up the performance of Maria Falconetti, Lubitsch said that it was conceived on the wrong plane. "I didn't believe her. She wasn't the Joan who rallied the routed French soldiers and defeated the English. We don't even get a glimpse of that part of her. We see only a despairing Joan."

Lubitsch invited Weinberg to a screening of Pudovkin's *Storm Over Asia*. During the screening, Lubitsch reacted negatively to a sequence showing the operation for the removal of a bullet. *"Schrecklich!* Why must he photograph the whole damn thing¿ He knows you can't show it! And who wants to see it¿ Is it necessary¿ *Meschenskind! Das is aber unmöglich!"* The film's climax, where the Mongols rise up against the British, was greeted with an approving *"Ach!* Terrific!"

Ernst's refusal to climb aboard the critical bandwagon that was applauding the austere Dreyer confirmed to Weinberg the singularity of his intelligence. In later years, Weinberg would become one of Lubitsch's fiercest acolytes and the author of *The Lubitsch Touch,* an elegant, enthusiastic, if factually improvisatory appreciation.

Maurice Chevalier was born in the working-class quarter of Paris known as Ménilmontant, on the right bank, west and north of Notre Dame. His upbringing made him the French equivalent of a Cockney, with the innately mocking manner and lack of concern for the future of the poor Parisian. He rose to fame as the partner and lover of the cabaret star Mistinguett, later going on to star alone at the Folies-Bergère and Casino de Paris.

The first move to sign Chevalier to a movie contract had been made by Irving Thalberg, but the deal came to nothing. A few weeks later, Jesse Lasky succeeded where Thalberg had failed. Thalberg and Lasky's ardor to sign the performer is a tribute to their confidence in their own judgment. Already nearly forty, Chevalier was not classically handsome and did not fit into any known category of leading man. Still, it was obvious that talkies were going to demand something different, although nobody seemed quite sure about the dimensions of the difference. The moguls guessed right about Chevalier; they guessed wrong about Harry Richman and Sophie Tucker, two other legendary cabaret entertainers they signed at the same time.

Despite his persona of carefree insouciance, Chevalier was prodigiously cheap and invariably withdrawn, a compulsive worrier, a neurotic man who saved all of his charm and most of his energy for the stage. "He would come on the set slouching," remembered Rouben Mamoulian, "sit in a corner looking as unhappy and worried as a homeless orphan . . . We started the camera . . . and then a complete transformation took place—

there he was: happy, debonaire, truly filled with that joy of living . . .
Then, as I said 'cut,' the light went out of him. He walked back to his
corner like a tired man, looking hopelessly miserable, as before."

Frankly scared about his entry into a new medium, he went around to
the reigning stars at the Paramount lot to get advice, the most valuable of
which came from Emil Jannings.

"Forget there is a camera," rumbled the actor in a German accent
Chevalier found difficult to penetrate. "Forget wrinkles and double chins
and profiles. The movies need more true personalities. Less empty beauty.
Forget everything except playing sincerely."

Chevalier's first film at Paramount, *Innocents of Paris,* was only so-so, but
the actor had been heartened by the reaction of the canny Adolphe
Menjou, who told him "I won't kid you, Maurice, the picture's not the
greatest. But you are going to be the greatest French success America will
ever see."

A few weeks later, Chevalier was stopped in a hallway at the studio by
what he remembered as "a small round figure . . . He looked a little like
a droll, cigar-smoking cherub." Ernst Lubitsch told Chevalier that "I am
walking around with a film musical in my head, Maurice. Now I will put
it on paper. I have found my hero." So far, so good. But Chevalier became
alarmed when Lubitsch explained that his hero was to be a prince.

"You see me as a prince?" asked the bewildered Chevalier. "I'm sorry,
I'm flattered, but that's impossible. A fisherman, yes, I could play, or any
other kind of man from a simple background. It's what I am and it's in
the way I talk and the way I walk and everything I like and understand.
But an aristocrat? Believe me, in a royal uniform I would make the most
ludicrous-looking prince on the screen."

Lubitsch convinced Chevalier to pose for some costume stills, which
Chevalier did, grumbling the whole time. The next day, Lubitsch charged
down the hallway from his office to grab Chevalier, shouting "Splendid,
Maurice, marvelous. You are a prince!"

Chevalier found Lubitsch to be "a man of strong, positive opinions
delivered in a deceptively mild fashion," but, from the first day of production on *The Love Parade,* they got along famously. Lubitsch loved the gleam
in the actor's eye, the way he could make even a straight line sound
risqué, while Chevalier's morose personality could be jollied along by
Lubitsch more effectively than anybody else.

"I found him an almost magic man to work with," wrote Chevalier in
his memoirs. "He was supposed to be a very difficult director with

American actors, but for me he seemed the easiest person in the world to understand. Just from the expression in his eye I could see what he wanted and somehow always produce it. And that bond of creative respect and sympathy seemed to affect the rest of the company as well."

But there would never be any particular affection between Chevalier and Jeanette MacDonald. People who worked on pictures with the two actors remember MacDonald with phrases like "a lovely lady," Chevalier with phrases like "he was all right, but he was a Frenchman."

Jeanette MacDonald was born in 1903 in Philadelphia; by the late 1920s she was starring in musicals for the Shuberts. In 1928, she had tested with Paramount for a film role opposite Richard Dix. She didn't get the part, but Ernst saw the test. Although he had been on the verge of signing Bebe Daniels for the lead in *The Love Parade,* he quickly reevaluated his options. "If she can sing and dance," he said, "I'd give her the part." She could; he did.

Ernst found that Jeanette was not only beautiful, eager, and hardworking with a joyous spirit he loved, but she possessed a stunning figure that he would always take special care to showcase, paying particular attention to her wardrobe. Since Lubitsch hated zippers, MacDonald always had to be buttoned into her costumes. At the beginning of the production of *The Love Parade,* Lubitsch called her "Mac," but she threatened to call him "Lu." He then started calling her "Donald," but stopped that when she threatened to call him "Itsch." Finally, he settled on "Jeanette," except when he slipped and called her "Mac."

In time, MacDonald would become one of Lubitsch's closest friends, at least partially because she could take a joke (Chevalier couldn't). During one of their musicals, Lubitsch directed MacDonald to walk across a room while singing, timing the end of the song to her arrival at a fireplace, where she was to let out a cry of anguish. MacDonald played the scene superbly, but the climactic shriek was more one of outrage than of anguish because Lubitsch had placed on the mantel a story from *Variety* announcing that the studio had just signed up Evelyn Laye, one of Mac-Donald's soprano rivals.

Chevalier seems to have been frankly jealous of the way MacDonald's winning personality compelled everyone to take her at face value. As late as 1964, after the actress had long been retired by a heart condition, he was telling interviewers that "She is a very sweet and talented girl, about twelve years younger than I am, although she always professed to being even younger than that . . . I never thought she had much of a sense of humor. When we worked together she always objected to anyone telling a risqué story."

In the early part of the twentieth century, musicals tended to fall into one of two camps: revue or operetta. Operetta featured sentimental stories, Mittel-Europa settings, songs with long, flowing melodic lines, traditional harmonies, and an overall mood of quiet melancholia. In operetta, music took precedence over words. The performers had to have large voices and perform with a good deal of dramatic fervor.

Revues, on the other hand, evolved out of vaudeville and minstrel shows. The music derived from ragtime or Tin Pan Alley, and usually had a healthy element of satire that was brought to bear on contemporary American life. The songs were partly sung, partly spoken, in a casual, humorous manner.

Ernst, an inveterate theatergoer, was intimately acquainted with both American and European performance styles. With the rare exception of a towering work like *Showboat,* American musicals utilized thumbnail plots that stopped when the music started. In particular, operettas used songs, as the musical historian Deena Rosenberg has written, "mostly . . . to heighten emotional moments or to create atmosphere." The revolutionary principles of Jerome Kern, who, as early as 1917, said that "the musical numbers should carry on the action of the play and should be representative of the personalities of the characters who sing them," were to take more than twenty years before they became accepted practice.

It was Lubitsch's idea to crossbreed these two hardy strains, to give the same emphasis to the lyrics as the music, to see if self-consciously satirical elements could be introduced into the operetta without consigning the audience's emotional interest in the characters to the ashcan.

Also tossed into the mix was Ernst's fondness for Viennese and Hungarian musicals from the Strauss-Kalman-Huszka cycle of composers. The librettos of these works had specific if limited aims: entertainment, amusement, enchantment. The story line of the Viennese/Hungarian operettas was invariably simple but usually touching, often funny, sometimes witty, occasionally inane. "But," said the critic Andrew Farkas, "the music was meant to carry the story and it was always melodious, sweet, caressing, or else the piece failed. If the plot was clever, or funny, or amusing—so much the better." And because Lubitsch was involving himself with operetta at the precise historical point at which it was beginning to decline, traces of parody couldn't help but season Lubitsch's invariable irony.

In retrospect, this was a risky experiment—a goulash, as it were—but, Paramount reasoned, if anybody could do it, Lubitsch could. He was given the go-ahead to make *The Love Parade*. Production began in June 1929.

Since sound was, at that point, virtually impossible to edit, and the script mandated a counterpoint duet between Chevalier/MacDonald and Lupino Lane/Lillian Roth that was supposed to be taking place in two separate parts of a palace, Ernst's fertile mind had to devise some way to make it work. The solution was simple, if cumbersome. The two sets were adjacent to each other, with the musicians—this was before the era of prerecording and lip-synching to the playback—just off-camera. Two soundproof booths, each containing a camera, were aimed at the couples. Lubitsch perched nervously on a stool between the booths, letting the technicians worry about the sound quality while he watched the performances and their timing with his customary sharp-eyed intensity. It worked; one sound track, one song, two locations, four voices. Lubitsch's first talkie wrapped production early in August.

We are deep in operetta country at the very beginning of *The Love Parade,* as Lupino Lane, setting out a full dinner service, sings "A little brandy, ooh la la," then finishes with a fine flourish by pulling the tablecloth out from under the setting he has so carefully laid out.

The moment has nothing to do with the plot or the characters; it is, rather, Lubitsch demonstrating with a flourish what he is about to do: make something very common seem very elevated, confer romance and aristocratic elegance on a medium newly hamstrung by plebian technical considerations. In short, spin gold from straw.

There is a loud argument going on behind closed doors. Chevalier opens the door, looks at the camera, and says "She's very jealous." It seems that the lady in question has found a garter that does not belong to her. It is a bad moment for the lady's husband to arrive, but that is what happens. It is one scandal too many for the military attaché from Sylvania; he is recalled home. There, he meets the queen, who is very happily unmarried.

At this point in the film, Lubitsch has already established the upstairs/downstairs duality of love as Chevalier's servant, Lupino Lane, romances MacDonald's maid, Lillian Roth. When Chevalier sings in the drawing room, the butler picks up the refrain in the garden and even the dog barks out a verse as they all say farewell to Paris.

Back in Sylvania, Old Europe is trying to promote itself as best it can;

a sight-seeing car emblazoned with "See Sylvania First" is filled with bored tourists who only perk up when the guide points out a castle that is reputed to be worth $110 million dollars. Huzzahs, uproar, much craning of heads.

The queen's attempted disciplining of her errant attaché rapidly turns into love, which quickly turns into marriage. But the relationship gets off on the wrong foot almost immediately; first, during the ceremony itself, he bridles at the phrase "obedient and docile husband." Then, on his wedding night, Chevalier is distracted by the incessant boom of celebratory cannons. He finds that he is nothing but a kept man, without status.

A trained soldier, he launches into a rear-guard action. He upstages the queen in front of her subjects at the ballet, arriving late and receiving the ovation that is rightfully hers. He taunts her by appreciatively ogling ballerinas through binoculars. When she pretends indifference to his presence, he makes a move to leave, but she asks him to stay for propriety's sake.

"Beg me to stay," he says. "Don't ask me. Beg me."

Finally, back at the palace, the arrogant queen capitulates to the rampant, charmingly swinish male.

"Where shall we live in Paris?" she meekly asks.

"We?"

"Wherever you go, I'll follow. You can't get rid of me."

With the issue of command at last decided, there's no sense in leaving Sylvania after all, especially when she addresses him as "My king." Chevalier closes the curtains of the bedroom so that the marriage can be put right.

With *The Love Parade,* Lubitsch casts off the lingering, heavy malaise that had affected his final silent movie. He is once again on his toes, moving lightly, nimbly, breathing new life into material that was old hat even in 1929. In Ethan Mordden's phrase, *The Love Parade* "[reduces] every event to its center, dressy, unblushing, velvet with bite."

158

And Lubitsch hits on the idea of using offstage space; for an all-important first dinner between the attaché and the queen, whom her advisors desperately want married, we never see the dinner itself, only the reactions of a series of onlookers and eavesdroppers. In an exhilarating precursor of *The Merry Widow,* a refrain of Victor Schertzinger's lovely melody "Dream Lover" is picked up by a chorus of lovers in a garden. And, most amusingly, just as a nervous Chevalier confronts his wedding day and confesses to a horror of cross-eyed people, who should promptly show up to announce the impending ceremony but—Ben Turpin!

Yet the servant subplot, while well done and not exactly filler, slows the picture's pace; 110 minutes is really too long for a screen operetta, even one as delightful as *The Love Parade*. (The silent version of the film, released to those theaters not yet wired for sound, seems to have run at least a half-hour less. The songs, of course, were missing, but as a result many scenes had to be restaged so that the audience would still be seeing a complete movie.)

While the typical Lubitsch sexuality and the mixture of two brilliant new personalities catapulted *The Love Parade* to fame, it also earned it a reputation it can't quite sustain today. Its lighter-than-air quality appealed mightily to no less than Jean Cocteau, who called it "a Lubitsch miracle, a mélange of Andersen fable and the brio of Strauss, not forgetting that extraordinary domestic couple right out of an opera-bouffe of Mozart."

Certainly, the film is an astonishing achievement for a movie shot in the summer of 1929; never does the viewer have to make allowances for any early-talkie primitiveness. *The Love Parade* could just as easily have been made in the summer of 1934, and, considering the paralytic style of most early talkies, that is high praise indeed.

The earliest screen musicals—the Marx Brothers' *The Cocoanuts* or the Goldwyn/Ziegfeld *Whoopee!* are particularly grim examples—did little but transpose the dreary conventions of the middle-brow Broadway show. Songs were not episodes in the action, they were interludes, pauses, and they contributed nothing to the movement of the story. As to the plots, simplistic boy-meets-girl premises were nothing but a shallow pretext for the stringing together of clunky production numbers.

Nor were those numbers ever direct, witty comments on the action, the story. With one film, Lubitsch changed all that, lifting the musical to a much higher level . . . *his* level. For one brief moment, it seemed that there would not have to be an impregnable, massive wall between the visual grace of silent films and an equivalent dynamism of sound.

Menjou's and Lubitsch's instincts about Chevalier were correct. When *The Love Parade* was previewed, Chevalier was on the boards in Paris. Lubitsch sent him a cable that ended "You are sitting on top of the world, Maurice."

When the film was released in November, the reviews hailed Lubitsch's achievement. *The New York Times* called it "finely directed," and said that "It is a real moving picture in the literal sense of the words," while *Photoplay* called it "sparkling as burgundy, and almost as intoxicating." James Shelley Hamilton in *Cinema* commented that the film was "excellent, gay entertainment, and a very sizeable step forward in the evolution of musical comedy on the screen." Rob Wagner's *Script* said that "Of course, Lubitsch had magnificent paints, but he always chooses his colors with intelligence."

Even before *The Love Parade* was released, Ernst and Chevalier were back in the studio in October, reunited for three sequences in the all-star revue *Paramount on Parade*. The most delightful is "The Origin of the Apache," in which Chevalier and the delectable Evelyn Brent begin the sequence in full evening dress, then become involved in an argument over another woman. Enraged, they begin to push and slap each other—on the musical beat, of course—then to rip off their clothes. As they are about to get to their underwear, the camera cuts to pieces of clothing flying through the air. But when the camera cuts back to Chevalier and Brent, they are again fully clothed and ready to go out for a night on the town.

Lubitsch had conquered sound the same way he had conquered silence, with clarity and a symmetrical grace . . . and by making it look very easy. He seemed to have everything, a flourishing career accompanied by critical praise and an equivalent standing among his peers. In 1930, he made *Film Daily*'s fifth annual list of the ten best directors for the fifth time, the only director to do so. He even had a happy domestic life. But that was about to be taken from him, and by someone he never would have suspected.

Patsy Ruth Miller, a frequent guest at Lubitsch's house in those days, remembered Hans Kräly as "at the house all the time. [Lubitsch] and Hans were so close." It was a strange pairing; despite their obviously similar sensibilities, Kräly was the direct physical and emotional antithesis of Lubitsch: tall, blond, and brutally handsome, not to mention quiet and withdrawn, so much so that only a few of Lubitsch's circle knew that Kräly had a wife in Berlin.

"His face was hewn out of stone like an unfinished Rodin," remembered Andrew Marton. "He had fallen arches and walked in a very funny way. Lubitsch ran—like a quicksilver ball. Even when he walked, you never saw his feet moving—just a blur . . . He had this twinkle, and Kräly was this solemn man carved out of stone."

Kräly was also one of the few people in Lubitsch's circle who would drink to excess. Once, at one of the Sunday afternoon parties, Kräly was lying down on a bench in the family room, unable to stand. When he asked Otto, the butler, for another drink, the saturnine servant replied in German, "Just please remain lying there, sir, and I'll pour it into you."

Despite the differences between Ernst and Kräly—or, perhaps, because of them—the relationship between Leni and the writer segued from friendship to passion.

"I liked Leni," remembered Patsy Ruth Miller. "We always got along, but she was not scintillating. She was a good hostess, her parties were pleasant, but she wasn't very colorful. And she made a mistake."

"She used to play a lot of tennis with Kräly," said Lupita Tovar Kohner. "You could feel that there was a close relationship there. But Lubitsch didn't see it. And I was so green that I was no judge. But later on, Paul [Kohner] told me that everybody knew about the affair."

In the latter part of May 1930, the normally quiet household was rocked by a series of explosive arguments. Eddie's bedroom was directly across the hall from his parents, and he heard the unfamiliar sound of Ernst's voice raised in anger.

On June 5, 1930, Lubitsch and Leni legally separated. Ernst came running down the steps with a packed suitcase in his hand. Eddie, standing at the foot of the steps, began to cry. Tommy, the chauffeur, tried to quiet the frightened child. "Don't worry, Eddie. He'll be back in a day or two."

Five days later, Leni filed for divorce under a suit charging cruel and inhuman treatment; obviously, a deal had been struck to minimize public humiliation. According to the divorce complaint, Lubitsch scolded and nagged her, insulted her friends in her home, and on many occasions would not speak to her at all.

Lubitsch was predictably furious when he found out that his friends had known about the affair. "Kohner, you never said a word!" the humiliated director said.

"How could I?" replied Kohner.

On June 12, when Eddie graduated from elementary school, Ernst sent him a letter of congratulations, telling him that even though they were living separately, they would remain the best of friends "forever." Lubitsch closed the letter with an admonition that Eddie should be good to his mother and give her a lot of pleasure. It was signed "Papa." The letter was intercepted by Leni, and Eddie would not discover it among her effects until 1990.

Over the next few months, Ernst would send Tommy over to 616 Beverly Drive to pick up Eddie and Heinz for a visit. Lubitsch would take the boys out to lunch or dinner, sit and talk with them, try to console the deeply unhappy Eddie.

Lubitsch took the separation very hard; he invited his sister Marga to come to Hollywood and keep him company. He was, he told her, terribly lonely. But the series of flights necessary to get from Germany to Hollywood and the fact that she didn't speak English very well scared her. She told Ernst she couldn't make the trip; some family members believe that, in a quiet, unspoken way, he never forgave her.

In August, Paramount announced that a large part of its production would be transferred to their Astoria studio in Queens, on Long Island, largely because of Astoria's proximity to the New York actors and playwrights that seemed necessary to talkie production. Ernst was appointed Astoria's supervising producer, with authority over stories, and on the way back east he took with him Ernest Vajda, who had worked on *The Love Parade,* and the young writer Samson Raphaelson.

A few months later, he was back in Hollywood. On Saturday, October 4, two months after the interlocutory divorce decree was granted, the situation exploded publicly. At an Embassy Club ball given by Mary Pickford and Douglas Fairbanks, Kräly attended with Leni, while Lubitsch was accompanied by actress Ona Munson.

At eleven o'clock, as he and Munson danced past Kräly and his ex-wife, Lubitsch suddenly left Munson, grabbed Kräly by the arm, and slapped him. A surprised Kräly stepped back, which gave Leni the opportunity to step forward and slap Lubitsch. At that point, Lubitsch's friends pulled him away from the scene to calm him down. An enraged Leni followed, screaming at Lubitsch until she too was pulled away.

Lupita Tower, who was in Lubitsch's party and was dancing with Paul Kohner across the room, remembered that "The whole room exploded. And they were all speaking German, which I didn't understand at that time. After Paul dragged him back to the table, Lubitsch left."

Lubitsch claimed that the scuffle had been the culmination of a campaign of whispers and snickers carried on by Leni and Kräly that included encounters at Malibu and at the Hollywood Roosevelt Hotel. The final straw at the Embassy Club had come when Lubitsch had noticed Leni and Kräly laughing about his dancing—the much larger Kräly had been dancing stooped over, pretending he was as short as his former friend.

The next day, Lupita Tower got a call from Leni, who told her that "If any reporters come asking questions, you know nothing." "As a matter of fact, I knew nothing," remembered Lupita.

Leni was deeply concerned about her image; that December, after *Photoplay* magazine ran a brief item about the fight, she responded with a letter to the magazine written on Christmas Eve regarding "this most unpleasant Embassy affair." Her main concern was the unflattering photo of her the magazine had run. "Would you please, in the meantime, accept a few pictures which were taken about three months ago. Maybe you could use those someday and give the world a different view of me."

The entire affair was regrettable and some of Lubitsch's friends thought it could easily have been avoided, even if Leni and Kräly were lovers. Charles Rosher, for one, thought that Lubitsch had turned irrationally jealous and believed more was going on than actually was, while Andrew Marton held to the unlikely view that Lubitsch had known about the affair all the time. But Lubitsch was a man, not a blithe, carefree character from one of his own movies.

Despite Leni's pleadings to her friends for privacy, she started talking to reporters and, for several months, didn't stop. She claimed that Lubitsch was still jealous of her and did not want other men paying attention to her. "No man or woman had anything to do with our divorce," she said. "If there had been a man, he had plenty of opportunity to so charge when the divorce was filed. He is just jealous."

Lubitsch remained defiant, sure he had done the right thing. "They continually taunt me," said Lubitsch, attempting to explain the incident. "This was the third time. They mimic me when I dance. They laugh at me. They make certain remarks that aren't in the dictionary as they passed me."

Kräly pretended innocence and said he had no idea what it was all about. When Leni announced that she expected to marry Kräly, Lubitsch exploded. "I shall send them a marvelous wedding present. I hope they are married a hundred years. He deserves it."

It would appear that Lubitsch was intent on punishing himself; a few days later he went to the opera, where Kräly and Leni were also in attendance. Although they brushed past each other a few times, only glares were exchanged. At that point, someone must have taken him aside, or his own instinct for dignified self-preservation must have finally manifested itself, for on October 9 he left for New York.

"They can have Hollywood all to themselves," he said of Kräly and Leni. "All I ask is peace—and as long as they give it to me there will be no trouble." Lubitsch had made up his mind to cut his losses, while Hollywood had made up its mind about who was to blame.

"Lubitsch would never have done to her what she did to him," believes Patsy Ruth Miller. "He liked to tease me, kid about my having boyfriends and all that, but there was always a certain old-fashioned respect for women in his attitude. I think he very much wanted to be a family man."

Although Lubitsch was the wounded party, he acted according to his best principles, undertaking to pay off the mortgage on 616 Beverly Drive and signing it over to Leni. (Since by June 10, 1930, there was only $2,288.58 left on the mortgage, Lubitsch must have been making double payments for some time.)

On Christmas Day 1930, a devastated Lubitsch was obviously still longing for his stepchildren, for he sent them a telegram in German wishing them a Happy Christmas "and everything good for the New Year."

The divorce became final in June 1931. Most of the couple's friends followed Lubitsch, but Mary Philbin remained loyal to Leni. Although everybody expected Leni and Kräly to marry, the relationship was based primarily on passion and quickly burned out.

About a year after the divorce, she sold the house on Beverly Drive because it was too expensive to maintain. On October 6, 1932, she eloped with Evan Lewis, a pilot for Transcontinental and Western Air Express. She promptly used part of her divorce settlement to buy Lewis his own airplane and used much of the rest, according to her son Eddie, "to invest in some of the lousiest property in Southern California."

In October 1933, Leni, through her lawyer, Milton Cohen, evidently made a rather bizarre overture to Lubitsch regarding her oldest child, Heinz, who was not even the director's favorite. On October 26, Lubitsch responded that, as much as he liked the boy, he was in no position to adopt the child because he was already considering adopting Hans, the son of his brother, Richard, who had recently died.

Thereafter, there was no contact between Lubitsch and Leni. She had a long and basically happy marriage with Lewis that only ended with her death in 1960. Over the years, she sold off most of the expensive jewelry that Lubitsch had bought so that she could maintain a standard of living beyond the reach of airline pilots. She did confess to her son Eddie on several occasions that losing Lubitsch "was the dumbest thing I ever did in my life."

The real loser in the messy triangle was Kräly; before the imbroglio, Kräly had been credited as writer on twenty-three films in the seven years since his arrival in Hollywood. Afterward, until his death in 1950, he was credited on precisely seven, with his last credit coming in 1943, on a Universal penny-dreadful called The Mad Ghoul.

"Leni was the death of Kräly," remembered Lupita Tovar Kohner. "Years later, Kräly was down and out. I remember he had a blond girlfriend, and they came to see us. On account of Leni, this man had become a nothing."

It is possible that Lubitsch expressly demanded Kräly's blackball, although such vindictiveness would have been out of character. It is more likely that the small community of the film industry decided that Kräly's violation of the trust of one of its most admired and respected men made him unworthy of employment.

After the initial attempts to maintain contact with Leni's sons, Ernst stopped calling. Aside from the fact that their existence could not help but remind him of what he had lost and how he had lost it, Lubitsch was inherently tough-minded and could make a clean break if he felt it necessary. As he had told his sister, "We Lubitschs are not sentimental people."

About four years after the divorce, Eddie wrote his former stepfather a letter. There was no response. Some time after that, his brother, Heinz, tried to contact Lubitsch personally. He found out the address of Lubitsch's new house in Bel Air and waited by the driveway for hours. Finally, Lubitsch's car drove out. It slowed down only slightly, just long enough for Ernst to recognize who was waiting to talk to him. The car sped up and drove away.

Lubitsch's emotional response to Leni's betrayal was covert. He referred to her only obliquely and never to what she had done. His practical response was to bury himself in his work. In 1932 alone, he produced and directed *The Man I Killed, One Hour with You,* and *Trouble in Paradise,* and supervised *If I Had a Million,* a backbreaking pace for a director who had previously contented himself with a leisurely regimen of one film per year. The pace becomes even more grueling when the long hours demanded by the studios in those pre-union days are taken into account. For instance: on Friday, June 21, 1929, while shooting *The Love Parade,* Lubitsch and his crew worked from nine in the morning till one the following morning. Work for Lubitsch was no longer merely a method of self-expression; it had become a means of escape.

Monte Carlo, produced at a cost of $726,465 and released on September 4, 1930, continued the innovations begun by *The Love Parade.* As critic Kenneth White wrote with stunned pleasure in *The Hound and Horn,* in Winter 1931, "objects about the players, an engine rushing through the countryside, the figure in a clocktower, became . . . instruments of musical and amusing comment. Sounds and music . . . perform the same function for the ear that the camera does for the eye. An auditory breadth and inclusiveness is achieved that could not possibly be obtained in any other representational art."

Every song in *Monte Carlo* either delineates character or advances the plot; songs not only arise naturally from the action, they *are* the action.

The film opens brilliantly, and without dialogue. It is a royal wedding, all pomp and circumstance, but as the celebrants troop into the church, the skies open up and a torrential rain begins, an ominous occurrence in light of a prominently displayed sign: "Happy Is the Bride the Sun Shines On." Claud Allister, the archetypal silly-ass Englishman, is the prospective groom, but he's interrupted by a maid as he's about to enter the church.

He rushes back to his room to find an abandoned wedding dress lying on the bed. He stumbles haphazardly around the room before uttering the film's first dialogue: "Papa! Papa!!"

Lubitsch has fun with his characters. As Allister sings a paean to himself ("I'm a simple-hearted soul . . .") the chorus responds, "He's a simp, he's a simp, he's a simple-hearted soul . . ."

The runaway bride (Jeanette MacDonald, in her underwear) is heading for Monte Carlo on a train. She's taken her last ten thousand francs and is hoping to parlay it into a stake so large she will never again have to contemplate marrying someone she doesn't love. As she hurtles toward freedom, the chugging of the train wheels begins to set a beat, accented by the whistle, and MacDonald swings into "Beyond the Blue Horizon," with peasants in the countryside picking up her refrain and forming a chorus. For all the number's reputation, it's surprisingly brief. Lubitsch contents himself with one verse and one chorus; he could milk it, but doesn't.

In Monte Carlo, MacDonald is spotted by Count Rudolph (Jack Buchanan), and they play yes-I-will-no-you-won't for six reels. Along the way, Ernst throws in a small homage to von Stroheim's *Foolish Wives*, as MacDonald spots a hunchback outside the casino. When she rubs his hump for luck, he turns and says "Fifty francs please, madame."

There is a particularly charming duet ("Give Me a Moment, Please") done while Buchanan and MacDonald talk on the phone, but *Monte Carlo* suffers from its leading man's lack of sexuality (presumably, Claud Allister was cast to make Jack Buchanan look more masculine). The casting throws the film off its needed erotic center. There is, after all, never any doubt that Chevalier knows what to do with a woman in bed; Jack Buchanan is thin, reedy, not uncharming, but essentially asexual, which renders all of Lubitsch's intimations of immorality rather moot. Buchanan lessens the genially erotic texture that make Lubitsch's operettas more than Romberg or Offenbach retreads.

Monte Carlo is more than good for an early talkie, but it's not quite good enough to make it a major Lubitsch film. It doesn't seem primitive so much as old-fashioned, as opposed to the classic timelessness of the best Lubitsch musicals. It lacks lilt.

Monte Carlo served at least one valuable purpose in introducing Ernst to the work of the lyricist Leo Robin. Robin's witty words would illuminate four more Lubitsch films, and he would remain the director's first choice on every musical project.

Since Robin was headquartered in New York, hiring him entailed extra trouble and expense. One day Robin asked Lubitsch why he chose him when there were superb lyricists in Hollywood. "I work with you because you do not make performers out of my characters," Lubitsch told him. "He felt," Robin said, "that with my style of integrating the lyrics with the book and everything, the character remained the same, instead of suddenly becoming a performer and walking out of the picture . . . Pictures [generally] weren't written that way, [but] I wrote it as if it were a show, with all the songs integrated."

By February 1931, Lubitsch had shifted his base of operations to the Astoria, New York, studios, and was in production on *The Smiling Lieutenant*. Quickly, he shot his version of Oscar Straus's operetta *A Waltz Dream,* which had been previously made in Germany in 1926 under its original title by Ludwig Berger. The film was not made under the most pleasing conditions; Lubitsch was still brooding over Leni's betrayal, while Chevalier was still grieving over the death of his mother some months earlier, and thereafter went through the motions with what even he recognized as a mechanical display of technique, what the performer called "smiles and cute winks of the eye."

"I was busy on the set," said Lubitsch, "but out of the corner of my eye I would see him sitting quietly in a corner; grave and serious. He never talked much or laughed with any of the others."

In addition, Lubitsch had to act as referee between Claudette Colbert and Miriam Hopkins, both of whom were determined that only the right sides of their faces would be photographed. Since the women were antagonists in the film, Lubitsch decided to encourage their dislike of each other.

As always, Lubitsch favored the blonde, invariably placing Hopkins on the left side of the frame so her favorite side would be photographed. The result was that "she was as pleased as a kitten with a new ball of yarn." Colbert didn't hold a grudge; she would always call Lubitsch her favorite director and say that he seemed to spend his entire day entertaining actors.

The Smiling Lieutenant opens promisingly as a bill collector for military uniforms rings fruitlessly outside an apartment door. Giving up, he walks down a long flight of stairs. A beautiful girl walks up the same flight of stairs, knocks twice, and the door opens immediately. Cut to a lamp over the door. As the light fades around it, the gaslight slowly comes on, then, as daylight arrives again, slowly goes out. The door opens and the girl, radiating a pleasurable languor, happily takes her leave.

Lubitsch cuts to an exhausted Chevalier, sitting in a rumpled robe and pajamas. He launches into "A Soldier's Work Is Never Done" ("we're the boudoir brigadiers"), with the actor rolling his eyes rather more than is absolutely necessary.

The plot kicks in when Miriam Hopkins, the lonely daughter of the king of a tiny Mittel-Europa country, imagines that the title character slights her during a royal trip to Vienna. Dislike, as it often does in the movies, turns to love. The lieutenant is far more interested in Claudette Colbert, the unpretentious, shyly sexual leader of an all-girl orchestra wonderfully named "The Viennese Swallows," but loyalty to their home-land's best interests demands sacrifices from all good soldiers.

Miriam Hopkins' character wants nobody but the lieutenant. She's so desperate she throws out the ultimate threat: if she doesn't get the man she wants, she'll marry an American. Her father, the king (George Barbier), looks crestfallen. Faced with such a dire possibility, he capitulates.

The Smiling Lieutenant offers some sparkling badinage between Chevalier and Colbert:

"So . . . you play the piano?"

"Uh-huh."

"Some day we may have a duet."

"I love chamber music!"

"We could have tea tomorrow afternoon."

"Why not breakfast tomorrow morning?"

"No. First tea, then dinner . . . then . . . maybe . . . breakfast."

Fade out.

Fade in to a valet flipping eggs.

In another brilliant sequence, alternate verses of the same song are done by cross-cutting from Chevalier and Colbert (vital, with brass and wood-winds) and Hopkins (sweet, passive, heavy on violins). Colbert sings in a faintly tremulous voice, but manages to hold a tune, and the Astoria studio's less than spacious confines are only slightly evident.

Despite the Viennese *Weltschmerz* and the brilliance of individual moments, *The Smiling Lieutenant* fails to coalesce. Ludwig Berger's version of the same material is ponderous, but Lubitsch goes too far in the other direction. *The Smiling Lieutenant* is too ooh-la-la by half, especially in comparison to the moving, welcome gravity of *The Student Prince,* or the romantic conviction that was evident in *The Merry Widow* three years later.

The primary problem is that the wrong girl gets the man. The always-wonderful Colbert, in a sisterhood-is-powerful moment, sings "Jazz Up Your Lingerie" to Hopkins, who plays a shrill, unsympathetic pill quite convincingly. The advice takes; Hopkins next appears in very sheer finery.

Ultimately, Colbert gives up her man because "girls who start with breakfast don't usually stay for supper." It's an oddly moralistic ending for a cheerfully amoral film.

Two months after Lubitsch finished shooting *The Smiling Lieutenant* in March, Paramount decided to close the Astoria studio; the East Coast studio had been an expensive satellite, and the financial condition of Paramount would not allow its continued operation. Lubitsch trooped back to Hollywood, returning to New York in May for the film's premiere.

In Hollywood, Lubitsch found a studio in decline. Paramount had aggressively pursued a theater chain (between September 1929 and May 1930 alone, they acquired some 500 theaters), and they had by far the largest group of theaters in the country. (Loew's vaunted chain numbered less than 200, but they were the right 200, half of them in and around New York, the other half strictly first-run houses in large eastern cities.)

When business was good, so were the profits, for Paramount had three profit centers: theaters, distribution, and production. In 1930, Paramount had profits of $25 million, more than any studio in Hollywood, even MGM, whose profits were $14.6 million.

But the following year, as the Depression deepened, theater attendance dropped off and Paramount suddenly found that, while they were property rich, they were growing cash poor. In 1931, Paramount profits shrank precipitously to $8.7 million, and the studio responded with a 33 percent cut in feature budgets and salary reductions. It didn't help. In 1932, theater grosses dropped by $25 million, and in 1933, the overly mortgaged studio was hit with a loss of more than $20 million. Paramount could no longer generate enough cash to pay off its mortgage holders and was thrown into bankruptcy.

For the next two and a half years, fifty-three different law firms, banks, committees, and consultants sliced, slashed, and patched at Paramount and its subsidiaries. The studio's largest asset was real estate, whose book value was some $150 million. The theaters were mortgaged for $58 million and there were $25 million in outstanding debentures, not to mention $13 million in debts to eleven different banks and $6 million owed to real estate firms. As *Fortune* magazine wryly observed, "The question of whether the company was solvent depended largely on the accuracy of the real-estate valuation. But it was an academic question in view of the fact that the company could not find enough cash to pay its bills."

Then, as if he wasn't sufficiently besieged already, Lubitsch was saddened by the sudden death of his older brother Richard. Ever the bohemian, Richard had been the center of a political roundtable in Cologne, an intimate of the intellectuals. Politically liberal, he was an ardent anti-Nazi. "He always opened his mouth," sighed his niece Evie. "If he would have lived to the Hitler period he would have disappeared [into a concentration camp]."

But Richard's end was considerably more pleasant than that; he had a sudden, fatal heart attack during a visit to a brothel. The family was, as the saying goes, shocked and appalled, but the location of Richard's death didn't faze his brother in the least. "Kings and princes die in whorehouses," he told his niece. "Why should we be ashamed?"

Lubitsch liked Miriam Hopkins; he may have been the only person in show business who did. Certainly, she was the right physical type to attract him, but it would seem that Hopkins managed to simultaneously entice him and keep him at arm's length.

There seems to have been an element of calculation in her behavior; Joel McCrea once wondered aloud about how "all those powerful men always wanted the women that rejected them . . . [Gregory] La Cava and Ginger [Rogers], Lubitsch and Miriam Hopkins." The photographer John Engstead referred to her as "that old . . . bitch. You should have seen how cute she was with Ernst Lubitsch. And Lubitsch never saw through [her]." His casting of Hopkins in *Trouble in Paradise* and *Design for Living,* after the springboard of *The Smiling Lieutenant,* gave her career a propulsive boost that carried her very close to the top rank of stars.

Still, if Lubitsch liked you, it was virtually guaranteed that he would occasionally tweak you. A year or so after *The Smiling Lieutenant,* Hopkins embarked on what she imagined to be a top-secret affair with King Vidor, who was directing her in *The Stranger's Return.* Lubitsch wanted Hopkins for the female lead in his adaptation of Noël Coward's *Design for Living* and sent her a script.

One night, after a tryst, Hopkins asked Vidor to read the script with her. They were both enchanted, at least until they got to the last page. There they found a scribbled note in Ernst's handwriting: "King—Any little changes you would like, I will be happy to make them. Ernst."

If the relationship between Lubitsch and Miriam Hopkins ever deviated from the strictly professional, she must not have been averse to sharing, for Ernst's relationship with Ona Munson, the actress who is best known today for her portrayal of Belle Watling, the good-hearted madame in *Gone With the Wind,* had become quite serious. Both newly divorced (Munson from the actor/director Edward Buzzell), the two would be on-and-off companions for the next several years. Intimate friends with whom Lubitsch and Munson spent time never doubted that he loved her. "When he looked at her," remembered Dorshka Raphaelson, the wife of writer Samson Raphaelson, "you could see a great glow of happiness in his eyes."

By 1932, Munson was spending weekends with Lubitsch at his Santa Monica beachhouse. One afternoon, Munson heard a knock, not at the door but on the window. A deep contralto voice asked if anybody was home. It was Greta Garbo, with her friend and lover Mercedes d'Acosta. They had been walking on the beach, passing the houses of Marion Davies, Irving Thalberg and Norma Shearer, when they came to Lubitsch's place. "That's Ernst Lubitsch's house," Garbo said. "He is the only great director out here. I would like you to meet him."

Lubitsch had been in the kitchen making drinks, but let out a great yell of happiness when he saw who his visitor was. "Mein Gott, Mein Gott, Mein Gott," he cried. "Greta, Greta, sit down and never go avay." He pushed her onto the sofa and plopped himself down beside her, holding her hand.

"Greta, why don't you tell those idiots in your studio to let us do a picture together. Gott, how I would love to direct a picture for you." Garbo brushed it aside, saying "You tell them. I am far too tired to have a conversation with any studio executive."

The two agreed that studio executives were fools, more to be scorned than pitied. "How vonderful Greta and I would be together," Lubitsch said. "We vould make a vonderful picture." Garbo sighed, and, according to d'Acosta, allowed Lubitsch to give her an affectionate kiss of farewell.

Despite the long weekends in Santa Monica and their sincere affection for each other, the Lubitsch/Munson relationship was never smooth. For one thing, Lubitsch may have been gun-shy after the debacle with Leni. For another, the affair lacked the element of sexual fantasia that Lubitsch thrived on. Munson was American, petite, and brunette, not one of the European blondes that could be relied upon to excite him.

There seems little question that Munson genuinely cared for Lubitsch, but his reciprocation did not seem to give her the necessary amount of nurturing. Mercedes d'Acosta, who became good friends with Munson in later years, remarked on her "very sad" eyes that "touched me very deeply."

The relationship, and Lubitsch's possessive friends, made the papers. On February 29, 1932, Julia Shawell of the New York *Evening Graphic* led her column with a blind item that could only be decoded one way.

"Let's call the director Othello and admit he's very much in love with Desdemona . . . It seems there's an Iago on the scene, a Russian artist, who told Othello that Desdemona had made some remarks that wounded Othello's feelings deeply.

"Desdemona never made the crack that Iago repeated. What is more she is still crazy about him and is actually sick over her loss . . . Noted for his great sense of humor on and off the screen, Othello this morning is a sad, sad figure."

Whatever story was whispered in his ear, Ernst took it to heart, for the next time Munson met with Dorshka Raphaelson at the Chateau Elysée, an apartment hotel in Hollywood, she began to cry. His German friends, she told Dorshka, thought she had only gotten involved with him to further her career. "Do they think so little of him that I couldn't love him for himself?" she asked Raphaelson.

Perhaps because monogamy didn't seem to be working out, Lubitsch embarked on a more Continental attitude toward women than he had previously allowed himself. "Like a sailor," remembered Jean Negulesco, "he had an official mistress in every port." Negulesco, a second-unit director who had been taken under Lubitsch's wing, got a call one day while working at Universal. "Call Mr. Lubitsch the moment you come in . . . urgent."

A worried Negulesco called back and was told by a distressed Lubitsch that his mistress in New York was arriving for a visit, and his Viennese

172

mistress had caught wind of it. Murder was in the air. "You have to come to dinner, make love to the New York mistress," implored Lubitsch.

Negulesco arrived and was doing just fine with the New York mistress—Lubitsch and he shared similar taste in women—when he felt a kick under the table. A surprised Negulesco looked up to see Lubitsch leaning over, whispering "Not so much!"

Some of Ernst's involvements were more redolent of subtle, humorous humiliation than subtle, humorous sophistication. Lubitsch told the composer Dimitri Tiomkin about one such disaster. It seemed that at a party in New York, Ernst found himself dancing with a young, very beautiful woman. He told her that he'd like to see her again, and mentioned the hotel where he was staying. A few days later, on a Sunday afternoon, the phone rang. It was the girl, asking if it would be all right if she came up.

Lubitsch hurried into his bedroom, put on his best silk robe. The girl arrived. He helped her out of her fur coat and watched as she excused herself to freshen up in the bathroom. That was just fine, for he had laid out a selection of the finest perfumes on the off-chance a lady guest might wish to use them.

He waited.

A long time.

Finally, the bathroom door opened and she came out, radiant and smelling delicious. She picked up her fur coat and put it on, explaining that there had been a women's convention in the hotel, and she hadn't been able to get into the ladies' room. "I thought you wouldn't mind," she said as she swept out the door.

Lubitch was never as interested in the brains or even the good looks of a prospective female partner as he was in her emotional coloring. "Charm is the most important thing in the world to a woman," he once told the wife of *Photoplay* editor James Quirk. "It is a composite quality, impossible to analyze. It takes a little part of so many things to produce charm."

Leni's betrayal meant that he would rarely grow too dependent on any one woman; once a relationship was over, Ernst was perfectly capable of offering avuncular advice. In later years, a former mistress who would go on to a medium-successful acting career married a wealthy man-about-town. "I want you to be a good girl," Lubitsch told her. "You've had your fun, you've been around a lot. Make this work."

. . .

As his romantic life solidified around one primary mistress surrounded by more transient relationships, Lubitsch's professional associations remained remarkably stable.

At home, serving as a combination butler/chauffeur/man Friday, was Otto Werner, a tough, phlegmatic man whose discretion and loyalty were beyond question. The secretary/amanuensis was Steffie Trondle, who gave Lubitsch an overbearing devotion that absorbed most of the oxygen in the room. Because of her dominating officiousness, she was more or less disliked by most of Lubitsch's friends ("a homely, pushy little woman who waited on him hand and foot and drove him nuts" was the way one described her).

Lubitsch would occasionally sigh, "Oh, if I could only get rid of Trondle," but he never did. He did not treat her with any particular lavishness, never paying her more than forty dollars a week, but in all probability he was as dependent on her as she was on him.

At the studio there was assistant director Eric Locke, a graduate in philosophy who also served as Lubitsch's business manager. Solid, tough-looking, with an interesting scar on his left cheek, Locke was the sort of man who carried cigarettes in one hand and a copy of Goethe in the other. Lubitsch trusted him sufficiently to give Locke the responsibility of shooting second-unit footage whenever it was required, either in America or Europe.

Surrounding these three members of his personal staff was the extended family at Paramount, such as Joe Youngerman, who began at the studio as a laborer in 1926, and would eventually rise to be assistant to studio chief Henry Ginsberg until 1950, when he left to run the Directors Guild. Youngerman worked for Lubitsch as both prop man and assistant director, and remembered him as "running a happy set. His rehearsals tended to run a little bit longer than other directors, but once he started shooting he was as fast as any director on the lot.

174

"He had a hell of a good sense of humor. He always had a cigar in his mouth, you know, but when he looked through the camera, he would lay the cigar down. To horse around, we always used to salt the cigar tip. Then he would pick it up and put it in his mouth and smack his lips and get this look on his face, but he never said a word about it. He knew what was going on, but he never said a word. He didn't mind being the butt of the joke."

To his crew, Lubitsch was completely approachable, putting on no airs, but Youngerman recalled that being the case with most directors, even

DeMille, "who was a terror on the set. One time I told DeMille, 'You know, I think you'd make better pictures if you did the long shots and Lubitsch did the close-ups.' And he said, 'Maybe that's so,' and laughed it off."

Lubitsch would usually invite selected members of the crew to previews of his pictures. After one preview, Lubitsch approached Youngerman and asked what he thought of the picture. Youngerman replied that he thought it was wonderful, but he suggested a few minor changes that he thought would make a big difference. Lubitsch listened and walked away.

A few days later, Lubitsch walked onto a set where Youngerman was working with Wesley Ruggles, sidled up to him and said, "Joe, you're crazy." The next day, the visit and the admonition were repeated. This went on regularly for the next several weeks until one day Lubitsch arrived, walked up to Youngerman, and, with an embarrassed shake of his head, said "Joe, you were right."

Of all Lubitsch's collaborators, the most significant were the writers. At first, Lubitsch attempted to replace Hans Kräly with a variety of talents, all solid professionals but none with the right bouquet. He even worked on two stories with Vicki Baum, the Viennese author of *Grand Hotel.* Although Baum was frankly uncomfortable with the scripting process, Lubitsch attempted to soothe her. "Don't worry. You write a short novel, in German, of course. I'll do the rest . . . You understand what's expected of you: another *Grand Hotel.* Lots of character woven into one plot, one pattern, one piece of fabric."

Lubitsch and Baum decided to place the action in a department store instead of a hotel. Paramount seemed pleased with the result, and, while mulling it over, extended Baum's contract for another six months. Ernst and Baum promptly went to work on a story for Maurice Chevalier, with music by Oscar Straus.

Baum adored Lubitsch ("the most loyal of friends," she wrote in her memoirs. "If you threw out a little line that gave him an idea for one of his famous 'touches' . . . you could actually see a tiny red flame kindle behind the black of the pupils"), but the Chevalier story was shelved, as was the department store idea. Paramount tried to cancel the remainder of Baum's $2,500 a week contract, but an angry Lubitsch forced them to honor the deal.

Replacing Kräly was made easier than it might have been by the fortuitous presence of Samson Raphaelson, "Rafe" to everybody but Lubitsch, who usually called him "Sem."

Raphaelson was born on March 30, 1896, on the lower East Side of New York. Given a classic Yiddish upbringing by his grandparents, he had no particular interest in being a writer. Raphaelson grew up loathing the people that surrounded him, immigrants and children of immigrants who freely and happily contemplated lives of factory jobs or waiting on tables. He dreamed of cars, servants, country estates, sleeping in late. "I had the makings of a nice little Fascist," he remembered drily.

"I had only one passion," he would recall in 1948, "to escape poverty. I had another passion—not to work hard." Since the most easily managed literary form seemed to be the short story, by the time he was nineteen Raphaelson had begun tinkering with fiction. After a short run as a police reporter for *The New York Times,* he began to work in the advertising business by day and to write by night.

Between 1922 and 1924, Raphaelson worked in the ad agency, read H. L. Mencken, *The Nation,* and *The New Republic,* and dedicated himself to the proposition that he was not a genius. He was existing, he remembered "in a nirvana of self-confessed mediocrity."

In January 1922, *Everybody's Magazine* published his story "The Day of Atonement." The story had been percolating for several years, ever since Raphaelson, then a senior at the University of Illinois, had seen Al Jolson in *Robinson Crusoe, Jr.* Raphaelson had instantly responded to the religious fervor implicit in Jolson's singing style, and constructed a story centering on the dramatic conflict between Old World roots and the temptations of assimilation.

Goaded by his secretary, Raphaelson adapted "The Day of Atonement" into a play. On September 14, 1925, Raphaelson's adaptation of his story opened on Broadway with George Jessel in the title role. It was called *The Jazz Singer* and had a very successful run of thirty-eight weeks, with the movie rights going to Warner Bros.

"I'm not ashamed of the play, but the movie embarrasses me," Raphaelson told Bill Moyers near the end of his life, and that was in spite of his admiration for Al Jolson.

But then, most movies embarrassed Raphaelson; as he would frankly tell Robert Carringer in 1973, "Pictures meant nothing to me. They were just like going to the circus. If I went to the circus I wouldn't envy Mr. Barnum, I'd say let him have his millions . . . And if someone would have to write a scenario for the tightrope walker—I wouldn't do it. I wouldn't want to be the one who did that. So that movies couldn't have meant less to me."

While the play and movie adaptation had put a good deal of money into Raphaelson's pocket—the movie rights alone brought fifty thousand dollars—the stock market crash of 1929 removed all of it and more. With a family to support (in 1928 Raphaelson married the former Dorshka Wegman, a performer in the Ziegfeld Follies; they had their first child a year later), there seemed only one obvious answer to the problem of making a living.

So it was that Samson Raphaelson made himself available to Hollywood, and would continue to do so for the next twenty-five years. Like Ben Hecht, like dozens of other writers, Raphaelson regarded screenwriting as a craft, a job of work that would finance a comfortable life for him and his family, sustaining him while he did what he regarded as his real work, his plays.

Raphaelson completed his first couple of assignments for Paramount without undue problems, but was dissatisfied. He was getting $750 a week from Paramount and had gone to B. P. Schulberg, head of the studio, to tell him "If you give me a $750 assignment, I'm not going to be any good. Give me a $2,500 assignment. You'll be saving a lot of money."

Schulberg had been courteous and said "I'll keep that in mind." Three days later he sent for Raphaelson and introduced him to Lubitsch. Raphaelson needed no background. "I admired him beyond any director whose work I had seen," he remembered in 1971. "I had seen *The Love Parade* . . . I was enchanted with it. High comedy. Style. It was a Lubitsch picture."

Although Raphaelson had totally forgotten about Lubitsch's interest in *The Jazz Singer,* Lubitsch had not forgotten about him. Ernst was considering material that called for the same kind of strongly emotional bonds between generations as *The Jazz Singer.*

Lubitsch immediately began telling Raphaelson the story of a European play called *The Man I Killed.* Within two minutes, Raphaelson broke in to criticize it. "As he went along, I had a feeling that this guy and I would get along. We both hollered, talked loud, and waved our hands. That was it. I was assigned to Lubitsch."

The two men quickly fell into step, complementing each other. "Lubitsch was concentratedly gentle," remembered Helen Vreeland Smith, Raphaelson's secretary. "But Rafe could be scathing and sarcastic. I remember that when I got married, it was on a Saturday, and Rafe got furious with me because I wouldn't run an errand for him that morning."

Raphaelson was particularly enchanted one day during the writing of *The Man I Killed,* as Lubitsch was acting out a scene in a graveyard. The scene called for a person on either side of a grave, and Lubitsch created the mood, even imitated the sound of a bird singing. When the time came to switch characters, he was living the moment so intensely that he began jumping over the grave, back and forth, hopping over a mound of fresh earth that existed only in his imagination.

Although *The Man I Killed* was written first (during October, November, and early December 1930), it was actually shot after *The Smiling Lieutenant.* Their collaborator on *The Man I Killed* was Ernest Vajda. According to Raphaelson, Vajda never presented a line or an idea. He would say "Our problem is . . ." and paraphrase what Lubitsch had been saying.

Without a break, as soon as *The Man I Killed* was written, the same three men collaborated on the script for *The Smiling Lieutenant.* On that picture, Raphaelson was no longer the insecure neophyte, and Lubitsch felt that Raphaelson was entitled to first script credit, which Vajda actively resisted.

"I only think it's right," Lubitsch told Vajda. "You got first credit on the other one."

"You do that and I don't work for you anymore," retorted Vajda.

"That's the chance I'll have to take," said Lubitsch. He gave Vajda the credit he wanted, but, except for a brief stint on *The Merry Widow* a few years later, never worked with him again.

Raphaelson, as well as many others, felt a slight queasiness about *The Man I Killed.* "I felt his whole attack on that picture was wrong. I came home and worried about it and then would go back and fight it out with him. He said, 'I know, I know. You stay with it this way and you'll see. It'll work out.'

"It didn't. It came out just as morbid and unattractive as I thought it would."

In spite of the indifferent results of their first collaboration, Raphaelson and Lubitsch quickly formed a professional bond that would never be broken. Over the next seventeen years, the two men would write nine pictures together, invariably following the same routine. They always worked in the same room, Monday through Friday, from nine to noon and two to six. In between the two sessions came lunch, a walk, and perhaps a catnap.

The script was not written so much as talked, with a secretary taking it all down. If the work was being done at Lubitsch's home rather than the studio, the writer would usually be invited to stay for dinner, in which case the only off-limits subject would be the script.

As the two men talked, it would usually fall to Lubitsch to outline a given scene. He was insistent on excellence—"Let's open different, better than anybody ever opened a goddamn picture," he once exulted.

Raphaelson never caught the director thinking formulaically, looking for hooks for his fabled "touches." "He wouldn't say, 'How can ve use a door in this scene?' " Raphaelson told Herman Weinberg. "He would face the problem and say, 'Vat do ve do here? How do ve lick dis? How do ve say it vit *style?* How do ve say it *different?* How do ve say it different and *good?* Different and true?' "

On those occasions when the two men would hit a dead end they could not evade, Lubitsch would suggest "Ve write it dull, like in life—just like people talk in real life—real dull—and see if ve get any ideas from dat." The process of creating a scene the wrong way would often point them toward the right way.

Raphaelson would do the actual writing—or, in his case, dictating. Verbally improvising, Raphaelson would dictate the scene, the secretary would take it down and type it up. The two men would then pore over the pages, adjusting, adding, subtracting, whatever. Brick by brick the script was built; there were no rewrites, no blue pages, no desperate on-the-set revisions. The first script was the only script.

"Lubitsch did need a writer," remembered Sam Raphaelson, "but he wasn't afraid of a good writer, which Hitchcock, I suspect, was, for very complex and obscure reasons. Lubitsch welcomed a good writer. That man had a sense of good writing second to none. If Shakespeare had been alive at his time, Lubitsch would have happily embraced him. And Shakespeare would have been a little better than he was . . . Lubitsch never cheapened you."

The partnership produced that odd, comforting feeling of a collaboration so intense it's virtually a symbiosis. As Raphaelson told Bill Moyers, "He wrote some of my best lines and I contributed more than a few of those silent things known as Lubitsch touches."

(Gottfried Reinhardt, son of Max, and a Lubitsch assistant, wasn't as sure as Raphaelson. "Lubitsch was 60 percent responsible for virtually every script he made," according to Reinhardt. "He needed writers for questions of linguistic style, for idiom. His accent always remained atrocious. Up to his last days, he would not say 'hundred' as in English, but *hundert* as in German.")

Once the script was finished, Raphaelson would usually head back east, but even when he didn't, he went on a movie set less than half a dozen times in his life, and then only because Lubitsch needed to change a line of dialogue. "There was nothing to learn by watching a three-minute scene being shot over and over," he would say.

"I've worked with directors before and since," Raphaelson recalled in 1959. "I worked with Hitchcock, I worked with Cukor . . . I worked with Frank Lloyd . . . Lubitsch towered above anybody, creatively, that I met in Hollywood; director, producer, and I would say writer, if you limited it to the screen. He was a man of enormous taste. He was a very creative man. I would nominate him and bet on it . . . that he was the greatest craftsman who ever lived . . . in the sense of knowing the most brilliant and original way to use the medium."

To a class of students in playwrighting, Raphaelson would exclaim that Lubitsch was "a very great craftsman. He was not a writer, but he was probably as good a half-writer as ever lived. Working with him, I learned enough technique to last a lifetime—too much technique. I became fascinated with the how and, for three years, lost all contact with the what."

Raphaelson gave Ernst a sympathetic collaborator, with a mind that could slip into lockstep with his own. Both of them believed implicitly in writing good acting parts, but Lubitsch pushed Raphaelson's writing far beyond the conventionalities it tended to live by. Left to his own devices, Raphaelson stopped at the point where Lubitsch began.

"I loved the guy," Raphaelson said. "He wasn't a warm man, no, but what I'd call a glowing man. He'd been trained in the tough world of German films and politics and he knew those tactics but he never used them."

In the beginning of their collaboration, it had never occurred to Raphaelson that he could be a writer of comedy. But as he would throw out ideas with a demurral like, "Here's an exaggeration, a kind of cheap belly laugh stuff that we ought to get, but with authenticity," Lubitsch would listen and respond with "What's the matter with that?"

"He made me realize," remembered Raphaelson, "that I'd been throwing away a lot of good material because I hadn't stayed with it and studied it and given character to it without losing it. That I was too 'earnest and sincere' and lost sparkle through it."

The two men even began socializing occasionally, Raphaelson accompanied by his beautiful, intelligent wife, Dorshka, Lubitsch by the actress Ona Munson. The two couples would often attend the Mayfair dance on Saturday nights at the Ritz Hotel. "He was a lovely dancer," remembered Dorshka Raphaelson, "and he and Ona were a darling couple. He had wonderful, sparkling dark eyes, and he was very mischievous and teased me a lot. 'You should be a good wife for Sam,' he would say. 'Take his shoes off when he gets home, bring him his slippers, light his pipe for him.' He would laugh as he said it. Rafe said that Lubitsch was bored by wives, but I don't think he was bored by me."

Yet, for all of their obvious sympatico, the two men never achieved a true intimacy as friends. When they worked together, their Christmas gifts to each other were strictly nominal tokens—boxes of candy, or baskets of fruit and nuts. In this period, Ernst's closest friends were Europeans like Paul Kohner and Henry Blanke, men as consumed by their work as Lubitsch.

"He always had a new project that he was moving toward after he completed the old project," remembered a good friend. "His life was an uninterrupted ribbon of film. He didn't talk about himself, he talked about people and situations." In other words, possible screen material. Friends, then, were mortar between the bricks. A man with the strong theatrical orientation of Sam Raphaelson didn't have the compulsive interest in the movie business shared by most of Ernst's friends.

Once, when Rafe and Dorshka arrived in Hollywood on a Sunday afternoon to begin work on a picture, Lubitsch called and invited them over after dinner. Upon their arrival, Lubitsch shook their hands and, saying "Now I tell you the story," sat Raphaelson down while Dorshka listened "like a good housewife." There was no small talk, no How-was-your-trip? preliminaries.

"I think I am possessed only of a fascination for the work I have chosen to do," Ernst wrote in 1938. "I am so engrossed by the production of a film that I literally think of nothing else. I have no hobby, no outside interests and want none."

In September 1931, nearly a year after he and Raphaelson wrote the script, Lubitsch finally began shooting *The Man I Killed,* finishing it forty-three days later. Although he had hoped to use Emil Jannings in the role of the German father, Jannings' unsuccessful tussles with English had forced him to beat a hasty retreat back to Germany, where he would become a primary cultural jewel in the propaganda films of the Third

Reich. Lubitsch replaced Jannings with Hollywood's all-purpose cranky old man, Lionel Barrymore.

The film opens with heavy music, and the image of a tolling bell clues the audience in that this is going to be a drama. The opening five minutes amplify hopes. In a rapid, impressionistic montage, Lubitsch shows a victory parade watched by a man with one leg, celebratory cannons scaring a bed-ridden patient in a veterans hospital, and, savagely, sabres dangling from officers' waists cluttering the aisle of a church. As the soldiers rise at the end of the service, the camera cranes down to a close-up of the desperately clasped hands of Paul (Phillips Holmes). "Father help me," he says. "I can't get away from his eyes."

We flashback from the eyes of Paul to the eyes of the man he killed in combat. He finds letters on the body and discovers that, like him, he was also a musician.

Back in present time, he makes his way to the cemetery to place flowers on the grave, where he meets the man's mother and fiancée. Lacking the courage to tell them he's responsible for the man's death, he lets them think that he and the dead man served together, whereupon they insist he come home with them and tell them about their beloved's time in the service.

The rest is easy to anticipate. The father (Lionel Barrymore) virtually adopts him, while the fiancée (Nancy Carroll) falls in love with him, all of which only increases his sense of guilt and unworthiness. Ultimately, he admits his responsibility for the son's death, whereupon Nancy Carroll refuses to let him return their lives to the darkness where they have been for the past three years. Barrymore gives Holmes his son's violin, and he and Nancy Carroll swing into a gentle duet, as the healing power of time and music hold gentle sway over all.

Lubitsch manages to accomplish some nice things in the film; there is a sense of European village life, as the shopkeepers rush from door to door telling each other to watch the young couple in love, and there are some moments of tart, observational truth as well. An eavesdropping old woman leaning out of a window darts out of the frame then comes back with a pillow to make her leaning more comfortable.

But Phillips Holmes is a moist actor (and, apparently, a vain one; Dorothy Coonan Wellman remembered the actor dyeing his hair orange, so it would photograph blonder) who was, for the most part, relegated to "sensitive" parts, and Lubitsch allows him to act in a hand-wringing, overwrought style. In addition, Holmes is supposed to be French, Lionel Barrymore German. Neither is remotely convincing.

The Man I Killed is a pocket drama, and a schematic, unorganic one at that. The heavy, barnstorming performances are out of synch with the material, which needs to be underplayed. For the only time in his American career, Lubitsch was attempting to be Significant, and it destroys the picture.

In the Yiddish theater, there was a moment in every play that was known as the "tablecloth speech," so called because it covered everything; there are several tablecloth speeches in *The Man I Killed*. Lionel Barrymore gets one ("We're too old to fight but we aren't too old to hate"); even Nancy Carroll gets one, which is unfortunate because not only does she move like a truckdriver, she acts like one.

Lubitsch makes *The Man I Killed* into a Stanley Kramer-style thesis film, and the sticky ending gives us a glimpse of what Lubitsch might have done with *The Jazz Singer,* draining the story of Jewish assimilation of all of its—and Jolson's—energetic show-biz vulgarity, which is to say, its very reason for being.

In attempting such a weighty subject, Lubitsch felt compelled to drop most of his characteristic sprightliness, his humor, his nimble way with actors. Part of the problem may have been an inability to establish a rapport with Nancy Carroll; Lubitsch told Miriam Hopkins that "she doesn't understand what I want her to do . . . she doesn't want direction . . . I said to her . . . 'If you would just put yourself in my arms' [hands]. And she said, 'That *I* should do that with you, [a] German?' "

The end result is one of his worst films. The reviews were respectful, the box office dire; Paramount began scrambling to try to recoup at least some of the weighty negative cost of $889,154.

"The thousands who have seen and been moved by *The Man I Killed,*" said an ad in *The New York Times* on February 9, 1932, "have taken such a personal interest in its success that they have actually insisted on a new title for the picture . . . one more worthy of the greatness of its drama and magnificent love story!

"In deference to these many requests, *The Man I Killed* is renamed *Broken Lullaby.*" It didn't help. *The Man I Killed/Broken Lullaby* was the biggest failure Lubitsch had had since the debacle of *Eternal Love.*

In 1932, after a courtship of nearly four years, Paul Kohner and Lupita Tovar were engaged. It seemed an odd match; Kohner was well known around town as a lover of beautiful women, while Tovar came from such a strict Latin environment that Kohner was the first man she had ever gone out with. The marriage was to be performed in Berlin, where Kohner would run the European office of Universal Pictures.

Just before they were to leave, Lubitsch sidled up to Tovar and said, "I think you're making a mistake. I give this marriage six months."

An astonished Lupita could only gasp, "Mr. Lubitsch!"

"Yes," he continued. "Paul is European, you're Mexican. He's Jewish, you're Catholic. Do you speak German?"

"No."

"Does he speak Spanish?"

"No."

"Well, how do you expect it to work? You're from two entirely different cultures. And you're still a little girl." Lubitsch reached into his pocket and pulled out a card. "I tell you, if you get in trouble, don't forget the number here. You call me."

After Kohner and Tovar had been married a short time, Lubitsch was making a brief return to Berlin when he attended a party thrown by Erich Pommer in his honor. He came over to the new Mrs. Kohner and, without preamble, said "Still happy?"

"But I've only been married a month . . ."

"Doesn't make any difference. Are you happy?"

"Very."

"You sure? You're not telling me a story?"

Despite his surface sophistication, Lubitsch's understanding of the complicated transaction known as marriage was essentially superficial. The Kohners would be married for fifty-six years. "I never stopped to think about the difference," remembered Lupita Tovar Kohner. "I was very much in love and apparently so was Paul. Those differences were never a problem. I learned German and he learned Spanish, and when we met, he could hardly speak English. We respected each other. If I had to do it all over again, I would."

Lupita Kohner smiled as she thought of her marriage. "We grew old," she said, "and we were still holding hands."

According to Sam Raphaelson, it was Paramount that nudged Lubitsch into a supervisory function, so that he could get more done each year and make more money as well. *Variety*, on the other hand, reported that Lubitsch's contract called for him to occasionally supervise the work of other directors without receiving any additional salary.

Since Lubitsch was heavily involved with *The Man I Killed*, Paramount decided that Lubitsch should only "supervise" the production of *One Hour with You*. Lubitsch's contract was due to expire on March 7, 1932, and

Paramount had scheduled Chevalier for two pictures: *One Hour with You* would begin production on October 26, 1931, and a second picture, to be directed by Lubitsch, was due to begin January 25, 1932. In essence, Paramount was squeezing as much work as possible out of Lubitsch before his contract expired.

George Cukor was assigned to *One Hour with You* on September 28. On October 22, Lubitsch completed shooting *The Man I Killed*, promptly sat down and took a look at the proposed script for *One Hour with You*, and just as promptly threw it out. A worried Lubitsch got the start date for *One Hour with You* pushed back to November, and quickly began work on a new script with Raphaelson.

Lubitsch and Raphaelson rewrote the old script for *The Marriage Circle*. As each sequence was completed, Lubitsch would invite Cukor (whose name he mispronounced "Kookor" instead of "Quekor") to hear the scene. "Cukor would applaud," remembered Raphaelson, "and very courteously thank him and say 'Great' and go. That was Cukor's total contribution to the script."

On November 12, the picture began shooting without a completed script (in fact, the film's script would not be finished until December 24, only two weeks before the picture was completed).

But while the Lubitsch touch could be present in the script, Lubitsch pictures could not be mass-produced. After two days of production, Lubitsch asked Raphaelson to come and look at the rushes, in itself an unusual occurrence. The scene Cukor was working on was near the beginning of the picture, when Chevalier comes out of the bedroom and explains to the audience that their lascivious thoughts are absurd, that the lady waiting for him is his wife.

"I sit there and I see Chevalier going up into the room . . . the door shuts, then he opens the door, *takes a cigarette from his pocket, lights it, and having lighted the cigarette and dropped the match into an ashtray on the little hall table, then* [emphasis Raphaelson's] he says, 'I know what you think, ladies and gentleman . . .'"

The result, according to Raphaelson, was the slaughtering of the scene's tempo for the sake of some casual stage business. "He was adding some goddamn obscure directorial touch to it," remembered Raphaelson. In a deposition taken for a resulting court case (*Cukor v. Paramount*, New York Supreme Court), Lubitsch said that Cukor's work lacked "the Continental flavor which was so essential to this type of picture. We felt also that the dialogue was not pointed in the right way and was not spoken as effectively as it should be. We particularly noticed that all of the actors over-acted their parts and in the silent parts were even grimacing."

Even Maurice Chevalier, hardly a team player, agreed, saying that "I was being directed much too broadly by Cukor and without any of the subtlety with which Lubitsch had directed me in *The Love Parade* and *The Smiling Lieutenant.*"

On the third day of production, Lubitsch began supervising camera placements and "conferring" with Cukor about the picture. The next day, Lubitsch reshot the offending scene, then with a profusion of "George, do you mind, I . . ." segued into rehearsing the actors before every scene. Beginning November 20, Lubitsch took the production over completely. For the next six weeks, Cukor sat quietly on the set, drawing his salary, confining most of his conversation to expressions of approval after each Lubitsch-directed scene.

In succeeding years, Cukor was always rather circumspect about this professional and personal humiliation, tending to ascribe the problem to the fact that, with Lubitsch, "everything was so carefully calculated in advance . . . everything was down pat, perfect. He knew exactly what was to be said and done. I'm not that rigid. In places I allow improvisation. I feel my way more."

One Hour with You was completed on January 7, 1932, at a very pricey cost of $1.1 million, although that figure also included a French-language version. Lubitsch took sole charge of the postproduction process. When the film was previewed on February 9, the credits read "An Ernst Lubitsch Production" and "Directed by George Cukor." Lubitsch waited for Cukor to come forth and refuse to take credit for a film that he had not in fact directed. A highly favorable review in *The Hollywood Reporter* of February 10, which gave credit to Cukor, finally got Lubitsch's back up.

The next day Lubitsch fired off an angry letter to B. P. Schulberg: ". . . after careful consideration, I came to the conclusion that it would be advisable for me to ask you to take my name entirely off the picture.

"From all I have heard so far the picture stands a chance to be rated as the best directed Chevalier picture, surpassing all my previous efforts . . . the spectator and the critics not familiar with the inside story will probably attribute the better direction to the help of George Cukor.

"As long as it is not possible for me to get full credit for my hard work on this picture, I think that at least I should not get any damage out of it. I believe that if my name is not mentioned in connection with the picture at all, I would at least be protected against any possible damage.

"I am confident that you will understand my point of view and will cooperate with me in this matter."

Lubitsch's fake *noblesse oblige* was a masterful bluff. Schulberg was hardly likely to snub one of his most valued directors—and one whose contract was about to expire—in favor of an untried talent like Cukor, no matter how promising. He promptly called Cukor in and asked him to take his name off the picture. Cukor refused. Schulberg responded by ordering his name removed from the picture, and Paramount sent out a "corrected billing" press sheet to exhibitors: "UNDER NO CIRCUMSTANCES IS GEORGE CUKOR'S NAME TO BE MENTIONED IN ANY WAY IN CONNECTION WITH ONE HOUR WITH YOU."

In the last week of February, Cukor filed suit to block the scheduled premiere of *One Hour with You* on March 23, 1932. Depositions were taken, and much dirty laundry was about to be publicly aired when a deal was cut. Paramount agreed to let Cukor out of his contract so he could go to work for his friend David Selznick at RKO. In return, Lubitsch got the credit to which he was entitled. The final credits read "Directed by Ernst Lubitsch." On another line, "Assisted by George Cukor."

Film historian Barry Sabath, after a painstaking perusal of Cukor's affadavits, estimates that Cukor's contribution to the finished film consists largely of single close-ups without dialogue, or shots of feet going up stairs, the sort of afterthought material that is often left to second units or assistant directors. For better or worse, then, *One Hour with You* is a Lubitsch film. George Cukor's own summation of the entire unfortunate affair seems eminently fair. "With the best intentions in the world," he told the critic and novelist Gavin Lambert, "I couldn't do a Lubitsch picture. Lubitsch was what they really wanted and what they should have had [from the beginning]."

One Hour with You opens in a park, with various couples necking. The only man not to panic when a flashlight falls on him is Chevalier. "You can't make love anywhere," says the policeman.

"But, officer, he can," says Jeanette MacDonald.

Enraptured by the compliment, Chevalier lights up: "Darling!"

Some of the piquancy is reduced when Chevalier addresses the camera a little later and informs us that "We really are married." *The Marriage Circle* plot is, for the most part, followed. Roland Young gets the Menjou part, but he lacks Menjou's delicious imperviousness, which is, after all, the essence of the joke.

The film even adopts rhyming dialogue briefly, which is unfortunate, as the meter is the same one later used by Dr. Seuss. While *One Hour with You* offers two good songs in "Oh, That Mitzi" and the title number, a few other songs are not as charming, and the rhymed dialogue quickly grows irritating. Mostly, it's a soufflé that obstinately refuses to rise, which, considering the difficulties of its production, is not too surprising.

The film does feature one priceless moment, when Charlie Ruggles, outfitted as some sort of Renaissance prince, arrives at a party to find it is not of the costume variety. Calling his valet, he asks why he told him it was a costume party.

"Ah, Monsieur, I did so want to see you in tights," replies the suddenly ardent servant.

Since Paramount did not hold an option, Lubitsch's services were definitely up for grabs as of the first week of March 1932. Paramount wanted to re-sign him, and discussed either eliminating his supervisory duties altogether or expanding them by giving him his own unit. Columbia and United Artists also expressed interest, but when Lubitsch arrived in New York on February 16, he announced that he was seriously interested in producing some Broadway shows in association with producer Walter Wanger, the composer Dimitri Tiomkin, and Tiomkin's wife, Albertina Rasch.

Lubitsch may have been bluffing; he also may have been entirely serious. He genuinely adored the theater, but it is a highly speculative business and Lubitsch, aside from taking money seriously, was far less sure of himself in the theater than he was in the cinema. Lubitsch once told Hedda Hopper that "[For] twenty years I wanted to [direct on the stage] but I never had the nerve to stick my neck out." The tentative thoughts about returning to his first love were closed out when Paramount made a preemptive strike that must have appealed to Ernst's considerable need for security and continuity.

Under the old contract, Lubitsch had been receiving $125,000 a picture for an average of two pictures a year. Under the new contract, he was to be paid a weekly salary that came to $225,000 a year for the same two pictures. It was a slight pay cut, but the difference in salary was offset by a provision that allowed Lubitsch to make one picture on loan-out.

Besides signing a new contract and seeing all the latest shows in New York, Lubitsch also shot a new ending for *One Hour with You* at the Astoria studio. On March 28, he returned to Hollywood to be met by Jeanette

MacDonald. He told waiting reporters that he had no plans to marry Ona Munson, that they were "just good friends."

When *One Hour with You* was released on March 25, it was greeted by the usual critical encomiums. *The New York Times* said that it was "an excellent production, with Lubitsch and Chevalier at the top of their form," while the *Los Angeles Times* wrote that "The Lubitsch touch, which has become more than a legend, is omnipresent in this production."

One day early in 1932, Lubitsch arrived at the Raphaelsons' house for lunch and told Rafe the story of their next film. It derived from a play called *The Honest Finder* by Laszlo Aladar. "No use reading the play, Sem. It's bad. We work with this material, you see." Later, Raphaelson did get a copy of the play but never bothered to read it.

Raphaelson was unaware of the fact that the central character of what became *Trouble in Paradise* was based on the famous Hungarian swindler and thief Georges Manolescu, whose 1907 *Memoirs* resulted in at least two silent films, one, in 1929, starring Ivan Mosjoukine, who was attempting to reestablish his European career after an unsuccessful sojourn with Universal.*

With his passion for all things Hungarian, Lubitsch probably knew of Manolescu, whose name, in the film, was slightly altered to Gaston Monescu. *Trouble in Paradise* continued Lubitsch's habit of latching on to an obscure, inferior play, usually Hungarian, and playing Pygmalion to its dog-eared Galatea. Although these works were nearly always structurally flawed ("You could have a play that fell apart and still have a success in Budapest," remembered Raphaelson), they invariably had an intriguing central situation and romantic characters. That was all Lubitsch needed. Psychologically, it made more sense to him to fix what was broken than to build from the ground up.

(In the fifteen years remaining to him, Lubitsch would produce only one entirely original script. Proving that he was a gifted creator as well as an interpreter, *To Be or Not to Be* was one of his greatest films.)

The central idea for the film was for a satirical treatment of a whodunit. Since neither Lubitsch or Raphaelson had ever done a whodunit or had

*Mosjoukine's only American film, Edward Sloman's *Surrender,* keeps threatening to become first-rate but never quite does; the star's American career was undoubtedly hampered by the fact that he bore a startling resemblance to the slapstick comedian Larry Semon.

any particular interest in the form, they called in a friendly contract hack named Grover Jones, who had matriculated in silent slapstick comedies. They promptly found that, as Raphaelson remembered, "We didn't need his savvy. He didn't know what the hell we were doing in our style, what we were after. We were so far away from him that he was cheerfully bewildered."

Jones sat there amiably spinning anecdotes at lunch while Lubitsch and Raphaelson wrote the script, and was rewarded with an "adaptation" credit. Some parts were written for specific actors such as Edward Everett Horton and Charlie Ruggles. The hushed, murmuring Herbert Marshall seems to have come in later in the casting process. Lubitsch must have been amused by Marshall's way with women; while very much married, Marshall managed affairs with both Kay Francis and Miriam Hopkins, as well as a serious relationship with Gloria Swanson, all within the space of a few years.

As always, Lubitsch and "Sem" slaved over the script. "We spent—oh, maybe three days, getting that opening shot," remembered Raphaelson. "He wouldn't be content unless we got a brilliant opening shot. We wanted to introduce Venice . . . Now, pictorially, the conventional way of saying that is to open on a long shot of Venice, medium shot of wherever you want to be, and close shot on the canal and the house, and then you go inside the house or hotel or whatever it is. That's [the] conventional way.

"Now, Lubitsch would sit and say, 'How do we do that, without doing that?' "

What Lubitsch and Raphaelson finally came up with was the famous opening where the singer of a glorious operatic air turns out to be a trash collector. Even in glorious, romantic Venice, someone has to pick up the garbage but, this being Venice—and Lubitsch—they must do it with panache. This sardonic undercutting of the ordinary is perhaps the quintessential "Lubitsch touch," but the director was careful not to overdo a good thing.

"Other times, he started [writing the script] right away," Raphaelson told Barry Sabath. "He didn't want to get a brilliant opening shot. Here, he felt he wanted it. He wanted to open with laughter and with style—and style, of course, is the essence of Lubitsch."

When the script was finished on July 15, 1932, Paramount notified Ernst that "the following players are available and should be considered: Adrienne Ames, Phillips Holmes, Charles Starrett, Irving Pichel, Cary

Grant." He promptly ignored all those possibilities and cast the picture his own way.

Ernst began shooting *The Honest Finder* the last week in July and finished in the first part of September. There were the usual minor complications, courtesy of the frantic Miriam Hopkins. In one scene, Hopkins ruthlessly upstaged Kay Francis by slowly turning the chair in which she was sitting until her profile had magically become her entire face. A furious Francis complained to Lubitsch, who assured her the problem would be solved in the next take. It was, by the simple expedient of nailing Hopkins' chair to the floor.

After the expenses of his last several pictures, Lubitsch cut back: *Trouble in Paradise* cost only $519,706. It was not until early October, nearly a month after the film finished production, that the film was finally titled *Trouble in Paradise,* which won out over temporary titles like *The Golden Widow, Thieves and Lovers,* and *A Very Private Scandal.* As was usually the case, Lubitsch came up with the title (the only title Raphaelson ever contributed to their collaborations was *The Smiling Lieutenant*).

Trouble in Paradise is the essence of middle-period Lubitsch. After the delectable opening, we see a man climb over a palazzo balcony, down a tree, and steal away into the night. There has been a jewel robbery.

Later, in another part of the hotel, Gaston (Herbert Marshall) is preparing for a tryst with Lily (Miriam Hopkins). "It must be the most marvelous supper," he tells the waiter. "We may not eat it, but it must be marvelous . . . You see that moon? I want to see that moon in the champagne."

"Yes, Baron," replies the waiter, writing down on the bill "Moon in champagne."

Gaston and Lily are a couple of blithe crooks—he committed the jewel robbery at the beginning of the film—and the success of their courtship is determined by a can-you-top-this demonstration of professional skill. Lubitsch and Raphaelson then introduce us to Colet and Company, successful French parfumiers. Company director Adolph Giron (C. Aubrey Smith) is saying that in times like these, salaries need to be cut. Madame Mariette Colet (Kay Francis), demurs, saying that business bores her.

Lubitsch brings these two plot strands together by having Gaston steal Madame Colet's jewel-encrusted purse at the opera, then returning it when she offers a reward large enough to enable Gaston and Lily to return to Venice for their anniversary. Gaston returns the purse, offers Madame some makeup advice, turns on his considerable charm, and soon is offered the job of Madame Colet's secretary, the perfect job for a man intending to steal someone blind.

But Gaston and Mariette begin to fall in love, and Lily and Mariette begin to fence knowingly over access to Gaston. Of course Mariette pursues him; of course, he lets her catch him. Ultimately, Gaston must choose between two women that he loves, one of whom is determined to rob the other as compensation for having her lover seduced.

The determining moment is Gaston's confession to Madame Colet. She has already been told of her secretary's true identity, and she is opening the safe to see if it can be true when he tells her that Adolph Giron has been embezzling money from the firm for years. She blanches and refuses to allow him to call the police. The scandal! The indignity!!

"You have to be in the social register to keep out of jail," Gaston says with a touch of bitterness. "But when a man starts at the bottom and works his way up—a self-made crook—then you say, 'Call the police! Put him behind bars! Lock him up!' "

So they part, he to be with Lily, whose larcenous heart is unsullied by false social poses. "Do you know what you're missing?" he asks Mariette at the door. She nods dreamily.

"No," he says, helpfully reaching into his pocket and pulling out a pearl necklace. *"That's* what you're missing . . . Your gift to her."

Mariette smiles and says graciously, "With the compliments of Colet and Company." In the cab, Gaston gives Lily the pearls. She pulls out Mariette's jeweled purse and drops the pearls in, then looks anxiously for something else. Gaston hands her the roll of money from Mariette's safe and they embrace. Love and larceny not only coexist, they positively bask in each other's company.

Lubitsch orchestrates his film with matchless grace and style to the nth degree, using all manner of optical devices—dissolves, wipes—even near-recitatives to move the film along on its toes. And, his professional luck was holding; *Trouble in Paradise* was released just a year and a half ahead of the imposition of the Production Code, which would have made a story centering on sexual swapping and resolutely unpunished crime impossible.

More heavily scored than most 1932 films, Lubitsch directs *Trouble in Paradise* as if it were an art deco musical, with the dialogue in place of lyrics and the characters as the elegant score. Miriam Hopkins runs at her usual frantic pace, but Herbert Marshall and the languid, knowing Kay Francis become the film's shimmering, tranquil erotic center.

Dignified, austere, Simon Lubitsch adored his younger son, Ernst, even though they had virtually nothing in common. Physically and emotionally, the boy took after his mother, Anna.

1. 2.

3.

Ernst Lubitsch (bottom row, third from right) in the days before he enjoyed having his picture taken, circa 1899.

4.

5.

(ABOVE) The aggressive, bumptious, overtly Jewish comic character Lubitsch created and played till shortly after the end of World War I.

(BOTTOM) A skinny Lubitsch (second from left) in a critical comic moment from *Meyer from Berlin*.

6.

7.

(ABOVE) Pola Negri as the spitfire Carmen.

(BOTTOM) Emil Jannings and minions in *The Loves of Pharaoh*.

8.

9.

(TOP) Lubitsch and his first wife, Leni, on their wedding day—Berlin, August 23, 1922.

(LEFT) Ernst and Leni on their honeymoon in Budapest, 1922.

(ABOVE RIGHT) Ernst and Leni visit with one of the locals while passing through Albuquerque, New Mexico.

Screenwriter Edward Knoblock (left), Douglas Fairbanks, Lubitsch, and Mary Pickford in a publicity still taken to mark the start of production on *Rosita*.

Lubitsch's struggle to extract authentic emotion from Mary Pickford is obvious in this shot from the pitched battle that was *Rosita*.

13.

After the successful release of *Rosita*, Ernst and Leni decided to stay in Hollywood. On December 20, 1923, Leni's sons, Heinz and Edmund, arrived from Germany; the family was now complete and ready to begin a new life.

Lubitsch and his new friend, Charlie Chaplin, shortly after Chaplin showed him *A Woman of Paris*.

14.

Lubitsch, Warner Baxter, and Adolphe Menjou during production of *The Marriage Circle*. After the first week, Lubitsch fired Baxter and replaced him with Warner Bros. contract player Monte Blue.

Lubitsch, flanked by Jack (left) and Harry Warner, signs with Warner Bros. He would prove a considerably more fractious employee than Rin Tin Tin, whose picture is on the wall behind Jack.

16.

The exquisite, difficult Pola Negri was perfectly complemented by the urbane Adolphe Menjou in *Forbidden Paradise,* one of Lubitsch's best silent films.

17.

Ernst instructs Lew Cody for a scene in *Three Women,* while Henry Blanke (sitting on stool) observes.

18.

19.

Ernst and Leni in front of their home, 616 Beverly Drive, in 1925.

20.

Ernst with Leni's two sons in 1925. "Ernst gave great love," said one family friend.

21.

Ernst and Leni enjoy a day at Santa Monica Beach, circa 1925.

Sunday afternoons a 616 Beverly Drive brought out Lubitsch's closest friends and most of the burgeoning German colony in Hollywood.

Lubitsch with Fritz Lang.

22.

23.

Trying on Lang's monocle.

24.

Josef von Sternberg.

25.

Lubitsch serenading Paul Kohner.

26.

Lubitsch and Rudolph (Papa) Schildkraut attempt to out-act each other.

Eric Locke (left) and Henry Blanke flank Lubitsch on what seems to have been a very hard day for all.

27.

Irene Rich (left) and May McAvoy amidst the classic symmetry of *Lady Windermere's Fan.*

28

Lubitsch and crew at the old Warner Bros. studio on Sunset
Boulevard during production of the party sequence of *Three Women*.

29

30

Clara Bow and Willard Louis in the now-lost *Kiss Me Again*.

31

The lavish, audacious ball sequence in *So This Is Paris,* the closest silent films would ever come to a musical number.

On the set of *The Student Prince,* Lubitsch obviously savors a visit from his mentor, Max Reinhardt (right), accompanied by the theatrical producer Morris Gest.

33.

Costume designer Ali Hubert arrives in Hollywood from Berlin on November 14, 1926, for the production of *The Student Prince*. From left, Eric Locke, Leni Lubitsch, Hubert, Lubitsch, and Hans Kräly.

34.

35.

(TOP) Lunch on the Laurel Canyon location of *The Student Prince*, February 1927. From left, Ramon Novarro, Norma Shearer, Eric Locke, Ali Hubert, Hans Kräly, Leni, and Ernst.

(BOTTOM) An ardent, love-struck Kathi (Norma Shearer) in one of Richard Day's remarkable studio sets for *The Student Prince*.

36

Lubitsch noodling on one of the portable organs used for mood music during the production of silent films.

37.

Ernst and Emil Jannings amusing themselves on the set of *The Patriot*.

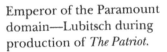

Emperor of the Paramount
domain—Lubitsch during
production of *The Patriot*.

Emil Jannings as the mad
Emperor of Russia in *The
Patriot*.

Jeanette MacDonald and
Maurice Chevalier in
Ernst's first talkie
feature, *The Love Parade*,
shot in mid-1929.

Jeanette MacDonald
singing "Beyond
the Blue Horizon" in
Lubitsch's *Monte Carlo*.

(TOP) Maurice Chevalier, *The Smiling Lieutenant,* and the reasons he's smiling: Miriam Hopkins and Claudette Colbert.

(BOTTOM) Miriam Hopkins and Herbert Marshall play can-you-top-this? amidst the shimmering perfection of *Trouble in Paradise.*

44.

45.

(TOP) The audacious opening scene of Lubitsch's adaptation of *Design for Living,* played in silence broken only by an occasional line in French.

(BOTTOM) Placid anonymity about to be shattered by an unexpected inheritance. Charles Laughton (near right row) in *If I Had a Million.*

After his acrimonious divorce from Leni, Lubitsch's most serious relationship was with the actress Ona Munson. Here they relax at his Santa Monica beach house, circa 1932.

Other, more transitory, relationships indicated he should have stayed with Ona Munson. Here, Lubitsch is photographed in Palm Springs with Greta Koerner, who sued the director in 1934 and forced him to pay a sizable settlement.

Lubitsch and his second wife, the beautiful, patrician Vivian, on their honeymoon.

(TOP) Beginning with his marriage to Vivian, Ernst began to mingle with a radically different group of friends. Here, Ernst and Vivian are bookended by Ouida and Basil Rathbone, social lions of Hollywood.

(BOTTOM) The backyard of Lubitsch's home at 268 Bel Air road.

Distraught assistant director Eric Locke finds Lubitsch asleep instead of ready to work. A gag shot, circa 1937.

52.

The 5'4" Lubitsch instructs the 6'4" Gary Cooper on the set of *Bluebeard's Eighth Wife*.

53.

Lubitsch conducts Garbo and Melvyn Douglas in a rehearsal for *Ninotchka*.

Ninotchka surrounded by her three lovable commissars (from left, Felix Bressart, Garbo, Sig Rumann, Alexander Granach).

Garbo and Melvyn Douglas in *Ninotchka*.

Lubitsch retrieves his daughter, Nicola, after the ship she had been traveling on was torpedoed by the German Navy.

(TOP) Maneuvering Margaret Sullavan and James Stewart through one of the most delicate scenes of *The Shop Around the Corner*.

(BOTTOM) Felix Bressart and James Stewart in the exquisite *The Shop Around the Corner*.

(TOP) Lubitsch and art director Vincent Korda inspecting the set designs for *To Be or Not to Be*.

(BOTTOM) The initial script reading for *To Be or Not to Be*, with Jack Benny engaged in a cigar competition with Lubitsch.

(RIGHT) Ernst (far right) shooting the opening scene of *To Be or Not to Be*.

62.

The bored Merle Oberon and the boring Melvyn Douglas in *That Uncertain Feeling*, the low point of Lubitsch's later career.

63.

Don Ameche and Gene Tierney court and fall in love in Lubitsch's *Heaven Can Wait*, the deeply affectionate—and affecting—story of a genial rake.

Charles Boyer and Jennifer Jones in the quiet, glowing *Cluny Brown*, Lubitsch's last completed picture.

64.

66

Although Ernst's second marriage failed, it produced his daughter, Nicola, whom Lubitsch regarded as the greatest happiness in his life. Here, with Charles Boyer, he gazes adoringly at her on the set of *Cluny Brown*.

65.

67.

68.

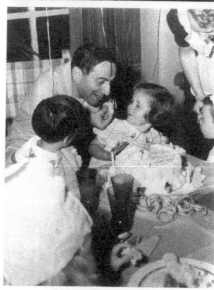

(ABOVE) While recuperating from his heart attack, Lubitsch, accompanied by his nurse (left) and his beautiful confidante Mary Loos (right), poses for a gag photo on the Santa Monica pier.

(MIDDLE RIGHT AND BOTTOM) Lubitsch's devotion to his daughter Nicola was a constant in his later years.

69.

A greatly aged Lubitsch in the midst of a severe angina attack at the
Academy Awards ceremony, six months before his death.

Lubitsch never tries to make the characters conventionally warm or likable. At one point, Lily tells Madame Colet that her mother is dead. "That's the trouble with mothers," Colet responds. "First you get to like them. Then they die." Gaston orders "deep red roses" for Mariette as a parting gift, but has them put on her tab. The characters' heartlessness is part of their charm. They may lie, but never to each other; unlike Giron, they're not hypocrites.

Trouble in Paradise is perhaps Lubitsch's clearest statement yet on the tenuous nature of romantic relationships, and on the necessity of variation and some gentle mutual deceit to stave off lethargy and boredom. It's a dazzling Möbius strip of erotic allusion, genial irony and dégagé visual lyricism and elegance. There's self-consciousness in the characters—their arch sophistication is always poised on the precipice of parody, yet never quite tumbles in—but there is no self-righteousness. Gaston may be cheerfully amoral, but he never mocks the pretensions and the vanities of the rich while he's stealing from them, because what he really wants is to live like them. It's nice work if you can get it.

At the same time, Lubitsch creates a world that, underneath the glowing surfaces of Hans Dreier's furniture and sets, is recognizably real. People steal while pretending to be honest, they fret more over a lost handbag than over the starving people they pass on the way to work. These ironies are never stated directly, but they're there nonetheless.

The rate of consumption of Madame Colet and her friends is so spectacular—and so casual—that Lubitsch's clear implication is that they deserve to be robbed. What sets Madame Colet apart is that she seems to realize it. That a man like Gaston Monescu is doing the robbing is merely poetic justice. Although without work or training, his industriousness marks him as their (im)moral superior. Equally ruthless, but swifter, more elegant, he is one of them.

The elegance that cascades off the screen in the Lubitsch films of the Paramount era, and their very specific texture, is partially the result of two men besides Ernst: the designer Hans Dreier and the costumer Travis Banton. Ernst had learned the importance of homogeneity in a theatrical presentation from Max Reinhardt, and had even hired Ernst Stern, Reinhardt's designer at the Deutsches Theater, to design several of his most visually inventive films. To achieve the look he wanted in his American films, it isn't surprising that Lubitsch would once again turn to his countrymen.

Hans Dreier was born in Bremen in 1885, and served with the Lancers during World War I. After the war, he joined UFA as an assistant designer, amassing thirty credits in the next four years for such designers as Erno Metzner and Paul Leni, later a brilliant director and intimate friend of Lubitsch's.

In 1924, Lubitsch brought Dreier to Paramount to design *Forbidden Paradise,* and the designer quickly demonstrated his great gift for subtle atmospherics. Although he rose to be the head of the Paramount art department by 1932—and would hold that position until his retirement in 1950—unlike his counterparts at RKO or MGM, Dreier continued to design specific films, among them most of the von Sternberg classics and many of Lubitsch's major efforts, including *Trouble in Paradise.*

Dreier's work consistently reflects a refined European sensibility and a belief in aesthetic unity. His designs for *Trouble in Paradise* are a stunning amalgam of art deco and Bauhaus and, in fact, Dreier used some of his own Bauhaus furniture on the sets. Personally, Dreier was charming, and he maintained the man/animal bond formed during his military service by owning a horse ranch in suburban Northridge. He had, however, a different face at work.

"Hans Dreier," remembered Boris Leven, "was a tall man, whose posture was ramrod-straight, a real military bearing . . . And he ran the Art Department at Paramount—where I began my movie career in 1933— as a kind of military hierarchy. You'd spend so many years as a private—a draftsman; then you'd become a corporal—an assistant art director; and so on."

"[He was] a good teacher," said Robert Clatworthy, who trained under Dreier and went on to design *Psycho* and win an Oscar for *Ship of Fools.* "Not only of work but of conduct—of discipline and responsibility . . . He really ran the department . . . it was punctuality, discipline. He was a taskmaster."

For Lubitsch, a set was much more than a backdrop before which the actors said their lines; a set was the frame for the picture, and it needed to reflect the subtext of the movie, what it was about. For Lubitsch, sets were a metaphor for the characters that inhabited them. Dreier responded by devising a rich, opulent, luminous surface that became the Paramount house style throughout the decade. As John Baxter wrote, "if Metro's films had polish, Paramount films had a glow. The best of them seem gilded . . . as rich and brocaded as a Renaissance tapestry."

Travis Banton was head costume designer at Paramount from 1928 to 1938. A heavy drinker, Banton's idea of a good time was to board a streetcar and ride all the way to the end of the line and back again, while Edith Head, his frantic assistant, would follow in an auto, desperately trying to ascertain which car he was in so she could lure him back to the office.

One of the main advantages Banton had was the quality of the actresses he had to dress. Paramount stars like Marlene Dietrich, Carole Lombard, and Miriam Hopkins had fabulous bodies. Over at Metro, the equally gifted Adrian had to engage in deceptions with oddly shaped women like Norma Shearer, Greta Garbo, and Joan Crawford. Crawford, for instance, had a large head, big shoulders, a large chest and rib cage, but was actually rather skinny from the waist down. Her asymmetrical body meant that she usually had to be photographed in medium shots and close-ups, which, of course, worked to her dramatic advantage.

For all of his brilliance, Banton did not do hats; on Lubitsch's production of *Desire,* a bunch of Lily Daché hats were brought to the set and Dietrich simply tried them on to see what she liked, without any particular discussion from anybody else.

Of the Paramount directors, only von Sternberg would involve himself heavily in the choice of costumes. In the early 1930s, the choice was largely up to the actress; much of the time, an actress would show up on the set wearing something the director had never seen. But as the decade wore on, the informality gradually dissipated; highly impressionistic costume sketches gave way to very specific drawings, and everybody at the studio tended to get more involved with costumes, which irritated pros like Banton.

In 1938, earning $1,000 a week, Banton's contract came up for renewal. Paramount, just getting out from under the sagging box office of Marlene Dietrich (temporary) and Mae West (permanent), was emphasizing new stars like Dorothy Lamour and Shirley Ross, people in whom Banton was frankly uninterested. He asked for $1,500 a week, was refused, and, after a brief fling with free-lancing, went over to Fox.

Filling out the Lubitsch frame were the miraculous character actors who remained a constant even when the stars varied; the gracious, serene, befuddled Charlie Ruggles and the nervous ditherer Edward Everett Horton. Horton discovered that Lubitsch always had the actor in mind when he was writing the part. Horton particularly liked the fact that Ernst insisted that the actors rehearse for an entire week on the sets before beginning photography. "No matter what you thought or what you wanted to do, Mr. Lubitsch had gone over it in his mind and had come to a conclusion," remembered Horton. "Just as soon as you could put yourself *en rapport* with him, you were very happy.

"He knew . . . actors very well," concluded Horton, "and he wanted something from them that even they didn't know they had. He was a genius, you see."

c h a p t e r   f i v e

Above all . . . power lies in seeming.

— a .   b a r t l e t t   g i a m a t t i

There is Paramount Paris and Metro Paris, and of course the real Paris. Paramount's is the most Parisian of all.

— e r n s t   l u b i t s c h

By the time they made *Trouble in Paradise,* Lubitsch and Raphaelson had an entirely secure working relationship. Once, when B. P. Schulberg, Paramount's head of production, asked him why he was shooting a scene a certain way, Ernst replied that he couldn't exactly remember, but "It is in the script, which is good enough for me. If I didn't have a good reason, it would not have been in there when Sam Raphaelson was writing it in the first place."

Yet it was during the writing of *Trouble in Paradise* that Raphaelson ran up against the tough, canny businessman that enabled Lubitsch to flourish amongst the carnivores.

On both *Broken Lullaby* and *The Smiling Lieutenant,* Raphaelson had worked with writer Ernest Vajda, the old hand who was, remembered Raphaelson, "one of the most charming fakes I've ever known." But Vajda was getting $2,500 a week while Raphaelson was doing all the work for $750 a week. Raphaelson waited for Lubitsch to stick up for him, to support the writer in his fight for more money. Nothing.

Jed Harris made Raphaelson an offer that would have meant the writer would have to return to New York, but Lubitsch asked him not to go. Raphaelson brought up the money question again and Lubitsch promised to take care of it "to your complete satisfaction." With that assurance, Raphaelson stayed to write *Trouble in Paradise.*

After a few weeks, and no raise, Raphaelson put a memo about the matter on Lubitsch's desk. Dated April 2, 1932, the memo outlines the problem. "I want either $1,250 a week for a year, or a contract to do three pictures a year at $15,000 per picture, in ten week periods . . . I feel, simply, that if you, as a director, need me on your picture, I am worth $15,000 against the budget. If you, as a director, do not need me $15,000 worth, then I suspect you don't need me at all. I know, at any rate, that I am not indispensable to you—that you can make as fine pictures without me as with me. The question is, can you replace me at $15,000—or would you [rather] have some other other person at $15,000 than me. Or would the studio. That is a pure business question and, I think, a very easy one to decide . . .

"If I am necessary as a writer to the extent of the figures I have named, then I ask only one thing of you as a friend rather than as writer to director: I ask that you present my problem to Mr. Schulberg rather than I. This is because I am a very bad representative of myself with Mr. Schulberg."

Lubitsch's response was, precisely, nothing.

"I couldn't have been more bitter, more resentful," remembered Raphaelson. "When we had lunch at the Santa Monica house, I had very little to say. I didn't go out of my way to be unpleasant, but I just wasn't buddies."

One day, Lubitsch asked Raphaelson if he wanted to go for a walk after lunch. Raphaelson refused. Lubitsch persisted in asking what was wrong and Raphaelson finally told him.

"Look . . . you know damn well you voluntarily got me into this. You promised me things. I put it in a memo . . . You have done nothing. I'm getting this salary and I'm doing the work that before you paid at least $2,500 plus $750 a week for. Let's drop it because it's too late now. If you go to the studio and say, 'Raphaelson has got me over a barrel, I'm in the middle of writing a picture,' I'll be a heel and you'll be the noble guy. I don't want you to be the noble guy, so forget it."

Lubitsch's head drooped, then he said "It's the first time in my life I ever have to acknowledge I have been unjust to somebody." Lubitsch said he would go to the studio, but Raphaelson refused to allow that. Raphaelson wrote *Trouble in Paradise* for $750 a week. The next time Lubitsch asked for Raphaelson, the writer informed the studio that the price was

Jeanette MacDonald and Maurice Chevalier in Lubitsch's musical masterpiece, The Merry Widow.

$2,500 a week. After some initial haggling, Raphaelson's price was met, a tacit acknowledgment by Lubitsch of the writer's worth.

In time, Raphaelson would witness other instances of this behavior. A few years later, Lubitsch wanted to buy the Hungarian play on which he and Raphaelson would base *The Shop Around the Corner*. Rather than bid on it under his own name, which would have driven the price up, Lubitsch used the agent Charles Feldman as a front, eventually paying about a fourth of what the play would have cost him otherwise.

"Lubitsch told me about that with a grin," remembered Raphaelson. "After a while, I could see how Lubitsch couldn't escape that kind of dealing . . . [but] I think you lose something as a person."

To the end of his life, Raphaelson wondered about these episodes, circling around how a basically warm, affectionate man could engage in psychologically debilitating financial subterfuges with people who were, at the very least, close collaborators and, at the most, good friends. "My guess would be that he was a cynical man, bred in a hard school . . . I think his attitude was 'On the day when Rafe quits, that's when I'll have to do something about it, and I will.' It may very well have been that he hated admitting that anyone [was] valuable to him."

"I don't believe he had any friendship that was more than what we had. I [just] think he was a completely politic man—a very decent one, as they go. I think he caught the hang of me and therefore was able, at certain times, to take advantage of me. He saw these frail postures that I took. He didn't deliberately, cruelly move in on them; he just didn't do anything about them until he had to."

On October 7, 1932, *Trouble in Paradise* was previewed in Hollywood and met with an enthusiastic response. Lubitsch thoughtfully wired congratulations to Raphaelson, who was back in New York. Once again he attempted to smooth over the rupture caused by Raphaelson's low salary by telling him he was looking forward to their next collaboration. A month later, when the film opened in New York, the critical reaction proved astonishingly obtuse. The New York *Herald Tribune* said that "it is far from being the best Lubitsch . . . average run-of-the mill for this extraordinary technician." *Photoplay,* as was not infrequent in these years, was more prescient, calling it "one of Lubitsch's best productions."

Although Lubitsch instinctively sensed the value of *Trouble in Paradise* ("As for pure style, I have done nothing better or as good as *Trouble in Paradise,*" he wrote in 1947), Raphaelson, as always the psychological realist, wasn't so sure. "It was just another job and it never occurred to me that I was making history," he told Robert Carringer in 1973. "I much more enjoyed and had much more respect for *Heaven Can Wait . . .* and *Shop Around the Corner* [which] dealt with sentiment, with emotions, with backgrounds, clerks—their slavishness, the tensions between them, their insecurity, romance on a level that I felt and respected . . . that had more body to me. I cared more about those people than I did about the people in *Trouble in Paradise.* I thought the people in *Trouble in Paradise* were just puppets."

Perhaps. But never have puppets been so brilliantly carved, so fault-lessly manipulated.

The omnibus film *If I Had a Million* has become justly celebrated for the W. C. Fields sequence (written by Joseph L. Mankiewicz) and Lubitsch's episode, which encompasses exactly eleven shots and an apotheosis of the director's point of view. An envelope bequeathing him a million dollars lands on the desk of clerk Charles Laughton. He brushes it aside to finish writing a number in a column (you can almost hear Lubitsch thinking, "Yah, that will keep it real . . .").

The clerk opens the envelope, reads it, and looks up with a completely dead nonreaction. He rises, goes out the office door, trudges up two flights of stairs and through a series of doors: "Secretary to the President," then "Private Secretary to the President," and so on.

Finally, he arrives at the sanctum sanctorum and opens the door.

"Mr. Brown?" he inquires, just before blowing a glorious raspberry.

All this takes about ninety seconds and one spoken sentence, but it is ninety seconds of perfection, Lubitsch's world view in microcosm.

"It didn't take more than two days to shoot," remembered Artie Jacobson, the assistant director on Lubitsch's segment. "He walked on the set and said, 'Everybody read the script? Anybody got any ideas? Let's hear them.' It could have been anybody, the guy that served the donuts. It was fantastic, wonderful moviemaking, all business with a great sense of humor. All he had time for was to make pictures."

As good as the episode is, it wasn't Ernst's first idea. The late writer John Bright, who wrote the George Raft segment of the film, recalled that Lubitsch's initial notion would have involved Marlene Dietrich and Lubitsch's return to acting.

The proposed scene opened with Dietrich in bed, angrily waiting for her errant husband to return home. Lubitsch comes home drunk and struggles to undress himself. As he comes to bed and makes a woozy pass at her, she pretends to be asleep. After he falls asleep and begins to snore, she gets out of bed and begins rummaging through his clothes, discovering the check for a million dollars. Her attitude instantly changes. She gets into bed, leans over his prone form, and says to him ardently, "Darling!" Fade out.*

201

*Another idea that Ernst tossed out at this time involved the Marx Brothers. The film would begin by following a man climbing stairs and going into a room. His wife is lying in bed and Groucho is hiding inside a closet. "Believe it or not,"

Even aside from the Lubitsch contribution, the episodic *If I Had a Million* is, for the most part, a very good picture, a trenchant pre-Production Code examination of a society made up predominantly of outcasts and losers overwhelmed by social oppression, as in the episode of the whore who, with her million dollars, rejects the brutish attentions of a sailor and elects to sleep alone.

The idea that the basis for behavior can be economic as well as genetic seems as if it could derive from Lubitsch via Karl Marx, but the episode was indeed directed by the unsung Stephen Roberts. In addition to the nine episodes in the finished film, Paramount prepared two others that were, apparently, never shot; one, by Harvey Thew, involved a bankrupt millionaire who receives his check and promptly drops dead, and another, by Walter DeLeon, involved a happily married blue-collar couple who get their check and immediately launch into a series of pitched battles over money.

By this time Lubitsch's influence was pandemic in Hollywood, and especially at Paramount, where his elegant, understated, allusive manner had become the house style. Outside Hollywood, he had become a household name. In New York on January 16, 1934, the popular novelty/cabaret act The Yacht Club Boys recorded a song called "The Super-Special Picture of the Year" for Columbia records. Benny Goodman, at the time a popular session musician, does an unmistakable, stylish clarinet solo at both the beginning and end of the song, but that's not its primary fascination.

The song involves a complicated series of interchanges by the chorus and the soloist:

CHORUS: Attention, please, attention, we just came back from the Coast.
We brought a big director who is California's toast.
He came from Germany and Mr. Zukor brought him fame.
He went to Hollywood and revolutionized the game.

Groucho would say, "I'm waiting for a streetcar." At that moment, a streetcar would clang into the frame and Groucho would jump on as the streetcar rolled out of the scene. Although Lubitsch correctly grasped the essentially surrealistic, cartoonish basis of the Marxian character, Groucho didn't care for the material, and the fascinating prospect of Lubitsch directing the Marx Brothers never materialized.

He's the king of all directors, would you like to meet him now?
Mr. Lubitsch, Mr Lubitsch, Mr. Lubitsch take a bow . . .
SOLO: . . . I'll show you how I make them, let's pretend this is a scene.
CHORUS: Everybody on the set, Mr. Lubitsch has begun.
SOLO: Lights, action, camera, we are shooting Number Vun.
I want a thousand airplanes to crack up in the sky,
To begin to shoot the picture as the pilots fall and die.
CHORUS: If you kill a thousand pilots, Mr. Zukor will get sore.
SOLO: The heck with him, I'm Lubitsch, kill me eighty pilots more . . .

One of The Yacht Club Boys does an amazingly accurate imitation of Lubitsch, right down to the timbre of his voice, the inimitable Berlin accent, and his gung-ho performing persona. Indeed, if it wasn't for the fact that a film survives of the group performing the song, an unwary listener could take the solo artist for Lubitsch himself.

Aside from humorous, public tributes to his bouncy personality, Ernst was also proving his efficiency. He had contributed some supervision to *If I Had a Million,* whose effortless production and low cost of $299,671 meant that it couldn't help but be profitable, thus recouping some of the ground lost by the expensive failure of *Broken Lullaby* and the overruns on *One Hour with You.*

The dispute with George Cukor that forced Lubitsch to take over *One Hour with You* meant that he had to pass up what he had planned as his next picture: *Love Me Tonight.* Nevertheless, Paramount was determined that *Love Me Tonight* would be made on the Lubitsch model.

While Ernst was in postproduction on *One Hour with You,* Sam Raphaelson began work on an early draft of *Love Me Tonight* with Rouben Mamoulian, who had taken over the project. But Raphaelson and Mamoulian didn't get along, and he left the picture. Mamoulian hired a succession of other writers and made what one critic partial to Mamoulian called "The Lubitsch film that Lubitsch was always trying to pull off but never quite did."

Mamoulian opens the film as the city slowly awakens to random morning sounds that become syncopated rhythms, which in turn become music. The director is helped by a largely wonderful Rodgers and Hart score, and he adds his usual (in this period) flash and filigree to the material. The first half-hour or so is a delight, buttressed by Myrna Loy as a frankly horny denizen of a stone castle populated by the aged and infirm, and the sight of C. Aubrey Smith singing and dancing.

In contrast to his later films, which often settle into a strenuous, slightly arty falsity, Mamoulian keeps *Love Me Tonight* afloat with some genuine fizz, as when Chevalier sings "Isn't It Romantic?" while reflected in a three-part mirror, and Mamoulian pans from mirror to mirror with each verse change.

But Mamoulian goes overboard and ends up imitating not Lubitsch but René Clair. The three fairy godmothers/witches are three too many, and speeding up the action so the actors move like the Keystone Cops, followed by slow motion, has the effect of yanking the audience out of the movie by screaming into their ears "Aren't I witty? Isn't this charming?"

Lubitsch, on the other hand, nudges, whispers. At his best, he directs comedy as if it were a musical *(Trouble in Paradise)* and a musical as if it were a comedy/drama *(The Merry Widow)*. While he never works terribly hard at making us suspend disbelief, irony and distance are achieved by a complicitous smile, a wink. "This," he says to the audience with the genial smile of the master confectioner, "is artificial, it is candy, and we both know it. But no one can make it like I can."

For the first five years or so of his career, Mamoulian proved himself a brilliant magpie. In *Love Me Tonight,* he takes Lubitsch's basic ideas and attitudes and smooths them out, just as, a few years later in *The Song of Songs,* he would take von Stroheim's corrosive, immensely strong and moving *The Wedding March,* do a light rewrite changing the milieu and the character of the swinish fiancé from a poor man to a rich man, and make a far more commercial if lightweight carbon.

But these are adept impressions of other movies, ersatz, and they lack a sense of authentic personality, as well as any sense of when enough is enough. *Love Me Tonight* may indeed be, as one critic has suggested, "one long unbroken production number," but 96-minute production numbers can be very tiring.

As *If I Had a Million* opened in New York on December 2, 1932, Ernst was arriving back in Berlin for what would prove to be his last visit to his hometown. The ostensible reason was to attend the Berlin premiere of *Trouble in Paradise,* but Ernst really just wanted to visit his old stomping grounds. He called his sisters from the boat; to forestall displays of the usual contentious Lubitsch temperaments, he told them in advance that "I want the sisters and children should be in peace together."

As usual, he stayed at the Adlon, and invited the extended family to dine with him in the hotel's elegant dining room. He never discussed show business or, for that matter, business of any kind. His two sisters asked him personal questions about old girlfriends like Hedy, or old wives like Leni. "Ernst, are you a millionaire?" was one teasing question, which made him laugh uproariously.

On December 14, Secretary of State Otto Meissner threw a party for him, much to the worried displeasure of Frau Meissner, who spent most of the night worrying that those invitees who were members of the Nazi party would look askance at celebrating a Jew who had bailed out of Germany a decade before. As it happened, Lubitsch turned on his considerable charm and defused any potential unpleasantness.

Lubitsch, however, was far from oblivious to what was going on. During the party, the society reporter for *Vossische Zeitung* asked Lubitsch why he no longer worked in Germany. "That's finished," he replied. "Nothing good is going to happen here for a long time." Although Lubitsch's friends never thought of him as being politically aware, he had sensed the prevailing Fascist winds; six weeks later, on January 30, 1933, at eleven o'clock in the morning, Adolf Hitler was appointed Chancellor of the German Reich by the senile President Hindenburg.

While in Germany, Lubitsch met Greta Koerner, the twenty-six-year-old daughter of a Vienna brewer. According to Evie Bettelheim-Bentley, Lubitsch's niece, "she was well known as an adventuress, a lady of the world, very beautiful." Maybe, maybe not. Lubitsch's physical taste in women was usually admirable, but surviving pictures of Greta Koerner indicate either an unphotogenic face or a lapse of taste. In any case, Lubitsch was swept off his feet; Koerner became his companion for the six-week stay. After he arrived back in America, he began pelting her with cables, letters, and gifts. But when Koerner arrived in America in December 1933, bearing Lubitsch's letters and an aggrieved expression, the director responded with embarrassment and mortification. "He didn't know how to get rid of her," remembered Evie.

There was only one reliable way. Pay her off.

Anita Loos was in Irving Thalberg's office one day during the preparation for *The Merry Widow* when Ernst came in chafing about being blackmailed for what Loos remembered as $50,000. "What's in those letters?" asked Thalberg. Ernst handed over some copies. After briefly perusing the contents, Thalberg handed them back and said, "Look, my friend, if you can keep those out of print for $50,000, you've got a bargain. Grab it!"

Money exchanged hands; somehow, the newspapers got wind of the affair and bruited about the absurd figure of $200,000. It was another public sexual embarrassment.

Early in 1933, Lubitsch was ensconced at the Ambassador Hotel in New York working with Ben Hecht on the script of *Design for Living,* his next picture. Paramount had paid $50,000 apiece to Noël Coward, for his play, and Hecht, for his dialogue. Lubitsch's first choice for the adaptation had been Sam Raphaelson, but he had turned him down, partly because he was still upset over the salary dispute, partly because he had grown slightly bored with Lubitsch's choice in material.

"I felt, 'What the hell can I do to add to Noël Coward?' " he remembered. "I was fed up with the whole milieu by then. I felt that he too should be, which was a little silly."

While Lubitsch was writing the script with Ben Hecht, he received a phone call from Max Reinhardt's son, Gottfried. "It was a very bad year," remembered Reinhardt, "the worst year of the Depression, nothing to do in the theater and my English was not too good. There was no possibility of a job. I heard that he was in town and I knew that he had acted under my father. In fact, my father had wanted to take me to the Berlin premiere of *Trouble in Paradise,* to get us acquainted, but I didn't go."

Lubitsch received the younger Reinhardt half-dressed and half-shaven. "You're early," Lubitsch said. "Well, come in. How's your father?"

As it happened, Max Reinhardt was not doing very well and, like many German artists and intellectuals, was about to do much worse. Lubitsch told the younger Reinhardt that he could come to work for him in Hollywood but that he would not be able to pay him anything. " 'There is a crisis in Hollywood,' he told me. Later, I was to learn that there is always a crisis in Hollywood. But I figured that by assisting him I could use it as a stepping stone, and that proved correct. I borrowed some money from friends and went west.

"He never believed that I had no money. For him, Max Reinhardt was, well, Max Reinhardt. After *Design for Living* was finally over, and we had become friends, I confronted him and told him the truth, that my father had lost every penny. I needed a job, so he picked up the phone and got me a job.

"He was actually a very nice man to work with, but you couldn't work for him because he didn't really need anybody. You worked under him. He was his own producer, and a perfect producer in that he never changed a line of a script. He didn't even change a camera angle, and he stuck to the budget. He was, in that respect, very responsible. He really did everything himself. He even cut the film himself; he may have been the only director who did that. I never met any director who actually went into the cutting room with scissors and cut their own films but Lubitsch."

Lubitsch was invariably kindly toward young Reinhardt, but one time his ambivalent feelings about Gottfried's father slipped out. Lubitsch and Gottfried were attending a lecture by Emil Ludwig at the Hillcrest Country Club. Although usually a light drinker, Lubitsch had a few glasses of whiskey and raised his glass to Gottfried with a sardonic toast: "To all the parts your father never gave me!"

Years later, Gottfried would claim that "My father did him a great favor never to give him those parts, otherwise he might never have gone into pictures. You see, the top people might have taken jobs in films but they did not make films their business."

At the same time, a few years later, when Warner Bros. announced that Max Reinhardt would direct a film of *A Midsummer Night's Dream* for them, a cynical guest at a Hollywood party was predicting disaster when an enraged Lubitsch turned on him. It was too bad, said Lubitsch, if a Hollywood that was swimming in riches could not afford to take a chance on the most imaginative and daring director in the world.

But *Dream* was lavishly budgeted and lavishly promoted; both the critics and, more predictably, the Warner brothers, were underwhelmed. The second picture under Reinhardt's contract was never made, and he settled into an uncomfortable, often financially perilous old age on the fringes of the theater.

"Reinhardt came to America when he was what, seventy?" commented Leon Askin. "It was such a different world. In Europe, the stage is a church. Once, during a rehearsal, an actor forgot to take his hat off and Reinhardt took it and threw it twenty yards. In Europe, nobody is allowed to eat on stage. These are small, little things, but they all contribute, and it is not so easy for an old man that is used to these things and so much else besides to adapt."

Lubitsch would back up his respect for Reinhardt with actions in 1942, when a desperate Reinhardt was attempting to launch a show on Broadway. Lubitsch cosigned a loan that enabled his destitute mentor to at least have lodgings worthy of his creative, if not financial, station.

The writing of *Design for Living* was initially hampered by Ben Hecht's studied pose, which combined the worst characteristics of a grumpy, high-priced, bang-it-out hack with those of the spoiled *artiste*. Lubitsch would later explain to Sam Raphaelson that "Ve vasn't used to each udder. I'd say to him, 'Look, de vay I usually vork, Ben, is ve get together, ve meet in the morning at a reasonable hour, ve have a secretary, and ve vork together.' "

Hecht's response was that he wasn't about to have anybody, even Lubitsch, tell him how to write his script. "I go home and I write the stuff and I bring it to you. Then, if you don't like it, we fight it out."

Lubitsch provisionally agreed. Two days later, Hecht returned with the opening of the film. "You know," Lubitsch told Raphaelson, "how can a man, in two days . . . do anything . . . anyvay I vas interested, so I read it and I say, 'Now come on, Ben, for God's sake, you don't call dis writing?' "

Hecht, presumably flabbergasted, and Lubitsch proceeded to "talk a little bit more." Soon, they were both getting together at nine every morning, in Lubitsch's usual working method. Sometime later, when Hecht made a suggestion Lubitsch didn't like, he flung his cigar into a wastebasket and said "That's the kind of suggestion grammar school children send in by mail."

The truth is that Hecht and Lubitsch weren't very well matched; Hecht once snarled to Miriam Hopkins that "If he grabs me once more to show me how Freddie March is supposed to embrace you, I'll turn pansy."

Years later, Lubitsch, accompanied by Raphaelson, ran into Hecht on the Fox lot. After a congenial exchange, they parted. Lubitsch turned to Raphaelson and said, "If dis man vould put half as much energy into writing a good script as he does into bamboozling everybody, he vould be a really great writer."

Lubitsch enjoyed making *Design for Living* and would always feel that it was sadly underrated because of an understandable critical bias toward the play and Noël Coward's lofty theatrical credentials. But the experience was not equally pleasant for everybody. During production, Miriam Hopkins, who had just ended her affair with King Vidor, would regularly turn up at Lubitsch's side and interrupt whoever he was talking to by saying "Leave them alone and amuse me, Ernst."

Truthfully, the film presented some serious problems. The budget was a very trim $563,000; once the decision to rewrite Coward had been made, Ernst then had to cast the picture. His first choice for the female lead was always Miriam Hopkins, but he wanted to star Ronald Colman and Leslie Howard opposite her. Colman, just escaping from his Goldwyn contract, was too expensive, and Leslie Howard didn't want to be placed in the position of being compared to either Noël Coward or Alfred Lunt.

Once Paramount contractee Fredric March was set for the part of the playwright, Lubitsch felt sufficiently freed up budgetarily to hire Douglas Fairbanks, Jr., for the part of the artist. But Fairbanks contracted pneumonia, and Ernst stunned everybody at Paramount by casting Gary Cooper, whose facility with dialogue had not been firmly established.

At the beginning of production, Lubitsch assembled his company. "The critics will not like our picture," he told them. "They will say we have ruined Noël Coward's play, and it is true that our picture will be quite different. But the people who do not read reviews or care about them will love it, and Noël Coward means nothing to most of them. Gary Cooper means something to them, and they will be happy to see that he is an accomplished light comedian."

An understandably nervous Cooper began production by rushing through his dialogue. Lubitsch took him aside and told him that "You play too feverishly, Gary. Don't anguish over your work, take your time. Look at Fredric; you can pause here and there. It shows me your value."

When the film was released in November 1933, Hecht wrote a typically overblown essay that contained flyspecks of accurate observation amid the oratory. Hecht noted Lubitsch's occasional harshness in judging the work of others, but also said that "If you sneer back at Mr. Lubitsch for anything he does he takes to his bed and is ill for a day . . . On such occasions he has to be coaxed out of his bed by questions about his early life as an actor . . . He is very modest but stubborn."

Gottfried Reinhardt agreed with the latter observation, noting that, although not egocentric in a conventional way, Lubitsch "was very sure of himself as a person. I never saw him apologetic, for instance. He was sure of his gifts."

In their script of *Design for Living*, Hecht and Lubitsch retained the central situation of Coward's play while altering its construction. The primary difference in terms of plot is that Coward's play begins when the girl leaves one artist for another, while Lubitsch includes all the "backstory," beginning the film when the three people first meet. (The film is slightly more than half over when it reaches the point at which the play begins.) The play involves only six long scenes, the film numerous short scenes. About a third of the play's scenes are included in the film, although each is seriously compressed.

Coward's characters, genial, monied Continental snobs who believe that the only sin is to lack taste or be a bore, are replaced by impoverished Americans with egalitarian attitudes and snappy patter—presumably, one of the reasons Lubitsch hired Hecht. They believe that unconventionality is the way to live because it's more fun, whereas Coward's characters live the way they do because it sets them apart from the lower classes.

Without really meaning to, Lubitsch was constructing a rough outline for the screwball comedies that would sweep the country in the next year or so. It was not a genre whose fullest flowerings he would ever have much sympathy for; too brassy, about ego and competitiveness more than sex.

Although Lubitsch came in for much knee-jerk criticism for daring to alter Noël Coward's play, both at the time and later, to him it seemed like he was only following his basic tenets of good picture-making. "When there is nothing happening between characters, and nothing needs to be talked about *now,* the camera must supply action, the action of their minds, faces, other people they are thinking about. And, especially, I think, the cinema should not talk about events in the past. That is why I have changed completely the beginning of the stage play. On the stage it was dull. One was told where they met, what they had done for many years, how they had loved. I must show these things, but in their proper order.

"The cinema should have nothing to do with the imperfect tense . . . film dialogue should deal with what is instead of what was." To Sidney Skolsky, Lubitsch eloquently stated, "I don't believe in reproducing a play on the screen exactly as it was done on the stage. Anyone can make a carbon copy. Carbons are always dull."

Lubitsch opens his film of *Design for Living* on a train. Two exuberantly awful *artistes,* George (Gary Cooper) and Tom (Fredric March), are asleep. Enter Gilda (Miriam Hopkins), who proceeds to sketch them. As if rewriting Noël Coward wasn't audacious enough, Lubitsch plays the first five minutes of the film either in dead silence or in French, without subtitles.

Lubitsch and Hecht announce their deviation from Coward almost immediately. "Don't let's be delicate,' says Tom. "Let's be crude and objectionable . . . delicacy is the banana peel under the feet of truth."

The marriage between Lubitsch's inferential visual style and Hecht's sonorous raucousness is not always comfortable. The lines have the usual Hecht touch, crinkly cellophane aphorisms that make every character sound like a literate but childish narcissist fending off self-awareness. Mostly, the words seem too harsh for the characters, not to mention the director.

Lubitsch even allows Hecht to introduce virtually the only plot Hecht ever had: a platonic love affair between men that uneasily expands to include a third party. While Hecht's other variations on this theme (such as *The Front Page* and *Gunga Din*) end with the men pushing out the intruder and once again joining their mutual battle, Lubitsch tempers that with his innate romanticism.

To forestall the obvious sexual charge that's in the air, Gilda vows to keep everything nonsexual and become a matron, as well as patron, of the arts. "We're going to concentrate on work. Your work." In short order, she's turned Tom into a successful London playwright ("I'm sure you'll adore it," says Gilda to a producer played by the eternally limp-wristed Franklin Pangborn. "It's a woman's play") and George into an in-demand society artist.

But while Tom is launching his show in London, she can no longer resist Gary Cooper's astonishing art deco beauty. "It's true we have a gentleman's agreement," she says, lying languidly across his bed. "But unfortunately, I'm no gentleman."

Once again, Lubitsch pays tribute to Chaplin. Gary Cooper throws a letter out a window as if he couldn't care less about the contents. Later, he rushes out and hungrily retrieves it, just as Edna Purviance had done with Adolphe Menjou's gift of a necklace in *A Woman of Paris*.

Caught between two swooningly attractive men, Hopkins deludes herself into thinking the middle ground is the place to be; she marries Lubitsch's favorite eunuch, Edward Everett Horton.

"Do you love me?" he asks.

"People should never ask that question on their wedding night," she tartly replies. "It's either too late or too early."

With Gilda caught in a passionless marriage, Lubitsch takes the opportunity to dramatize the conflict between messy but exuberant nonconformity and the living death of stuffy social correctness. With little warning, George and Tom appear at her door, indulge in some graceful physical clowning, and spirit Gilda off, with all three lovers once again vowing to keep another highly unlikely gentleman's agreement.

While *Design for Living* lacks the clockwork logic of Lubitsch's best work, and nobody would make a claim for it as being among his higher achievements, it's far from the runt of the Lubitsch litter. The essential problem is the misalliance between Ernst's irony, Coward's urbanity, and Hecht's coarse clownishness.

The critics reacted pretty much as Lubitsch had predicted. Jack Alicoate in *Film Daily* seemed at cross-purposes, first saying that the play "has fallen victim to the celebrated Lubitsch touch . . . in place of thin ice we now have fields of sterilized spring flowers," but concluding his notice by paraphrasing the company's motto, saying that *"Design for Living* is immense and should have no trouble in clicking. It's a Paramount picture and one of the best in town."

Richard Watts, Jr., in the New York *Herald Tribune,* lacked any trace of boosterism. "The filmed *Design for Living,* if anything, [is] even more superficial than the original . . . You could hardly expect Mr. Cooper to be properly at home as a witty sophisticate, and I fear that he isn't."

Although financial information on individual Paramount releases of the period is fragmentary, it is obvious that Lubitsch was not scoring box-office triumphs. Take, for instance, Lubitsch's record during 1932. *Broken Lullaby* cost $890,000 and grossed only $815,000, posting a loss of $501,000. *One Hour with You* lost nearly $300,000. Finally, *Trouble in Paradise* grossed only $475,000 domestically, $45,000 less than it cost, for a net loss of $135,000 (which was probably made up in Europe). The only bright spot was *If I Had a Million,* which earned a profit of $65,000.

In short, within one year, Lubitsch lost Paramount, in round numbers, $870,000. He responded by retrenching; while von Sternberg was spending more than $800,000 on matchless exercises in exotic erotica like *Shanghai Express* and *The Scarlet Empress,* Lubitsch reduced his negative costs to an average of slightly more than $500,000 in the same period.

Still, the economic realities were dismal. How was it, then, that Lubitsch's power and prestige were never seriously threatened?

Partially, it was the times. In 1932, there were no hits at all in the film industry, and the years from 1932 to 1934 were the deepest depths of the Depression. George Schaefer, head of Paramount's distribution arm, wrote a memo late in 1932 articulating the problem. "Many of the important key situations throughout the country find it very difficult to do any downtown business. Chicago is simply deserted at night and in New York you are lucky to get three weeks on a [first] run picture at the Rivoli or Rialto. There is no such thing as a first run in Boston, Philadelphia, Pittsburgh or Washington . . . Neighborhood and suburban houses are cutting their prices fast, some of them going as low as 10 and 15 cents. My opinion is that you cannot stop that trend . . .

"The only out . . . is to make a severe cut in negative costs. I am as certain as I am of sitting here, that the time is past when outstanding pictures costing more than $500,000 can make a profit. I think that we have to get back to an average negative cost of $200,000 or $250,000, and that only when we have a picture like *A Farewell to Arms,* or a Chevalier or Dietrich, can we go to $500,000. Negatives costing $750,000 and $800,000 are out for many years to come."

Lubitsch, then, was insulated from the austerity by dint of the fact that he was one of the elite directors who made the Chevalier and Dietrich pictures. Each studio, then or now, aimed for variety in their release schedule. When a sophisticated comedy hits, it hits nicely, and Lubitsch was at the top of the list when it came to directors of sophisticated comedy.

Also, it's highly likely that the management of Paramount thought of Lubitsch as a prestige loss-leader, a critical caretaker. Because everybody knew there was no real money to be made, there was little at stake. Paramount had the small consolation of knowing that Lubitsch was making quality goods, even if buyers were not lined up outside the store.

"Lubitsch was cerebrally way beyond the ordinary director," remembered J. J. Cohn, general manager of Metro-Goldwyn-Mayer for years. "And the studios did respect talent. For instance, a lesser director might be paired off with an important producer. But someone like Lubitsch, he had his own unit at both Paramount and later at MGM."

"There is no question that he was treated specially," said Gottfried Reinhardt. "Partially because his films were more successful in Europe than in the U.S. European income was very important to the studios. But what also played a part was that he lent prestige. It is a mistaken idea that Hollywood in those days was only a commercial factory; they allowed themselves prestige and Lubitsch symbolized that. And he was reliable; once a budget was set, he didn't go over."

Also contributing was the fact that Paramount, more than any other studio in Hollywood, was a director's studio. Elite talent like DeMille, von Sternberg, and Lubitsch functioned as their own producers, without much interference from a centralized front office. Even directors on the tier beneath them—Wesley Ruggles, Norman Taurog or, somewhat later, Mark Sandrich—worked with a great deal of freedom.

"One time I was working with William Wellman," remembered Joe Youngerman. "He rehearsed the actors, then went and sat down to wait for the lighting. Fifteen minutes later, the cameraman comes to me and says 'Joe, we're ready.' I go tell Wellman and he says, 'Oh no, we're not ready. See that man standing at the door there? We're not ready until he gets off this stage.' The guy in the doorway was Sam Jaffe, the production manager of Paramount studios. Wellman would not shoot until he was gone."

But what might have been equally important was the fact that Lubitsch, alone among the upper echelon of directors who commanded respect, did not come on like a highbrow. To the European Jews that created and ran the movie business, he was a *Landsmann*. His homely looks, everpresent cigar, and bubbling humor made him seem unthreatening, one of their own, which entitled him to a far longer leash than a New York highbrow, even if that New York highbrow had been exhibiting precisely the same gourmet tastes by making precisely the same films.

While in New York in 1934, Lubitsch was the guest of honor at one of Elsa Maxwell's posh parties at the Waldorf Towers. Maxwell, a bovine, good-hearted creature, had promised a young, aspiring English actor named David Niven that she would introduce him to Lubitsch. Niven, as much of a naif as he was a sexual athlete, found himself standing next to a man he remembered as "a little dark man with a pale face, slicked down black hair and a huge cigar."

"Which is Lubitsch?" he asked.

"I am," said Lubitsch, as he moved away from yet another pursuer.

Another invitation came from George Gershwin, who was completing his opera *Porgy and Bess*. An inveterate appreciator of his own work, Gershwin played some of the music for Lubitsch, who responded with suggestions for the staging. The settings, he said, should be "just a bit off realism." To amplify the drama of the material, Lubitsch advised Gershwin that his director should make free use of lighting effects. Gershwin liked Lubitsch's ideas and, judging from photographs of the original production, used them.

Throughout this period, there is no record of any reaction from Lubitsch to the spreading squalor of the Depression. As sensitive as he was to individuals, he could be remarkably oblivious to the world stage. Adding to his imperviousness was his native caution, a survivor's instinct that was pandemic in Hollywood, even among the more enlightened members of the movie community.

In 1932, when Sergei Eisenstein was stranded in Mexico while filming *Que Viva Mexico!*, the editors of the magazine *Experimental Cinema* sent telegrams to the Secretary of Labor asking the government to grant

Eisenstein a temporary visa. Cables to enlist support were also sent to Lubitsch, Chaplin, von Sternberg, Douglas Fairbanks, Lewis Milestone, King Vidor, Irving Thalberg, and John Barrymore, among others. Only von Sternberg responded.

Ernst would invariably shy away from political involvement. In late 1935, twelve directors, including Henry King, William Wellman, Howard Hawks, Rouben Mamoulian, and Frank Borzage attended a meeting at the home of King Vidor for the purposes of forming the Screen Directors Guild, which was incorporated in January 1936. Although undoubtedly solicited—the support of a director as prestigious and trusted as he, would have been enormously helpful to the fledgling union—Lubitsch did not attend and took no particular part in Guild operations in the coming years. This may have been the result of an inherent solipsism similar to Chaplin's, who simply felt that he didn't need a union, or a function of the well-honed survivor's instincts that told this particular paying guest not to alienate his hosts.

Irving Thalberg had been mulling over a remake of *The Merry Widow* for years. It was no wonder, for *The Merry Widow* had been a success ever since its Vienna premiere in 1905. Even the 1925 MGM version directed by the defiantly uncommercial Erich von Stroheim had turned a clear profit of $758,000.

In the MGM script files at the University of Southern California there is a segment of a *Merry Widow* script by Harry Beaumont dated June 27, 1929. Another, uncredited script for a musical version was prepared in mid-1930, with different plot machinations and more musical numbers.

But MGM at this point was not well-stocked with musical performers, largely making do with falling stars like Ramon Novarro. Clearly, a production of *The Merry Widow* would require someone more serious than Novarro. So Thalberg, who had a superb eye for talent that had been misused or prematurely tossed aside by others, signed up Maurice Chevalier, who had been jettisoned by Paramount in the wake of the declining box office of the Lubitsch musicals.

But success, or the thought of working for Thalberg, had not relaxed Chevalier at all. One night at a party, Greta Garbo asked him if he knew how to swim. Yes, of course. "Then let's go for a dip in the ocean right now."

Chevalier drew back in horror. "But it's midnight. *Le Pacifique est glacial!*" Garbo walked away and never spoke to him again.

For his new picture, Chevalier wanted Grace Moore for his costar, but

Thalberg said that he wanted the Widow to be played by someone "extraordinary and beautiful and dynamic and unknown." Actually, he wanted the Widow to be played by Joan Crawford, who, in November and December 1933, was diligently taking voice lessons so she could clomp over Lehár the way she had clomped over Rodgers and Hart in *Dancing Lady.* Chevalier capitulated to Thalberg's wishes; his contract states that "His name and the name of Joan Crawford shall be displayed in type of the same size."

After feinting Chevalier out, Thalberg promptly signed Jeanette Mac-Donald for the part, sending Chevalier into a towering snit. "She was exquisite and talented," remembered Chevalier, "but we had already done three pictures together. Wasn't it time for each of us to have a new partner?" What Chevalier probably didn't know was that Thalberg had tried to sign MacDonald to a contract as early as January 1932, with one of the planned projects to be a production of *The Merry Widow* costarring Ramon Novarro. MacDonald, of course, was not ecstatic either; her opinion of Chevalier remained tart: "The fastest derriere pincher in Hollywood."

Thalberg put the project on the front burner, assigning writers as varied as Rowland Leigh, Vicki Baum, and even Ernst's ex-best friend Hans Kräly to the project. (Thalberg was insistent on devising an entirely new scenario in order to avoid paying royalties to Erich von Stroheim, who had authored the scenario of the 1925 version, on which he was a profit participant.)

Kräly's material was essentially a variation on the 1930 script, while Vicki Baum outlined a dramatic script that was neither comic nor musical in any sense. In December 1933, Anita Loos tried her hand at a scene in which Danilo tries to get Sonja to show him her face, and she responds by running rose thorns through his hands. It is the first sign of the picture that would become *The Merry Widow,* for by this time Lubitsch and Ernest Vajda were already hard at work.

Initially, Thalberg had intended the film to be directed by Sidney Franklin, an option that the producer must have kept in the back of his mind, for when the negotiations for Lubitsch's loan-out began, the director made demands that were unheard of for an MGM employee.

According to an MGM interoffice memo, "Mr. Lubitsch wanted a contract with the exact terms and conditions of his present contract with Paramount. Mr. Thalberg attempted to have Lubitsch agree to certain modifications including the main modification that our decision would be final.

"Mr. Thalberg's thought," says another memo, "is that we should, if legally consistent, draft the provisions in such a way that [Lubitsch] will not lose face and yet we would have the control that we desire."

Ultimately, Lubitsch refused to accept any provisions other than those of his Paramount contract. Mayer and Thalberg conferred, then capitulated. Among Lubitsch's contractual rights under his Paramount contract were the right to have sole charge of the entire film and to make whatever retakes he considered necessary. Ultimately, Lubitsch's contract for *The Merry Widow* stipulated "that no changes, interpolations, modifications, additions or eliminations of any kind shall be made in the negatives or positive prints of the photoplay," other than censorship cuts, after Lubitsch signed off the final print.

Furthermore, MGM agreed that no scenes from *The Merry Widow* could be utilized in any other film. These were provisions that, to Thalberg's mind, were anathema and his rightful responsibility. (Over at RKO, the young George Stevens was already proving to be so single-minded and contractually demanding that his bosses referred to him, with some exasperation, as "the young Lubitsch.")

Lubitsch signed to direct *The Merry Widow* on December 4, 1933. The contract mandated that he be paid $83,333.33 for 17⅓ weeks of work beginning December 4. If the film entailed work beyond 17⅓ weeks, he was to receive $1,000 a week for the next 4⅓ weeks. After May 3, 1934, MGM had to pay him $5,000 a week.

To add to his discontent over MacDonald, Chevalier was not thrilled to be working with Lubitsch again either. Information began leaking into the gossip columns that Chevalier didn't want to be directed by Lubitsch or act with MacDonald. None of the items were followed by denials from Chevalier.

Finally, rather obviously prompted by a Thalberg ultimatum, Chevalier issued a statement saying that he was delighted about everything. Lubitsch, who had not adopted a subservient posture with Negri and wasn't about to do it with Chevalier, responded by saying "I wish he had expressed the same views before, as it would have saved a great deal of embarrassment."

The Merry Widow would be their last picture together, to both men's evident relief. In time, Chevalier would become one of the few men that Lubitsch didn't even pretend to like; when the actor was accused of collaborating with the Germans during World War II, Lubitsch freely said that he had no doubt that the charges were true.

Now that he had the director he wanted, Thalberg set about trying to get him to work within the MGM system. Although Lubitsch's manner of scriptwriting was to enlist his chosen writers and then be left alone, Thalberg assigned Anita Loos to doctor the work of the official team of Ernest Vajda and Samson Raphaelson. Although he must have been fuming, Lubitsch gave Loos what she recalled as "grudging" acceptance, and the large number of script drafts and alternate versions of scenes attest to the fact that Thalberg was having his way with the writing process.

Thalberg told Loos about Lubitsch's tendency to neglect "the human element" in any given story. He told Loos that she was to keep an eye on his tendency to cut away from the lovers to a closing door or a pair of bedroom slippers, that the plot of *The Merry Widow* concerned the human heart far more than it did the MGM prop department.

Loos found that Lubitsch quickly reverted to form and became fascinated by the idea of the Widow having a pair of poodles, one black, one white. To divert his attention, she came up with a particularly unlikely if witty line of dialogue for Chevalier: "You have brought a ray of moonlight into my life!"

Sitting in the rushes with Thalberg, Loos's line was spoken. Thalberg winced and muttered, "There goes our love story." Loos didn't have the nerve to tell him she had written the line.

Although time has not dealt kindly with Jeanette MacDonald, largely because of her insufferably coy performances in the films she did with Nelson Eddy, stolid operettas that obliterated the considerable sexuality Lubitsch so charmingly displayed, she was one of the few actors Lubitsch considered a friend.

When working with Lubitsch, she tended to be docile, but the temperament that caused her to be known as "The Iron Butterfly" could not be completely banked. Lubitsch was particularly fond of a specific "soft" look in her eyes, and one sure way to achieve it was to upset her so she would begin to cry. His method of doing this was to storm at her after a take, shouting "That was terrible! Rotten!!" The genteel MacDonald would become upset and her eyes would well up, whereupon Lubitsch would yell gleefully, "She's crying, she's crying!"

"The day she comes in and won't cry, I feel defeated," Lubitsch would confess. Lubitsch believed MacDonald had grown as both actress and woman in the years since *The Love Parade*. "She was still an ingenue [then]," he would tell one writer. "She was very, very pretty and knew it. Her beauty and voice had given her some success on the stage, but she was undeveloped within. She did not make you feel." On *The Merry Widow,* making the audience feel was to be important.

MacDonald was not without weapons of her own, but Lubitsch was adept at turning them against her. Once, when Lubitsch ordered a retake, she threw down her script and stalked off the set. When the script girl went to pick up the script, Lubitsch forbade it, then threw five more scripts down on the floor and told the cast and crew to take a break.

After an hour, MacDonald came back on the set and sweetly asked "Shall we continue?" "When you pick up the scripts you threw down," said Lubitsch, lighting a cigar. MacDonald blushed, picked up the scripts, including the five she hadn't thrown, and shooting continued.

Maurice Chevalier was less temperamental, but he had one particular foible that Lubitsch delighted in tweaking: he was cheap, cheap beyond all imagining. Some mornings, Lubitsch would devote a good deal of his time to devising methods that would force Chevalier to pick up the check for lunch. In a good week, he could manage the feat about twice; whenever he succeeded, he would send Chevalier an autographed picture of himself as reimbursement. Chevalier was not amused but couldn't think of a way to stop him.

The actor had his revenge, albeit unintentionally. He gave Lubitsch a coffeepot made out of inferior Dutch silver, with a handle that would get hot whenever the pot did. Lubitsch had to use a napkin to pick it up. "Damn that cheapskate Chevalier," he would invariably mutter.

Ernst's relations with his crew at MGM were every bit as congenial as at Paramount. Joseph M. Newman, assistant director on *The Merry Widow,* said that Lubitsch "had the greatest sense of humor of any individual I've ever met. The actors all loved him. He had a very . . . human quality about him. He was the type of man that became your friend after you met him once. A great man."

Production on *The Merry Widow* began the week of April 9, 1934, and dragged on for thirteen weeks, with separate French and Belgian versions being produced, as well as a version for English audiences that changed the ruler of Marshovia from a king to a general, so as not to antagonize the evidently hypersensitive royal family.

Many at the studio thought the foreign-language versions an unnecessary expense, but, as Thalberg explained in a cable to Arthur Loew, "IF WE ABANDON WE WILL BE OUT OF POCKET $30,000 IN COMMITMENTS TO ACTORS WRITERS ETC. STOP . . . FROM WHAT I UNDERSTAND FRENCH PUBLIC RESENTS

CHEVALIER NOT SPEAKING FRENCH STOP . . . STRONGLY RECOMMEND FOR 50 OR 60 THOUSAND EXTRA WE MAKE IT NOW AS BELIEVE CHEVALIER NEEDS EXTRA HELP EVEN IN FRANCE STOP CABLE QUICKLY ALSO WHETHER WOULD BE WORTH $30,000 TO HAVE SONGS SUNG IN SPANISH AND $30,000 FOR GERMAN. RE-GARDS, IRVING."

The Spanish and German versions were never made; the French version—with the exception of some additional business within some scenes—largely mimics the English version. In early August, the MGM hierarchy suddenly became concerned about whether or not they could use any of Lubitsch's literary material "and all ideas written, prepared or suggested by him" in any future remake of the property. His contract seemed ambiguous on the point, so the MGM legal department contacted Henry Herzbrun, head legal counsel at Paramount. Herzbrun's professional allegiances took precedence over his friendship with Lubitsch; he informed MGM that he would assist them in getting a release from Lubitsch as "he and Lubitsch are very good friends and Herzbrun thinks he might do it better than we."

By September 10, a rough cut had been prepared, and Thalberg terminated Lubitsch's salary. But Ernst was still fussing over editing details and worked out a remarkable agreement, as Thalberg acknowledged in a memo of September 21: "Have arranged with Mr. Lubitsch that he will complete his agreement with us as of last Saturday September 15. He will stay here until he finishes all of the work on the picture, [but] his salary will stop as of that date.

"Mr. Lubitsch requested, however, that nothing be said to Paramount as to when his salary stopped."

In short, Lubitsch worked at least one week for free, an unheard-of situation for either MGM, Paramount, or Lubitsch, and a mark of how deeply committed he was to the film.

MGM's satisfaction with the movie that emerged from this mélange of cross purposes was manifested when they released a lavish production trailer about the film, entitled *Happy Days Are Here Again*. The film begins with clips from past MGM classics such as *Ben-Hur*, *The Big Parade*, *Broadway Melody*, *Grand Hotel*, and *Dinner at Eight*, offers a clip of costume designer Ali Hubert saying that, in the film, "My Vienna lives again," and shows Ernst directing on the set while the narrator refers to him as "the premier genius." Thalberg even dispatched a camera crew to Europe to shoot the cherubic, smiling Franz Lehár, who is shown conducting and saying, in good English, "Ladies and Gentlemen, I greet you on the thirtieth anniversary of my Merry Widow."

The narrator winds up *Happy Days Are Here Again* by calling *The Merry Widow,* "the supreme triumph of the art of motion picture entertainment." But even as the short was whetting the appetites of audiences and exhibitors, *The Merry Widow* was encountering Lubitsch's most panic-stricken sessions with the censors of the Production Code and the newly energized Legion of Decency.

Although the film had been passed for exhibition in September by West Coast Production Code administrator and noted, if private, anti-Semite Joseph Breen, at its New York premiere on October 11, Will Hays and Martin Quigley, the arch-conservative publisher of the *Motion Picture Herald,* were outraged. Quigley especially viewed the film as an "industry double-cross" and singled out Irving Thalberg, who "deliberately introduced a lot of filth" into an operetta.

Will Hays contacted MGM's New York office and expressed concern over "several suggestive sequences," then called Joseph Breen on the carpet. Breen backpedaled, admitting that, yes, the film was "typical French farce that is definitely bawdy and offensively—in spots—suggestive."

According to the predominantly Catholic censors, the problem was in Danilo's carefree pleasure in his cocksmanship. This was immoral and unacceptable. They proposed thirteen cuts to modify the character, as well as eliminating the impression that Maxim's was nothing but a whorehouse, and trimming a scene of Sonia partially undressed.

Thalberg had little choice but to capitulate, but the primary problem was how to make the cuts, since all the prints had already been made. MGM had to wire every local exchange office in the country to make the cuts before releasing the film to the theaters. On November 1, Will Hays approved the reedited *The Merry Widow* for release.

The rash of cuts totaled slightly more than three minutes. Fortunately, however, the 1962 reissue, and successive releases for TV and videocassette, are Lubitsch's original version, because they derive from the original printing negative that was never actually tampered with.

Lubitsch's attitude toward censors was to pretend they weren't there. "Everything is fine," he told a reporter who inquired about the relationship. "I am having no trouble with anyone at all. You get nothing out of me on that subject."

The critical response to *The Merry Widow* was incomprehensibly lacking in enthusiasm. Although *The New York Times* called it "witty and incandescent," William Boehnel in The New York *World Telegram* said that it "is no improvement on the original . . . indeed . . . it is on the whole, just a torpid affectation." But Rob Wagner, who had worked for Lubitsch on *So This Is Paris,* was considerably kinder in his magazine *Script,* saying that, although the material was "dated in costume and humor—and somewhat in music [!!!] . . . our greatest director of sophisticated comedy has brought it to life with a gorgeous bang."

The Merry Widow cost slightly more than $1.6 million, a very high budget for the time and only $300,000 less than *Mutiny on the Bounty.* Although the picture attracted large audiences in Europe, where it grossed $1.7 million, twice as much money as it made in America, it lacked "crossover" appeal and ended up losing $113,000. A 1949 European reissue made up all but $1,000 of the loss.

After *The Merry Widow*'s musical opening that establishes Chevalier's character as the *bon vivant* with the most *joi de vivre,* Lubitsch shifts to an air of romance and mystery. The gypsies of the tiny central European country of Marshovia, who regularly serenade themselves, abruptly stop when they see Sonia. "You may continue," she tells them as she walks by, isolated and obviously lonely. The violins and chorus return, welling up around her, but we aren't told why she walks alone.

When Chevalier's Prince Danilo sees her, he interrupts her reverie to begin his pursuit. Lubitsch crossbreeds mystery and ardor; Sonia refuses to remove her veil. She would, she offers, if she had reason, or temptation, but . . .

"Not terrific," she says in frank appraisal of Danilo. "Not even colossal."

It is gradually revealed that Sonia has been a widow for ten months and is thinking of leaving Marshovia to live in Paris. As she is the richest person in the country, this would mean economic disaster for Marshovia, so the king assigns Danilo to marry her. Danilo is obviously the right man for the job because the king has already discovered him in the queen's bedroom, and with his sword-belt off!

When Danilo and Sonia meet at Maxim's in Paris, he doesn't know she's the woman he's been assigned to marry and pursues her out of chemical attraction rather than duty. The first time we—and they—hear the "Merry Widow Waltz," it is in a small private dining room, and Lubitsch choreographs a stunning scene that seems to be a throwaway but isn't. As she hears the music, Sonia begins dancing by herself, the camera moving around her in a half-circle; Danilo rises and pursues her, then they waltz together in a *pas de deux* of desire, of hesitance and gentle pursuit. She sings, then moves away from him. He pursues her, kisses her; they recline on the couch.

"Do you love me?" she asks.

"Certainly. Why not?" He evades the underlying seriousness of her question and she responds with predictable hurt. "You don't even know what love is!" she charges.

As written, this is a conventional scene of the complex female need for emotional commitment colliding with the basic male need for sex. But Lubitsch throws the emotional weight of the scene to the music, makes his actors and his camera move with it, so that Lehár's romance, lilt, and gravity ground the conventional dramatics. In the regret the scene imparts, it points the way to the heartbreak and conviction of the great Lubitsch films of the 1940s.

Later in the film, at the Embassy Ball, Danilo realizes that the woman he fell in love with at Maxim's is the same woman he was ordered to marry. Standing in the garden, he tells her he loves her. They argue. He is about to leave, when the "Merry Widow Waltz" begins. Again, the music impels them to dance as they're magically enveloped by dozens of couples waltzing onto the terrace. Danilo and Sonia meld together and dance throughout the entire number, alternately lost in the crowds of dancers and isolated as they introduce the movement into room after room of the palace. The waltz seals their relationship, consummates their attraction. For the first time in a Lubitsch musical, music is not a metaphor for sex, but for love.

There is more to the film—a reel of largely extraneous plot convolutions—but the film's emotional core has been revealed. The score is a masterpiece and Lubitsch is its equal, adapting his cutting strategies to the rhythm of the music; when MacDonald's solo on "Vilia" reaches its release, Lubitsch cuts to an expansive long shot of her on a balcony, with the Marshovian mountains in the background. The sense of freedom, of film perfectly timed to the mathematics of the music, is exhilarating.

The Merry Widow is playful, but only on the surface, in the reflexive Lubitsch tradition; Sonia may be a widow, but that merely means that Lubitsch can outfit MacDonald in black negligee and bustier, so as to contrast all the more with her creamy white bedroom. "Vilia" and the "Merry Widow Waltz" do not merely symbolize the alternatives of the heart's yearning and the heart's fulfillment, they *are* that yearning and fulfillment, the things themselves, sensual forces against which Danilo and Sonia are helpless.

At the same time, while the music the characters respond to is deeply emotional and authentic, hence lending meaning to their slightly written characters, Lubitsch—and, undoubtedly, Thalberg—is not only rethinking the material, but also the traditional Lubitsch approach. The previous Lubitsch/Chevalier films had endorsed the sexual smugness that was so prominent a part of the actor's screen personality, but in *The Merry Widow* that smugness is turned on its head; it is Danilo who is humiliated and ultimately capitulates, not Sonia.

Early in the film, Danilo says that "Any man who could waltz through life with hundreds of women and is willing to walk through life with one should be hanged." At the end, Sonia repeats the damningly arrogant line only to have Danilo replace "should be hanged" with "should be married!"

The premise is the same as the Lehár original, but the new lyrics by Gus Kahn and Lorenz Hart carefully adapt themselves to Lubitsch's main point, that music is romance made audible. MacDonald's song "Tonight Will Teach Me to Forget" is taken from a duet that, in the original Lehár show, is sung by two supporting characters. Lubitsch gives it an up-tempo treatment, and directs MacDonald to sing it with resignation but without melancholy. The result is the creation of a magical set piece out of what had been a virtual throwaway.

In addition, where Lubitsch had previously tended to alternate musical numbers with straight book numbers, *The Merry Widow* bunches most of its songs in the first half, which, to paraphrase William Paul, makes a musical of songs a musical of dances and emotions.

But the commercial disappointment of *The Merry Widow* was the harbinger of different times, and a difficult period for Lubitsch. In film critic Andrew Sarris's words, "The resurgence of censorship, the delayed realization that breadlines and Continental sophistication didn't mix and that a wink was no match for a wisecrack, and the pervasive humorlessness of both the left and right brought hard times for . . . stylistically playful directors."

Not only that, but indigenously American rowdies like Frank Capra and Leo McCarey began to redefine the terms of prestige comedy; movies began to turn away from swanky high-life to a very conscious emphasis on the middle class. When the rich, or those who aspired to be rich, were

l a u g h t e r

in paradise

the central characters of a comedy, as in *My Man Godfrey* or *Holiday,* they would often be characterized as self-absorbed, fatuous dopes; America's favorite Frenchman would no longer be the playful Chevalier but the more restrained, slightly mournful Charles Boyer.

Ultimately, Lubitsch was too deeply committed to the exploration of the enchanted world he had created to make more than the most cursory gestures toward commercial accommodation. There would be virtually no margin for error; once and for all, Lubitsch had defined his parameters as an artist: charm, wit, insouciance, the tantalizing possibilities of sexual enticement and love. With one exception, there would be no recourse to action, to battle scenes, or thundering orchestral chords to jack up the energy level.

Amidst the rubble of *Broken Lullaby,* Lubitsch had set himself the task of creating lyrics of tart romance, and in *The Merry Widow* he succeeded as well as he ever would. Future attempts would not always be this great film's equal, but they would always be his.

Following the release of *The Merry Widow,* Lubitsch stayed in New York until the first week of November. He attended parties and the theater, including Norman Krasna's play *Small Miracle,* which Paramount had bought and which Lubitsch was thinking of turning into a film. But all production plans suddenly came to a halt on February 4, 1935, when Lubitsch was named production head at Paramount.

As far as Hollywood was concerned, Lubitsch's uncommercial track record made him a very strange selection to lead a struggling company out of bankruptcy. "I remember that all of Hollywood thought it was a weird choice," said Gottfried Reinhardt. "Not that this was Paramount's only weird choice." Indeed. With the sole exception of Jesse Lasky, Paramount production heads had tended to be an entertaining assortment of egomaniacs, clowns, and fools. One, Charles Eyton, was never too busy to referee a good prize fight; another, Emanuel Cohen, who preceded Lubitsch, ran a newsreel company in the silent days, and, after ascending to the job of production head, signed up Paramount stars like Mae West and Bing Crosby to personal service contracts. When Cohen was fired after two and a half years on the job, not only did Paramount have to pay him off to the tune of $360,000, they had to fund his personal productions starring West or Crosby and share the profits with him!

Lubitsch had been assigned production duties as early as 1929, when Paramount, worried about their highly strung star Clara Bow, made Ernst the producer for her second talkie, *Dangerous Curves*. He had the script rewritten and the actors recast, and assigned the direction to his old schoolmate Lothar Mendes. Despite a temporary collapse brought on by a bad case of mike fright, Bow gave a good, relaxed performance, and Lubitsch's influence was felt in the bright, inventive film.

That had been followed by random production duties on films such as *If I Had a Million* and *One Hour with You*. Clearly, Lubitsch was no tyro when it came to nursing a film through the production process, and his respect for budgets and overall professionalism was well known. The choice may not have been that strange after all, especially considering an interview he had given just two years before, in which he groused about the "tczarist" system of production heads, men who supervised fifty or sixty pictures every year, but, according to Lubitsch, "couldn't do one properly." He complained about the producers' habit of assigning as many as ten writers to a script, saying that resulted in stories without "concentration of thought, no definite evolution . . . no logical development . . . the story becomes a hodgepodge."

The change in status naturally threatened to cause a change in attitudes. The affable, friendly Lubitsch considered himself to be a writer and was accepted as such. In fact, he usually sat at the writers' table in the Paramount commissary. But now he was the Boss, the Chief. One day, shortly after Ernst was named production head, a writer named William Slavens McNutt seated himself in the commissary chair usually occupied by Lubitsch. When Ernst arrived for lunch, McNutt handed him his hat and said, "Hang that up for me, will you, Ernst?" Lubitsch did, then returned to the table to find that all the seats were filled. He sat down at a nearby, unoccupied table, all by himself.

McNutt called over, "You're no longer a writer, Ernst; you're a big executive—a success!" And Lubitsch yelled right back: "You're wrong on both counts. I'll always be a writer, and I'll never be a big success until I can handle a baton like a bandmaster back in Berlin!"

As far as Lubitsch was concerned, his biggest immediate problem was figuring out which telephone to pick up when one of the several on his desk would begin ringing (he had extension numbers 636 and 637 on the studio phone system). As far as the other directors on the Paramount lot were concerned, their biggest immediate problem was their fear that Lubitsch would attempt to impose his style on them, a notion he did his best to downplay. "The screen would be pretty dull if all directors made pictures alike," he said. "I haven't any intention of injecting my personal tastes into anyone's work.'

Shortly after he became production chief, the company signed King Vidor, Lewis Milestone, and Frank Borzage. It would, Lubitsch said, "be presumptuous of me to try and dictate to these three. In the first place, they wouldn't stand for it and, secondly, I admire their brains and experience too much to interfere with their work. If I had ever wanted to subject directors to my way of making pictures, I wouldn't have picked the three most successful ones in the business. I'd be too shrewd for that."

There were, he went on to explain, two kinds of directors: there were the script-shooters, those who essentially set the camera up, make sure the shot is reasonably composed, and have the actors do what the script tells them to do. And then there is the creative filmmaker. The perennial problem, recognized Lubitsch, was that "there aren't enough of the latter to make a fraction of the films. For the others [the script-shooters] we will attempt to provide a balance. Those who can work with writers will operate that way. Those who can take an intelligent script and get a . . . story out of it won't have to bother with the writing. Directing at Paramount will be entirely a matter of personal taste and ability."

He likened his position to that of the chief resident of a hospital medical staff, someone with a broad, sympathetic knowledge of many branches of medicine, with a sense of which specialist needs to be called in to tend which patient. "Motion pictures are also a science," he said. "A director is a specialist who should bring understanding and sympathy . . .

"If I try to do everything, I'll do nothing. I can't contribute much to sixty pictures a year, but I can give a little to each."

Brave words, but, considering Lubitsch's character, improbable. According to Gottfried Reinhardt, "Lubitsch was a particularly bad idea [as production head] because he was incapable of delegating authority. He proved that when he took Cukor off [*One Hour with You*]. He was a loner, and he couldn't stand criticism. After a preview of one of his pictures he would disappear and never talk to any of the executives about his picture. He wouldn't accept criticism of a script, even from a man like Irving Thalberg. He was a loner, he had to be a loner, to work his own way."

But if Ernst was a loner, he wasn't necessarily in sympathy with other loners. Grover Jones, the writer who had proven such an entertaining companion while Ernst and Raphaelson were writing *Trouble in Paradise,* once noted that some people on the Paramount lot thought that Lubitsch

eyman

scott

had a Napoleon complex and believed him to be an autocrat devoid of sentiment. "Friendship ceases when it gets in the way of Lubitsch's art," wrote Jones.

Now that he was production head, Ernst had to set up realistic parameters of what was directorially acceptable, as well as assure New York that they hadn't made a mistake in hiring him. "There was a time when directors thought that by making silly camera angles and dissolves they were geniuses," he told one reporter. "They didn't know how to tell a story and they covered up with pseudo-artistry. Perhaps they would shoot a scene from under a table, when that scene, for proper story value, should have been made on top of the table . . . No man is a genius unless he can deliver honest entertainment."

Given Paramount's recent history, Lubitsch could hardly have been talking about anybody but Josef von Sternberg, whose deliriously visual films with Marlene Dietrich had become increasingly unacceptable in commercial terms. The relationship between the two men had been quietly antagonistic since Emil Jannings asked von Sternberg his opinion of his performance in *The Patriot*. "*Scheisse,*" replied the pithy von Sternberg.

Jannings promptly informed Lubitsch of the remark. According to von Sternberg's memoirs, Lubitsch upbraided him "for not behaving like a colleague." Von Sternberg claimed that Lubitsch said that he, von Sternberg, had not heard the last of the affair, and went on to use "his remarkable sense of humor, all his bite and venom to discredit me . . . The making of films became secondary for him."

But stories of such vindictiveness probably derive more from von Sternberg's thwarted, magnificent megalomania than Lubitsch's purported jealousy. Von Sternberg's problem wasn't merely his mania for the perfect line reading interacting with the perfectly lit shot (Dick Moore distinctly remembers seeing "take #149" on a slate during production of *Blonde Venus*). It was his attitude.

"Von Sternberg was a son of a bitch," said the normally benign Cesar Romero, who received a considerable career boost when he replaced Joel McCrea in the male lead opposite Dietrich in *The Devil Is a Woman*. "He used to bawl her out in German and she would cry. Her German maid would stand on the sidelines, and while he was yelling at her, the maid would be holding her face going 'Oh! Oh!!!' The things he must have been saying to her . . .

"He made things very difficult for people. He was a little king; he controlled everything, and his word was law. He would sit down in front of the camera, and she would have a little thing to say: 'I love you.' He would keep the camera rolling and he would repeat the line to her behind the camera. 'I love you,' she would say, and he would say 'I *love* you.' 'I *love* you,' she would repeat. This would go on for fifty or sixty times. It was incredible.

"At Christmas time, the crew would line up, and he would come out with Miss Dietrich, and they would sit down in chairs. He would call each person's name and they would go up and be handed their Christmas gift. I didn't get anything, but the crew would."

"One day Dietrich came up to me and asked if I was finding things difficult. I said, well, yes. And she told him. He said, 'So, you told Miss Dietrich that I'm difficult to work with?' And he proceeded to get back at me.

"I had to run down a flight of stairs, and I had Cuban heels on my boots. I did it once. He said "Do it faster.' He made me do it about fifteen times, and every time he would say 'faster,' until it got to the point where I was leaping them four and five at a time. Finally I fell and damn near broke my neck. The next day I went to see the rushes and I was sitting in back of him. He watched all those takes of me going down the stairs, then turned to the script clerk and said 'Print take two.' He was just a difficult man and he didn't make things easy at all."

In a town of ravenous sharks, von Sternberg was distinguished both by his enormous talent and by being one of the most disliked people around, although some of the stories were almost certainly apocryphal. (Von Sternberg would occasionally play poker with Herman Mankiewicz, who would boast of starting negative stories as part of "Get von Sternberg Week.")

A poignant story is told by Artie Jacobson, who knew von Sternberg well, serving as his assistant director on *An American Tragedy,* among others. "We were shooting the location footage at Lake Arrowhead. A couple of days after we arrived, I found my girlfriend, who I later married, standing in the hotel lobby holding a long-stemmed red rose.

" 'You'll never guess who's admiring me,' she said. 'The boss.' " An unbelieving Jacobson, who had known von Sternberg since he reshot a third of *Children of Divorce* in six days back in 1927, stared at her. She went on to explain that she had smiled at him as he passed her a few minutes earlier. He had stopped, plucked the rose out of a vase, and handed it to her, saying "That's for the only smile I'll get today."

That Lubitsch and von Sternberg didn't get along is not hard to believe, for their internal chemistries and basic beliefs were very different. Von Sternberg took the smoky mysteries of sex and eroticism seriously; Lubitsch believed only in love . . . but not all the time. "Most of the films he made failed to appeal to me," von Sternberg wrote in his memoirs. "When Lubitsch was serious, not trying to indulge in little drolleries, he could make something unbelievably bad, like *The Man I Killed.*"

Lubitsch had taken it on himself to tweak von Sternberg's eccentric poses at least once before, when von Sternberg and Paramount were embroiled in a dispute over *Blonde Venus.* According to von Sternberg, the script had been foisted on him by B. P. Schulberg; according to Schulberg, the script was von Sternberg's own invention. Both parties insisted the story was trash.

Lubitsch, like all of Hollywood, knew that the story for *Blonde Venus* was indeed von Sternberg's, and went out of his way to tell reporters. "I think when a man does something he should stand by it," Lubitsch said, with what must have been a fairly convincing display of wide-eyed innocence. Indeed, it was common knowledge that nobody had forced story material on the moody autocrat since von Sternberg's first success at the studio with *Underworld,* derived from a Ben Hecht story.

With Lubitsch assuming production control at Paramount, there was some clock-watching to see just how long it would take for the two strong-willed men to clash. As it turned out, not long. Lubitsch promptly changed the title of von Sternberg's final flourish of Dietrichian exotica from *Capriccio Espagnole* to *The Devil Is a Woman,* on the theory that the public wouldn't pay money to see a movie with a title most of them couldn't pronounce.

The retitling of his film seemed proof to von Sternberg that Lubitsch had "liquidated" him at the studio. But, as von Sternberg had alienated virtually everybody with whom he'd come in contact, all Lubitsch could really be accused of was making sure the door was open so the long-established waves of animosity could wash von Sternberg off the lot. As von Sternberg finished up *The Devil Is a Woman,* he summoned the strength to simultaneously end his emotionally masochistic relationship with Dietrich, and avoid any further confrontations with a competitor who had been transformed into his boss.

"I am tired, beloved," von Sternberg wrote Dietrich. "I can no longer fight with you, with Lubitsch, who despises me almost as much as I detest him. And I can add nothing to you. I'm only plagiarizing myself."

"Jo was his own best invention, just as Orson (Welles) was," remembered Maria Riva, the daughter of Marlene Dietrich, and a particularly clear-eyed observer. "You have these talents that are so vulnerable that they invent a persona for the world so they can't be hurt or have their fragility damaged—extremely talented people but without emotional stamina.

"Lubitsch was an ambitious man, a manipulator. He knew how to present his talent. He was very clever, with a lot of the qualities von Sternberg would have liked to have had. A great deal of Jo's antagonism was because he knew he didn't have Lubitsch's personal skills."

In later years, the two men established a cordial social relationship, based partly in their mutual membership in the Hollywood Chess Club at Cherokee Avenue and Hollywood Boulevard. By that time, with the fires of mutual competition long since banked by von Sternberg's professional eclipse, he could accept Lubitsch's considerable warmth at face value. "Jo liked Lubitsch," remembered his widow, Meri von Sternberg. "He had no grudges against anybody except for Charles Laughton. Him, he wished he'd never met."

Ernst's relationship with the other major directorial force on the lot was considerably less strained. Ernst had no quarrel with Cecil B. DeMille, for the two men shared what DeMille categorized as "a high and healthy respect for each other. Our pictures were different indeed, but I recognized Lubitsch as the top director in his field, and he apparently thought that I did well in mine."

DeMille remembered that whenever he went to Ernst for production decisions, the putative studio head would respond by getting flustered and obviously embarrassed. Yet the surviving correspondence indicates that DeMille, while never servile, was certainly eager to try to please Lubitsch, and appeared in need of feedback and stroking.

DeMille would forward laudatory reviews from critics and exhibitors up the chain of command to Lubitsch. On November 15, 1935, DeMille sent Lubitsch a rough outline of *Samson and Delilah* and asked him to try to read the material over the weekend. Ernst responded four days later by telling him he had been too busy preparing for a Paramount sales convention to read it, but would get to it as soon as he could. That same day, DeMille replied that Lubitsch didn't have to hurry but that he, DeMille, was "very anxious to get your reaction and advice on the treatment."

In return, Ernst did his best to place old friends. On June 24, 1935, he wrote DeMille asking if it would be convenient for him to interview his old friend and associate, the costume designer Ali Hubert, with an eye to a place on DeMille's staff.

While DeMille was shooting *The Crusades,* Lubitsch would often take a break from his executive duties and go down to the set and watch. One day, DeMille came over and complimented Ernst on *Trouble in Paradise,* saying that it was like "a present from Cartier's with the tissue paper just removed." Then DeMille inquired as to what Lubitsch found so fascinating about his set. Ernst replied by saying, "I'm *hypnotized.* There isn't a cocktail shaker or tuxedo in sight."

Among Lubitsch's priorities were several reclamation projects. The steady decline in the returns for the von Sternberg/Dietrich films made a change of image for the actress mandatory, so Lubitsch began carefully handcrafting the film that was to be called *Desire.* He also took special care with Carole Lombard, whose performance opposite the maniacally inspired John Barrymore in *Twentieth Century* had opened up undreamt-of career avenues for her, an actress who had always been cast against her nature as a languorous glamour girl. Lubitsch gave Lombard a couple of months off while he had a script entitled *Hands Across the Table,* originally written for Claudette Colbert, rewritten for her.

He came across a play entitled *The Milky Way,* about a meek milkman who becomes a boxing champion, and declared that "Only one man can play this in pictures. Harold Lloyd. But he isn't under contract to us." For $125,000 plus 50 percent of the profits—a very rich deal for a star who was obviously in decline—Lloyd signed to do the picture.

In June 1935, Paramount Publix Corporation reemerged from bankruptcy as Paramount Pictures, Inc., carrying debts of $96 million. As if running a company with that kind of debt wasn't burden enough, Ernst began a serious relationship with a beautiful young female agent named Vivian Gaye, whom he met when she sold him the story that became *Desire.*

Lubitsch also had to contend with a striking insult from his native country. On January 28, 1935, Germany revoked Lubitsch's citizenship as well as that of 207 other naturalized Russian and Polish Jews and others deemed "dangerous to the state." Appeal was impossible and citizenship in any other German state was forbidden. He had been back home only three years before; although he had long been a *de facto* American, it must have come as a jarring blow. Ernst admitted to being "mildly surprised," but pointed out that he had already applied for American citizenship.

The Nazi campaign against Ernst had actually begun in 1933, with an anonymous article in the Berlin *Film Courier* that slightingly referred to Ernst as "an amusingly low-grade entertainer; the sham who created dubious eroticism." Lubitsch films made after Hitler assumed the chancellorship (such as *The Merry Widow* and *Angel*) were not shown in Germany.

The slander would culminate by singling out Lubitsch in the infamously vicious 1940 "documentary" *The Eternal Jew*, directed by one Fritz Hippler. The narration, outrageous in content but coolly contained in tone, runs under a montage showing Jews in the German arts, and the degrading effect the "foreign Jew, the deadly enemy of [the German] race," had on the fatherland.

"The Jew," the narrator says, "is interested instinctively in everything abnormal and depraved. He senses the chance to corrode the healthy judgment of a nation." The film interpolates scenes of a screaming Peter Lorre from the trial scene of Fritz Lang's *M*. "Believing that it is not the murderer but his victim who is guilty, an attempt is made to twist normal judgment and, by presenting the criminal sympathetically, to excuse the crime.

"Too many Jews were considered outstanding people, portrayed by their fellow Jews in newspapers and newsreels as German artists and representatives of German culture," the narrator continues. The film cuts together a montage featuring Richard Tauber; Emil Ludwig-Cohn, "the Jew Chaplin"; and Lubitsch. At least he was in good company.

Then, in a newsreel shot made during his visit to Berlin in 1932, Lubitsch is seen sitting in a chair and accepting a cigar. He reaches into his pocket for a light, and the film cuts to a close-up. Lubitsch lights the cigar, puffs four times, takes the cigar out of his mouth and says, in German, "I'm glad to be back in Germany and my hometown, Berlin."

Out of this innocuous material, diseased minds constructed bogeymen. Whether or not Lubitsch knew of his inclusion in *The Eternal Jew* is uncertain, but a man with his sensitive antennae could hardly fail to be aware that he was on the special list of the likes of Hitler and Goebbels.

Lubitsch now began working in earnest to get his family out of Germany. Hans, the son of his late brother, Richard, was already living with him when, on May 1, 1935, his sister Marga, her daughter Ruth, and Ruth's husband arrived in America. Lubitsch paid their fares and picked them up in a car so new he wouldn't allow any baggage to be piled on the roof. Lubitsch was pleased at how his niece had blossomed and told his sister that "Ruth is very beautiful." Once they were ensconced at the Château Marmont, they went to his new house on Bel Air Road for dinner. When they pulled up in the driveway, Lubitsch's niece Ruth saw all the other cars and thought it was going to be a big party. "No," Lubitsch explained gently, "those are all for my employees."

The émigrés were primed for a splendid German feast, but Ernst, perhaps with Vivian Gaye in mind, turned out to be very concerned about his waistline; most of what he served was suitable for those on a strict diet. A hungry Ruth Hall went in search of something sweet and found peppermint ice cream that she thought horrible, grossly inferior to the luscious torts of Berlin. Truly, Ernst had become an American.

Soon, it was time to show them his adopted homeland. He took them to the Hollywood Bowl, where they heard a concert by Yehudi Menuhin. Ernst gave a large party to welcome them and Ruth got a chance to meet Cary Grant, who was virtually unknown to her. Lubitsch gave them a guided tour of Paramount, where they were introduced to Bing Crosby, who, he told Ruth, "was going to be a great artist," and Marlene Dietrich. In the studio dining room, a waitress spilled a tray of dishes on the floor and Ruth was astonished to see Dietrich leap from her chair and help clean up the mess.

And he took Vivian and his newly transplanted family on a trip to Lake Arrowhead, where he swam very strenuously in what Marga thought was an obvious attempt to impress Vivian. "She had eyes like a cold mountain lake," remembered Ruth Hall. He also took care to introduce his family to Ona Munson, who was still very important to him and, thought his niece, was "the only one who wasn't after his money."

The twenty-five-year-old Ruth Hall appraised her famous uncle as "a simple man, a very natural man. I always was in awe of him. I never talked. I was very timid and never spoke up." She noted that, although his mind was Americanized, "his accent was so Berlin it was awful."

Until they were on their economic and social feet, Lubitsch took complete care of Marga and Elsa and their families, sending $300 a month to each of his sisters once they relocated to New York. Marga preferred to stay in hotels, but out of her $300 a month she managed to save enough money to go to Europe nearly every year.

Ernst's niece Ruth had married a man named Ernest Halitzki—later Anglicized to Hall—and Ernst rented them an apartment at the Hotel Meurice on 58th Street, four rooms with a piano. He made some phone calls and got Ruth's husband an opportunity with the Emerson Corporation, where he eventually became vice president. Even after the life of the Halls had stabilized, Ernst continued to support his sisters.

"He never said, 'You're making money now, you can support your mother,'" remembered Ruth Hall. "He was so wonderful, we really never suffered." Although free with his money to those of the blood, Ruth noticed that, while he obviously loved his family, he loved them best at a distance. "He didn't like them around too much; he wasn't really a family man. He wanted the family in New York, not Hollywood."

He asked his sister to do him only one favor during her five-week stay in California: "Bake me an apple cake the way Mother baked it." Marga did her best, but she made the tort with strips across the top; Lubitsch remembered his mother making it with a solid crust, and he ate only one piece.

In years to come, as a ritualistic part of his annual trip to New York, he would take his niece Ruth and her husband out to the restaurant "21," and to the theater. At "21," he could be imperious; once he thought it was too cold and asked the management to turn off the air-conditioning. When they did, every other customer in the restaurant began to complain, but the air-conditioning stayed off.

In 1937, they all went to see George M. Cohan in *I'd Rather Be Right;* in 1941, it was *Arsenic and Old Lace.* Ruth hadn't been in the country long enough to be fully attuned to the American sense of humor; she thought that poor old ladies killing people was sad, pathetic. Ernst thought it was wonderful.

Sam Raphaelson would write with precision and wit about Ernst's taste in women: "A wife to him meant a lady, and as much of a lady as the 1930s would tolerate . . . Any female with the icy look of ancestry . . . made him stop, look, and listen."

Vivian Gaye was the right woman with the right look at the right time. On July 27, 1935, Lubitsch and Vivian charted a TWA plane and flew to Phoenix, accompanied by Vivian's friend Sari Maritza; her husband, Sam Katz; Vivian's mother; Hans Lubitsch; and a couple of friends.

The marriage was, as they say, sudden, and the press reacted accordingly. The New York *Daily News* noted that the groom was forty-three and "none too handsome." Vivian was twenty-seven and very much in line with Lubitsch's taste in women: tall, slender, and blond.

The *Daily News* went to the trouble of contacting Leni Lubitsch Lewis, who responded with appalling frankness. "I wish I'd never left Mr. Lubitsch," she said. "I had clothes, money, maids, everything then." Evan Lewis must have been greatly comforted by his wife's words.

Vivian had been born Sanya Bezencenet—the name under which she signed the marriage license and by which many of her old friends always referred to her—in 1908. "Sanya was a mysterious creature who appeared one day in Hollywood with Sari Maritza," remembered Gottfried Reinhardt. "They were living together. I had no idea who Sari Maritza was and then Sanya introduced herself to me as Sari Maritza's secretary, which made it even more mystifying." The exotic aura projected by the name "Sari Maritza" might have been considerably lessened had she kept her original name of Patricia Nathan.

Actually, Vivian appears to have acted as Maritza's agent, helping her achieve a brief vogue in such forgotten pictures of the early Depression years as *Monte Carlo Madness, Evenings for Sale,* and the slightly less obscure *International House.* Vivian and Maritza had been acquainted with the Raphaelsons long before Vivian met Ernst, when her name was still Sanya. They were good enough social friends that she would bring over beaus like Randolph Scott for a casual afternoon.

"She was sort of, almost a friend," remembered Dorshka Raphaelson. "But there was always something about Sanya . . ." There was, for instance, a time in the winter of 1933, when she and Sari Maritza came to the Raphaelsons for tea. Sam Raphaelson's mother was also visiting when, suddenly, Vivian and Maritza began talking to each other in French. A surprised Dorshka said nothing, but managed to catch a few of the things they were discussing—trivial chitchat. Dorshka and her mother-in-law continued sipping tea. After a while the two women stopped speaking French and resumed English.

After they left, Sam Raphaelson's mother said simply, "Those two, they're so pretty, and they were so very rude." "To this day," says one friend of Lubitsch's, "I think they were a couple of adventuresses." There was indeed a common belief in Hollywood that Sari and Vivian had taken a page from Anita Loos and came to Hollywood for the express purpose of marrying rich movie executives.

In time, Vivian would come to be almost universally loathed by Lubitsch's friends. "She is a very intelligent person, a very cultivated person," says Gottfried Reinhardt. "She had good schooling, spoke languages, and she has always been a kind of mystery to me.

"She was most disliked by almost everybody. Lubitsch had a lot of friends and friends dislike wives who come into a life and take a man away. Since he had the reputation of being with gold diggers, everybody cast aspersions on her. Whether they were correct or not I cannot tell you, but I never joined the anti-Vivian brigade. I can tell you that she was a tremendous snob, a climber, and suddenly his parties changed. The Jules Steins started coming."

As Paramount emerged from bankruptcy, the presidency was assumed by a man named John Otterson, who moved to California to offer Lubitsch the benefits of his newfound expertise in motion picture production. Behind Ernst's back, Otterson began making overtures to lure a disgruntled Irving Thalberg from MGM.

On January 24, 1936, Lubitsch made official the allegiance that had long been obvious, when he became an American citizen. As it turned out, Lubitsch didn't have much time to savor his new status. Two weeks later, on February 7, he was removed as head of production at Paramount and replaced by William LeBaron. Lubitsch told several different stories about the inelegant firing, one being that he was informed of his dismissal by the studio barber, the other involving a conference in his office.

In the latter version, Lubitsch called in a producer to administer a tongue-lashing when Lubitsch noted that the producer hadn't taken his eyes off a trade paper he had brought in with him. Stopping his tirade—proof enough that the normally mild-mannered director had no business in the job—Lubitsch looked at the headline to read "Lubitsch Out at Paramount."

Actually, Lubitsch's stories were metaphorical variations on the theme of his very real humiliation. "I happened to be at his house on a Sunday," remembered Gottfried Reinhardt. "He was called in to the phone and when he came out his face was literally green. I asked him if anything was wrong, and he took my arm, drew me aside and told me that he had been fired. He had learned it from Louella Parsons, not from anybody at the studio. He took it hard. He was not used to failure, but he was also not used to that type of Hollywood treatment. He was always treated as special . . . but he was very unceremoniously bid good-bye by Mr. Zukor."

The new Paramount regime planted stories in the trade papers, saying the change was necessitated by rising costs coupled with substantial losses, "since January 1935." "It was immediately following Emanuel Cohen's resignation as studio head, early in 1935," reported *Variety* on May 6, 1936, "that production costs began to rise, finally resulting in the current perplexing situation." The trade papers backed up their claims with numbers: *The Big Broadcast of 1936,* made under Lubitsch, had cost $1.2 million and lost $337,000. The next year's entry, *The Big Broadcast of*

1937, made under William LeBaron, cost $847,000 and made a profit of $450,000. *Variety* also helpfully pointed out that, under Cohen, studio morale was high and costs were low, clearly implying that the opposite had been true under Cohen's successor. Lubitsch's name was never mentioned.

Mostly, Lubitsch seems to have found the job a hornet's nest of egos and frustrations. Not only did he have to deal with administrative and financial details that he had no interest in, on at least one occasion he also had to soothe governmental egos. In November 1935, the trade papers reported that FBI director J. Edgar Hoover had retained an agent for purposes of selling stories to the movies. At the same time, *The Hollywood Reporter* ran an item about Melvin Purvis, the former head of the FBI's Chicago office who had resigned following a clash with a Hoover perturbed over Purvis's growing fame. The item said that Purvis was being solicited to run a protection service for the motion picture industry.

The paranoid Hoover had the head of the Los Angeles FBI office canvas all studio heads in order to ascertain the degree of their loyalty to the FBI. Lubitsch, along with Mayer, Warner, and the rest, assured the government that, in the words of agent J. E. P. Dunn, "it would be the constant purpose of their organization to cooperate fully at all times with this Bureau." The Purvis item had been planted by Sam Goldwyn's press agent, prompted by Purvis's friend Jack LaRue. Clearly, Hoover wanted to discourage any studio from hiring Purvis.

Back on the Marathon Street Paramount lot, and away from the internecine political affairs that he had never had an interest in, Lubitsch had been astonished at how many directors could only helplessly follow a script, were unable to add any *frissons* from the camera or the actors, bring anything extra to what was on the page. "It was one long headache," he remembered later. "Trouble in the morning, trouble at lunch, trouble all afternoon—and even at night."

238

Certainly, he could have had little taste for the bureaucratic niceties of the job, such as an October 31, 1935, memo he sent out mandating the prerecording of all musical numbers, rather than the more time-consuming direct, live recording of the music while the scene is being shot. "[Live recording] means not only a great loss of money, but a great loss of quality," he wrote, undoubtedly hoping no one would point out that he had done his share of live recording in movies like *The Love Parade* and *Monte Carlo*, with no particular loss in sound quality.

Lubitsch's most serious imbroglio was with Mae West, who didn't take sex seriously but took herself very seriously indeed, to the point of claiming screenplay credits on films for which she contributed only bare plot outlines, leaving the (invariably uncredited) grunt work to seasoned professionals like John Bright.

West grew angry because Lubitsch refused to give her the cameraman she wanted for *Klondike Annie,* in addition to objecting to her idea of a script, in which everybody besides the star was a stooge. Lubitsch wanted to pair the purring pouter pigeon with a bona fide male star, but no male star was going to undertake a part that consisted of little besides feeding straight lines.

Two weeks after Lubitsch was out of the way, Jim Timony, Mae West's lover of record as well as manager, had the bad grace to go public with West's disagreement with Lubitsch, saying that "She was in the show business long before he ever thought of being. Lubitsch thought he could push Miss West around, but he was the one that got pushed around."

Having decided to get out of town until the gossip moved on to some other subject, Lubitsch was in Chicago when he heard of Timony's remarks. Just before catching a train to New York with Vivian, Lubitsch snorted, "Try to push her around, did I? She's much too heavy." As to the crack about West's greater experience, Lubitsch pointed out, ungallantly but correctly, that the lady was, after all, older than he was. With that, he and Vivian boarded the train for New York.

A week later, they were on the *Berengaria* for a three-month belated European honeymoon where he promised Vivian that there would be "No picture talk." But already Lubitsch was floating possible ideas for movies, including a remake of *The Patriot* to star Charles Laughton. In any case, Lubitsch was a man whose entire reason for being was making pictures; to Ernst's friends and acquaintances, the question of just what he and Vivian would talk about seemed uncomfortably vague.

Although his year as production head could not be considered a triumph, Lubitsch was defensive about the common perception that he had failed in the job. The pictures he had scheduled for production in the coming year suggest that he had indeed found his sea legs; among them were *National Velvet,* W. C. Fields' *Poppy, The Count of Luxembourg* (music by Franz Lehár), and the Pulitzer Prize–winning *The Old Maid.* All but *Poppy* were canceled or sold to other studios.

"I never was allowed complete control," he explained to the *Los Angeles*

Times' Philip Scheuer in March 1937, pointing out that the selection of stories and stars for the release program was well under way when he took the job. Sixty pictures had been scheduled, sixty release dates committed to.

"I remember that once I called off two B pictures because I thought they were too awful for words. The New York office wanted to know if a crazy man was running the studio. I do not consider that I failed—for a year or less is no real test of executive value. Had I remained, the second year would have told the story."

To another reporter, he said that "A supervisor should be a person who likes to give cursory glances and invaluable advice—not one who likes to do it all, and can't possibly under the circumstances."

During Lubitsch's tenure, Paramount produced and released pictures like DeMille's *The Plainsman, Valiant Is the Word for Carrie,* and *Swing High, Swing Low.* But he also had to bear responsibility for expensive failures like Harold Lloyd's *The Milky Way,* a delightful picture hung out to dry by lack of audience interest in its aging star. It grossed $1.1 million, just slightly more than it cost; Paramount figured the loss at $250,000, but at least it confirmed to Lubitsch the great gifts of its director, Leo McCarey, whom he called "brilliant . . . one of the best directors in Hollywood."

Two directors he respected, King Vidor and Lewis Milestone, let him down by making, respectively, *So Red the Rose* and *Anything Goes.* With all this, the fact was that Paramount's profits for 1936, with a slate of films mostly planned by Lubitsch, totaled $4 million dollars.

His taste was triumphantly vindicated yet again when *Desire* was released in April 1936. Still smarting from the critical reception of *Design for Living,* Gary Cooper had hesitated to play in another sophisticated comedy, with dialogue that was too "clever." Having second thoughts, Cooper told Lubitsch he was willing to work with Dietrich now that the dreaded von Sternberg was no longer around. Ultimately, Lubitsch convinced him by saying, "Very well, Gary, do not try to be clever. Just say the lines straight and give them your own sweet personality, and they will be excellent comedy lines."

Cross-pollinating Lubitsch's taste in plot and characters with director Frank Borzage's ability to articulate emotional resonance, *Desire* is fascinating for the considerable influence that the film had on Preston Sturges, for it is a very clear, dry run for *The Lady Eve.*

Madeleine (Dietrich) and Charles (John Halliday, in a part intended for John Gilbert, Dietrich's current lover, who had a heart attack just before production began) are high-line jewel thieves/con artists working the luxury spots of Europe. Dietrich has dropped a string of pearls in the pocket of Tom (Gary Cooper), a credulous but jaunty American tourist. As Dietrich tries to get back her pearls, she begins to fall in love. Each, in their own way, lets their guard down by demonstrating their skills. She sings him a song; he offers to walk on his hands.

The actors get more close-ups than Lubitsch might have given them if he'd directed the film himself, but Borzage's gentle eroticism matches up nicely with the usual Lubitsch playfulness, and the dialogue by Edwin Justus Mayer, Waldemar Young, and Samuel Hoffenstein sparkles with an elegant melancholy. "These are not pearls," notes one character, "they are the tears of mermaids." At another point, John Halliday says off-handedly that "people wouldn't be so afraid of dying if they could take a bottle of brandy with them."

Although Dietrich never found Gary Cooper sexually attractive, she covers her disinterest very well indeed, perhaps because John Gilbert, an intelligent, deeply self-destructive man whose nascent ambition was to be an expert director, was giving her notes on her performance.

"Remember . . ." he wrote her, "Keep Alive!

"No Placidity in scenes!

"No white mystery!

"No ghost!

"No matter what happens to us—please remain an alive animal . . ."

The film's final fifteen minutes flirt oddly and unsuccessfully with melodrama—at one point a gun is drawn—but *Desire* is still a delight and one of the better films of its decade, even though its production cost of $1.2 million rendered it of dubious profit potential. It was a factor that would become an increasing problem for Lubitsch in the next several years.

Marlene Dietrich was nothing if not loyal. If her professional relationship with Josef von Sternberg was at an end, then Lubitsch was a reasonable substitute. She was mightily upset by Lubitsch's removal as production head, and seemed determined to make Paramount pay. Immediately after finishing *Desire*, Lubitsch had cast her in a remake of the Pola Negri silent *Hotel Imperial*, to be directed by Henry Hathaway. Lubitsch once explained to the writer Norman Krasna the secret for working with Dietrich: "Miriam Hopkins talks all the time and everything is witty. But when you come to Dietrich, watch; the big trick with her is you think she is going to say 'no' and by God she says 'yes.' It's what has to be built up for her."

Hathaway's concept for the film would have continued the remodeling of the actress's image along more accessible lines. His idea was to de-glamorize Dietrich, make her someone the public could relate to, and hopefully win back some of the audience that had been alienated by von Sternberg's relentless excursions into arabesques of pure style and sub-limated sexual masochism. But, as Hathaway remembered, "Each time we began rehearsals she was a little more dressed up than I wanted her to be. I always won because I'd go to Lubitsch and he would tell her what to do."

With Lubitsch gone, Dietrich refused to allow herself to be dowdily costumed, and refused to follow Hathaway's instructions. Finally, she said that if Lubitsch was not going to produce the movie, then Paramount had violated her contract; she walked off the picture. Paramount quickly recast it with Margaret Sullavan, but after less than a week of shooting she fell on the set and broke her arm. Taking the hint, Paramount canceled *Hotel Imperial* and wrote off some $300,000.

Although Lubitsch's assuming responsibility for sixty pictures had worked out badly, and was not an experiment he ever thought of repeat-ing, his instincts for the crucial details of film production never failed him.

Shortly after he was deposed as production head, Heinz Herald and Geza Herczeg, two old friends from the Reinhardt days, went to Lubitsch with a ten-page synopsis for a movie about Émile Zola and the Dreyfus case. Lubitsch read the synopsis, liked it, and insisted they take it to Henry Blanke at Warner Bros. Blanke and Warners, he insisted, had the only actor who could play Émile Zola: Paul Muni. *The Life of Émile Zola* was made with Muni and directed by fellow Reinhardt alumnus William Dieterle. Not only did it make money, it won Muni the Academy Award for Best Actor and Warner Bros. the award for Best Picture.

And, a few years after that, when Lubitsch heard that Howard Hawks had embarked on a remake of *The Front Page,* except with the character of Hildy Johnson turned into a woman, he murmured, "A stroke of genius."

c h a p t e r   s i x

The so-called happy ending of a high comedy should have a sardonic overtone
. . . because there is no such thing as a happy ending for an intelligent writer.

— s a m s o n   r a p h a e l s o n

Ernst and Vivian's honeymoon trip stretched on. There was Vienna, where Ernst's niece Evie had moved after her father landed a job with Metro-Goldwyn-Mayer. Ernst introduced Vivian to his niece, and they got on quite well. Vivian and Evie would go shopping together and the new wife would talk to Evie about how important it was that a woman work "and not loaf around." Vivian was impressed by Evie's command of English and suggested she should think about being a tourist guide. At the end of her stay in Vienna, she gave Evie a letter to take to American Express saying that she could highly recommend her as a guide.

When Ernst and his bride got together with composer Oscar Straus, the meshing of personalities was less satisfactory; Vivian didn't care for him. Ernst paid a call on a young writer named Walter Reisch, who was working at the Sascha Studio. Lubitsch had seen some of Reisch's films, liked what he saw, and discussed the possibility of Reisch writing a script of *Der Rosenkavalier,* which Lubitsch wanted to direct with Jeanette Mac-Donald, and, possibly, Emil Jannings as the baron.

The two men got on well, and Ernst told him they would talk again in eight weeks, when he returned from Moscow and Leningrad. In mid-April, Lubitsch and his wife arrived in Moscow for what he said was a "purely private" visit. Vivian's mother was Russian, her father Swiss. Never having seen her mother's homeland, she was curious. In Moscow, they were feted by Boris Shumyatsky, head of the Soviet Film Industry, but overall the trip was kept rigorously low-key. The Soviet film magazine *Kino* announced Ernst's presence on April 17 with a brief item: "Ernst Lubitsch, a well-known German director working in Hollywood for the last fourteen years, is in Moscow now. Our film-goers must know his films *Spanish Dancer* [the Russian title for *Rosita*] and *The Marriage Circle*. Ernst Lubitsch will spend some days in Moscow and then leave for Hollywood where he plans to start shooting a new film right away."

As they were disembarking at the train station, Ernst and Vivian were spotted by a friend of Gustav von Wangenheim, an old colleague from the Reinhardt days who had acted for Ernst in his two Shakespearean pastiches, *Romeo and Juliet in the Snow* and *Kohlhiesel's Daughter*. Von Wangenheim and his wife, Inge, had been living in Moscow since 1933, and they immediately set out to find Lubitsch.

Ernst was staying at the Hotel Metropol and was overjoyed to see his old friend. Inge von Wangenheim appraised Vivian as "a beautiful American WASP, stiff and quiet, who appeared to have just thawed." Ernst struck her as "alert, lively, piercing . . . truly nice, without guile or pretension." The newlyweds accepted an invitation to dinner at von Wangenheim's house on Kouznetski Most. The spread was bountiful: ham and caviar, food so good it melted even Vivian's formidable reserve.

The conversation turned to the great Socialist experiment, and Inge von Wangenheim, a committed Communist, went into a long, humorless diatribe. What was happening in Russia, she declared, would be of enormous importance for the entire world, and she failed to understand how a man of culture and experience like Lubitsch could believe that there was anything more important than the effort to build a new world. Certainly, she said, "the dream machine lubricated by dollars" seemed a paltry, insufficient world in which to spend one's life.

Ernst listened attentively, never interrupting let alone contradicting, black eyes dancing, clearly growing more and more amused. So this was what had replaced the dirt and squalor of czarist Russia from which his father had escaped! He could understand why the lower and working classes preferred life under communism—it held the promise of improvement. But for an artist?

At the end of the evening, Ernst grabbed his old friend by the arm and asked him bluntly, "Now tell me honestly, Gustav: are you happy here?"

An expectant Garbo and her bemused director on the set of Ninotchka.

The answer was affirmative—von Wangenheim and his wife would only
return to Germany in 1945—but Lubitsch was clearly bewildered by his
friend's enthusiasm.

The evening was far from a total loss, however, for in the stentorian,
mechanical-minded Inge von Wangenheim, Lubitsch discovered the matrix for the title character of what would become his most famous film:
Ninotchka.

Ernst and Vivian had been forewarned about Russian attitudes toward
wealthy American capitalists—it was the peak of a xenophobic period in
Russia, so an imperialist Hollywood director would have been regarded

as a virtual provocation. Ernst and Vivian took care to dress very plainly and kept a low profile. All this probably explains why the official Russian record is so spotty; the files of the Krasnogorsk Archives for Documentary Films and Photographs feature bountiful coverage of the 1931 Russian visit by DeMille, for instance, but nothing on Lubitsch's visit five years later.

Despite Ernst's care, there was trouble; Ernst had his gold watch taken away at the border and only got it back on his return. In what Walter Reisch would remember as nineteen days instead of eight weeks, Lubitsch and Vivian were back in Vienna. He would not discuss what he had seen and done in Russia, telling Reisch only that he was "committed to silence."

On their return to Hollywood, Lubitsch moved Vivian into the house at 268 Bel Air Road he had built in 1934. Walter Laemmle remembered that "the Bel Air house was much smaller than the Beverly Drive house, which was a big colonial. The Bel Air house didn't even have a very big back yard." Still, the house on Bel Air Road had been built to Lubitsch's specifications and was a clear reflection of his desires.

The man who slaved over every sentence of a script, every shot of a film, had approached his living environment with a perverse casualness. Lubitsch commissioned the design of the house from Walter Willrich, a friend who wasn't even a professional architect. A hybrid of Mediterranean and Spanish styles, the house had an asymmetrical but not unattractive façade, with a two-story entrance hall, red tile floors, and hand-smoothed white plaster walls.

For the interior, Lubitsch hired his old art director Harold Grieve, who had abandoned art direction in 1927 when union restrictions placed what he considered to be outrageous strictures on his profession. Grieve quickly became a fashionable designer, decorating houses for Norma Shearer and Irving Thalberg, John Gilbert, James Stewart, and seven houses for Bing Crosby.

Taking his cue from the roughhewn brick exterior, Grieve furnished the Lubitsch house in what might be called Hollywood rustic: studded leather furniture, iron and tin wall fixtures, lampshades with suede stitching. There were ceramic tiles on the walls and ceilings, exposed beams, and a split-level living room. The lower level offered a bare wood floor, while the upper level was tiled. There was a fireplace, a baby grand piano, and a large armoire that concealed a radio and a lavish record player that was almost a mini-jukebox.

The back windows looked out over the pool and cabana. Lubitsch's own bedroom was almost spartan, with bare walls, and furnishings limited to a bed, chest of drawers, and daybed. The overall effect was clean, uncluttered, homey, noticeably unostentatious and basically pleasing, a functional proscenium for the personalities that would inhabit it.

Apparently, Vivian was none too thrilled with the house. The layout was awkward—there were far more halls than were necessary and no service staircase—and her bedroom was situated directly over the kitchen.

Very soon, Hollywood was none too thrilled with Vivian. Lubitsch's friends were quickly shut out. "She ruled his life," remembered one, claiming it was common knowledge that Vivian's morning routine involved the servants trooping in to stand by her bed while she gave them their orders for the day. One old acquaintance of Lubitsch's looked under a desk blotter during an infrequent visit to the house and discovered Vivian's household budget.

"You never saw such a heavy-handed thing in your life," remembered the friend. "Chocolates, $50; cigarettes, $40; florist, $200; and liquor and wine way, way, way above what they should have been."

The trip to Russia disabused Lubitsch of any romantic feelings he might have had about socialism in any form. Soon after his return, he told Salka Viertel, a screenwriter and good friend of Garbo's, to take his name off the roster of the Hollywood Anti-Nazi League, saying it was a tool of the Communists. As an alternative, beginning in October 1939, Ernst became actively involved in a project called the European Film Fund, jointly spearheaded by him and Paul Kohner. Essentially the idea of Charlotte (Mrs. William) Dieterle and Lisl (Mrs. Bruno) Frank, the fund's committee consisted of Curtis Bernhardt, William Dieterle, Lothar Mendes, Gottfried Reinhardt, Bruno Frank, Erica Mann, Walter Reisch, Salka Viertel, and Conrad Veidt.

Successful émigrés working in Hollywood would tithe between 1 percent and 5 percent of their pay to a central fund. Paul Kohner's office served as the headquarters, with Kohner as the main muscle. When émigrés arrived in Hollywood with little but their reputations and the clothes they were wearing, the fund would disburse a weekly stipend, sometimes as little as the forty dollars a month Ludwig Marcuse received. Occasionally, individual members of the fund would underwrite what amounted to a scholarship for a specific émigré, as William Dieterle did for Max Reinhardt.

In addition, Kohner functioned as virtually a one-man relief agency. During his daily contacts with the studios as an agent, Kohner would apply pressure on behalf of recently arrived émigrés. For a writer or actor, for instance, he would ask for a six-month or one-year contract at a minimum salary, generally a hundred dollars a week.

"He would regularly place people at MGM, Columbia, Universal," remembered Lupita Tovar Kohner. "He was such a hard worker, and a marvelous salesman. He could sell you anything, but he worked extra hard on this because for a lot of these people, it was a matter of life and death." Among the people that he placed at the studios were Alfred Döblin, the author of *Berlin Alexanderplatz,* and Walter Mehring, a founder of the Dadaist poetry movement.

Most of the Europeans who were already working in Hollywood were willing to help, but they were not always as generous as Kohner thought they could be. "That guy could afford to give me more than five hundred dollars," he'd say, but his wife would calm him. "Be grateful for the five hundred. Even if they are making a lot of money, people have obligations that go with it."

Lubitsch would regularly attend the board meetings of the fund, but he rarely approached people for contributions or contracts. "It was awkward for Mr. Lubitsch," remembered Lupita Kohner. "Some people can approach anybody, as long as it's for somebody else, but Lubitsch couldn't."

When he did choose to help, he often made sure his actions were surreptitious, which led old acquaintances like Ernst Mátray to claim that he didn't really want to help any of the emigrants. According to Mátray, when Max Reinhardt arrived in Hollywood, Lubitsch's only response to his mentor's presence was to ask friends "What does he want here?" Similarly, when Erich Pommer arrived back in Hollywood in 1934, the friendship between him and Lubitsch had cooled. "He was so successful here and my father wasn't," said John Pommer. "You must remember that there was a lot of infighting then. Tigers were about."

248

But Max Reinhardt's son disagrees. "Lubitsch was one of those Europeans who were fully cognizant of the fact they had to be firmly established in America," said Gottfried Reinhardt. "Except for private relationships, he almost never helped during the immigration to get jobs. He had a way of helping through others. For instance, when I produced *The Great Waltz,* he called me up one day and said 'I've got the conductor for you.' It was a man called Arthur Gutman, who had conducted at the UFA-Palast in Berlin. Lubitsch would never have hired him himself, but he would call me and recommend him. That was his way."

At times, Lubitsch would get directly involved. As early as 1933, he was soliciting funds for the United Jewish Appeal, putting a gentle but firm arm on Paramount peers like Cecil B. DeMille. Two-thirds of the money went to the Joint Distribution Committee, expressly for German Jews, while the rest went to the Jewish Agency for Palestine. "It is needless for me to elaborate upon the need for funds in this emergency," Lubitsch wrote DeMille on July 6. "The condition of the Jews in Germany today is one of distress. At such a time long speeches and lengthy pleas are superfluous."

Yet, Ernst's feelings about the great waves of Jewish intelligentsia that came flooding out of Germany after 1933 were deeply ambivalent. For Lubitsch, men like Thomas Mann and Bruno Frank were unreachable heroes who could only remind him of his own lack of a distinguished academic background. Like Max Reinhardt, they made him slightly uncomfortable.

"Funnily enough, there was actually much more common ground between Lubitsch and the Americans than between Lubitsch and the Europeans," remembered Gottfried Reinhardt. "There was not that gulf. He was very natural; he liked to sit down and play the piano—badly, but with fervor. And he was unreflective, like most Americans. Americans like that [kind of person]. Europeans—not necessarily."

Back in Hollywood, it was time to get back to work. Now Lubitsch had everything he wanted: a beautiful young wife, a fine new house, with a built-in gym where his trainer, Terry Hunt, could give him the strenuous massages he liked. And there was Otto Werner, on board as chauffeur—Lubitsch did not drive—who would also become an indispensable right arm at home, just as Steffie Trondle was at the studio.

Basking in his successful middle age, Lubitsch was now smoking at least a dozen cigars every day and favored Viennese cooking, so long as it didn't include cheese, which he loathed. Jewelry was limited to a watch, drinking to wine and beer. Sports bored him, with the exception of boxing. He favored showers over baths and was quite ticklish. He wore black silk pajamas, but when he wasn't working he would occasionally get up, have breakfast, and, after a walk, decide to go back to bed.

Although he enjoyed horseback riding, he was no more at home with the natural world than the character he had played in *Meyer from Berlin*. One night, about the time he met Vivian, he was dining at home and heard strange noises from outside. "Otto, what is that?"

"Those are frogs in the pond, sir."

Taking that under advisement, Lubitsch listened for a while, then said, "Otto, is this necessary?"

Lubitsch returned to the Paramount lot, twenty-seven acres in the heart of Hollywood illuminated, at one time or another, by practically every famous name in movie history. By this time, Paramount had assumed the realm of a cozy cocoon for Lubitsch, and for hundreds of others as well. Inside the big iron gate off Bronson Avenue there was a shoeshine stand run by a black man named Oscar Smith, who had arrived on the lot in 1919 through the good offices of Wallace Reid. Besides being the studio's unofficial jester and mascot, Smith's stand was Gossip Central and a primary gathering place for some of the highest-priced talent in Hollywood, including Bing Crosby and a young, comparatively low-priced contract writer named Billy Wilder.

In the center of the lot, right in front of the production office, was a pond, filled with goldfish. "It was a country club," remembered Bob Hope, who arrived at Paramount in time to make *The Big Broadcast of 1938* and stayed for the next twenty-one years. "They were all country clubs. There was no hustle-bustle, 'get it done this week' attitude. They didn't even care that much if you were over budget. It wasn't a national disaster. Really, it was gorgeous; everybody was so relaxed."

Dorothy Lamour, who came to the studio in 1936, remembered it as "a family. It really was, from the front office on down. One New Year's Eve, it was raining. I had a date to go out and my hairdresser was washing my hair. I heard some music and I said, 'Elaine, what's that?' She looked out and began wrapping a towel around my head. 'You've got to see this,' she said.

"Outside, standing in the rain, were all the guys from the set, the grips, the carpenters. They were on a flatbed and they were singing 'Girl of My Dreams' to me, on New Year's Eve! It was that kind of place."

As with any family, there was always time for a playful joke or two. When illness struck Henry Herzbrun, who had handled the money while Lubitsch had functioned as production chief, Ernst called the writer Claude Binyon and asked him to write a funny telegram he could send Herzbrun to cheer him up. A few days later, Binyon got a call from Herzbrun, who asked him to write a funny telegram so that he could send it to Lubitsch. "I'll try," gulped Binyon. The next day, Lubitsch, carrying Binyon's response to his own joke, ran into the writer. "Claude," he exclaimed, "he topped us!"

The friendly atmosphere was a necessary corollary to the fact that, for the blue-collar workers at least, the hours were backbreaking. It was a six-day week, with unlimited hours, and Saturday shooting might go to very early Sunday morning.

"It was rough but nice," remembered Jack Barry, who started out in the mailroom in the 1930s and, by the 1970s, had risen to the rank of production manager. "If you went to work at Paramount, you worked there the rest of your life."

For his first picture since being deposed by William LeBaron, Lubitsch chose to adapt *Angel,* a play by Melchior Lengyel that had already been produced in English, courtesy of a script by Guy Bolton and Russell Medcraft. Lubitsch began writing the screenplay for *Angel* with the successful boulevard playwright Frederick Lonsdale, author of *The Last of Mrs. Cheyney,* but Lonsdale left the project after three weeks over what *The New York Times* called censorship problems. A disturbed Lubitsch called on Sam Raphaelson to take over, but Raphaelson was in New York working on a play. Two days after Raphaelson turned the job down, Lubitsch was on the phone saying "I'm coming to New York." Lubitsch brought his entourage, immensely flattering Raphaelson, who worked days with Lubitsch and nights at the theater, rewriting and rehearsing.

In his reflective old age, Raphaelson once asked himself why he never quite realized that to work with Lubitsch was to be in writer's heaven. Unlike most writers, Raphaelson was objective enough to realize that he lacked the capacity for self-laceration necessary if his work was going to last beyond that Broadway season.

"I don't know," he said. "I wanted to be sole author. [I should have] forgotten my ego and said, 'I'll work for you the rest of my life.'"

Again, Raphaelson was nervous about the material of *Angel;* "Whenever you hit a stronger emotion than was called for in usual high comedy," he remembered, "Lubitsch was in danger of going wrong . . . I didn't think it was a good picture."

Gottfried Reinhardt explained the nature of Lubitsch's limitations, which were becoming increasingly evident. "His interest in films was enormously limited. Basically, he [adapted] Hungarian comedies, and that was the extent of his knowledge. He never read a book in his life, which was another misunderstanding between Hollywood and Lubitsch. If someone has an accent, the average Hollywoodian think's he's very cultured. But Lubitsch wasn't. He had no idea about anything. Politically, he was liberal, but naive.

"Once, I was sitting in the Trocadero with some people and he came through with a dinner jacket on. He passed my table, said hello, and I said 'Why the jacket, what was the affair?' It turned out that Hal Roach had invited him to a reception for the son of Mussolini. And he had gone! 'Ernst,' I said, 'are you crazy? How can you go to this Fascist thing?' When I explained it to him, he was rather embarrassed that he had gone. The most sophisticated director in Hollywood was, politically and erotically, the most naive man you can imagine."

As *Angel* began production late in March 1937, Lubitsch and Dietrich crossed swords more than they ever had before. "Ernst wanted [her] to maintain the ladylike front," Melvyn Douglas told Charles Higham. "There was some conflict between them as he reminded her constantly, 'This is a *lady* you're playing, not a demimondaine.' "

Trained to withstand the inordinate number of takes demanded by von Sternberg, Dietrich thought Lubitsch worked a little too fast. One day she asked for an extra take in a scene. "I'm not satisfied with it," she explained.

"You're not satisfied with it?" said an incredulous Lubitsch. "Well, you go right ahead and make the scene until you are satisfied with it. I'm going home." By the end of production, Lubitsch and Dietrich were not speaking.

A reporter for the New York *World Telegram* visited the set and took down Lubitsch's instructions verbatim, even reproducing, however crudely, Ernst's thick Berlin dialect. Although the actors had presumably studied their scripts in order to memorize the dialogue, Lubitsch left nothing to chance or improvisation, and felt compelled to give them the entire backstory of the scene and of their characters.

"Vatch how I do it, Melvyn," he said to Melvyn Douglas. "Now, I am a romantic young man who iss smitten—absolutely smitten with this voomans. She is driving me crazy. I am in loff with her and I don't even know who she is. I don't know if she loffs me. I don't know if she has a husband even. You see, Melvyn?"

"All right. Ve proceed. I am going to take this voomans in my arms and kiss her passionately." Lubitsch seized Dietrich, and spoke Douglas's lines: " 'Who *are* you. I must know.' Do you follow me, Melvyn?"

Turning to Dietrich, he said, "Now you, Marlene, you are a neglected wife who iss in Paris on a stolen holiday. You loff your husband, but he is paying to you no attention. At this moment he iss off in Geneva settling the Yugoslavia question vile you are starfing for his loff. Do you see the possibilities? . . .

in paradise

"Camera! Action!!"

Despite a fine cast, a provocative central situation, and his painstaking directorial attention, Lubitsch's rhythm was alarmingly off; *Angel* was to be his most disappointing picture since *Eternal Love.*

Marlene Dietrich is Maria, the neglected wife of international diplomat Sir Frederick Barker (Herbert Marshall). She encounters Anthony Halton (Melvyn Douglas) at a salon presided over by Laura Hope Crews, apparently doing an Elsa Maxwell imitation. Halton mistakes Maria for the mistress of the house and immediately tries to make her the mistress of his house.

"I've found through life the days take care of themselves," he tells her. "It's the evenings that are so difficult." She won't tell him her name, so he settles on calling her Angel. They agree to meet again in a week. Back at home with her overbooked husband, we see that it is a marriage beset by equal parts ennui (hers) and too many distractions (his). When she asks him what he'd do if she fell in love with somebody else and left him, he replies, "I certainly wouldn't quarrel. It would be too late." Snore.

As Melchior Lengyel's long arm of coincidence would have it, Sir Frederick and Anthony meet at a dinner party, where it turns out they had the same mistress during World War I. Anthony tells Frederick of his infatuation for Angel; back home, Sir Frederick tells Dietrich of his new-found friend and his odd love affair.

Lubitsch devises one masterstroke for a dinner party at which the ardent lover realizes he is trying to cuckold a friend. When Anthony gets up to look at a picture of Barker's wife, Lubitsch first holds the camera on Barker mixing a drink, then cuts to Dietrich coming down the stairs to face what she knows will be a contretemps between her husband and her lover. Lubitsch withholds the conventional shocked reaction shot, and stimulates anticipation for the confrontation to come.

Played faster, for confusion and duplicity, the story of *Angel* could have been the premise for a fine screwball comedy. Played with more inflection, with more expressive leading men, or more of a sense of emotional commitment, it could have been a moving, albeit contrived, romantic drama.

But the characters are written and played to reflect little more than polished surfaces. Barker and Halton are supposed to be instant fast friends, but Lubitsch and Raphaelson's way of indicating male bonding is by having one man refer to the other as "Old Man." The psychological constriction is palpable, and probably derives from Ernst's own discomfort with intimacy.

Many of Lubitsch's "touches"—playing out a scene of Douglas looking for Angel entirely through a reaction shot of an old flower seller—seem strained, touches in search of something meaningful to touch upon. For virtually the only time in his career, Lubitsch here verges on the insulting affectation of style disassociated from content. What with Barker's servants commenting on the manners and breeding of their overstuffed masters, and the have-it-all sexual politics of the central characters, *Angel* plays as Lubitsch's most reactionary movie, which could hardly have been his intention.

In the end, the Barkers confront each other at the Paris salon. He knows she has been unfaithful, but she denies it by saying that Angel is in the next room. He begins to go toward it. "Frederick," she says, "if you go into that room, I'm afraid our marriage is over. If you find Angel in there, you'll be happy that I'm not Angel and want to continue our old life. But that would not be satisfactory to me."

"And if I don't find Angel?"

"In that case, I think you'll want to see your lawyer as soon as possible. If you don't go in at all, you'll be a little uncertain. You won't be quite so sure of yourself. And that might be wonderful."

Barker goes to the door and enters the room. It is empty. Anthony Halton arrives to take Angel away, but is interrupted by Barker. "I've met her," he says. "In the last few moments, I've thought more about our married life than in all the years we've been together. And all I know is—the train to Venice leaves at ten . . . Well, I've said good-bye to Angel and so must you, Maria." As he walks toward the door, Maria joins him and they leave together.

Frederick, of course, has it both ways, as does Lubitsch. Barker throws his lack of trust in his wife's face even though she has threatened to leave him if he does, which makes the happy ending seem forced and irritating. Lubitsch seems to mean the ending to be movingly redemptive, but the actors and the director's attitudes are far too aloof, the resolution nothing but a victory for the status quo.

By any standard, *Angel* is a failure, but it is nevertheless a key transitional work. For the first time Lubitsch is attempting, however unsuccessfully, to deal with the emotional results of infidelity, and the internal dynamics of his characters. But the mechanism of the story is at odds with the cast and treatment. Ernst was still more comfortable with polished puppets than with real people.

The die had been firmly cast when Lubitsch enlisted the smooth, superficial Frederick Lonsdale to work, however briefly, on the script. Ultimately, the film doesn't work because Lubitsch and Raphaelson don't dig deep enough, and they didn't cast actors who could suggest deep emotional confusion underneath the requisite placid surface.

In spite of the evident uncertainty of *Angel,* Lubitsch was glad to be back directing. "The official billing on the picture," he explained, "[is] 'Marlene Dietrich in an Ernst Lubitsch Production, *Angel,* directed by Ernst Lubitsch.' All of the honor is in the first phrase, my agent tells me, but all of the fun is in the second."

Angel was an aesthetic mistake and, at the very pricey cost of $1.4 million, a commercial blunder as well. As the New York *World Telegram* wrote, "After the madcap comedy that has been so popular with audiences lately, the suaver nuances of . . . Lubitsch's brittle little comedy drama may seem quite tame." It was not a mistake Lubitsch would repeat; the next time he attempted to make a film about real people with real emotions, he would achieve perfection.

By the mid-1930s, the only competition the Foreign Legion had was the English colony, whose main members were actors like Ronald Colman, Cedric Hardwicke (who would fix a kipper breakfast for his countrymen on Sunday mornings), C. Aubrey Smith, and Boris Karloff, as well as young renegades like David Niven and Errol Flynn. Unlike the Foreign Legion, who tended to be writers and directors, the English were usually actors and banded together at least partly to preserve the most valuable of their attributes: their Englishness. Since few of them were really good actors, they had to count on their national identity to carry them through.

"In those days," remembered Vincent Price, "the English Colony really ran Hollywood. There was the [old] guard up in the hills and then down by the beach Niven and Flynn, living at the house they called Cirrhosis-by-the-Sea. In between there were middle-range people like Reggie Gardiner, who eventually took to sounding so desperately clipped and stiff-upper-lipped that not even English audiences could ever understand a word he said. The colony . . . had considerable grandeur, especially Ouida Rathbone, who behaved like some manic duchess and used to fill the swimming pool with gardenias every time Basil had a party. The smell was really appalling."

While the English were basking in an environment hospitable to Anglophilia, the German colony was besieged by dozens of recent arrivals. Hitler's appointment as chancellor in 1933 was the cause; the wholesale fleeing of hundreds of people from Germany's literary, film, and theatrical worlds was the effect.

The main difference between the two primary colonies was the fact that the vast majority of the Germans were refugees in need, while the English were in Hollywood by choice or by invitation, and were mostly without the strong emotional need to band together in a new environment.

In varying degrees, the Germans found it difficult to make their way, both practically and psychologically. Actors, writers, and directors who had achieved at least recognition and, in many cases, renown, were once again virtual tyros, forced to justify their existence to often skeptical domestic talent. A sad, metaphorical joke spread quickly through the German colony, about a refugee walking his little dog who meets another refugee on the street. "Nice dog," says the second refugee. "Ach," says the owner sadly, "back home he was a Saint Bernard."

Billy Wilder was born in Sucha, a small town one hundred miles east of Vienna, in 1906. Although his father had hoped he would be a lawyer, after a year at the University of Vienna Wilder opted for a job as a reporter on *Die Stunde* and, in Berlin, *B.Z. am Mittag*. On the side, Wilder moonlighted on movie scripts, including the minor classic *People on Sunday*. Leaving Berlin after the Reichstag fire ("It seemed the wise thing for a Jew to do"), he made his way to Paris, where a script he wrote attracted the attention of director Joe May. The script was never produced, but the money from its sale got Wilder to Hollywood. After the usual period of adjustment, that is to say total and complete impoverishment, Wilder landed at Paramount, where he once claimed to have made so little of an impression that he was seriously studying the want ads.

It was at that point that Paramount story editor Manny Wolf introduced him to Charles Brackett, a patrician from the Eastern Seaboard. "From now on," Wolf told them, "you're a team." At Wolf's suggestion, Lubitsch took them on to write *Bluebeard's Eighth Wife*. It is highly probable that, by matching Lubitsch with some younger talent, Paramount was trying to ease him into a more *au courant* mode than had been represented by *Angel*.

At the first meeting, Lubitsch posed the elemental question: "How do the boy and the girl get together?" Wilder immediately suggested that the film open in the men's department of a department store. "The boy is trying to buy a pajama, but he only sleeps in the tops. He is thrifty so he insists on buying only the tops. The clerk says he must buy the pants, too. It looks like a catastrophe. Then the girl comes into the shop and buys the pants because she sleeps only in the pants."

Lubitsch was enthralled. Where had this diminutive man with a slanted mind been all his life? It wasn't until some months later that Wilder confessed that, in fact, he wore only pajama tops to bed, and he'd been carrying the situation around for a long time waiting for an opportunity to use it.

Wilder, whose ambitions to direct would shortly be jump-started by having Mitchell Leisen ("That fag who ruined my scripts") direct his material, immediately fell into a student/teacher relationship with Lubitsch, who taught him things he would remember the rest of his life.

"His technique was totally subordinated to storytelling," Wilder would remember, pacing back and forth in his office, occasionally stopping to whack his thigh with a riding crop. "His theory—and mine—is that if you notice direction, you have failed. You have to hide your technique. No dolly shot should be so overwhelming that you say, 'My God, look at that.' Look at the story, look at the characters, and make the technique become part of the action."

Beyond niceties like plot and character, Lubitsch gave Wilder an underlying attitude, an aesthetic belief system: let the audience write the script with the filmmaker. "Don't spell it out, like they're a bunch of idiots. Keep it just slightly above their station. He would not say to the audience, 'Now listen to me, you idiots! Two plus two equals four! And three plus one equals four!! And one plus one plus one plus one equals four!!!' Big deal.

"No. You give them two plus two and let *them* add it up. They'll have fun and they'll play the game with you.

"Lubitsch would have laughed if you had suggested making a film with no cuts in it, or making a film with just ten setups, like Hitchcock did in *Rope*. Those are exercises in masturbation and it would never occur to him. The living room should not be shot through a fireplace unless it is from the point of view of Santa Claus and he's a character in the film."

Lubitsch also bequeathed to Wilder his affection for obscure source material. "I don't like taking a big hit and making a movie out of it," Wilder remembered. "It's too easy, too uninteresting. I couldn't fuck it up. I like to work either with original stories or some obscure story that you just use a notion from, nothing very substantial."

While writing *Bluebeard's Eighth Wife,* Brackett and Wilder noticed that Lubitsch composed his pictures in segments rather than all in one piece. They also noticed that whenever Jack Barry would stop by to drop off the mail, he would be subjected to a quiz about the picture business or the theater. If he knew the answer, Brackett, Wilder, and Lubitsch would pay him double the cost of the paper or magazines he was delivering. If he didn't know the answer he got nothing.

Lubitsch valued Barry for his common-man persona and would occasionally ask him to pass on a situation or word in the evolving script that he feared might be too arcane for general understanding, as in the time he asked Barry if he knew what "chapeau" meant.

The writing did not always go completely smoothly; once, working with Brackett and Wilder, the story sessions seemed to be erupting with material they thought was consistently hilarious. But Lubitsch's new secretary just sat there, impassively taking her shorthand. Gradually, the secretary's stony nonreactions began to affect the work. After a line that slayed the three men, Lubitsch finally turned on the secretary and asked her point blank, "Don't you think that's a funny line?"

"This is the funniest script I've ever worked on," she replied.

"Then why don't you laugh?"

"Perhaps later, I might laugh. Just now . . ." Lubitsch, assuming some recent tragedy, backed off and began treating her with solemn deference. Two weeks later, in the middle of another story session, the secretary broke into hearty howls of laughter. Lubitsch asked what had happened to change her mood.

For the first time, the secretary smiled. "The dentist removed my braces," she said.

Lubitsch proved himself a relentless polisher, always saying "Is this the best we can do? Does it ring the bell? When it's right, it rings the bell." For a scene in which Claudette Colbert, pursued by Gary Cooper, was to dive into the Mediterranean, Lubitsch wanted Colbert to yell something before she dived. Just one word. Nobody could think of the right word. Over and over, Lubitsch would pantomine Colbert's dive, then look at Brackett and Wilder imploringly, waiting for the *mot juste.* Long after they had given up and moved on to other scenes, Lubitsch would suddenly go back to it. "Does it ring the bell? *Is it the best we can do?*" (In fact, they never found the word, an ominous portent of the finished film.)

In the script sessions, Lubitsch would act out each part as he tested the lines, playing not only Cooper and Colbert but David Niven and Herman Bing. Wilder thought Lubitsch did Bing better than Bing did Bing, and his performances invariably reduced the writer to helpless hysterics. Even the reserved, well-bred Brackett would break up.

"If the truth were known," remembered Wilder, "he was the best writer that ever lived. Most of the 'Lubitsch touches' came from him. I remember in *Bluebeard,* the script had a scene where Gary Cooper walks into a department store in Nice and sees some signs. One of them says 'Se Habla Espanol,' another one says 'English Spoken Here.' [Lubitsch] took a pencil and wrote underneath that 'American understood.' A tiny little joke, but it meant everything."

Lubitsch sent Eric Locke to Budapest, Vienna, Prague, Paris, and the Riviera to shoot background footage for the process photography, and began production in Hollywood on October 11, 1937, two weeks before *Angel* was released. And Lubitsch showed he had no hard feelings toward the ambitious young man who had been lying in wait for him at Elsa Maxwell's party four years before, by casting David Niven in a good-sized part in *Bluebeard's Eighth Wife.*

"Lubitsch sat," wrote Niven in his memoirs, "like a little gnome, beside the camera, perched on a small stepladder, giggling and hugging himself at all his own wonderful inventiveness . . . He was patient, understanding, and encouraging; what more could any actor ask?"

Niven confessed that one of the reasons he became such an adept farceur were those few months with the first great director with whom he would work. Niven always treasured something that Lubitsch told him: "Nobody should try to play comedy unless they have a circus going on inside."

The film wrapped in January at a final cost of $1.3 million and was quickly cut together in time for its New York premiere on March 23. Despite the hilarity and good fellowship that prevailed during the picture's writing and production, the critical response was muted, and properly so. *The New York Times'* Frank Nugent wrote that "it's not a bad comedy by our current depressed standards [!!!], [but] it has the dickens of a time trying to pass off Gary Cooper as a multi-marrying millionaire." The New York *Sun* was similarly strained, calling the picture "slim but funny," while *Variety* said that it was "a light and sometimes bright entertainment, but gets a bit tiresome, despite its comparatively moderate running time of 85 minutes."

It was one, unspecified review that particularly jarred Lubitsch. The critic, although professing to enjoy the picture, wondered whether in these days audiences were kindly disposed toward people who didn't work.

With a start, Lubitsch suddenly realized that the world had changed around him. He could no longer get away with the delightful irresponsibilities displayed by the characters in *Trouble in Paradise*. "We must show people living in the real world," he would tell the New York *Sun* in November 1939. "No one used to care how characters made their living—if the picture was amusing. Now they do care. They want their stories tied up to life . . . Now [a character] must have a job, or else the fact that he doesn't work becomes the important thing about him."

After the opening scene of *Bluebeard's Eighth Wife,* easily the greatest meet-cute in Hollywood history, the film settles down to a misalliance between Gary Cooper's dreamily truculent, much-married tycoon and Claudette Colbert's impoverished aristocrat. The buoyant first half gradually loses its sparkle just about the time their marriage does—on their honeymoon in Venice, they take separate gondolas—and thereafter proceeds in contrived fits and starts.

Part of the problem is that Lubitsch is attempting to accommodate the impulses of screwball comedy without having the necessary rambunctious temperament (at one point, Gary Cooper's character has a stunningly unlikely nervous breakdown and is confined to a straitjacket). Lubitsch's element is not savagery but satire, not chaos but control. Great screwball directors like Capra, Hawks, McCarey, and La Cava were either alcoholic wild men or craftsmen who could allow themselves to be far more improvisatory in their methods and attitudes than could Lubitsch. With the exception of *To Be or Not to Be,* Lubitsch films never subject their characters to gleeful ridicule, let alone the ritual humiliation that is the raison d'être of screwball comedy.

There are Lubitsch films where the internal mechanism peters out before the end title, but *Bluebeard's Eighth Wife* was the first Lubitsch film to have no mechanism at all. It is the emptiest movie he ever made.

All of Lubitsch's friends were pleased by his obvious pride in Vivian's blond beauty, her aloof air, her aristocratic bearing. But virtually the kindest judgment any of Lubitsch's friends would be able to summon was Lupita Tovar Kohner, who said that, "She was much more attractive than Leni. But Vivian was a snob. It became an entirely different life. She didn't like the people that had been his friends before. By the time they married

I could speak some German and I remember one of Lubitsch's friends saying, 'The lovely days are over.' Because of all this, we didn't see them very often. She did have a party for his twenty-fifth anniversary in films. It was very nice, but otherwise . . . I think she kept in touch with the Wylers more than anybody else."

Well, not really. Margaret Tallichet married William Wyler in 1938 and was quickly introduced into Lubitsch's circle. She found the Lubitsch marriage strange. "They never seemed suited to each other. I don't know whether they liked or were interested in the same things. They just always seemed to me like they came from the opposite ends of space. Forget about passion; I never even felt any intimacy there, that ease you can feel between a couple who really like each other."

Sam Raphaelson, normally a gracious man, said that "she was a calculating bitch. I thought she treated him terribly. Of course, he wanted to be treated terribly. He liked women who treated him badly." In 1981 Raphaelson would write succinctly that "The lady may have been the choicest of choice womanhood, but in my eyes she was not good enough for him."

It was apparent to her intimates that Vivian simply hated Hollywood and, presumably, most of the people in it, which was sometimes manifested in an embarrassing way. Once, Ernst invited some friends to come to the house for dinner, followed by a night out at a preview screening. The guests arrived, but Vivian was nowhere in sight, and the house was very quiet. Finally, Vivian came down and sat with them with her hair in a towel. "Aren't you coming to the preview, Vivian?" inquired one friend. "No," she replied curtly. The coldness was palpable.

Sam Raphaelson would write that he thought the marriage went dead after about three years, which seems to be remarkably accurate; by 1940, when Ernst and Vivian would attend a party, he did not bother to conceal his interest in other women. "He was unable to keep his eyes off Fay [Wray]," Clifford Odets reported to his diary on October 19, "who he likes and obviously would like to have. This seemed to amuse his wife, who seemed often on the point of making sharp remarks but did not." Odets didn't mind Lubitsch's attentions to his current lover. Later in the night they drew each other aside for a talk about actors and the war. "The quality of his mind did not attract me," concluded Odets. "His personality . . . witty . . . keen, appetites sharp . . . always did."

At about the same time, Ernst and Vivian went to a dinner party with the Raphaelsons. Lubitsch and Dorshka were out on the dance floor, and

Sam and Vivian began talking. Vivian began praising the American melting pot. "I'm all in favor," she commented, "of mixing the blood of the aristocrat with the blood of the peasant."

Raphaelson couldn't pass up the opportunity. "I know just what you mean, Vivian. You are, of course, referring to Ernst and yourself—he the aristocrat, and you the party of the second part."

Raphaelson remembered that they both laughed, pretending nothing vicious had been said. Lubitsch came back to the table and the conversation moved on to other things. But Sam Raphaelson was never invited back to the Lubitsch house until after Vivian moved out.

The consecutive failures of *Angel* and *Bluebeard's Eighth Wife* made Lubitsch's position at Paramount untenable. As always, the studio had given him the casts of his choice and acquiesced to his taste in material. The results had been two expensive—and not very good—pictures. Casting about for possible explanations, Lubitsch decided the fault was not in the movies but in changing times.

"Comedy on the screen can no longer be charming," he told Philip Scheuer. "People aren't interested in just charming humor any more. They want to be shocked and surprised in order to laugh. It is the spirit of the age. I could not make a picture today the way I made *The Marriage Circle*. Such comedy would be too delicate to appeal to the public."

Lubitsch was right; films like *Midnight* and *My Man Godfrey* took the old Lubitsch smoothness and suggestiveness and mixed it with a very American snap, crackle, and pop. If all this wasn't ominous enough, even the critics were turning on him. Lewis Jacobs' influential 1939 book *The Rise of the American Film* noted that recent Lubitsch pictures "show a significant loss of vitality and timeliness . . . his films seem static . . . his most recent films do not show that he is keeping abreast with the swiftly changing times." Suddenly, Lubitsch seemed in danger of both commercial and aesthetic obsolescence.

In March 1938, the break was made official. After ten years, thirteen influential films, and one of the most mutually productive relationships between a director and a studio in Hollywood history, Lubitsch left Paramount.

There were some initial feelers from Warner Bros., but nothing came of them. Instead, in July, Lubitsch decided to take the plunge into independent production and formed Ernst Lubitsch Productions, Inc., with Myron Selznick, the gifted but self-destructive agent and brother of David O.

Selznick. The first production was slated to be a property called *The Shop Around the Corner,* and Lubitsch enlisted Samson Raphaelson to write the script, personally paying him the modest up-front stipend of $1,000 a week in return for a 5 percent share of the gross after Lubitsch took $50,000 in profits. If the deal to produce the film independently fell through and Lubitsch produced the script with an established company, Raphaelson was to receive a fifth of whatever Lubitsch was paid.

The Shop Around the Corner originated in a Hungarian play entitled *Parfumerie* that had opened in Budapest on March 31, 1937. Although the script was originally offered to MGM, they passed, and in July 1938, the play was sold to Lubitsch, working through a front to keep the price down. Steffie Trondle translated the play into English, and Lubitsch and Raphaelson began the adaptation.

At the time the script was being written (late 1938–early 1939) the star was to be Dolly Haas, a gifted actress who had starred in the British remake of Griffith's *Broken Blossoms* and would later marry artist Al Hirschfeld. According to Lubitsch's plans, the film was to be released either through United Artists or MGM, although MGM was a very farfetched possibility, if only because they rarely handled the product of outside producers.

It was all highly speculative, but Lubitsch could afford a small gamble; in 1937, Paramount had paid him $260,833, the same salary he had made as production chief. It was $12,000 more than they paid Claudette Colbert, but $110,000 less than Marlene Dietrich, and far more than any other producer/director in the industry. (In 1937, for example, Howard Hawks made $130,000; Henry King, $157,444. Even independent producers like David Selznick—at $203,500—and Sam Goldwyn—at $189,000—took less salary than Lubitsch, although, unlike Lubitsch, they owned their films.)

In the words of film historian Barry Sabath, *Parfumerie* "provided an excellent blueprint for the script; it is like a good solid first draft. The narrative events of the film are all present in the play to a certain extent, but they await color, nuance, wit and characterization." Structurally, the play has the female lead already working in the shop at the beginning. Also, the circumstances by which the male lead discovers that he has fallen in love with the woman he can't stand to work with are different.

Otherwise, Lubitsch and Raphaelson retained the original structure, but made multiple improvements, streamlining lengthy speeches and lucidly polishing the dialogue, as in the heartrending scene in which the great

Frank Morgan says of his broken marriage, "Twenty-two years we've been married. Twenty-two years I was proud of my wife. Well . . . she didn't want to grow old with me." In the original play, the dialogue is: "For thirty-two years I believed in my family, my happiness and my children . . . She doesn't want to grow old with me."

Mostly, Lubitsch and Raphaelson added wit and humanity to the characters. Specific additions to the script include the ritualistic morning openings of the shop; the running gags about the music boxes that play "O Chi Tchornya"; Klara procuring her job; the meeting at the cafe; the invented story of how the mysterious correspondent is a fat, unemployed, depressed man; and the final reconciliation of the lovers.

When the script was finished, Lubitsch regarded it as one of the best he had ever been associated with. But it quickly became clear that Myron Selznick couldn't find the capital to back even one modest production, let alone an entire slate of pictures, probably because of Lubitsch's recent losing streak at the box office and Selznick's well-known unreliability. Moreover, Lubitsch didn't like Dolly Haas's tests for the part. According to Raphaelson, "Lubitsch lost his nerve, that's all. She was a European star, not widely known in the U.S., perfect for the part, heaven-sent. But [Lubitsch] got nervous . . . He felt a movie was at best such a gamble that he wanted to play safe at every point where he could get established pros.

"Anyway, he asked me to see the test. At once it was obvious that Dolly was agonizingly self-conscious—she must have sensed Lubitsch's insecurity—and I told him so. 'The fact of the test is demoralizing her,' I said. 'Start the picture. She can't miss.' Well, he didn't."

Lubitsch's crisis of confidence was made worse by the fact that there weren't a lot of free-lance stars around whom he could afford and who could also carry the picture. He began taking the property to other studios, including Paramount, but, as The Hollywood Reporter (January 24, 1940) would say, "He could not get one of the major companies interested . . . principally because they were not interested in Lubitsch." The perceived failure as production head and the consecutive flops of Angel and Bluebeard's Eighth Wife had cost him dearly.

As all this frustration was getting under way, on October 27, 1938, Vivian gave him the greatest gift of his life, an eight-pound, two-ounce daughter they named Nicola Anne Patricia Lubitsch.

While Ernst and Vivian may have been the biological parents, the child actually owed her existence to Dorshka Raphaelson. Shortly after Vivian and Ernst married, Vivian came to Dorshka's rented Hollywood house for tea. During the conversation, Dorshka said, more as a statement than a question, "You're going to have children."

"Oh, no," replied Vivian. "Ernst doesn't like children. He doesn't want any."

Dorshka, remembering Ernst's absolute delight in her infant daughter Naomi years before, couldn't believe what she was hearing. "Get pregnant, Vivian," she advised. "Have a baby. Pay no attention to him saying that; he'll be very pleased."

A month and a day after Nicola's birth, Lubitsch wrote to Raphaelson that, while Nicola was fine, healthy, and already developing a personality, *The Shop Around the Corner,* which he called "the best script I have had in a long time in my hands," seemed to be dead in the water, slowly losing momentum through constant postponement. It began to look like if he wanted to make the movie, he'd have to take a deal—and not necessarily the best deal—at a studio.

As far back as 1929, Greta Garbo had been vocal in her enthusiasm for the idea of being directed by an artist, as opposed to the craftsmen of various abilities who were employed at MGM. Specifically, she was enthusiastic about working with either Lubitsch or Erich von Stroheim. In 1933, Louis B. Mayer had dangled the possibility of borrowing Ernst from Paramount to direct *Queen Christina,* which led Garbo to cable on April 1, "PREFER LUBITSCH. ALSO HAPPY FOR [EDMUND] GOULDING." But Ernst was too deeply involved in preparing *Design for Living,* which began shooting in the first part of July. The tantalizing partnership had to be put off for a few more years.

The story for *Ninotchka* had been brought to MGM in 1937 by Gottfried Reinhardt, who was then working as assistant to Sidney Franklin. Melchior Lengyel's original story was obviously written with Garbo in mind but is highly conventional. Its springboard was a three-sentence memo scrawled in a notebook: "Russian girl saturated with Bolshevist ideals goes to fearful, capitalistic, monopolistic Paris. She meets romance and has an uproarious good time. Capitalism not so bad after all."

In Lengyel's original story, the three commissars are not comic (they're played straight), and there is nothing about jewels. Leon, the male lead, becomes a drunkard when a business deal falls through and, at the end, he accompanies Ninotchka to Moscow. The foundation of the finished film is there—a political anal-retentive loosened up by love—but the story is plot-heavy. It reads like a nominal Sidney Franklin production.

Lengyel completed a portion of a shooting script on January 7, 1938. The three delegates have become five but they're still played straight. Leon is to be played by William Powell. The addition of Powell's polished but antic humor and sex appeal might have done a great deal to add sparkle to what was, at this point, a slightly flat script.

During the latter part of 1938, Gottfried Reinhardt collaborated on two scripts for the film, one with Jacques Deval, who wrote *Tovarich,* the other with S. N. Behrman. At this point, the film was scheduled to be directed by George Cukor. Surviving script material from these drafts indicates a lack of real progress; as late as November 30, the commissars are still not being used as comic relief.

While Reinhardt was in New York working with Behrman, he heard that Cukor had backed out of *Ninotchka* to devote his full energies to *Gone With the Wind.* It was bad timing, at least for Reinhardt and Behrman, for it seemed that they were turning the corner on the script; in a script dated 12-15-38, scenes at the Eiffel Tower and Leon's apartment are fleshed out. More important, Behrman and Reinhardt have invented the restaurant scene as the moment where Ninotchka's glacial reserve finally cracks.

Responding to Cukor's defection, Garbo, who had *de facto* director approval, gave MGM two choices: Edmund Goulding or Lubitsch. As far as MGM was concerned, Goulding was out of the question, tired and passé. (That same year Goulding would direct—rather well—*Dark Victory,* and would go on to make several more major pictures, among them *The Razor's Edge* and *Nightmare Alley,* all combining to suggest that what was passé was Louis B. Mayer's taste in directors.) MGM's enthusiasm for Lubitsch was muted, if only because he had lost them a great deal of money on *The Merry Widow.* Still, he seemed a more felicitous choice than Goulding.

Negotiations were concluded on December 30, 1938. As part of the arrangement, MGM agreed to take over *The Shop Around the Corner,* for which they paid Lubitsch $62,500 (he had paid $16,500 for the story, and was thus making a tidy profit). In addition, MGM agreed to pay Lubitsch $147,500 in fifty-two weekly installments for the next year of his professional life, during which time he would make two pictures. The main proviso was that *Ninotchka* would come first, although the studio tried to calm the nervous director by inserting a clause allowing for the cancellation of the Garbo picture which "shall not affect our respective rights and obligations with regard to . . . *Shop Around the Corner.*" The studio agreed to supply James Stewart and Margaret Sullavan for the picture. MGM had five months from January 14 to determine whether or not Lubitsch actually held the rights to *Parfumerie*. If the rights were determined to be not completely cleared, the studio had the right to cancel the remainder of the contract and get their $62,500 back.

"The minute Lubitsch took over, I told Behrman we might as well forget the whole thing," remembered Reinhardt. Lubitsch reported to the lot on February 8, 1939, and, just as Reinhardt had guessed, promptly informed Sidney Franklin that he didn't like the script. Franklin thought the script was fine, and for a while the project seemed to be verging on dissolution; in March, *The Hollywood Reporter* announced that MGM was considering William Wyler to direct the picture, but a reconciliation was effected (probably to placate Garbo), and Lubitsch began to work on the script.

By this time, Gottfried Reinhardt had arrived back in Hollywood to find Lubitsch completely in charge and already working with Walter Reisch. "We were in Sidney Franklin's office and we started arguing about the jewelry business Walter Reisch had brought into the script [the Behrman script involved a nickel mine]. I thought [the jewelry subplot] cheapened it. Well, Lubitsch stopped and asked Franklin if he could take me out and talk to me. Franklin said of course.

" 'Gottfried,' he said, 'don't make a mistake. Don't fight me on this. You'll lose.' Lubitsch was a very nice man but he was a very tough man. But he made a very good film." (When S. N. Behrman made similar noises about the jewelry business, Lubitsch, with unassailable logic, pointed out that "The nice thing about jewels is that they are photogenic.")

Work resumed on the script, and again Wilder and Brackett were called in to help . . . and to be amazed. "He wasn't just a gagman," remembered Wilder, "he was the best creator of toppers. You would come up with a funny bit to end a scene, and he would create a better one. I think he thought up the bit where the picture of Lenin smiles back at Garbo, [but] I can't be too sure. He would look at our stuff and go 'Ho-ho, very good,' and scratch out the next line. He'd read a bit more, go 'Ho-ho,' and scratch out another line. What he did was purify, and that was what made him a great writer.' "

By April 8, the script was very close to the finished shooting script; dialogue and scenes are largely intact. The script gives credit to Lubitsch as well as Wilder, Brackett, and Walter Reisch, who wrote a memo to MGM saying that all three writers felt Lubitsch was more than entitled to a credit. On April 12, Lubitsch wrote Raphaelson that work on the script was proceeding smoothly and that he certainly would have wanted Raphaelson to work on the project if he hadn't been busy with a play. He told him that he was disappointed that he hadn't been able to get more money for the MGM deal, but that the outlook for the Lubitsch/Selznick company had become so dim that he had been forced to compromise.

With the script approaching its final stages, it was time for Lubitsch to convince Garbo that she could do the film. (Although she had actually signed a one-picture contract in December 1938 for $125,000, a steep drop from her mammoth salary of $275,000 for *Anna Karenina,* Garbo always reserved the right to walk, which accounted for the cancellation clause in MGM's contract with Lubitsch.)

She drove to MGM for a conference but didn't want to get out of her car. An obliging Lubitsch got into the passenger seat and sat with her for the next two hours. The actress's main fears revolved around the drunk scene; she thought it was not right for her and, she admitted, she was also ashamed to act drunk in front of other actors. After much coaxing, she agreed to try the scene, and the film.

Production began on May 31 and continued for fifty-eight days. As always, Garbo's insecurity manifested itself as paranoia; anybody who wasn't absolutely necessary to the production was barred from the set. Nevertheless, Billy Wilder would sneak on the soundstage to watch Lubitsch direct surrounded by a skeleton crew. One day Wilder was at least thirty feet away, not making a sound, when everything suddenly got very quiet and two grips put a blackboard in front of him. "Nobody said for me to leave, they just put this here, and I knew that Garbo had felt my presence."

Lubitsch put the drunk scene off for virtually the entire production, waiting to do it until Garbo felt completely secure with him and the film. "I believe [she] is the most inhibited person I have ever worked with," Lubitsch said. When she came to him and said she didn't think she could play the scene, Lubitsch had to put his foot down.

" 'Look here, I'll do anything you want; I'll change the script, the dialogue, but this can't be changed. Too much depends on it. You must make up your mind that you'll have to play it' . . . When we did get to it she was very—afraid is too strong a word—timid. But finally I got her to relax completely by talking to her and being patient."

As Garbo started the scene, Lubitsch began modifying it, saying casually as he walked past her, "Very good, but if you could just do . . ." Lubitsch found that Garbo didn't rely on technique—it is entirely possible she had none—but had to emotionally feel a scene in order to play it.

Although they had known each other for years, Garbo seems to have been uncomfortable working with Lubitsch. Years later, she told Gavin Lambert that she hadn't enjoyed making the picture, found Lubitsch vulgar and had little rapport with him.

"How strange that I got mixed up in that business, but I did," she told Cecil Beaton in 1947. She did admit that she thought that Lubitsch was a much better actor than any of the people in the cast. "I remember, one morning, going in, and seeing him, cigar in mouth, with my big leading man, running through a scene on the sofa that I was to do. He was being so funny! But underneath he was a vulgar little man."

According to Hedda Hopper, Lubitsch was working at a faster tempo than Garbo was accustomed to, leading her to ask him one day, "What next, Mr. Van Dyke?" a reference to "One-Take" Woody Van Dyke, an MGM director famed for his slapdash speed on the set. Garbo's most frequent director, Clarence Brown, always directed her in whispers, and she had obviously gotten used to it. At one point, Garbo became ruffled by the steady high energy and accented expostulations, and spoke to Lubitsch in German: "Please, when you speak to me, please speak more softly." A startled Lubitsch modulated his voice.

"Garbo didn't care for him," confirmed Gottfried Reinhardt, who produced *Two-Faced Woman,* her last, disastrous picture. "I wouldn't be surprised if it was Salka Viertel who suggested Lubitsch to her for the film. Garbo was strange; many good directors she didn't like. She liked directors who left her alone, like Clarence Brown. She didn't care for directors who directed her. She had some kind of somnambulistic instinct for her effect on the camera. Whoever tried to interfere with that she instinctively fought. You couldn't really direct Garbo. And, if you look at her films, you find that she is always more or less the same, including *Ninotchka.*"

Yet, like many actresses, Garbo seems to have tailored her reactions—indeed, her personality—to the company in which she found herself. With Reinhardt or Cecil Beaton, she would claim that she had been uncomfortable with Lubitsch. Yet, she told Raymond Daum, who regularly accompanied her on her endless, post-retirement walks through Manhattan, that Lubitsch was "a marvelous little man," and she told the journalist Sven Broman that Lubitsch treated her "like a loving father." With her lover Mercedes d'Acosta, she was exuberantly happy.

"Never since I had known her had she been in such good spirits," wrote d'Acosta of Garbo during the production of *Ninotchka.* "[It is] the first time I have had a great director since I am in Hollywood," she told d'Acosta, who called her "a changed person. She used to come for me as usual after shooting, and we walked in the hills. At least I walked, but she more often ran and danced. She laughed constantly and she used to repeat the question 'Why' as she did in the picture. She would imitate Lubitsch's accent and ask over and over again, 'Vhy? Vhy?' "

Sometimes Garbo even acted out scenes from the picture for d'Acosta. "It was fascinating to see how by playing a gay role rather than a sad one her personality changed."

If Lubitsch sensed Garbo's periodic unease, he didn't let on; for him, there was no ambivalence, no vacillating about what he thought of this deeply moody, anomalous creature. "I wouldn't have done it if Garbo hadn't been cast for it—and without Garbo I don't think it would have meant a thing . . . She made age-old gags seem brand-new. She understood perfectly what I wanted, and performed exquisitely."

Privately, Lubitsch's mood during the production of *Ninotchka* was testy. He didn't trust Metro and Metro was not thrilled with him either. Although *Ninotchka* would (apparently) renew Garbo's commercial viability, the start of World War II divested MGM of the European market, which accounted for nearly 40 percent of their revenues. It was a particularly dire situation for a star like Garbo, whose domestic appeal was largely urban. As Gottfried Reinhardt said, "Garbo was a money star only in Europe."

Lubitsch obviously sensed the emotional misalliance between himself and the studio. On February 7, 1939, the day before he reported to the studio, an MGM memo stated that "[head of the MGM legal department] Floyd Hendrikson is having a helluva time with Lubitsch. The latter is a very suspicious individual and, for some reason or other thinks that Metro signed him up merely to do the Garbo picture and that it will attempt to avoid its obligation to have him do *The Shop Around the Corner*. The latter apparently is the apple of his directorial eye and he is so anxious to be sure that the title is cleared up that he has hired Louis Swartz to make an independent investigation of the title."

Exactly a week later, Lubitsch's ire had grown to the point where MGM was saying that "although we do have until sometime in June to clear the title it would make matters much more pleasant for the studio . . . if this title could be cleared in the near future." They took their sweet time; as late as April 15, a memo was saying that "Lubitsch is supposed to be working on the Garbo picture but is probably devoting most of his time to worrying about whether or not we intend to go ahead with the other picture which is the one he really wants to do."

The grumpiness extended even into his private life. In May 1939, when David Selznick invited Ernst to a dinner party for his new discovery Ingrid Bergman, Lubitsch was heard to mutter unkindly, "She's such a big peasant." By the end of the evening, however, Ernst had been charmed by Bergman's glowing, ingenuous femininity. "Don't let this get you down," he told her. "We all came to Hollywood for the first time, and it was hard for all of us." Selznick tried to promote Bergman to Lubitsch; indeed, she would have been wonderful for *The Shop Around the Corner,* but the part had already been promised to Margaret Sullavan.

Lubitsch's old, touchy relationship with Norma Shearer sparked again when he attended the wrap party for *The Women,* which had once been floated as a Lubitsch project. As Rosalind Russell got up to dance with George Cukor, Lubitsch sidled up to her and said, "If you want all your close-ups to stay in the picture, better dance with Norma." Russell promptly reported the crack to Shearer, who was secure enough to laugh, hold out her arms, and dance with Russell right past Lubitsch. There is no record of who led.

At a preview of *Ninotchka,* Lubitsch brought along Charlie Brackett, Billy Wilder, Walter Reisch, and a few studio executives. The film seemed to go well, with laughter in all the right places. After the film ended, Lubitsch swooped down on the filled-out preview cards and took them back to the studio limousine, refusing to let anybody else look at them.

"He had this very serious expression as he was reading," remembered Billy Wilder, "and you could tell that it was pretty positive. Well, he gets to this one card and he just stares at it for a while and then he breaks into this howl of laughter. He was rocking back and forth on the seat and pounding it with one hand. We were looking at each other and wondering what the hell was so funny. Finally, he hands me the card and this is what it said:

" 'Great picture. Funniest film I ever saw. I laughed so hard, I peed in my girlfriend's hand.' "

Although Garbo later claimed that she put off seeing *Ninotchka* for three years, Lubitsch clearly remembered her attending a preview with him in Long Beach, and of her shocked surprise at hearing people laugh at one of her movies. "She was *so* excited," he told the *New York Post*'s Michel Mok. "She is the only star I ever worked with I did not have to drag away from the mirror."

The tortuous preproduction process of the film was matched by

Metro's agonizing over the right title. In March 1939, the provisional title was *We Want to Be Alone,* but by the time the film was in production the title was *Give Us This Day,* which nobody in the New York office liked. *A Kiss from Moscow* was offered up as a substitute, but publicity director Howard Dietz pooh-poohed that and suggested *Intrigue in Paris.*

The list of possibilities also included *This Time for Keeps, The Love Axis, Time Out for Love, A Kiss for the Commissar, A Foreign Affair,* and *A Kiss in the Dark.* Finally, Nicholas Schenck, the president of Loew's, Inc., and a native Russian, ordered that the epochal Lubitsch/Garbo collaboration would be known as *Ninotchka.*

Ninotchka is the story of three hapless Russian commissars sent to Paris to sell some jewels to raise money for the state, and of the woman sent to fetch them when they are slowly seduced by the pleasures of the West. For Lubitsch, who could make masterpieces like *Trouble in Paradise* out of moonbeams and charm, this was a very strong, almost top-heavy premise, but he managed not to be overwhelmed by it.

There are a few Lubitsch touches in the visuals: the transition of the commissars from loyal apparatchiks to sybarites is effortlessly visualized by dissolving from their battered headwarmers on a rack to their shiny bowlers and top hats on the same rack.

And, of course, there is no shortage of verbal wit; Ina Claire refers to her lover, Melvyn Douglas, as ''My vulgar boatman,'' and Lubitsch takes some free swings from both sides of the political fence. The Russians are portrayed as fetishistic about their drabness, and self-righteous about their alliance with the proletariat. When Ninotchka goes into a restaurant and orders raw beets and carrots, the owner replies, ''Madame, this is a restaurant, not a meadow.''

As for the capitalists, a conniving, poor-mouthing middleman is capsized by the knowing remark, ''Capitalistic methods—they accumulate millions by taking loss after loss.'' And, just to prove that the Production Code held few terrors for Lubitsch, he gets away with an outrageous double entendre, when Ninotchka says to Leon, ''I was a sergeant in the third cavalry brigade. Would you like to see my wound?''

As always, nuance is all. When three leggy cigarette girls come striding in to the hotel room, Ninotchka deadpans to the commissars, ''Comrades, you must have been smoking a lot.'' She does not say ''smoking a great deal,'' even though her character's formality might make that a more realistic line. But the blunt, explosive sound of ''a lot'' is, simply, funnier.

Ninotchka's world is one of feckless aristocrats, of rich and poor, of sexual struggle symbolized by political roles. It's a von Stroheim world really, but instead of emphasizing morbidity and tragedy, Lubitsch plays it for laughter and wit. Never before was he so adept at creating recognizable types, then delighting us with variations on our expectations: not merely reverses, but sideways shuffles, sweeps around end, every possible dodging permutation.

Lubitsch is giving Metro an unaccustomed *brio*—MGM's idea of a comedy director was Jack Conway—and he manages to endow the film with more visual variety than Metro's preferred procession of medium shots, usually adopted in order to make reshooting and reediting easier. But Metro is affecting Lubitsch as well. There are vast amounts of white light cascading in from over the top of the sets; the incandescent Paramount glow that seemed to emanate from the characters instead of being applied by a thick brush is sorely missed.

More important, the film runs 110 minutes, much closer to the typically stately MGM idea of pacing than the Paramount ideal of 85 minutes and out. As with *The Merry Widow*, Lubitsch's previous MGM film, there is a distinct *longueur* toward the end of the third act, when the dramatic and sexual tension dissipates and Lubitsch and the writers slog through the film's Russian sequences, which are nearly as dreary as the environment they portray, before we get to the inevitable reconciliation at the end.

If it did nothing else, *Ninotchka* would confirm Lubitsch's gifts with actors. He lures, *seduces*, Garbo into playing a marvelously delicate, lilting drunk scene, and she appears enchantingly, radiantly relaxed as she was only once before—for George Cukor in *Camille*. When Leon sends Ninotchka a large bouquet with a jar of goat's milk inside it, Garbo seems to cry real tears, and the moment is ineffably moving because of the authenticity of emotion; people *are* moved to tears by silly but appropriate gifts that tell them that someone genuinely knows and understands them. Garbo's tears are not the tears of a goddess, but those of a woman, and Lubitsch manages to effect this transition while leaving the essential mystery of the actress intact.

There are cavils, however. Several times Lubitsch indulges himself by using a subjective camera from the inside of a safe: Ina Claire has beautiful diction and timing but, to be polite, she seems at least a decade too old for her part. And Melvyn Douglas, while polished and likable, lacks sufficient variety. More important, he lacks sexuality. There was always something redolent of pipe and slippers about Melvyn Douglas, and, while he doesn't hurt the film, he doesn't give it the antic, erotic charge that William Powell or Cary Grant would have. (According to Billy Wilder, Lubitsch in fact offered the part to Grant but was turned down.)

Ninotchka marks the beginning of Lubitsch's richest period, when he would examine with a remarkable, tender humor the ways in which the life of the mind yields to the life of the heart; communism yields, not to capitalism, but to copulation. "No one can be so happy without being punished," Ninotchka wails at one point, but in the benevolent world of Lubitsch, no one is punished and nothing is punishable except cruelty.

Commercially, *Ninotchka* returned worldwide rentals to MGM of $2.2 million on a cost of $1.3 million. The tally was all the more impressive because countries as various as Italy, Estonia, Lithuania, Bulgaria, and France banned the film because of its satire on communism (France's ban was lifted on appeal).

Domestically, the picture grossed only $1.1 million; the total profit was a mild $138,000 (a 1952 reissue made another $416,000, most of it from Europe). MGM was obviously concerned about the costs of *Ninotchka,* for, in a September 16, 1939, memo, they told Ernst that $110,721.10 of his total salary of $147,500 would be charged to the modest production budget of *Shop Around the Corner.*

Ninotchka's financial returns were less than those of the year's biggest hit, *Mr. Smith Goes to Washington,* which made $3.5 million, but considerably more than other hits like *The Old Maid* ($1.4 million), *Only Angels Have Wings* ($1.1 million), or *The Rains Came* ($1.65 million).

As far as Louis B. Mayer was concerned, it didn't seem like the picture was worth all the trouble. "*Ninotchka* got everything but money," he groused. "A[n] [Andy] Hardy picture cost $25,000 less than Lubitsch was paid alone. But any good Hardy picture made $500,000 more than *Ninotchka* made."

Still, *Ninotchka*'s commercial and critical response was more than sufficient to refloat the endangered careers of both director and star. Frank Nugent in *The New York Times* wrote that *Ninotchka* was "one of the sprightliest comedies of the year, a gay and impertinent and malicious show which never pulls the punch lines . . . and finds the screen's austere first lady of drama playing in deadpan comedy with the assurance of Buster Keaton." Howard Barnes of the *Herald Tribune* chimed in saying that Garbo "floods the production with her timeless . . . beauty, giving a rich and haunting quality to the romantic scenes and a moving intensity to the few passages of straight drama. There is an added verve and color to her personality . . . which makes her even more magically lovely than in the past." *Variety* said that "Selection of Ernst Lubitsch to pilot Garbo in her first light performance in pictures proves a bull's-eye. Deft and amusing touches and switches are there in goodly numbers . . . there's some bright and eyebrow-lifting dialogue, delivered in typical Lubitsch fashion."

Despite having been squeezed out of the project, S. N. Behrman was also thrilled with the picture, and with the performance Lubitsch got out of Garbo. Behrman told Lubitsch that she had given a first-rate high-comedy performance and must continue along those lines. Lubitsch replied that he had some ideas for more films with Garbo, but he could not get her on the telephone.

So there would be only the one collaboration; then or now, one can do little more than echo one of the commissars when he first spies the luxury hotel in the City of Light: "Comrades, why should we lie to each other. It's wonderful!"

In early September 1939, two months before *Ninotchka* was released, Vivian was in London with her daughter. She put Nicola, along with her nurse, on board the *Athena* for the long voyage home. Later, Vivian would claim that she had been unable to obtain passage for herself. Two hundred miles off the coast of Ireland, the ship was struck by a German torpedo. Many of the children on board went down with the ship because at the time of the explosion the adults were in the dining room. Immediately, they were ordered not to go below to their cabins; those that did were met by upsurging water.

In America, it was Labor Day, and the normal radio programming was interrupted for bulletins by, among others, Walter Winchell. When the passenger list was read over the air, MGM executive Sam Katz heard the name "Nicola Lubitsch" and rushed over to Lubitsch's house to break the news, picking up Walter Reisch on the way.

After he was told, an aghast Lubitsch leaned against the piano in the living room, clinging to a silver-framed picture of his daughter. Katz began working the phones. Five MGM employees were called and ordered to work *their* phones. The words "Metro-Goldwyn-Mayer" opened many doors. For hours, Lubitsch remained standing by the piano, clinging to his daughter's photograph.

Finally, a call came from the MGM office in New York. Katz offered the phone to Ernst, but, in Reisch's words, "he was incapable of holding the receiver." Otto took the call.

The information was courtesy of Lord Beaverbrook. When the explosion vibrated through the ship, Nicola's nurse had snatched the child with one hand and a life-preserver with the other and rushed topside. Both of them were immediately put in a lifeboat. For ten hours, they drifted; there was no milk on the lifeboat, so Nicola subsisted on chowder, ginger ale, and potatoes. Finally, they were sighted by the yacht *Southern Cross,* whose propeller wash capsized the lifeboat. Nicola and her nurse were both alive and in fine shape.

Ernst staggered away from the piano and went into his study, locking the door behind him, "without his cigars, without finding any words, without a smile," according to Walter Reisch.

"Baby stays right here after this," Lubitsch declared once Nicola was home on September 18. "No more monkey business. She stays here in America, where she'll be safe."

After Nicola was back home, Lubitsch became even more obsessive about her, sometimes even having his meals in her nursery. Doting, loving, he was bending over the crib one day when he suddenly turned to Vivian and said, "You know, for all she's been through she hasn't much personality."

Another marriage might have been strengthened by the crisis, but not this one. "One of the reasons Vivian was in England was the [rocky marriage]," said Gottfried Reinhardt. "Everybody blamed her for not being with the child, but that saved the child's life, because the nurse acted so correctly."

A few years later, Dorshka Raphaelson was at the train station to pick up her daughter, when Ernst arrived to meet Nicola, who was then about five. The train came in, passengers began moving up the ramp, and Lubitsch turned to Dorshka and said, "This child has been the greatest happiness I have known in my life. Vivien told me you are responsible for us having her."

His attention was diverted by the sight of his daughter coming toward him. "When she came up the aisle," remembered Dorshka Raphaelson, "his face just ate up her darlingness and happiness. That's the one time I saw him when he wasn't the concentrated working man."

It was Vivian who suggested the title for her husband's next film, but her wording was *The Little Shop Around the Corner,* which she thought was worth $500. Lubitsch left out *Little,* and believed that made the title his. Whatever the title, Lubitsch was attracted to the story by its simplicity, its authentic emotions. "I have known just such a little shop in Budapest," he would explain when the finished film premiered in New York. "The feeling between the boss and those who work for him is pretty much the same the world over, it seems to me. Everyone is afraid of losing his job and everyone knows how little human worries can affect his job. If the boss has a touch of dyspepsia, better be careful not to step on his toes; when things have gone well with him, the whole staff reflects his good humor."

Lubitsch would claim that James Stewart had popped into his head when he and Raphaelson were writing the script, partially because of his grace as an instinctive actor, but mostly because he was "the antithesis of the old-time matinee idol; he holds his public by his very lack of a handsome face or a suave manner."

Lubitsch had gotten very lucky with the casting of Stewart, for there were few actors who could pull off the part of Alfred Kralik, and there was only one on the Metro lot.

Lubitsch approached production with a full measure of obsessive care for the external details. Metro's researcher Henry Noerdlinger, who would later become DeMille's head researcher, obtained an inventory from a Budapest leather store, which revealed that most of the leather sold in Hungary was from America and that tan suitcases were particularly popular. When Margaret Sullavan asked for his approval for a simple $1.98 dress she had bought for the part, Lubitsch said it was "Too smart for a clerk looking for a job." He had it altered so it didn't fit quite so neatly, and left out in the sun until it was slightly faded.

Ernst didn't wait to see what the public response to *Ninotchka* would be; by the time it opened in New York on November 9, he had already begun production on *The Shop Around the Corner.* Working quickly, the film he was making matched up to the film in his mind with an astonishing clarity; the movie was completed in twenty-seven days at a cost of $474,000.

The Shop Around the Corner is the story of Matuschek and Company, leather goods merchants, who are, an opening title tells us, "just around the corner from Andrassy Street—on Balta Street in Budapest, Hungary." The film begins as the employees' day begins, with the ritual gathering outside the shop, as everybody waits for Mr. Matuschek to open the store.

They banter, inquire after each other's children, Alfred Kralik (James

Stewart), the head clerk, had dinner the night before with the boss and his wife. The women clerks wonder if the boss's wife has had her face lifted. "How old did she look last night?" one inquires of Kralik. "Forty" he says. "She's had her face lifted," is the decisive response.

The opening scene sets the characters: Frank Morgan's Matuschek, kindly but preoccupied; Joseph Schildkraut's Vadas, conceited, conniving, and relentlessly sycophantic; Felix Bressart's Pirovitch, happy in his life, content in his job, but careful not to stick his head up above the crowd; and William Tracy's Pepi, a brash and blunt errand boy, unbound by the conventions that bind the others.

Into this comfortable, flourishing family comes Klara, a new clerk who promotes herself into a job even though Matuschek and Company is already overstocked with help. Unbeknownst to either of them, Kralik and Klara have been corresponding, addressing each other as "Dear Friend," and have fallen in love with what they imagine to be the other person. Face to face, however, because of their differing status, their mutual competitiveness, and because each idealizes the person reflected in their letters, they can't see each other clearly. Actually, they actively dislike each other.

Lubitsch and Raphaelson masterfully integrate other strands into the story—Matuschek's indecision about whether or not to sell the store, his fears that his wife is having an affair. And Lubitsch works in moments that surely derive from his days at S. Lubitsch, as when a customer inquires, "How much is that belt in the window, the one that says $2.95?"

Mostly though, it is a film of ambience and intimacy about men and women who are happy to be middle class and trying to stay that way—the clerks' quiet desperation to please each customer, and to not displease Mr. Matuschek; the way each of the correspondents is slightly afraid to meet the other one for fear of the ideal of perfection being sullied by grim reality.

Before their official meeting can take place, Kralik is fired by Matuschek, who wrongly believes him to be having an affair with his wife. When Matuschek finds that the real culprit is Vadas, the old man attempts suicide but is stopped by Pepi. Kralik, who now knows that Klara is his beloved, is brought back to manage the store.

It is Christmas Eve. A deep, heavy snow is falling, but inside Matuschek and Company are celebrating, for they have had the best sales since Christmas Eve of 1928. Pepi has been promoted to clerk and takes full advantage of his new position to terrorize the new errand boy. Klara still has her defenses up toward Alfred, hiding behind feigned arrogance and a patronizing air, but, as they sit in the darkened store, he calls her his "Dear Friend." At last, she knows, and the embrace that they have denied themselves for so long finally takes place. In a perfectly paced diminuendo, dreams meld with reality, and harmony is once again restored to Matuschek and Company.

The Shop Around the Corner is immensely ingratiating, but it never condescends to its characters or to us. Part of its strength is its concentrated unity. Lubitsch rigorously excludes everybody outside the immediate family of Matuschek and Company; we never see the home life of Pirovitch, we never see the duplicitous Mrs. Matuschek.

Ernst gives the people at Matuschek and Company the full measure of his respect and affection. Through the dignity with which he treats them, the film becomes a celebration of the ordinary, gently honoring the extraordinary qualities that lie within the most common of us. As Alfred Kralik says, "People seldom go to the trouble of scratching the surface of things to find the inner truth." *The Shop Around the Corner* is the most meaningful tribute possible to the owner and employees of the long-vanished Berlin clothing firm of S. Lubitsch.

"*The Shop Around the Corner* could have been anywhere," pointed out Samson Raphaelson. "It was a shop in the mood and atmosphere of the early 1900s, and that I remember, you see. I had worked in The [World's] Fair in Chicago as a salesman . . . as an extra on Saturdays. I knew and felt the whole atmosphere behind the counter, and Lubitsch as a kid had worked as a helper in [his father's] shop. We just smelled our way through."

The serenity, the ease, and, above all, the tenderness of the picture are astonishing, especially when contrasted with its 1949 musical remake, *In the Good Old Summertime*, pointlessly moved to turn-of-the-century Chicago, with the characters' reality obliterated by their amplification into recognizable musical comedy types. (A 1963 Broadway adaptation, *She Loves Me*, by Jerry Bock and Sheldon Harnick, was considerably better; Broadway musical authority Miles Kreuger calls it "the best musical of the '60s.")

When *The Shop Around the Corner* was released in January 1940, *Variety* called it "smart and clever . . . with all the vivaciousness and piquant humor" expected of Lubitsch. Ironically, *Ninotchka*, which Lubitsch hadn't particularly wanted to make, was less successful than *The Shop Around the Corner*, which Louis B. Mayer hadn't particularly wanted to make.

The film ended up amassing a world gross of $1.3 million and a

$380,000 profit, helped along by a delightful trailer in which Lubitsch made an appearance. Frank Morgan, in character, introduces his establishment—"It's the kind of shop where you get a $3.50 value for $3.48."—and, via clips from the film, the people that work for him. Suddenly, Lubitsch enters the frame, taps Morgan on the shoulder, and points to his watch. "I thought you were a customer," says Morgan, who then introduces Lubitsch. The nattily attired director impatiently acknowledges the camera and takes a puff on his cigar. "The man," says Morgan, "who gave you a Garbo in *Ninotchka* who could make you laugh now gives you a Morgan who can make you laugh." Lubitsch snorts and says "I hope!"

Although Raphaelson was in for a share of any profits on *The Shop Around the Corner,* all he ever saw on top of his $1,000 a week salary was $5,000. "I should have gotten a hell of a lot out of it," he commented in 1971, "but Leland Hayward had not made a good contract for me. I didn't read the fine print. Lubitsch hadn't done the right thing by me. I am sure he didn't."

Lubitsch's two-picture stint at MGM, undertaken because none of the other major studios would have him, began the great, final flourishing of his genius, when he began creating character and story of a sudden, intermingled poignance and vulnerability. Lubitsch's style had long since been pared down to an unobtrusive classicism that usually avoided fancy angles and seldom utilized any but the most rudimentary editing. Other than a more leisurely cutting scheme, Lubitsch's style stopped evolving by 1935, but, perhaps as compensation, what suddenly began to evolve was a deep understanding of people, a more humane view of life.

Sam Raphaelson had a pet theory that one's secret vices have more to do with talent than one's known virtues. "If you have a tendency toward murder and larceny," he explained, "it would be advisable to repress that tendency in your life and to grow into a decent person, but don't repress it in your writing. Let go to the limit—enjoy yourself without the faintest qualm of conscience."

Long before he had ever met Raphaelson, Ernst had been carrying out that dictum, filling his movies with ironic boulevardiers, the sophisticated drawing room swordsmen that he would have liked to have been. No more.

From now on, Ernst Lubitsch would not make movies about the man he wanted to be, or the social set he quietly wished he had been born into. Now, he would make movies about the people he knew, the man he was. The mysterious chemistry of age would make him less German, more

Jewish; he would look beyond the story, through it, and in so doing begin to capture the gentle but palpable wing-beat of life itself.

For nearly twenty years he had divided his male characters into Leading Men and Comic Caricatures. But now, the traits began to blend together. In films like *The Shop Around the Corner, To Be or Not to Be,* and *Heaven Can Wait,* the leading men are both cordial *and* crusty, sincere *and* duplicitous, noble *and* foolish. Partially this was because of his continued reliance on Raphaelson, partly because Ernst was now a middle-aged father with one failed marriage and one that was none too healthy, living in a world that was shortly to begin savagely tearing at itself. The Lubitsch of 1939 was not the Lubitsch of 1931, as Sam Raphaelson was finding out.

"[In the early days] when I'd say, 'Look, we're losing emotion, we don't care anymore,' he used to say . . . 'That's all right, Sam. We get a big laugh here, we pull back into that mood, we dissolve back and we get that mood.' But when he found that that did not happen, he began to pay more attention. Lubitsch's great problem was that he would run empty after a while because he had no lifeline to emotion; his life outside of his work was an increasingly empty one. He had . . . a wretched, meaningless home life. His whole life was his work. He was a sad man to contemplate. I don't think he realized it, because he was a fully successful man and a very wealthy one. But . . . through our experience together, he began to value emotion."

"Which of his movies is most like him?" Lubitsch's niece Ruth Hall considered the question in her small, neat Florida apartment. *"The Shop Around the Corner.* It's so European; it contains the most of what he was, all the types, the people that were his friends, the people he loved."

The lesson of *Broken Lullaby* had taken a long time to percolate, but Lubitsch had learned that great, lasting truths didn't have to be revealed on a battlefield or in a church confessional. They could just as easily be discovered in a little leather goods shop, just around the corner from Andrassy Street—on Balta Street, in Budapest, Hungary.

Although it had been the largesse of studio production that made it possible for Ernst to realize his dream of making *The Shop Around the Corner,* he still felt the need to attempt independent production. In March 1939, while still working on the script of *Ninotchka,* Lubitsch formed an alliance with producer Sol Lesser.

"Sol," remembered Paul Lazarus, Jr., head of advertising and publicity at United Artists, "was one of the merchant princes. He was commercial, but he fancied himself an artist. He really should have been in the clothing business."

Born in Spokane in 1890, by 1939 Lesser's film credentials were minor—some Jackie Coogan silents, some George O'Brien B Westerns, and *Thunder in the Sun,* the feature carved out of Eisenstein's aborted *Que Viva Mexico!* An alliance with Lubitsch was a coup for a man widely regarded as a B-movie producer. "You've got to understand the Hollywood mentality," says Lazarus. "All of the moguls and many of the independents like Lesser were people of no education, out of middle Europe. Anything that could give them an aura of culture or improve their social status was very desirable. Making a deal with Lubitsch, who was a mythical character, would lift him onto another plateau." Not only that, but, as Lesser put it, "Lubitsch was conscientous and dependable as to budget requirements."

Lubitsch was betting that Lesser would give him the money to make his movies in peace; besides that, he was very much the kind of man Lubitsch liked; a *haimish,* unpretentious character and an extraordinarily good businessman who negotiated the deals for the purchases of the land on which the Academy of Motion Picture Arts and Sciences, and the Motion Picture Country Home, would be built.

Lubitsch signed a four-picture contract with Lesser on March 20, 1939. He would receive 50 percent of the stock of Ernst Lubitsch Productions, Inc., even though the vast majority of the firm's financing was supplied by Lesser. There were only 100 shares of stock, 50 of Class A, 50 of Class B, all priced at $10. The company was to be a frugal operation; budgets were set at about $400,000, "unless some well-known star or stars shall be engaged . . . in which event the cost shall be proportionately increased."

Either partner had the option of terminating the agreement after the first or second picture, although United Artists had the option of picking up Lubitsch's option for the second picture. The contract mandated that "Lubitsch shall be in complete charge of the making of the pictures" and that "Each picture shall be advertised as an Ernst Lubitsch production, the name of Ernst Lubitsch to be displayed in letters larger than any other name including the names of the artists participating in such picture, unless such artists shall be stars recognized and advertised as such, in which case the name of Ernst Lubitsch shall be in letters at least as large of as those of the star."

The implications of the contract were clear: Lesser needed him more than he needed Lesser. Lesser's own five-year contract with United Artists, signed on May 12, was very clear on the point that the first picture in the deal had to be directed by Lubitsch.

At last, Ernst would achieve his dream and be fully independent, but not without some sacrifice; in return for ownership of the product, and a percentage of the profits, Lubitsch was working for a guarantee of only $30,000 a picture, the smallest salary he had made since leaving Germany.

Still, it was a coup for Lesser and he knew it. The trade papers were soon featuring full-page photos of Lubitsch, with copy announcing "Sol Lesser presents an ERNST LUBITSCH production." Neither story or stars were mentioned, just the filmmaker. That was enough.

Lubitsch's initial idea for his first independent production was based on a tale that David Selznick's story editor had told him. It involved a governess who takes the job of teaching a reputedly difficult twelve-year-old whose mother has died. After she begins her instructions, she discovers that the problem seems to be with the girl's father, not the girl. Unfortunately, the story editor could remember neither the title nor the author.

Lesser was complaining to his sister-in-law about their dilemma when she recognized the story as a magazine serial written by Rose Franken. After purchasing the story for $25,000, the two partners got on a plane for Los Angeles, with Lubitsch settling down to read the story. After a while, an obviously alarmed Lubitsch turned to Lesser. "This is not a comedy," he said. "Instead it's quite a serious drama. That won't do for me." He continued reading and discovered that the child turned out to be a psychotic who accuses her father of killing her mother. Appalled, he threw the story aside and told his chagrined partner "We must keep on looking for a story." Lesser was out $25,000.

Neither Ernst nor Lesser could find a new story that was to their liking, but their dilemma was eased by Alexander Korda, who was looking for a project for his wife, Merle Oberon. MGM, who owed Korda a favor, gave him a picture commitment from Melvyn Douglas as payment. Korda offered Lesser the two stars and a partial script that had been written around the story of Ernst's 1925 picture *Kiss Me Again,* for what Lesser remembered as "a fair price."

Feeling pressure to get the new venture off dead center, Ernst decided to proceed. Lubitsch assigned Walter Reisch the job of adapting the story, while Lesser negotiated a $500,000 loan from the Bank of America.

Just before production got under way on the picture the partners had provisionally titled *Divorces* but would soon be renamed *That Uncertain Feeling,* Lubitsch embarked on his first acting chore in years. The vehicle was a "Screen Guild Playhouse" radio show on October 20, 1940. The premise of the show was simplicity itself: Lubitsch is directing a radio show with Basil Rathbone and Claudette Colbert. Enter Jack Benny, desperate to broaden his nonexistent range and improve his dismal reputation. "If you can make Garbo laugh, you can make me cry," he explains.

Lubitsch's performance and timing are expert and he gets every laugh that's in the script. His voice is less booming than stage Germans like Sig Rumann, more jovial, but the accent is similar. Obviously, the actor in him was still fairly close to the surface, but he had avoided indulging it for a very long time.*

Lubitsch's performance on "Screen Guild Theater" is consistently hilarious and certainly shows that his gusto for acting had not diminished over time. Moreover, it provokes regret that more opportunities for performing did not present themselves over the years, other than occasional appearances in the trailers for some of his movies. "He probably would have been very good," theorized his friend Mary Loos, "but I think he might have been too involved with his own creativity to step in and do a little vignette for someone else."

That Uncertain Feeling was shot quickly and effortlessly between October and December 1940, and released the following April. Burgess Meredith noted Lubitsch's habit of "just before you [were] going in on a scene of breaking you up [with] a whispered comment. Lubitsch was most amusing, dry . . . He was quietly very witty—always working precisely, softly and swiftly. Between takes . . . he often played the piano quietly in the corner of our soundstage."

Overall, for Meredith, making the picture was "a haunting experience.

*In 1923, just about the time Lubitsch began directing *Rosita,* he had done one day's work playing himself in Rupert Hughes's *Souls for Sale,* a drama about Hollywood (most of the film survives, but Lubitsch's sequence is apparently lost). There were other acting offers over the years; in 1937/38, DeMille had offered him the part of Napoleon in *The Buccaneer.* Although the resemblance was obviously there, and Lubitsch had expressed interest in the part, he ended up passing. In 1945, he was costumed and made up to appear in a scene in Gregory Ratoff's *Where Do We Go From Here.* Although stills exist of Lubitsch on the set, a thorough search of the finished picture fails to disclose Lubitsch anywhere in it.

He'd act everything out for you, because he loved the part, and he'd act it out so funny, and so definitely, that I would stand there as an audience. The reason that it didn't bother me . . . [is] that he would act it out in such a way, and so hilariously, that he would give you the idea of what he wanted without expecting you to do it, because first of all he had a horrendous accent, and he would stop in the middle of when he was acting my lines and make some crack about my brother, who I was having trouble with then, or some purely personal thing which in some psychic way he knew I was undergoing. He was a very psychic man."

There was one amusing, if unexpected sidelight. Merle Oberon, who remembered it as "the happiest picture I ever made," found Lubitsch's methods irresistible; she made it a habit to ask him to act out every scene for her. Months later, when her husband, Alexander Korda, arrived from England, she asked his opinion of the picture. "Oh, fine. You played it beautifully, like a little Jewish girl."

That Uncertain Feeling returns to *Kiss Me Again* not just in plot outline but in theme, of not being able to take any sexual relationship for granted, of the necessity of stoking love's fires with risk, even, if necessary, lubriciousness.

Merle Oberon is Jill, a bored wife plagued by hiccups who goes to a psychiatrist to determine the cause of her malaise.

"Age?" he asks her.

"Twenty-two."

"I am your doctor, Mrs. Baker."

"Thank you," she says, whereupon he writes "24?" on his notepad.

The session continues, with the doctor attempting to get her to breach her own defenses. "Wouldn't you like to meet you?" he asks.

"No. You see, I'm a little shy."

It's no use. At the doctor's office she meets Alexander Sebastian (Burgess Meredith), a blocked concert pianist who can only play well in a studio or in private. "I'm against anything and anybody," he snarls. "I hate my fellow man and he hates me." Later, they go to an art gallery, where Jill asks about the creator of a particularly strong painting. "A woman," snaps Sebastian. "No man could be so malicious."

Jill and Sebastian fall in love, but life with a compulsively self-absorbed, would-be artist/egomaniac can be exhausting, and Baker reverts to her nice, dull husband.

The blatantly antisocial Sebastian promises to perk the movie up, but the triangle of Oberon, Douglas, and Meredith simply fails to ignite. Melvyn Douglas has a nice line in squeamish, uneasy smiles, but it is never a good idea to cast a dutiful, slightly dull actor as a dutiful, slightly dull character, and neither of the other two leads is quite strong enough to carry off the deadpan, somewhat saturnine treatment Lubitsch imposes on the material.

In its portrayal of women as cossetted pets good only for frequenting Elizabeth Arden or trading wisecracks about men and marriage, *That Uncertain Feeling,* is vaguely reminiscent of *The Women,* but it has more damaging internal contradictions. Structurally, Oberon's Jill Baker is rebelling against being treated dismissively as a mere wife, but, as written and directed, that's all she is, and Oberon is not a forceful enough actress to transfer her own strength of personality to her character.

Obviously, after the renewal represented by the two MGM films, Lubitsch's energy was again flagging. He resorts to a variation of Chaplin's famous inferential direction in *A Woman of Paris,* in which Adolphe Menjou takes a large man's handkerchief from a drawer in Edna Purviance's apartment and we know they are living together. Here, Douglas is on the phone when a girl comes in. He goes over to his desk, shuffles around among some papers, and hands her her purse.

Oberon delivers her punch lines effectively enough, but she lacks the requisite lightness of spirit, and she has no inner life. The film could definitely use more close-ups, and, in an odd lapse for a painstaking craftsman like Lubitsch, there are some mismatched cuts. The photography of the normally superb George Barnes lacks the lustre of either the MGM high-key lighting or the Paramount glow, which is unfortunate because the script needs all the help it can get. Clearly, the enforced restrictions of a modest budget were telling on Lubitsch.

The viewer is forced to cling to little in-jokes, as with a character named Kafka who works for Universal Mattress. Except for a funny running joke about a vase that Sebastian finds offensively hideous, the film plays like a mild, innocuous comedy that could have been directed by any number of second-rank filmmakers.

Appropriately enough, both the reviews and the commercial returns were pallid, with a world gross of $848,000 ($585,000 domestic). Sol Lesser said that the film produced a "reasonable profit," but he had been hoping for something more. *Variety* said that "The famed Lubitsch touch is there but the entertainment value isn't . . . as a whole, it is tiring, very slow . . . and embraces numerous situations that are basically weak." The mild picture's mild success would probably have been greater had it not been for World War II closing off most of the European market, a problem of considerable significance for a director like Lubitsch.

Ernst's share of the $100,000 profit was not enough to compensate him for the added grief of assuming far more risk for far less money. Sol Lesser seems to have become quickly disillusioned; certainly he regarded the picture as a bad lot. In September 1941, when the copyright materials necessary to register *That Uncertain Feeling* in England were lost at sea, Lesser told U.A. not to bother spending an additional $28.76. "We do not feel it necessary to copyright the story of *Uncertain Feeling* in England," he wrote the distributor. "The picture is already in distribution and . . . we feel that the expenditure is unnecessary at this time."

Even before Lesser's letter to the U.A. management, he and Ernst had made the decision to go their separate ways. "The marriage wasn't a happy one," said Paul Lazarus. "Sol would have let him do almost anything he wanted, but he also wanted the money coming in regularly." As far as Lesser was concerned, "Ernst required too much of my time, which I could employ to better use." Also, there was no doubt in his mind that his time could bring "better results from a profit point of view."

Soon, Lesser would take over production of the Tarzan pictures from MGM and continue the profitable series while occasionally attempting an upscale effort like *Our Town, Stage Door Canteen,* or *The Red House.* "But," says Lazarus, "he always had a couple of Tarzans in the background." Lubitsch and Lesser maintained a warm social relationship, but, as Lesser's son Julian points out, Sol Lesser never made another romantic comedy.

"After long and careful consideration," Lubitsch wrote United Artist's Arthur Kelly on August 27, 1941, "we both came to the conclusion that with our financial arrangements and limitations we would not be able to make any kind of a picture that would be profitable to us or to the exhibitors. The lack of sufficient funds and the impossibility of casting the [next] picture with important names could only have produced a picture which would have been a great disappointment."

Lubitsch went on to say that he felt it imperative that his next picture "should be a very important one with a high budget." Ernst Lubitsch Productions was dissolved in 1943; Lubitsch and Sol Lesser each received a final disbursement of $10,000 and 50 percent of the rights to *That Uncertain Feeling.*

That Uncertain Feeling was copyrighted by Ernst Lubitsch Productions, but, when the time came to renew the copyright, Lubitsch was long dead, and Lesser wasn't paying attention. As a result, the film fell into the public domain. Thus, one of Lubitsch's worst pictures became one of his most frequently seen.

After what must have been a considerable creative and financial disappointment, Lubitsch pulled himself together and regrouped. Even while he was writing the letter to Arthur Kelly, he was working on the script for the "very important" picture. Since everybody in Hollywood was making an anti-Nazi picture, he would too. But unlike all the others, his would be a masterpiece.

chapter seven

There's a revolution on in the world. Is laughter to depart? Is gracious and
graceful living, wit and the jocund interplay, the amusing warfare of man and
woman all to vanish? Must I weep for the world that was and not be permitted
to re-create it? Devoutly I hope not. For then I should not desire to make more
films. I should be content to die."

— e r n s t   l u b i t s c h ,   j u l y   1 9 4 3

In March 1941, Ernst decided to return to the security of the studios—
and a steady paycheck—by signing a three-year contract at 20th Century-
Fox. He planned to report to the lot by mid to late summer, as soon as
he had his second United Artists picture out of the way. It wouldn't be
that simple.

To Be or Not to Be began life as the second commitment under Lubitsch's
partnership with Sol Lesser. When Ernst Lubitsch Productions was dissolved, United Artists gave the picture to Walter Wanger, but that producer's recent films had been largely unsuccessful, leaving him unable to
finance his portion of the $1 million movie. The production was passed
on to Alexander Korda.

Ernst and Korda had been acquaintances since the late 1920s, when
Alex had arrived in Hollywood and promptly served as the butt of one
of Lubitsch's practical jokes. During a Sunday afternoon stroll, Lubitsch
and a writer friend named Heinrich Fraenkel came upon Korda's house.
Knocking, they found the door open and nobody home. Mischievously,
Lubitsch decided to fake a burglary. Ashtrays, books, anything movable
was stuffed under the couch. The carpet was yanked up and furniture was
shoved around, after which Lubitsch and Fraenkel quickly left.

When they arrived back at Lubitsch's house, they enlisted an actress friend to call Korda, who had arrived home by then. Pretending to be a reporter from the *Los Angeles Times,* she told Korda that a burglary had just been reported at that address. An appalled Korda confirmed that, yes, he had been robbed. The reporter asked him for a recapitulation of his career, and a list of things that had been stolen.

Five minutes later, another Lubitsch friend called, and then another, each one pretending to be a reporter, each asking exactly the same questions: his previous career, how he liked it in Hollywood, whether American women were prettier than European women, and, by the way, what had been stolen?

By the third call, Korda's dramatic imagination had kicked in, and he was reporting that his wife's pearl necklace had been stolen, even though Lubitsch and Fraenkel had never come near it. Lubitsch snatched the telephone, barked "Man, just have a peep under the sofa," in rough Berlin slang, and hung up.

Korda's initial stint in Hollywood had been a failure, but, in England, he struck gold with *The Private Life of Henry VIII,* the momentum of which carried him through a slate of expensive pictures that almost invariably failed. As a British subject, Korda had returned to America with the sanction of the British government, but since most of Korda's films were financed by the Bank of England, he had to keep the British Foreign Exchange Control Board happy; the principal, and most of the resulting profits of films like *The Thief of Baghdad, That Hamilton Woman,* and *The Jungle Book,* were earmarked to be returned to England.

The Jungle Book had run over budget, necessitating additional financing. The banks chose not to indulge Korda and refused to finance anything beyond the Kipling project, which put the Lubitsch venture in sudden jeopardy. Although Korda had invested some $100,000 in start-up costs on the new Lubitsch picture, he lacked sufficient liquidity to continue.

However, as Korda was a co-owner of United Artists, the company, for reasons both legal and psychological, was forced to pick up his commitment with Lubitsch. All this finagling over financing meant that Ernst had to put his commitment to 20th Century-Fox off for nearly a year.

The original story for *To Be or Not to Be* derived largely from Lubitsch himself, although he worked in collaboration with Melchior Lengyel, who reported that "Writing for Lubitsch is just kibitzing." Ernst's first impulse seems to have been to structure the picture as a comeback vehicle for Maurice Chevalier, who had returned to Europe shortly after *The Merry*

Ernst Lubitsch (far right) and the rest of the people making To Be or Not to Be *try to restrain their laughter at the least likely Hamlet in theatrical history.*

Widow. The resulting pictures had received scant distribution in the U.S. Director Robert Florey remembered Chevalier in Paris hoping for the call from Lubitsch that would bring him back to Hollywood. The call never came.

Beyond that, however, Ernst was consciously going to try something different. "I was tired of the two established, recognized recipes," he would write in *The New York Times* of March 29, 1942. "Drama with comedy relief and comedy with dramatic relief. I had made up my mind to make a picture with no attempt to relieve anybody from anything at any time."

The scriptwriter, Edwin Justus Mayer, had previously collaborated with him on *Desire*. Mayer began his creative life as another intellectual New York playwright who had the bad luck to write a scathingly contemptuous piece about movies, the medium in which he would spend the better part of his working life. In an October 1923 issue of *The New York Times*, Mayer referred to Hollywood as "The abode of prosperous failure . . . the retreat of intellectual beachcombers . . . the first refuge of a scoundrel . . . the capital of defeat . . . an outlet of stereotyped forms and sentimental postures."

At the time, Mayer could afford those lofty sentiments, for his play about Benvenuto Cellini, *The Firebrand,* was about to open and be acclaimed as one of the ten best plays of the 1924–25 season. Brooks Atkinson would call him "a writer of originality and taste"; George Jean Nathan said he was "a writer of dignity . . . who tickles the ear with a skillful and fanciful pen."

But Mayer's later plays, such as *Children of Darkness,* although praised for their mordant humor, were financial failures, and by 1927 he was scavenging for jobs alongside the rest of Hollywood's intellectual beachcombers. As usual, Lubitsch chose his collaborator well.

"Eddie Mayer was a far more sophisticated writer and man than Raphaelson," remembered Gottfried Reinhardt. "Mayer was among the intellectuals, part of the clique around Herman Mankiewicz: Hecht and MacArthur, S. N. Behrman, Louis Weitzenkorn and Mayer. In Europe it would have been a coffeehouse atmosphere. They all had wit. In Germany you had nobody in films and hardly anybody in the theater like that, except Brecht, who had a political horizon, which made him much too serious for a man like Lubitsch."

Mayer's script for *To Be or Not to Be* shares with *The Firebrand* and *Children of Darkness* a sense of black comedy, of each character's absurdity, with characterizations defined via sardonic asides. All three scripts revolve around monstrous egos, but there is a difference. Mayer's plays are almost brilliantly written, but they're metallic, lacking in humanity, cold. *To Be or Not to Be* is warm, and no matter how absurd "that great, great Polish actor" Josef Tura may be, there is something very needy, very recognizably human in his actorish vanity. That was the true Lubitsch touch.

· · ·

Lubitsch's contract with United Artists for *To Be or Not to Be* was signed on August 5, 1941. With the proviso that Lubitsch could work for Fox under his preexisting contract with them so long as it would not substantially interfere with work on *To Be or Not to Be,* the contract guaranteed that he "shall not be subject to the supervision or control of any office or employee of any producer except Alexander Korda or any Executive Producer who may succeed Alexander Korda."

Again, Lubitsch was working for less than his usual salary, this time getting $60,000 up front, with another $50,000 payable out of the net profits over the next five years, and 25 percent of any net after $130,000 in profits. (He and Melchior Lengyel received $10,500 for the original story in October 1941, with Lengyel getting $7,000 of that and sole story credit. Edwin Justus Mayer received $2,500 a week to write the shooting script.)

Lubitsch had writer approval, cast approval, and his usual final cut. Clause 24 of Lubitsch's contract states that "The director shall have complete and final control over the production of said photoplay . . . and shall have complete and final control over the cutting and editing." U.A. would only be allowed to interfere with the form of the picture if censorship boards demanded changes as a condition for release.

Eager to work for a great director, Jack Benny came on board for $125,000 plus 10 percent of the distributor's world gross in excess of $1,250,000. Before the deal was signed, an obviously embarrassed Lubitsch asked Benny to make a test in Nazi regalia to see if he could play one of the scenes where Josef Tura goes undercover. Benny didn't mind the test and passed with flying colors.

While the money was good, it wasn't why Benny was eager to make the movie. Benny had told Lubitsch over a year before, long before the script was even written, that he'd do the film. "If you want me for a picture, I want to be in it," he had told Lubitsch. "It was always impossible for comedians like me or Hope to get a good director for a movie," Benny remembered in 1973. "That's why we made lousy movies—and here was *Ernst Lubitsch* for God's sake, calling to ask if I'd do a picture with him. Who *cares* what the script is!" Benny said that Lubitsch was "the greatest comedy director that ever lived," and the only other director to whom he would have given an automatic "yes" was Leo McCarey.

Although Ernst played around with the idea of Miriam Hopkins opposite Benny, she and the comedian had an uneasy relationship. Moreover, as soon as Hopkins heard of Lubitsch's interest, she began pushing to have her part built up. Benny began campaigning for Carole Lombard, but Korda passed the buck to Lubitsch, and Lubitsch passed it right back to Korda. Finally, Korda and Benny went out one night in New York, with Korda getting very drunk. After some minor cajoling by Benny, Korda wired U.A. to hire Lombard.

Ernst had been good friends with Carole Lombard since her earliest days at Paramount. Although he had never cast her in one of his own pictures, and had even stated, upon becoming production head at Paramount, that the studio's only long-range female assets were Claudette Colbert and Marlene Dietrich, they remained close. Lombard once told the director Sidney Salkow that she had attempted to persuade Lubitsch to direct her in a film entitled *Love for Breakfast*. He wasn't convinced. "I don't think it's going to be a success," Lubitsch said.

Desperate, Lombard countered with the only thing at her disposal. "If it turns out to be a stinker, you can have your way with me." Ernst's face broke into a smile at the thought, but Lombard reached over the desk and snatched the cigar from his mouth. "And if it's a hit," she said, "I'll shove this black thing up your ass."

Although Lombard's husband, Clark Gable, was unenthusiastic about both the script of *To Be or Not to Be* and Lubitsch (whom Gable supposedly referred to as "the horny Hun"), Lombard signed on anyway, for $75,000 in cash, with an additional $75,000 to be paid out of 4.0837 percent of the producer's profits. The only unusual clause in Lombard's contract was one specifying that Irene design her wardrobe, "if Irene is reasonably available." Irene was; Irene did.

United Artists agreed to undertake production of the film themselves, something they had traditionally worked very hard to avoid. Then as now, film production can easily turn into a financial bloodbath, while film distribution is a virtual license to print money.

On August 26, U.A. formed Romaine Film Corporation and secured a loan from the Bank of America for $1,200,000. Production began on November 6, and was completed in forty-two days, although the last work day for Carole Lombard was New Year's Eve, when she did a day's work posing for stills shot by Robert Coburn.

Initially, the production was hampered by Jack Benny's nervousness. Benny was an innately modest man with a string of so-so movies behind him that were rarely as bad as he pretended they were. "I made twenty-two [movies]," he admitted at the end of his life. "And most of 'em were good." Nevertheless, he was mystified as to why Lubitsch had expressly chosen him for the part of Josef Tura.

"You think you are a comedian," responded Lubitsch. "You are not a comedian. You are not even a clown. You are fooling the public for thirty years. You are fooling even yourself. A clown—he is a performer what is doing funny things. A comedian—he is a performer what is saying funny things. But you, Jack, you are an actor, you are an actor playing the part of a comedian and this you are doing very well. But do not worry, I keep your secret to myself."

Although Benny had never thought of it that way, he had to admit that Lubitsch was right. The painstakingly developed character of a cheap, vain, petty, mean man who played the violin badly was not at all like the real Benny . . . except for the part about the violin.

Although Benny loved the part of Josef Tura and loved Lubitsch ("He'd have done anything for Lubitsch," remembered Benny's daughter, Joan. "He thought he was the best"), he was extremely uncertain all through production. "Jack was an innocent," recalled Robert Stack, who had the difficult job of playing Carole Lombard's young lover, in spite of the fact he had known her since he was a child. "He'd never done a movie that worked. He'd always ask me, 'Is it funny?' and I'd say, 'Jesus, don't ask me.' 'But you're an actor,' he'd say. Basically, he was scared to death."

Benny did not seem bothered by Lubitsch's habit of acting out every comedy scene, not from the point of view of a director but that of an actor, a "corny comedian," in Benny's words. "Lubitsch was about the only director who ever really directed me," Benny explained to Milt Josefsberg, one of his writers. "In practically all of my earlier pictures the directors would say, 'Jack, you know so much more about comedy than I do, play the scene the way you feel it.' The only trouble was that I knew lots about radio comedy, a little about stage comedy, and nothing about movies."

As if the problems of the picture's financing and its worried star were not omens enough, there were more harbingers of trouble. On the day Lubitsch was shooting a scene of storm troopers marching down the street, a visitor on the set, a woman who had just come out of occupied Poland, fainted dead away. Behind the scenes, there was only one outbreak of hostilities. Miklos Rozsa, musical director for the Korda operation, had originally been scheduled to score the picture, but he was appalled by the script's satirical take on the Nazis and flatly refused to participate. Korda and Lubitsch assigned the musical score to Werner Heymann.

During one scene, Stack was having trouble, which Lubitsch's sense of precision could not allow. Putting his hands behind his back, he walked back and forth for a bit, then walked into the set. "Bobby, try this," he said, and played Stack's part himself.

"He exaggerated the key to the scene," remembered Stack. "He caricatured it and I saw it at once and it became easy. He didn't play it naturalistically, he made it larger, so I'd get the sense of it. After that, it flew like a bird."

Stack found that the basis of Lubitsch's gift was his ability to take and maintain control. "He was a Renaissance man. He could do it all. He was an actor, a writer, a cameraman, an art director. He did not allocate responsibility. You must remember, that didn't happen in those days. Everybody was in a box. The writer did what he did, the art director did what he did. For instance, I worked with Frank Borzage on *The Mortal Storm*. Borzage didn't do *anything*. He'd set up the shot, make sure it was composed, tamp down his pipe, turn his back and smoke and let the actors do the scene. He pretty much let them take over. But he cast the film perfectly. Now, if less gifted people try that, they won't get away with it.

"But there was no ego working with Lubitsch. He never manifested any himself and he obviously loved actors. He could be a little rough, yes. Jack was not an actor per se, and sometimes [Lubitsch] made him do a lot of takes. Specifically, the scene where Jack comes home and finds me in his bed asleep and does a series of double takes, he made Jack do at least thirty takes on that scene."

Despite Lubitsch's demands, the picture was made in an atmosphere of affection and warmth. Even if Carole Lombard was not scheduled to work, she would drive into Hollywood from her ranch in the San Fernando Valley to sit on the set and watch Lubitsch work. "Everyone was in awe of him," remembered Jack Benny, "[but] we did nothing but laugh." Stills of the production, whether of script conferences or just the cast and crew waiting between shots, show virtually everybody laughing uproariously.

Although the script was sacrosanct, Lubitsch dreamed up a few additional laughs on the set. The film offers a running gag involving Sig Rumann's officious Nazi (the immortal Concentration Camp Ehrhardt) screaming for his assistant Schultz. At the end of the picture, a distraught Ehrhardt goes behind a closed door to commit suicide. There is a shot, and the camera holds on the door for a few seconds, only to have the silence broken by Ehrhardt again screaming for "Schultz!," a topper added on the set.

The director was no more given to compromising quality than before. At one point, Lubitsch asked Benny to take a look at the rough edit of a scene they had just completed. Although Benny was unsure of his expertise in film comedy, he told Lubitsch that he thought it could be better. Lubitsch promptly interrupted the shooting schedule to redo the scene. "Everything had to be just so," remembered Benny.

As the production wrapped just before Christmas, Carole Lombard delighted Benny by promising to guest on his radio show as soon as she returned from a bond-selling tour in mid-January. Beyond that, she was planning to spend some time tending to her marriage, which was currently going through a rocky phase.

"I think the marriage would have survived," says Robert Stack, who knew both partners well. "I know they had a fight before she left on the bond-selling trip. But I don't think any [other] woman was going to do for [Clark Gable] what Carole did. She became one of the guys, completely adjusted to him, learned to shoot, go out in duck-blinds, all that."

As Lubitsch began to edit the picture in the early part of January, United Artists began to make throat-clearing noises about the title. The Shakespearean reference contained in the title *To Be or Not to Be* was, they felt, too highbrow, possibly misleading, and this was, after all, a commercial venture. Lubitsch, undoubtedly with tongue planted deeply in his cheek, suggested as an alternative *The Censor Forbids,* which promptly drew angry cables from Benny and Lombard.

"IN THE INTEREST OF A PICTURE IN WHICH I AM AN INVESTOR AS WELL AS A PARTICIPANT," wired Lombard to U.A. president Grad Sears on January 13, "I FEEL THAT MY INVESTMENT IS JEOPARDIZED BY THE PROPOSED TITLE CHANGE. I CONSIDER THE TITLE 'THE CENSOR FORBIDS' SUGGESTIVE AND DEFINITELY QUESTION ITS GOOD TASTE. IT IN NO WAY CONVEYS THE SPIRIT OF THE PICTURE AND IS UNBECOMING TO AN ORGANIZATION AS IMPORTANT AS UNITED ARTISTS. SO STRONGLY DO I FEEL ABOUT THIS THAT HAD THE PICTURE BEEN OFFERED TO ME UNDER [THAT] TITLE, I DEFINITELY WOULD NOT HAVE ACCEPTED THE ENGAGEMENT NOR WOULD I HAVE INVESTED IN THE VENTURE UNDER ANY CIRCUMSTANCES WHATSOEVER. I STRONGLY RECOMMEND THAT NO CHANGE BE MADE FROM THE ORIGINAL TITLE . . . WHICH IN MY OPINION FITS THE PICTURE, THE STORY AND THE SITUATION. WILL YOU PLEASE ADVISE ME."

Jack Benny's protests were no less virulent: "I PROTEST MOST EMPHATICALLY AGAINST CHANGING THE TITLE . . . WHICH I CONSIDER HIGHLY SUGGESTIVE

AND CONTRARY TO THE SPIRIT OF MY EMPLOYMENT CONTRACT. I HAVE TRIED FOR YEARS TO BUILD UP A REPUTATION FOR CLEAN HUMOR OVER THE RADIO AND THE RELEASE FOR ANY PICTURE THAT COUPLES MY NAME WITH A TITLE OF THIS KIND CANNOT BUT DO ME IRREPARABLE DAMAGE . . . I EARNESTLY URGE YOU TO RECONSIDER AND TO GIVE THIS PICTURE A TITLE WHICH HONESTLY REFLECTS ITS TONE OF WHOLESOME HUMOR. I HAVE NEVER HAD TO STOOP TO SENSATIONALISM TO ATTRACT AN AUDIENCE. PLEASE ADVISE."

Grad Sears sent beseeching letters to both Lombard and Benny insisting that *The Censor Forbids* had been Lubitsch's idea, but that he was willing to discuss any proposed title change, although he was "absolutely certain that the title *To Be or Not to Be* is not box office."

That same day, Lubitsch wired Sears that he wanted to withdraw his alternate title. "I FEEL THAT INASMUCH AS BOTH [Lombard and Benny] ARE INVESTORS AND PARTICIPANTS WE HAVE TO CONSIDER THEM PARTICULARLY AS IT WAS ONLY THROUGH THEIR MARVELOUS COOPERATION THAT WE COULD BRING IN THE PICTURE FOR THAT PRICE . . . THEY NOT ONLY DISLIKE THE TITLE BUT ARE AFRAID THAT THE VAST MAJORITY OF EXHIBITORS IN ADVERTISING WILL USE THIS TITLE FOR UNDIGNIFIED SEXUAL EXPLOITATION AND I CANNOT DENY THAT SUCH A POSSIBILITY EXISTS. BENNY'S ADVERTISING OF OUR PICTURE OVER RADIO IS OF TREMENDOUS VALUE AND . . . HE FLATLY REFUSES TO MENTION 'THE CENSOR FORBIDS' IN HIS BROADCASTS . . . I HAVE NEVER WEAKENED ON 'TO BE OR NOT TO BE' DESPITE RESISTANCE BY SALES DEPARTMENT BECAUSE I KNOW THAT ANY-THING UNUSUAL ALWAYS MEETS WITH RESISTANCE. THIS TITLE NOT ONLY FITS THE PICTURE BUT I FIRMLY BELIEVE THAT THE STRENGTH OF SEVERAL SCENES IN PICTURE WOULD BE ENHANCED BY ORIGINAL TITLE.

"IF FOR INSTANCE PAUL MUNI WOULD APPEAR IN 'THE DICTATOR' AUDIENCE WOULD ENTER THE THEATER WITH ENTIRELY DIFFERENT EXPECTATIONS AS IF CHARLIE CHAPLIN APPEARS UNDER THE SAME TITLE, AND IF JACK BENNY APPEARS IN 'TO BE OR NOT TO BE' I DON'T BELIEVE THAT ANYBODY WOULD GET THE IMPRESSION HE WANTS TO RIVAL JACK BARRYMORE OR JOHN GIELGUD BUT AM SURE THAT AUDIENCES EVERYWHERE ANTICIPATE A LOT OF FUN ESPECIALLY AS HE IS ABLE TO EXPLAIN THAT BEFOREHAND TO GREATEST LISTENING AUDIENCE IN THIS COUNTRY. REGARDS."

Lubitsch's alternate title was indeed awful, so awful it couldn't have been an accident. Faced with the rather obviously orchestrated wrath of the picture's stars, and Benny's threat to withhold valuable plugs on his radio show, U.A. had no choice but to capitulate and leave *To Be or Not to Be* as the title.

But the picture's troubles weren't over yet. As the picture was being scored, Lubitsch was outraged to discover that Werner Heymann had "Mickey Moused" a highly dramatic scene, that is, had musically mimicked the physical action of the actors, thereby cheapening the scene. Miklos Rozsa was called to the studio and confronted by a furious Lubitsch, who told him that he, Rozsa, was the musical director on the picture, his supervision had been lacking, and what exactly did he intend to do about it?

It was ten in the morning, the musicians were waiting on the recording stage, and there wasn't money in the budget to go so far as five minutes past six that night. Rozsa looked at the scene, timed it, went back to his office, called for copyists and orchestrators, and began writing music. By four o'clock, the scene was written and recorded, all three minutes of it. Lubitsch was happy, and Werner Heymann gave Rozsa a boxer puppy as thanks for bailing him out of trouble.

On January 16, 1942, Carole Lombard and her mother got on a plane in Indianapolis for a multiple-stop flight that was supposed to end seventeen hours later in Los Angeles. But a few minutes after 7 P.M., the plane slammed into Olcott Mountain, a few miles west of Las Vegas, instantly killing all twenty-two people on board.

It had been such a near thing; the plane impacted only 120 feet from the top of the mountain. The flight had been originally scheduled to go from Albuquerque to Boulder, but the Boulder airport was a daylight-only field. Since night would have fallen by the time they got to Boulder, pilot Wayne Williams made the decision to head for Las Vegas. A later inquiry determined that Williams had strayed off course, probably in an attempt to make up lost time and get to Los Angeles on schedule.

Lubitsch's ex-stepson Eddie was by then a meteorologist working for TWA airlines and a good friend of the pilot. Wayne Williams was widely regarded as a superb pilot, so the accident caused consternation among his friends. Gradually, they came around to the idea that the 120-foot shortfall might have occurred because Williams had been in the back of the plane talking to Lombard. In any case, the FAA raised the minimum altitude for planes in the area by a full 1,000 feet.

In addition to his grief, Clark Gable's reaction was complicated by a full measure of guilt. "If Clark didn't have a death wish after that, it was certainly close," said Robert Stack. "His attitude became 'I don't care if I die.' He had terrible guilt. Much later, he married Kay [Spreckels], and she was a great deal like Carole."

Lombard's death necessitated some slight reediting in *To Be or Not to Be* to cover the deletion of a particularly unfortunate line: "What can happen in a plane?" That added another $35,000 to the budget. The total cost of *To Be or Not to Be* came to $1,022,000.

The death of a star before the release of a picture has traditionally been considered a harbinger of financial disaster, although for every *The Misfits,* there is a *Son of the Sheik.* Certainly, U.A. seemed more than slightly confused. The company archives are rife with correspondence over whether or not Lombard's death invalidated the contractual provision by which one-half of 1 percent of her percentage of the picture was to be donated to the Motion Picture Relief Fund.

The film was released on March 6, 1942, but two weeks before that, U.A. had already made plans to dissolve the Romaine Film Corporation, which actually happened on June 30, as the picture was still playing around the country. Not only that, but they adopted the "cost recovery basis" for figuring the financial returns, meaning they deducted their costs from the gross in an amount sufficient to reimburse their negative cost before even reporting any income.

Not surprisingly, they declared a loss on the film, in spite of the fact that their own records showed a worldwide gross of $2.1 million, which would, under "conventional" motion picture accounting methods, have produced a profit somewhere over $300,000. Lubitsch was not paid the remaining $50,000 due him until late in 1943, and not until he wrote a slightly plaintive letter to U.A.'s Arthur Kelly, who had mentioned signing a dividend check for him when the two men ran into each other one night at New York's "21." "Were you kidding or was it serious?" asked Lubitsch. Before he died, Lubitsch collected another $27,000 in small chunks, while Lombard's estate only got $57,307 of the $75,000 in profits she was contractually entitled to.

Eventually, the Internal Revenue Service took United Artists to tax court over their manipulation of the Romaine Film Corporation. U.A. had to admit that they had indeed paid Lubitsch his $50,000 share of the profits, not to mention $58,000 to Benny for his share of the profits, all of which made their contention that there were no profits slightly suspect.

In tax court, U.A. argued that the entire picture had been a salvage operation, that Lombard's death had raised serious doubts in the company's mind as to the possibility of success, and that the theme of the picture was a humorous treatment of Nazis. "During the early portion of 1942," the company stated in a brief, "due to the success of Germany in the war, the Nazis were not humorous characters and the producers of the picture had serious doubts as to the reception, in view of the world situation, a picture kidding the Nazis would receive."

For a company with a reputation for financial maladroitness, it was a pretty fair piece of sharp dealing, but the government charged that the Romaine Film Corporation owed taxes totaling at least $74,067.21, a figure that, after some serious negotiating and much interoffice correspondence among lawyers and accountants, was reduced to $21,746.41. It was not until February 1949 that the case would be decided, with the court determining that United Artists owed the government $11,200, along with a 25 percent penalty.

Variety said that *To Be or Not to Be* was "typically Lubitsch . . . one of his best productions in a number of years" and "an excellent box-office attraction." *The National Board of Review Magazine* liked the film, but against their better judgment, calling it "an . . . incongruous mixture . . . which many people will protest against, warmly and sincerely . . . There's no escaping what, to use the gentlest terms for it, must be called a lapse of taste in the picture. There have been, and will be, harsher words for it."

Like, for instance, those chosen by The New York *Morning Telegraph,* which said that Lubitsch had devised "a sly approach, and a cute idea, and if it were laid in any place but Warsaw, it would have been among the best things Lubitsch has ever done." The man who was often derided for concentrating on the trivialities of the boudoir was now being slammed for assigning himself a morbid, serious subject and setting, especially by the reliably dreary Bosley Crowther of *The New York Times,* who called it "a callous comedy . . . a shocking confusion of realism and romance . . . Frankly, this corner is unable even remotely to comprehend the humor . . . in such a juxtaposition of fancy and fact. Where is the point of contact between an utterly artificial plot and the anguish of a nation which is one of the great tragedies of our time? . . . You might almost think Mr. Lubitsch had the attitude of 'anything for a laugh.' "

"It was tragic," remembered Robert Stack. "The press just did a terrible number on Lubitsch, and the arrogance he supposedly had in making fun of the Polish situation. But he was a Jew from the Old Country himself! It was the best satire and put-down of Nazism that's ever been done, but they weren't hip enough to pick up on what he was doing."

The press weren't the only ones. At the preview of *To Be or Not to Be* at the Village Theater in Westwood, on came the scene in which Concentration Camp Ehrhardt offers a scabrous one-liner about Josef Tura: "What he did to Shakespeare we are doing now to Poland." The line was met with dead silence.

After the preview, Lubitsch, Vivian, Charlie Brackett, Billy Wilder, Alexander Korda, Henry Blanke, and Walter Reisch went to a nightclub on Sunset Boulevard for a post-mortem. After much throat-clearing and many noncommittal sounds, Vivian finally suggested eliminating the line. Everybody else immediately concurred. Walter Reisch remembered that Ernst was "aghast . . . to be accused of lack of taste made his face waxen and the long cigar tremble in his mouth."

Despite the virtually unanimous opinion of his closest friends, the line stayed in the picture. After *To Be or Not to Be* was released, Ernst was genuinely wounded by the adverse comments and sprang to his own defense with an article in *The New York Times.* "I admit," he wrote, "that I have not resorted to the methods usually employed . . . to depict Nazi terror. No actual torture chamber is photographed, no flogging is shown, no close-ups of excited Nazis using their whips and rolling their eyes in lust. My Nazis are different; they passed that stage long ago. Brutality, flogging and torture have become their daily routine. They talk about it the same way as a salesman referring to the sale of a handbag. Their humor is built around concentration camps, around the sufferings of their victims."

Although Lubitsch always prided himself on the decorousness of his films, the true genesis of *To Be or Not to Be,* its daring analogy between the rape of a nation with the aesthetic rape of a playwright, was unknowingly inspired by the savagely misanthropic W. C. Fields.

Over a year later, as Ernst was awaiting the release of his next picture, the wounds had healed sufficiently so that Lubitsch could talk about the original idea for his most daring film. He explained to a reporter that he used to have a hard and fast rule regarding jokes about blindness. Blindness, Lubitsch believed, was the most terrible affliction that could be visited upon man and was therefore off-limits. But, he explained, one day at Paramount he had seen a movie with a blind man (Fields' *It's a Gift*) "with comedy all about this blind man. I laughed and I laughed. Then I realized there can be no rules. It must depend on how it is done.

"It seemed to me that the only way to get people to hear about the miseries of Poland was to make a comedy. Audiences would feel sympathy and admiration for people who could still laugh in their tragedy."

Then, as always, he indicated that he knew the true worth of what he had created, despite the carpings of his contemporaries. "What is the only picture that is still remembered from the last war? It's not Griffith's *Hearts of the World,* or any of those sad ones. It's Chaplin's *Shoulder Arms.*"

To Be or Not to Be opens with the words "An Ernst Lubitsch Production," with Lubitsch's handwritten signature in place of type. It's the story of the feckless theatrical troupe headed by Josef and Maria Tura, the Lunt and Fontanne of Warsaw. They are, of course, genial egomaniacs—Maria tells her distraught husband that she'd kiss him but it would spoil her makeup—and she is carrying on a heavy flirtation with a handsome young bomber pilot (Robert Stack) who leaves for their trysts by conspicuously stomping out of the theater whenever Tura goes into his "To be or not to be" soliloquy. It's the one thing that shakes Tura's preening self-regard, inducing a state bordering on nervous collapse.

In Maria's dressing room, the lovestruck pilot moons. "This is the first time I ever met an actress," he exclaims.

"Lieutenant, this is the first time I ever met a man who could drop three tons of dynamite in two minutes," she responds.

Even the small-part actors have caught the Turas' virus of pompousness. "It'll get a laugh," says one about a piece of business, but the director explodes. "I don't want a laugh there." A philosophical spear-carrier who yearns to play Shylock (the wonderful Felix Bressart, serving as Lubitsch's mouthpiece) interjects himself into the argument. "A laugh," he says, "is nothing to be sneezed at."

However, in August 1939, even genial egomaniacs cannot ignore the real world. An anti-Nazi play they have been rehearsing is forbidden to open, so they hurriedly substitute *Hamlet.* And that too has a shortened run, as Warsaw is occupied by Nazi troops.

Back in England, Professor Siletsky, a Nazi masquerading as a Polish patriot, leaves for home with a list of the members of the Polish underground; the Turas and their bedraggled troupe are enlisted to kill the traitor and keep the renegades of Poland alive.

To Be or Not to Be begins as backstage farce, turns into wartime melodrama, then begins intermingling the strands until, finally, it returns to farce at the end. Through it all, Lubitsch never drops a thread in this, the most intricate, least foolproof script he ever attempted.

Lubitsch adopts the same central theme that enabled him to break through to the emotionally nurturing characters in *The Shop Around the*

Corner: a cohesive but endangered community, a small band of brothers whose primary allegiance is to each other. Tura and company may be bad actors, but they are very good friends, freely risking their lives for each other and for their country, and all through using the tools of their trade: makeup, spotlights, curtains. In a word, artifice.

As usual, Lubitsch casts actors who bring very specific characterizations with them: Benny's invariably aggrieved vanity, Lombard's glistening earthiness and her airy, surprising line readings (she says "Bye!" with a lilt, like a tinkling bell), Lionel Atwill's fustian hamming.

Lubitsch carefully constructs his film so that the laughs derive far more from character than they do from situations. But the situations—Benny's immortal "So, they call me Concentration Camp Erhardt!" *pas de deux* with Sig Rumann—intensify the traits of the characters; vanity flares up at the most inopportune moments, as when Tura, masquerading as a Nazi, can't resist fishing for compliments (unsuccessfully) for "that great, great actor Josef Tura." Emotional imperatives, no matter how greatly they increase the potential for disaster, are too strong to deny.

This, and the large glistening patch of blood on the coat of the dying Siletsky, make *To Be or Not to Be* oddly realistic despite the preponderance of studio sets. Josef and Maria find in war the glory that had always been denied them in the theater. *To Be or Not to Be* is consistently hilarious, but Lubitsch's sense of commitment, of engagement, is matched by his characters'; they become moving because they put aside their petty individual grievances for the collective good. Through their absurd but authentic bravery, they find a grandeur, a nobility they never could have achieved through their acting.

At its comic heart, with lines like "What he did to Shakespeare we are doing now to Poland," *To Be or Not to Be* is black comedy, and, as James Harvey has pointed out, its coarseness, its moments of low vaudeville, are "not slapdash and inadvertent but aggressive and purposeful, aimed at all forms and degrees of power worship . . . The Nazis in this film *are* like ordinary people. They are also monsters. Evil is clearly named; but it is also brought closer to familiar feelings and situations than people expected it to be in such a film."

The critical trouble Lubitsch encountered derived from the simple fact that black comedy wouldn't be invented for twenty more years. While other directors—good ones—like George Stevens *(The More the Merrier)* or Leo McCarey *(Once Upon a Honeymoon)* were playing the war safe, sappy, and, ultimately, sentimental, Lubitsch dared to satirize oppressor and victim alike.

Whatever the critics thought about *To Be or Not to Be,* it didn't affect the mutual admiration between Lubitsch and Jack Benny. In the first week of November 1942, Ernst directed a week of retakes and a few added scenes on Benny's vehicle *The Meanest Man in the World.* Although Lubitsch was far beyond doing uncredited retakes even as a favor to Darryl Zanuck, he willingly undertook the job because of his affection for Benny. His handling of the scenes between Benny and Eddie "Rochester" Anderson provided the charming if brief little film with its sole reason for existence. In later years, Benny admitted that he only really liked three of his movies—*Charley's Aunt, George Washington Slept Here, The Meanest Man in the World.* And, he would say, he only loved one—*To Be or Not to Be.*

Ernst finally reported to 20th Century-Fox in February 1942, nearly a year after he had signed his original three-year deal. Fox was the domain of two men: Darryl Zanuck and, behind the scenes, Joseph Schenck. Writer/director Philip Dunne called Darryl Zanuck "the Knute Rockne of studio heads, always driving, always encouraging . . . always trying to make the picture better, to move it faster." A little bull of a man with a sharp, needling sense of humor, Zanuck viewed women the way Caesar viewed Gaul; the producer once described a tender love scene as being one where the hero "rams his tongue down her throat."

The men who worked for Zanuck remember him with phrases like "the executive par excellence." Elia Kazan, a dominating man without much stomach for other dominating men, said in his memoirs that "Everyone who worked for him respected him. So did I." Joseph Silver, the son of Zanuck's barber, who eventually became head of postproduction at Fox, said that "If you were part of his team, he was very loyal. He was very rough, but never with little people . . . producers, directors, he could be very rough [with], but he never, ever yelled at underlings."

Everybody agreed that Zanuck's great gift was in editing. "He truly knew all about film editing," remembered Silver. "He had a [photographic] memory. He looked at every foot of dailies that [were] shot . . . He did the final editing on every show." Zanuck was something of a nocturnal creature and wouldn't watch rushes till late at night, usually starting about 11 P.M., with a resulting flood of (invariably pointed) notes and memos landing in studio mailboxes the next day.

One of Zanuck's most admirable qualities was the fact that he would listen. Joe Silver's father was usually invited to screenings of rough cuts, so Zanuck could get the opinion of someone who wasn't in the industry and had no vested interest in a given picture's success or failure. "He would accept ideas from anybody, including the cop at the front gate," said producer David Brown, who was his story editor for years, "and he would always admit it when he was wrong. A strong man like Otto Preminger could even talk him out of something, but if a director was indecisive or didn't know what he wanted, Darryl would walk all over him."

Zanuck's great liability was the fact that Fox was light on stars. After Shirley Temple hit puberty and saw her career disappear, about all Zanuck could offer were Tyrone Power, Alice Faye, Betty Grable, or Don Ameche, most of whom would have been lucky to get second leads at Metro. This meant that the script, the story, had to be the star of a Zanuck picture. For Zanuck, stars were incidental, and he would rather have a good story with a mediocre cast than a yeoman effort on flawed content.

If he liked and respected you, Zanuck could be an admirable mensch. If a few writers had done good work, Zanuck would instruct them to borrow some skiing clothes from the wardrobe department and fly up to Sun Valley for a story conference for a week. As there was rarely more than a single story conference during the week, it was Zanuck's way of saying thank you.

"One time," remembered composer David Raksin, "I did something absolutely contrary to his wishes and I thought it was the end of my career. I was scoring a Western for him and he wanted the aftermath of a Indian massacre to be scored with 'Bury Me Not on the Lone Prairie.' I thought what he wanted was vulgar."

Raksin scored the film his own way. At the studio screening, Zanuck asked him why he hadn't used "Bury Me Not on the Lone Prairie." Raksin explained and Zanuck said that he wanted the scene rescored, which meant the picture would miss its scheduled release date.

"I was going out the door when Zanuck stopped me and ostentatiously said, so the other people in the room could hear it, 'Don't worry about this. When I make a mistake, it costs the studio a half million dollars.' "

While Zanuck made the pictures, Joe Schenck, chairman of the board, worked behind the scenes. Zanuck set policy but Schenck made sure that the policy could be enforced. "Schneck was the money man," remembered David Brown, "but he was not only the catalyst. He put things together. I don't think he ever read a script; Darryl would never ask his opinion on an individual picture, but he would ask his opinion on deals. He was a godfather, an elder statesman, a problem solver when costs got out of line. Uncle Joe was totally loyal, a crony loyalty. You could go to him with a problem and he'd solve it.

"Every highly visible person in Hollywood has an invisible partner who is never a threat creatively but makes it happen financially. That was Uncle Joe."

A gifted filmmaker in his own right, Schenck was one of the few moguls who was loved for his decency rather than feared for his power. In the silent days, he had fallen in love with and eventually married the actress Norma Talmadge. In order to keep Norma's mother, Peg, happy, Schenck assigned Constance Talmadge, the flighty but delightful sister nicknamed Dutch, to Anita Loos and her husband, John Emerson. Their assignment was to keep Dutch busy and construct a series of comedies that would be a distaff version of the breezy, exuberant, successful Douglas Fairbanks films.

One day Schenck called Loos and Emerson in to his office and said, "When I put Dutch into your hands, it was only to satisfy Peg. I never expected to make money on the deal. But the pictures have turned out to be gold mines, so I want you two to have a little bonus." He handed them a check for $50,000.

Universally remembered as a quiet, gentle man, Schenck lavished attention and gifts on his butler's daughter, who was treated as if she were his own child. Although, by the time Lubitsch went to work at Fox, Schenck had been divorced from Norma Talmadge for ten years, Schenck's enormous Spanish stucco mansion in Beverly Hills was dominated by a full-length portrait of the actress that hung in the living room. But Schenck was a pragmatist; whatever his lingering feelings for Talmadge, he was well-known for his enjoyment of the services of the more compliant Fox starlets.

So it was that Lubitsch found himself at a studio bound on one side by a serene old capo and on the other by a nervous, energetic firecracker. Because of Zanuck's overwhelming certitude and ego-driven dominance, 20th Century-Fox didn't make a habit of giving directors the kind of latitude they had at, say, Paramount. Long-term directors at Fox were competent professionals like Walter Lang or, on a higher level, Henry Hathaway or Henry King. In Lubitsch's well-chosen phrase, they were script-shooters, but with unfailing picture sense. In most cases, the director's job ended when shooting did, with Zanuck taking over the postproduction process.

"Zanuck looked on [the director] as a necessary evil," remembered Philip Dunne. Not only was the director forbidden from working on the final editing, he was rarely involved in developing the script. Yet, according to Dunne, "Zanuck really understood people who worked for him.

He knew which ones had to be cajoled, and which ones had to be bullied. I saw him treat Mike Curtiz like a slave. But he wouldn't do that with Nunnally Johnson and he wouldn't do that with me, or certainly not with Lubitsch. He had the great executive knack of knowing how to get the best out of each person." Zanuck, then, was a secure enough man to give a berth to a powerhouse director if he respected him. John Ford, say, or Joseph L. Mankiewicz . . . or Ernst Lubitsch.

With all the *sturm und drang* over *To Be or Not to Be,* Lubitsch was forced to begin his tenure at Fox from a standing start, spending several months just looking for a story. A project with Ginger Rogers called *A Self-Made Cinderella* didn't get made; Fox bought the hit Broadway play *Margin for Error* for him, but he shied away and it was made by Otto Preminger, who had also directed it on the stage.

Then Lubitsch hit upon the idea of making a drama centered on the lives of New York's oldest mercantile families, but that mutated into something else entirely once he discovered a 1934 play by Laszlo Bus-Feketé entitled *Birthday.* Lubitsch and Sam Raphaelson, once more brought on board to script, changed the title to *Heaven Can Wait.*

As before, the strengths of the play were maintained, the weaknesses banished. Bus-Feketé opened *Birthday* at the main character's fifteenth birthday, and the characterization of Grandpa is about the same, as are the fearsome Strables, although in the play they are named Gyurkovics. But there is a harshness to the main character that Lubitsch felt obliged to soften; in the play, he sleeps with his wife's younger sister and, after his wife dies, marries her.

In retrospect, Lubitsch would claim that, after twenty years in America, he felt comfortable enough with the country and its people to approach an American subject, a point of view that conveniently overlooked *Three Women,* not to mention *That Uncertain Feeling,* made only a few years before. But those films didn't have to be set in America, while *Heaven Can Wait* did, if only for the central character of Henry Van Cleve, who mixes lecherous calculation and ingenuousness in a way that is peculiarly American.

The writing of *Heaven Can Wait* occupied Lubitsch and Raphaelson for several months, all of it done in exquisite comfort at Ernst's house at 268 Bel Air Road, with Sam remembering that he often put down his pipe for one of Lubitsch's favorite Upmann cigars.

Raphaelson was once again *persona grata* at Lubitsch's house, because Vivian was no longer living there. On April 22, 1942, Lubitsch and Vivian had separated, with Ernst leaving the house to take up residence at the Beverly Wilshire Hotel for a short time. It was typical of the oddly formal, impersonal nature of their relationship that Lubitsch had originally planned to move out a day earlier, but stayed because Vivian had planned a dinner party.

"I don't like to dramatize anything like this," he explained to reporters. "It would only build up the scene." Vivian filed for divorce on May 19, 1943, charging cruelty.

During the trial the following month, Vivian testified that Lubitsch would "sleep all day Sunday" and offered her no companionship. "I was forced to spend my life almost completely by myself. I seldom saw Mr. Lubitsch except when we went out with other people, and when we would come home he would not speak to me. I was really living like a stranger in my own house." She also said that Lubitsch objected to her friends. "It got so about all we were saying to each other was 'Good night.'"

Vivian had a point and Lubitsch knew it. "When I am working at the studio, I forget everything," he had told Louella Parsons the year before. "I've worked right through the dinner hour without even realizing it." As Ernst's niece Ruth Hall would say, "I don't think he was a marrying man; I think she wanted to make him a real husband and he liked to be with his cronies." On the other hand, Vivian had known what she was getting when she married him.

It was all reasonably cordial, but there was no reason it shouldn't have been. Under the terms of the final divorce decree of August 4, 1944, Vivian received a lump sum of $28,500, a percentage of her ex-husband's earnings (probate records indicate a monthly alimony of $3,709.22), plus $150 a month for Nicola.

According to Nicola, Lubitsch promised her that she would never have any other mother but Vivian, that he would never remarry. Nicola also avers that her father always carried a torch for Vivian, which is possible, if only because of the generous settlement and the fact that Lubitsch made her a beneficiary in his will. Yet, after Lubitsch's health began to fail, friends of Lubitsch's did their utmost to keep Vivian away from him because, as Mary Loos put it, "They didn't like each other very much."

One day Lubitsch and Raphaelson were having lunch at the Fox commissary when they ran into Darryl Zanuck. "How's it going, Ernst?" inquired Zanuck. "Vell, I tell you," said Ernst, "slow but good." "That's fine," replied Zanuck. "The only thing I'd rather hear than that is—*very slow and great!*"

During the writing of *Heaven Can Wait*, Lubitsch was fascinated by the idea of depicting "an age that has vanished, when it was possible to live for the charm of living." The key to the humor of Henry Van Cleve, the central character in *Heaven Can Wait*, was that, sexually speaking, he was "fifteen years ahead of his time, all the time." The central comic idea was that 1920s callous sexual misdemeanor is 1935s convention. When the script was done, Ernst and Sam both thought it was faultless.*

After the script of *Heaven Can Wait* was completed, Lubitsch took time out to prepare a propaganda film for Lieutenant Colonel Frank Capra entitled *Know Your Enemy: Germany*. The film was shot in one week in October 1942, on the back lot at Fox. It was completed and previewed, but never released, and Lubitsch's script appears not to have survived. Other internal documents have, however, and reveal that Lubitsch made his movie in seven days on a succession of revamped and standing sets, for a cost of $37,692.85.

Lubitsch's idea was to trace the rise of modern Germany through one Karl Schmidt, who was to be shown at various ages. According to the trade papers, *Know Your Enemy: Germany* opened with Wagnerian music and involved some fairly static philosophical discussions. In any case, the Army rejected the film and it was never distributed.

Two years later, the project was reactivated, rewritten, and assigned to Gottfried Reinhardt, Anthony Veiller, and William L. Shirer. The final result, titled *Here Is Germany*, wasn't released until 1945, and retained the character of Karl Schmidt. Although some of Lubitsch's footage was cannibalized for the new film, most of the picture was cobbled together

---

*It was not achieved without a lengthy wrong turn in the narrative that was unprecedented for the two men. The first draft script, completed August 24, 1942, featured a twenty-two-page sequence showing Henry Van Cleve marrying a second time. The young gold digger is named Pearl, and, in addition to her acquisitiveness, she brings into the Van Cleve house an obnoxious pair of siblings. The sequence dwells rather too heavily on Henry's naïveté and resultant humiliation. It all ends in a fistfight, and leads into the scene of a chastened Henry asking his son about the possibility of having an older woman come read to him. In addition to being out of character for Henry—up to this point, he has evinced no interest in being married to anyone but Martha, his fascination with other women having nothing to do with marriage—the sequence is very long and drags the film down. The scene never made it in to the film.

from a wide variety of German films, from costume dramas to old newsreels, in the by-now standard style of the *Why We Fight* films.

Following the divorce from Vivian, Lubitsch made tentative moves toward the social circle she had alienated. Since Willy Wyler had gone off to war, leaving a large gap in the Wyler house in Bel Air, Lubitsch began inviting Wyler's wife, Talli, to accompany him and a few other friends on regular trips to a newsreel theater on Hollywood Boulevard, where they would bring themselves up to date on the latest war news.

He also volunteered as an air-raid warden for his neighborhood. One night he was making the rounds during a blackout. Noticing a light on at Walter Reisch's house, Ernst yelled out, "Valter, Valter, there's a light on in the second floor." Reisch responded by yelling out "Right avay, Ernst." Next door, Laurence Olivier leaned out of the window. "My God," he bellowed, "are the fucking Germans here already?"

Lubitsch was unambivalent about the war between his native country and his adopted one. "That war people didn't have any difficulty about," remembered Talli Wyler. "Especially if you were European or Jewish, you weren't torn. You knew exactly how you felt." Although a congenital nonjoiner, Ernst allowed his name to be used as a sponsor for both Russian War Relief and the Hollywood Anti-Nazi League, groups largely made up of liberals like Donald Ogden Stewart, Charlie Chaplin, Lillian Hellman, John Huston, and Thomas Mann.

As they spent more and more time together, Talli Wyler found that Lubitsch was a good listener, "unlike Chaplin. He was always on, to the point where I found it exhausting." Although most wives of famous and powerful men grow used to being treated politely but rather blankly as "the wife," Lubitsch, she remembered, "had that particular sparkle, that twinkle, that told you that you and he were relating as people.

"With Ernst you always got a sense that he was sitting back watching what was happening, pulling a little string here and a little string there. He loved gossip, who was sleeping with who. And if somebody wasn't sleeping with somebody, he would do his best to promote it. Irna, his cook, would fix a dessert I've never had since, some sort of essence of berries, pressed and made into sort of a jelly. It was fabulous. He was a very good friend when Willy was away."

Not everybody pulled together in the war. Herman Mankiewicz, a friend of Ernst's since the Paramount days, had become an isolationist in the mold of Lindbergh, but with a strong tinge of the anti-Semitic Jew. He blamed Communists for leading America into a war he believed America could not win. "All the doctors, lawyers, and professional men in Germany were Jews," Mankiewicz told Eleanor Boardman, "and they were getting too strong a hold." One day at a party at Ernst's house, Mankiewicz went into one of his diatribes; Ernst grew so angry he ordered Mankiewicz to leave.

At night, Lubitsch often went to The Blue Danube, a Hungarian restaurant opened by Mia and Joe May after their movie careers bottomed out. The Danube became a popular meeting place for the German and Hungarian colonies. And, of course, he remained highly attentive to his friends. In 1942, when Billy Wilder was about to start his initial directing job on *The Major and the Minor,* the younger man came to his mentor and confessed that not only was he terrified, he was also beset by a nervous diarrhea.

Lubitsch put an arm around Wilder. "I have directed fifty pictures," he said, "and I'm still crapping in my pants on the first day." On the first day of production for *The Major and the Minor,* Lubitsch showed up on the set with every German director in Hollywood (including Dupont, Dieterle, and Koster, with the Hungarian Michael Curtiz in on a pass) to wish Wilder *bon voyage* in his new venture.

And Lubitsch returned to his bachelor ways. "He was a chaser," remembered Gottfried Reinhardt. "He was constantly interested in these sort of sexpots. None of them very young or attractive. He had a carelessness about sex. Ernst Lubitsch had only one interest: films. Then he rode horseback and he got massages and he went fucking. He did these things secondarily. There was really nothing in his life but the movies."

While Lubitsch and Raphaelson were thrilled with their script for *Heaven Can Wait,* Zanuck wasn't entirely sure. He was evidently nonplussed by the amiable lethargy of the lead character, for, in Lubitsch's words, "The hero was a man only interested in good living with no aim of accomplishing anything, or of doing anything noble."

When he was asked why he wanted to make "such a pointless picture," Lubitsch answered by saying that he wanted to introduce the audience to some people, and that if the people should find them likable, then the picture would be a success.

Lubitsch and Raphaelson had written the script with either Fredric March or Rex Harrison in mind, but, once it was finished, Zanuck asked the director if, as a personal favor, he would test Don Ameche for the part of Henry Van Cleve.

A few days later, Lubitsch invited Raphaelson to look at the test, "because I think we're in trouble." Raphaelson was amazed; Lubitsch had managed to pull a scene of remarkable depth and subtlety out of the actor. Lubitsch glumly agreed. "Isn't that the vorst luck in the world? Vat are we going to do, the guy is good. Ve're in a spot!" Ameche got the job.

On February 1, the first day of production, Lubitsch gathered the actors around him. Pointing to the script, he said "These are the facts. I beg you don't change anything, because this is the way I would like it." As always, he was single-minded in achieving what he wanted, which affected some actors more than others. "Gene Tierney couldn't quite come to one scene," remembered Don Ameche, "and he just kept at her and at her until he broke her completely down. When, shortly after, she straightened herself around, he rolled the camera and got exactly what he wanted. He knew how to do it. He didn't do it unless he had to, but he was a man totally dedicated to his art."

To Ameche he was "dedicated"; to Tierney he was "a tyrant." Tierney was seraphically beautiful but deeply closeted emotionally, and invariably seemed to be acting in a glazed trance. Around the Fox lot, she had a reputation for responding to any emotional scenes by going slightly over the top in a cloying, sentimental way. In trying to spark some emotional immediacy out of her, Lubitsch had terrified the actress. The day after their contretemps, Tierney sought him out and explained that "I'm willing to do my best, but I just can't go on working on this picture if you're going to keep shouting at me."

"I'm paid to shout at you," he retorted.

"Yes, and I'm paid to take it—but not enough." They laughed, and Lubitsch modulated his approach for the rest of the shooting.

The young actor Dick Moore, making an uneasy transition from child stardom, was playing the adolescent Henry Van Cleve, and found Lubitsch to be "a dear, dear man. I remember being on the set with him and Signe Hasso for a scene where I'm supposed to take a cigar out of my pocket. I took the cigar out of my trouser pocket when it should have been in the breast pocket. I caught a look between Lubitsch and Hasso at my inexperience at putting a cigar in my pants pocket. I knew I had done something to cause their amusement and I was mortified." Moore also noted Lubitsch's habit of wearing old sweaters smelling vaguely of mothballs, something Vivian would assuredly never have permitted.

Moore sensed that Lubitsch saw the character as much looser than he was able to play him, but that was probably due more to Moore's increasing sense of emotional constriction than to any shortcomings in his performance; as past history showed, if Lubitsch was dissatisfied with an actor, he would quickly recast the part.

One of the few problems of the production involved Louis Calhern. His first shot involved him coming down a winding staircase, leaning over the bannister, and calling to Spring Byington. But Calhern had a very difficult time finding his key light, for the Technicolor cameras demanded such a high degree of illumination that the entire set was hot, not just the area illuminated by the key light.

"We must have shot it ten or fifteen times and Calhern was very angry with himself," remembered Dick Moore, "but Lubitsch never displayed any impatience with anybody. He had infallible courtesy, never raised his voice, and was always very gay. Ebullient, in a quiet sort of way. He knew exactly what he wanted. It was a chess game and he knew every move he was going to make. He gave it an improvisational feel, but it wasn't improvisational at all."

As always, Lubitsch entertained himself by playing the piano while the crew was setting up the next shot. One day, Moore asked him how he found time to keep in practice. "Oh, Dickie, I've always loved music," he replied. "But you know Hollywood is a funny business, a funny town. We never know what's going to happen. I always like to keep up with my music because someday I may have to play in a cafe."

Another day on the set he sidled up to Moore and said "Someday you may want to become a director. This Technicolor is interesting, perfect for this kind of picture, wonderful for musicals and comedy. But permit me to give you a word of advice: never shoot a drama or a mystery in Technicolor."

"So," says Dick Moore, "I look now at films like *The Maltese Falcon* and the rest of the wonderful dramas that [Ted] Turner is [colorizing and] fucking up, and Lubitsch was absolutely right; it's fifty years later and he's still right."

As he completed production of *Heaven Can Wait,* Lubitsch seemed to be in fine fettle. He was still never without his omnipresent cigar, and eating and drinking as he pleased ("must I handicap myself?"), but he tried to maintain an even keel by exercising, in particular walking. "I cherish the illusion," he told Hedda Hopper that July, "that I feel as young as I did that day in 1922 when I stepped off the train in Los Angeles, thanking my stars for a woman named Mary Pickford."

Taking a paternal pride in his twenty-one years of working in American studios, Lubitsch played the Grand Seigneur and again emphasized the view that movies were a thing of the moment. "Fundamentals don't change. Only externals change. Styles in acting, styles in writing, styles even in photography and lighting. A picture made ten years ago looks hammy today, no matter how great it was then."

Lubitsch should have known better, but it was evidently the way he truly felt. "A movie," he once told Sam Raphaelson, "any movie, good or bad, ends up in a tin can in a warehouse; in ten years it's dust. You're smart that you stick with the theater, Sam. What college teaches movies? But drama is literature. Your plays are published. Someday a student gets around to you—you have a fighting chance."

But Lubitsch was also careful to hew to the no-one-here-but-us-hard-working-carpenters line that even the best directors of the era put out. He had seen firsthand how the system had crushed Rex Ingram, Maurice Tourneur, Josef von Sternberg, and Erich von Stroheim, with, it is true, considerable assists from all of those brilliant but iconoclastic, self-destructive men. He had no wish to set himself up for a fall by proclaiming himself an artist.

The gentle nostalgic tone of *Heaven Can Wait* is set by the music under the credits: "By the Light of the Silvery Moon." Henry Van Cleve, having just died, presents himself "where so many people had told him to go." He tells His Excellency (Laird Cregar, with an amusingly malevolent gleam in his eye), that he had just finished his dinner. "A good one, I hope," says His Excellency. "Excellent," says Henry. "I ate everything the doctor forbade."

The mood is elegant, serene but regretful. "There are several people up there I would love to see," Henry says, "particularly one—a very dear one. But I haven't a chance." His Excellency asks for some specific credential that would entitle Van Cleve entrance to his domain. A heinous crime, perhaps?

"Crime—crime . . . well I'm afraid I can't think of any. But I can safely say that my whole life has been one continuous misdemeanor." Henry goes on to tell his story, which tends to involve more lecherous intent than penetrating accomplishment. Henry is initiated by a French maid who takes a look at her young charge and instinctively understands that here is a man whose sexual expressiveness is yearning to breathe free. As she puts it, "His soul his bigger than his pants."

Young Henry is morose; he feels he has to marry a local girl simply because he has kissed her. Rushing to enlighten him, Mademoiselle (Signe

Hasso) tells him that it is not necessary to marry everybody you kiss. "Kiss is like candy," she says. "You eat candy for the beautiful taste—and this is enough reason to eat candy." With his social and sexual boundaries newly enlarged, young Henry is promised even more valuable knowledge at his first French lesson.

The years go by in the house at 921 Fifth Avenue. Henry is entranced by the gorgeous Martha (Gene Tierney), unaccountably sprung from the grotesque loins of "one of the great meat-packers of our time," the entirely dreadful, nouveau-riche Mr. and Mrs. E. F. Strable, played to hideous perfection by the porcine Eugene Pallette and Marjorie Main. In spite of her parents and the attentions of his prosaic cousin Albert (Allyn Joslyn, whom Lubitsch had loved in the Broadway production of *Arsenic and Old Lace*), Henry elopes with Martha.

After ten years of marriage and one child, Martha leaves—a messy business about an expensive bracelet given to somebody besides Martha— and goes back to Kansas. Henry and his beloved Grandpa follow her and win her back. As always, Henry is the sincere romantic; as always, Grandpa is the pragmatist. "Come on, sweep her off her feet," he snaps, "or we'll miss the next train."

And so Henry Van Cleve turns fifty, and we find him still dressing in the formal fashions of his youth and wearing pince-nez glasses. The times are passing him by. He clumsily tries to con a showgirl his son is seeing, so as to prove her unworthy. But she doesn't want romance, just money. He coughs up $25,000, only to find out that his son had grown bored with the girl anyway.

Abashed, a little embarrassed, he asks his wife if she thinks he's getting too heavy. "As a matter of fact, I like it," she replies. "Let me tell you something. Nearly fifteen years ago, when you and Grandfather brought me back from Kansas, I still didn't feel that you really belonged to me—and only to me. I can't put my finger on anything definite. But still, whenever I wasn't with you, I was always uncertain and nervous about my little Casanova. And one day I noticed that you began to have a little—well, just a little tummy. *Then I knew I was safe.* From that moment on, you were really mine. You had settled down."

At their twenty-fifth wedding anniversary, Martha tells Henry that she has had to see a doctor. But all she wants to do is dance. As she and Henry gently waltz in the empty entrance hall of their home, the camera pulls up and away as we watch a loving, committed husband and his wife dance together for the last time.

316

l a u g h t e r

in paradise

As a widower, Henry reverts. He comes in late, he cadges money from relatives. Women call the house asking for "Pookie." His son is a work-oriented sobersides and seems frankly alarmed.

Henry's sprightliness is stifled only by his age. In 1942, Henry is seventy and weakening. He wakes up and tells his nurse about a dream he just had. The door opened and a man stepped out of a rowboat and said he was going to take Henry on a long trip from which he would not come back. Henry responds by saying "If I ever take a trip like that, it'll be in a deluxe cabin and not in a dinky little rowboat that doesn't even have a bar." He throws him out.

But the man comes back with a luxury liner floating on an ocean of whiskey and soda. Instead of smokestacks there are cigars. In a lifeboat there is a beautiful blonde wearing a Merry Widow costume. The man plays the "Merry Widow Waltz" on the accordion, and Henry and the girl are about to dance . . . when he wakes up.

The nursing shift changes; outside in the hallway we see the new nurse come on duty and check her appearance in a mirror. She is a luscious blonde. She goes in Henry's bedroom. The camera holds, holds, then, as we begin to hear the "Merry Widow Waltz" played on an accordion, the camera slowly pulls back and down as we return to Henry and His Excellency.

"Who could ask for a more beautiful death?" asks Van Cleve. Although Henry is prepared for the worst, His Excellency has to inform him that, "Sorry, Mr. Van Cleve, we don't cater to your class of people." As he walks him to the elevator, he suggests that Henry get some character references from some young ladies that might be in the other place. Or Grandfather. "And," he adds, "There is someone else . . . She will plead for you."

"Do you think so?"

"You know she will." As Lubitsch's last masterpiece concludes, His Excellency sends Henry Van Cleve, not down, but up.

From its opening scene, there is no question that *Heaven Can Wait* is the work of a master in such total command of his craft that he doesn't have to flaunt it. The mood is loving, relaxed, richly nostalgic, and assured. Lubitsch even includes flashbacks within flashbacks and never loses narrative lucidity and logic.

And because the film's framework is that of a dead man's reminiscences, and because the story of any long life is full of friends and family peeling off into the grave, *Heaven Can Wait* is grounded by an omnipresent sense of mortality underlying Henry's scampish infidelities.

Henry Van Cleve is a benign sexual Bad Seed, whose bedroom instincts arouse only outraged middle-class propriety on the part of his family. His antic genes derive from his grandfather (the foxy Charles Coburn), who admits that he had them but, to his devout regret, never acted on them.

Yet, while Henry thinks he always gets his way, throughout the film women tend to control him. His subterfuges are obvious, his infidelities, either actual or attempted—the film goes a little vague about specifics—are rather charmingly pokey. He is an early example of the species Boy/Man and Lubitsch is equally fond of both aspects, a partiality he passes on to most of the female characters.

Lubitsch obviously knows that Henry is a problematic character; he polishes him up by contrasting him with a procession of males who are either sexless sticks, like cousin Albert, or charmless grotesques, like the Strabels. Likewise, Lubitsch makes Henry empathetic by directing all the older actors in the film to perform in a theatrical, declamatory style, while asking for—and getting—quiet, naturalistic underplaying from Ameche and Tierney.

With the exception of the far more flamboyant *Trouble in Paradise*, Lubitsch's sense of decor has never been seen to finer advantage; he defines character largely through art direction; the dignified, subtly designed and decorated house at 921 Fifth Avenue lends its dignity to the lives it contains, and contrasts sharply with the Strabels' Kansas house, a nightmare of overstuffed Edwardian bric-a-brac, brocades, and statuary, not unlike the interiors of German films circa 1915.

Yet, even characters who are little more than narrative necessities are granted a humanity and believability, as when the Strabels, after some brief posturing, quietly help their daughter, Martha, up to her room after she has left Henry. Throughout the film, Lubitsch belittles only priggishness and unsightly vanity; an old woman displaying her varicose-veined legs to His Excellency prompts him to instantly hit the trap door, consigning her to a screaming Hell.

For his first film in Technicolor, Lubitsch utilizes a very restrained palette, especially compared to Fox's penchant for glaring, heavily contrasting colors. His most lavish stroke is outfitting Tierney in various shades of blue or lavender.

While Don Ameche lacks the kinetic, purring sexuality of a Rex Harrison, his courtly, elegantly voiced performance hits every note that Lubitsch and the script demand (Ameche would call Lubitsch the only actor's director he ever worked with, as well as the only genius); it is the performance that will earn him a spot in Actor's Heaven.

Heaven Can Wait was praised by a large cross-section of critics, but the most sensitive notice was from James Agee, who wrote that, while it was not up to Lubitsch's best (he preferred the silent Lubitsch), "It has a good deal of the dry sparkle, the shrewd business, and the exquisite timing . . . It brought back a time when people really made good movies . . . the sets, costumes and props are something for history . . . [and] the period work, in these respects—as in Lubitsch's modulations in styles of posture and movement—was about the prettiest and the most quietly witty I had ever seen." Even D. W. Griffith put aside his old jealousy to pay tribute when he told Ezra Goodman that "I liked the way Lubitsch used color in *Heaven Can Wait*. And the way he used sound, too."

As Andrew Sarris has observed of *Heaven Can Wait*, "the timing of every shot, every gesture, every movement was so impeccably precise and economically expressive that an entire classical tradition unfolded . . . Contemporary sloppiness of construction brought on by the blind worship of 'energy' as an end to itself make it almost too easy to appreciate Lubitsch's uncanny sense of the stylized limits of a civilized taste. Almost any old movie looks classical today: Lubitsch's movies are nothing short of sublime."

Heaven Can Wait encapsulates the values Lubitsch's late work embodies: elegance, charm, beauty, impudent wit moving hand in hand with spiritual transcendence, and, above all, the idea that the gift of laughter entitles the bearer to their own special morality, their own particular goodness, and their own valid pass to the Elysian fields.

Surely that gentle playboy Henry Van Cleve is Lubitsch's ideal image of himself, and the beautiful, forgiving Martha is the mate he was never lucky enough to find. To die in the arms of a beautiful blonde with the "Merry Widow Waltz" welling up around you is not a bad way to check out, although Lubitsch had no way of knowing that he would in fact go Henry Van Cleve one better. If *Heaven Can Wait* isn't quite Lubitsch's last will and testament, it's his best will and testament.

The success of *Heaven Can Wait* (its domestic return to Fox was $2.37 million against a production cost of $1.1. million, a very economical budget for a Technicolor film) temporarily displaced whatever free-flowing anxiety Lubitsch had about pleasing his new boss. One day at lunch in the executive dining room, Zanuck was pontificating about art. "I've seen the Louvre fifty times and I studied the *Mona Lisa* fifty times," he proclaimed, "and I have yet to see what's so great about the *Mona Lisa.*"

Lubitsch puffed on his cigar, his eyes darting around the room to see if anybody was going to contradict Zanuck. No one did. "There are three pictures I would like to have," he began. "One, I would like to have the *Mona Lisa;* two, I would like to have a picture of Darryl Zanuck looking at the *Mona Lisa;* three, I would like to have a picture of the *Mona Lisa* looking at Darryl Zanuck."

The laughter at the table was minimal, but Lubitsch turned to the columnist Leonard Lyons, who had enjoyed the deflation of the mogul's pretensions, and said "I give a dinner for you. Thursday. 8:15. Black tie."

At the dinner, Lyons noticed that each of the water glasses had a different set of initials on it. Lubitsch explained that a friend had once given him the glasses, each of which carried the initials of one of his closest friends. But such was the casualty rate in Hollywood, that he could no longer remember the names of all twelve people. "In fact, I even forget who gave me the twelve glasses."

Jeanette MacDonald, sitting across the table, jogged his memory. "I gave them to you, Ernst."

The subdued sadness of the aging Berliner was coming closer to the surface. That night, Lubitsch accompanied Lyons home. As they drove past the Beverly Wilshire Hotel, Lubitsch said "It happens to us all here. We arrive from all over the world, carrying a small bag and check into this hotel. Then, if our movies are good, we buy paintings and move into a house. The house is too big for one person so we marry. Then comes the divorce, and we take a small bag and check into the Beverly Wilshire, buy paintings, move into a house, it's too big . . . around and around and around."

320

As a followup to *Heaven Can Wait*, Lubitsch felt secure enough in his adopted country to tackle a contemporary subject. The project was entitled *All Out Arlene*, about the WACS. He made a short tour of WAC camps to gather some background, and even went to Washington to talk to Colonel Oveta Culp Hobby, the WAC commander. It was obvious that Lubitsch's taste in women hadn't changed.

"You expect to find two cannons and a man behind the desk with a revolver," Lubitsch reported. "Instead, behind the desk is the most beautiful little girl, the most polite and charming little blonde girl I ever see. That could only happen in this country.

"Here they show you what we are fighting for. In other countries, they show you what they are fighting with."

Lubitsch's writers on the project were Henry and Phoebe Ephron, two young transplants from Broadway. They noted his elegant dress, his habit of pacing while writing, and his specific way of approaching a script. The original story by Hi Phillips was basically *See Here, Private Hargrove* with the genders switched. "It's not a masterpiece," he told them. "It's not even good. It's like starting with one sentence, but I've done that often. Also, I like the title."

Lubitsch told the Ephrons to write with Gary Cooper and Claudette Colbert in mind, to ignore the book's plot and concentrate on the central situation: "An engaged couple are in the Army. She is a lieutenant and he is a private. Their love affair has been interrupted by the war. The rest is up to us."

The Ephrons came up with the idea of emphasizing another male character in the book in order to make the script's central situation a triangle. Lubitsch liked the idea and, at the end of their first script session, Lubitsch had stopped calling them "Mr. Ephron" or "Mrs. Ephron" and begun calling them Henry and Phoebe.

Three weeks later, Lubitsch was impatient to go from script notes direct to screenplay. The Ephrons protested that they didn't have an ending. "There'll be a third act," Lubitsch told them. "There might even be two third acts. Even three. We can make a choice."

"Who does Arlene end up with?" asked Henry Ephron.

"I don't know."

The Ephrons went back to their offices awash in dreamy happiness at working for a man who, as Henry Ephron put it, was "a gentleman and a creative human being."

321

He had always loved to dance. But, he would lament, he was always behind in learning the latest steps. By the time he had mastered the two-step, everybody else had moved on to the Charleston. Adding the Charleston, everybody else was doing the Black Bottom. By the early 1940s, he had achieved competence in the rumba, only to find that the new rage was the conga.

On the night of September 1, 1943, Lubitsch was attending a tent party at the home of Sonja Henie and having, as he usually did, a fine time, when he suddenly collapsed. Dr. Joel Pressman, the husband of Claudette Colbert, got him home and, together with Otto, decided to let him take it easy overnight and see how he felt the next morning.

On the morning of September 2, Otto phoned Ernst's friend Mary Loos and said they were going to take him to the hospital. "Who's going with him?" Loos wanted to know. "I don't know," replied Otto. Loos thought he should have some company so she drove over to the house where she found him alone, except for Otto and the housekeeper. Lubitsch, she remembered, looked "green, as if he wasn't going to make it."

Otto drove Loos's car while she accompanied Lubitsch in the ambulance. Once admitted, he was sedated, but when he came to he wanted to know what he was doing in the hospital. Loos explained that he had had a little heart trouble, but was going to be just fine. She compared it to a wound that had to be left alone until it healed. In fact, he had had a massive heart attack.

Word quickly spread around town. Sam Raphaelson's secretary called Lubitsch's house and found Steffie Trondle in a state combining hysteria and efficiency, talking about coffins and choosing pallbearers. The next day, Lubitsch's illness had made the papers; back at the hospital, Ernst was concerned over whether or not Zanuck had called. Loos said, yes, of course, even though he hadn't. After Lubitsch drifted off to sleep, she called Harry Brand, director of publicity at Fox, to explain to him that Lubitsch needed the reassurance of a telegram from his boss. The wire arrived quickly.

As far as the doctors were concerned, this was Lubitsch's first cardiac episode, but the possibility exists that there had been a precedent. During the year that he had been production head at Paramount, Ernst had been forced to take a plane to a preview of a Mae West picture. A very nervous flyer at the best of times, Lubitsch blanched when, during a bit of turbulence, the pilot's cabin door flew open and two men ran down the aisle and opened the exit. "We don't know what you're going to do, but we're getting the hell out of here," they yelled just before they jumped.

It was, of course, a practical joke, but Jesse Lasky, Jr., reported that Lubitsch actually had a minor heart attack on the spot and lost consciousness. If Lasky's story is true, it was a very expensive joke.

On the second day after his heart attack, Dr. Morris Nathanson, who would become his cardiologist, was trying to cheer him up. "You mustn't worry," said the doctor. "Lots of people have had this ailment and recovered. Why, you wouldn't believe it, but one of my patients is the composer, Jerome Kern." Lubitsch opened his eyes and gave the doctor a quizzical, sharp look. "And what did he write afterward?"

Sam Raphaelson also visited and found a very pale Lubitsch under doctor's orders to refrain from any and all unnecessary movements, up to and including the use of his hands. Raphaelson tried to reassure him, pointing out that Broadway producer John Golden had made a roaring comeback after a stroke. "I know, I know," muttered the shaken man. "But when I die, this is what I'll die of."

At the studio, Henry and Phoebe Ephron were stunned by the news of Lubitsch's collapse. At the writer's table at Fox, F. Hugh Herbert snarled, "Well, well, how are the writers who gave Lubitsch a heart attack?" George Seaton tried to soften the remark by telling them it wasn't their fault, that "it was one of the two beautiful sisters," a reference to an aspiring young actress whom Lubitsch had been seeing. She was, of course, blonde.

Lubitsch remained in the hospital for an endless seven weeks. By the first week in November he was home, surrounded by two nurses and Steffie Trondle to boot. He was allowed to take rides and little walks. Doctor Nathanson had told him that there was a good chance for a full recovery, but that he would not be able to return to the studio till after the first of the year.

With the initial danger past, Lubitsch began to fret over the enforced inactivity. For one thing, he didn't really feel sick, but Nathanson explained that he had to spend the next several months building up a reserve to draw on in the future. Even reading was beyond him, as the medication made it hard for him to concentrate. The whirl of life that he had always taken pride in being able to regulate had slowed to where he was a motionless centerpiece for what he called "a kind of rococo salon."

After every visitor, one of the nurses would take his pulse; the only one who raised it to alarming heights was Miriam Hopkins, although Lubitsch assured Sam Raphaelson that it was only because of the stress of trying to follow her rapid speech pattern. He would later say that the only thing that could save him from a pulse rate of 125 after a visit from Hopkins was a visit from the quiet Charles Brackett, who could send Ernst's pulse plunging to around 68. For stimulation, he was limited to gossip. "If only I were an Englishman I could recover twice as fast," he complained.

After three weeks at home, he called the Ephrons and told them to come to his house. The young writers were impressed by his fine art collection. Unlike many in Hollywood, Lubitsch had no art adviser and bought paintings on his own. By this time he had developed a rather good eye. (Once, after returning from New York, he dropped into a friend's house and presented them with a Lautrec etching, saying only "Here's something I got in a gallery.")

Lubitsch told the Ephrons that "There are supposed to be more El Grecos in Bel Air than there are in the Louvre." He pointed to a small mahogany box on a bookshelf. "My cigars. I'm not allowed to smoke them anymore. But, I have some good news for you. Zanuck loves the pages you wrote and wants to put *All Out Arlene* back in work."

That was all well and good, but during the two months since Lubitsch's heart attack, the Ephrons had been assigned to B-picture producer Bryan (Brynie) Foy, who wanted them to write *Rip Goes to War,* a remake of *To the Shores of Tripoli,* with John Payne's part being taken by a dog.

Lubitsch groaned. "You want to get off it?" he asked. "Tell me, children, can you write bad? You write a fifteen-page scene of the family that owns Rip. They are deciding whether to send the poor dog to war or what. You have uncles, aunts, cousins, the boy who owns the dog, the mother, the father, a few neighbors—you write dialogue for everybody. No close-ups, no fade-ins, no cut-tos, no fade-outs—just dialogue. If there's one thing Brynie hates, its dialogue."

The scene took a day and a half to write, and quickly got the Ephrons booted off *Rip Goes to War;* they sent a dozen roses to Lubitsch's house. But Zanuck assigned Otto Preminger to pick up *All Out Arlene,* and the Ephrons found him unbearable. "Every morning," wrote Henry Ephron in his memoirs, "he was on the phone for an hour trying to buy a used car, or sell the one he'd just bought, quarreling with his cook over Saturday night's menu or arguing with his tailor . . . His manner of working was madness. If one of us came up with an amusing line, he would never laugh. He would simply nod his head and say 'That's funny.' But he never smiled, he never chuckled, and there was never any encouraging laughter . . . Where was that wonderful, free Lubitsch laugh that filled you with enthusiasm and made you try harder and be even funnier?"

Preminger asked for other writers; the Ephrons moved on to other scripts and more amiable coworkers; *All Out Arlene* was never made.

Lubitsch began to resume physical activity slowly. Lonely in the big, empty house, he wrote to his niece Ruth and asked her to come for a visit. But she was afraid to fly and begged off; she spent the rest of her life regretting her decision, for he had never denied her or her husband anything.

It was too much change too fast and it was all for the worse; the divorce meant that his adored Nicola wasn't around most of the time, and now the roaring vitality he had always taken for granted was removed with a sudden hammer-blow. Although Lubitsch would recover a certain amount of momentum, he would never have the emotional security of good health again, would always be noticeably more subdued. His friends missed the full measure of his bustling energy, but those qualities were replaced by a certain contemplative gentleness that seemed to be a new arrival.

Walking with his nurse in a park one day, he passed a large flower, which, blown by the wind, seemed to nod at him. Twenty minutes later, they were back at the same spot, and the flower once more was nodding in the breeze. "Thank you very much," said Lubitsch, bowing slightly. "I saw you the first time, too."

chapter eight

DOCTOR: *Very little meat, no fancy sauces, no champagne, wine, whiskey. All that is out of the question. I repeat, no excitement . . . You'll live to be 100.*

HENRY: *Doctor, promise me one thing. If, after living 30 years like that, I should still be alive and 100, bury me anyway!*

— a   d e l e t e d   s c e n e   f r o m   *h e a v e n*
c a n   w a i t

Lubitsch's marriage to Vivian had displaced the Foreign Legion, while his heart attack and lengthy recuperation had prevented any further reunions. At the same time, Hollywood was undergoing a remarkable transformation as mysteriously inevitable as the darkening and deepening of Lubitsch's own films. The quiet, sleepy little company town, where the studios were never very far from orange groves that scented the air, had become a metropolitan city; traffic was noticeably heavier, and the red streetcars that Universal apprentices like Ernst Laemmle and William Wyler used to take were becoming scarce.

Walter Laemmle had returned to Munich in 1926, been arrested by the Gestapo shortly after *Kristallnacht,* and finally came to America for good in 1938. "Paul [Kohner] was still here," remembered Laemmle, "my brother was still here and Henry Blanke was still here, but that world of the Foreign Legion had drifted apart. Times had changed. We had all grown up. It was a different life now."

Many of the European intellectual elite—Aldous Huxley, Salka Viertel, Vicki Baum, and Thomas Mann—settled in and around Santa Monica, or Amalfi Drive in Pacific Palisades. For people used to spending time in Spain or Italy, Southern California was an acceptable substitute, and the rents in the Palisades and environs were far more reasonable than in Beverly Hills or Bel Air.

In addition, the atmosphere was more casual than in those ostentatious enclaves. The actor Leo Carillo thought nothing of riding his horse into a neighbor's house, sweeping up a friend he had not seen in what he thought was too long a time, and taking the captive back to his house for a friendly visit. Dolores Del Rio also lived in the neighborhood and would get furious with her mother for taking her cast-off shoes to the market to swap for eggs.

Salka Viertel's Sunday salon quickly became the left-wing literary equivalent of Sunday afternoon at Ernst's, with regular guests including Bertolt Brecht, Lion Feuchtwanger, Christopher Isherwood, Charlie Chaplin, and Hanns Eisler. Thomas Mann's daughter Erika noted in her diary that "All of [the Germans and Austrians] are working hard, all of them are learning English furiously, and all of them have exactly two topics in which they are interested—film and politics."

For a writer like S. N. Behrman, the Hollywood of this period was "a kind of Athens. It was as crowded with artists as Renaissance Florence. It was a golden era." Of course, it all depended on your point of view. One night, Joseph L. Mankiewicz and his friend Hume Cronyn were flying into Los Angeles. They beheld the city exploding with lights—except for one dead, dark spot in the middle of all the glitter. Cronyn idly wondered what the dark spot was.

"The public library," snarled Mankiewicz.

The German colony's Sunday afternoon *Kaffeeklatches* had moved up Bel Air Road to the home of Walter Reisch, who, after the success of *Ninotchka,* went on to a long career as a writer/producer, primarily at Fox. Ernst became a regular guest during these Sunday gatherings. Although to a visitor from Germany like Lilli Palmer they seemed to be "a village full of professionals in desperate search of an audience," to the members themselves it was a welcome return to normal. Since there was a war on, they even managed to overlook the traditional dislike between Germans and Austrians. "You know," said the Austrian Lisl (Mrs. Walter) Reisch, "if a German comedian comes to Austria, nobody laughs."

The environment was equally ambiguous for Jean Gabin, then in the midst of an affair with Marlene Dietrich. One Sunday afternoon, Gabin accompanied Dietrich to the Reischs and the subject turned to opera, which usually put Gabin to sleep. "I don't like opera," he said. "It's stupid. Nobody sings when he's dying." Lubitsch responded by saying "A swan doesn't dance when its dying but that doesn't invalidate ballet." Gabin, yet another grumpy Frenchman, stalked out of the party.

Although the Reischs had been having a Sunday open house long before they moved to Bel Air, their home in the 300 block of Bel Air Road was centrally located for the European contingent. Lubitsch lived at 268 Bel Air Road; the corner house of the 300 block was Otto Preminger's, and directly across from him were the Reischs. On the facing corner was the home of Alexander Korda and Merle Oberon, while around the corner on Copa de Oro was the home of Willy and Talli Wyler.

This close feeling of community resulted in a lot of jobs being passed around, but not always the requisite amount of money. When Walter Reisch did an uncredited rewrite on Sam Spiegel's *Tales of Manhattan*, Spiegel didn't pay him, but rather gave him an expensive record player that, after playing one side, turned the record over so that it could play the other side. It was a machine that demanded much fascinated study by the émigrés, but unfortunately this marvelous invention was accompanied by a grinding of industrial gears more appropriate to the harvesting of wheat.

Technically, the Sunday afternoons at the Reischs started at 3 P.M. with coffee and cake, some drinks, and maybe a bite to eat later. Although Lubitsch owned two cars (a 1941 Buick sedan and a 1941 Super Deluxe Ford Tudor sedan), he would usually walk over between 11 and noon, with Nicola in tow. The early arrival and the presence of his daughter meant he could leave a little early; "Ernst enjoyed meeting people," remembered Lisl Reisch, "but not too often; he liked parties, but not too big." While Lubitsch and Walter Reisch talked, Lisl Reisch would entertain Nicola. "I used to be a dancer and I would show Nicola some steps; she was pretty good at some things, so we had something in common."

On those Sunday afternoons, there were no stars, no particular agenda, and the mood was completely relaxed. Even Garbo would occasionally drop in, with her hair in becoming curls. At 6 P.M. the party would halt while everybody listened to Walter Winchell on the radio. Afterwards, Gottfried Reinhardt or Helmut Dantine might start a chess game while, in another corner, Bronislau Kaper might play the piano. The topic of conversation was rarely the movies, usually the war. Sometimes Marlene Dietrich would come with a stack of her records under her arm. "But," remembered Lisl Reich, "when I would go into the kitchen she would turn off the records so I wouldn't miss a note of her singing."

Lisl Reich found that Lubitsch adored her Austrian cooking: Wiener schnitzel, veal in sauce, mushrooms in sauce, sour cream, dumplings, chocolate cake, all undoubtedly delicious but a disastrous diet for a recovering heart patient. He especially adored *Lubitschkoch,* a pudding dessert of eggs, wine sauce, and steamed walnuts that Lisl named after him because he loved it so. The only problem with *Lubitschkoch* was that it required a double boiler, which, on top of all the other cooking Lisl did, meant that another pair of hands was mandatory. That was where Dietrich ("an excellent cook, a top cook, and a dear, great friend") came in.

On those occasions when Walter Reisch was out of town, Lubitsch would send Otto Werner to fetch Lisl, and they would have dinner at his house followed by a night at a concert (Ernst was especially fond of Vladimir Horowitz). Once again, Ernst's great gift for friendship came to the fore, his particular ability to have friends love him and care for him, perhaps because they perceived the vulnerability and loneliness that he ordinarily masked from lovers and people at the studio.

"He was so special," remembered Lisl Reich. "What made him special? My daughter is named Maria Francesca; Ernst gave her that name. We simply had to call her Maria, he said. Upstairs, in his house, he had an electric kitchen installed. A stove, an oven, a refrigerator. When my daughter was born, he suddenly decided he didn't need the kitchen anymore and gave it all to us. We installed it in a big linen closet we had. We called it the Lubitsch kitchen."

As far as any meaningful professional activity, Ernst was forced to bide his time, waiting for the go-ahead from Dr. Nathanson. He began casting around for likely diversions. For a while, a very good friend of his and the friend's mistress stayed with Ernst as houseguests. The friend had only recently left his wife, and the rumor around town was that he had become a practicing masochist at the hands of his coldly beautiful girlfriend. Lubitsch heard the talk and told a few friends that he had spent a good deal of time "looking for the vhip. I vunder vere he keeps it?"

Increasingly, he came to rely on two beautiful young women. One was Nicola. Once, at a dinner party, he proudly introduced his daughter to the guests. She mentioned a children's party she had attended at Jack Warner's house. Knowing her father liked paintings, she described Warner's Impressionist collection. Mr. Warner, Lubitsch explained, is a wealthy man.

"Daddy, you're as rich as Jack Warner," she said, but Lubitsch demurred.

The little girl persisted, and Lubitsch pointed out that some very great men had very little money. Like, for instance, Mr. Einstein.

"Who's he?"

"He's a scientist, a great, great scientist."

"What did he do?"

"He discovered the theory of relativity."

"What's that?"

A long stare. "All right then. I *am* as rich as Jack Warner."

The other was Mary Loos, the niece of Anita Loos. Loos had had a successful public relations firm in New York, then came back to Los Angeles and went to work for Howard Strickling at MGM. Besides tending to her publicity chores, Loos began writing fiction on the side. Because of her Aunt Anita, she was privy to a social circle that other MGM publicists weren't.

Lubitsch had originally met Mary at a party at Jules Stein's house. He was still married at the time and was accompanied by Vivian. Loos immediately noticed the trademark Lubitsch sprightliness. "He was a sparrow," she remembered, "eyes darting around, taking everything in. He walked with his toes out, with a quick shuffle. The trigger of his charm was his attitude toward life. I used to say that he looked like a bird, checking everything out."

That first night, Loos told him that "I know you're just a little German boy from Berlin, but sometimes you act like a Spanish grandee." He was impressed—and flattered—by the simile. After his divorce from Vivian, Lubitsch called Loos up and asked her to dinner. Unbeknownst to Lubitsch, she was living with her father, a successful doctor. When Otto drove up to a big, beautiful canyon house with a long winding driveway, Ernst was taken aback.

Loos quickly became Ernst's confidante, an intellectually compatible companion with whom he could gossip and exchange jokes and ideas without having to worry about sex corrupting the sympatico relationship. "He took out lots of beautiful women," remembered Loos, "but when it came time to go out to the Goldwyns or the Mayers, I'd get invited. It was very flattering to me, and I was very fortunate to have that relationship in my life. I learned a lot."

(One day at MGM, Loos returned from lunch to find an amazed phone operator. "There are three messages for you," the operator deadpanned. "Mamoulian called; Lubitsch called; God called.")

At gatherings of the high and mighty, Loos noticed that the moguls tended to fawn over Lubitsch rather than the other way around. "He was the center of attention; he never just sat back and chatted. He was *there*. He had magic, imagination, wit, charisma."

Mainly, Lubitsch and Loos had a great bond of laughter, and she was enchanted by the essential duality of his character: the ardent romantic and the knowing cynic, which made it possible for him to capture both the sentimentality and absurdity of love, the ridiculous, endearing vanity of human nature. When Sam Spiegel, worried about a possible wave of anti-German feeling in the wake of World War II, changed his name to the thunderingly patriotic S. P. Eagle, Lubitsch laughed for weeks. Nor did he have much respect for the way business was usually done in Hollywood, once telling Loos that "every time Molnár writes a play, eight Hollywood Hungarians are employed to steal the plot."

"We'd have the greatest time just sitting in nightclubs watching people," remembered Loos. Once, at a nightclub, Lubitsch and Loos eyed the slinky French star Simone Simon come waltzing by on the arm of Robert Hakim. Despite her demure image, Simon was a lusty girl, well-known for her sexual exploits with Darryl Zanuck, among others. "Robert was dancing cheek to cheek. Simone looked like a beautiful peach blossom and everybody knew what a tramp she was. Ernst watched them go by and then said, 'I vunder if he's had a Vasserman?' [a test for venereal disease]. I just fell on the floor laughing."

Loos found that Lubitsch delighted in practical jokes. When a couple of friends left for a European cruise, Ernst sent them a long cable with explicit instructions about where to go, what to do, and whom to see. The only problem was that most of the telegram was made up of deliberately garbled words that reduced the instructions to gibberish. The couple spent their vacation worrying about how they would break the news to Lubitsch that they hadn't been able to do any of the things he'd wanted them to do.

Loos found that the quietly attentive and effusive Lubitsch could be guarded in his opinions about other filmmakers, or the talents of his friends. He refused to read any of Loos's early attempts at scriptwriting or fiction because he wasn't sure she was a good writer; if she wasn't, he didn't want to risk embarrassing her, not to mention himself.

When it came to directors, Lubitsch was franker about his likes than his dislikes. He liked Hitchcock's work and attended several of the Englishman's dinner parties. At one, Sir Cedric Hardwicke, a prig known to the genial rounders led by John Barrymore and Gene Fowler as "Sir Seldom Hardprick," was expounding on the subject of English cooking, which Lubitsch abhorred.

"Well, it all depends on one's taste," offered Hardwicke. "For instance, in women, there are women who are perfumed and made-up and their clothes expensively designed for them—and there are other women, wholesome and artless and healthy and simple . . . " "Who vants dat?" interjected Lubitsch, breaking up Hardwicke's threnody and the party.

At another party, Hitchcock brought out his private stock of cigars, and gave some to Lubitsch. Lubitsch lit up the prime leaf, savored it, and finally said, "Alfred, for this cigar, I'm going to give you a secret dissolve!"

He also "revered" Willy Wyler, and, surprisingly for a man with such a respect for budgets and shooting schedules, had enormous respect for Erich von Stroheim, whose wanton expenditures of money and time had rendered him unemployable as anything but an actor.

Loos protested that von Stroheim's temperament and perfectionism led him to absurd excess. "That's the way it should be," Lubitsch maintained. "All the rest of us make the equivalent of novellas, or short stories. The story moves from the beginning to the end, in one direction. Von Stroheim is the only filmmaker who really wrote a novel when he directed. A maid doesn't just come in with a tray of fish; you see where the maid comes from, and where she got the fish!"

Loos was a good audience, but she knew her friend; since Lubitsch loved to schmooze, she wasn't offended by his habit of taking her to a party and then rushing off to a corner to talk to the men. Since Willy Wyler would often be at the same parties—usually sitting at a card table playing gin—Loos and the beautiful, bright Talli Wyler would end up having a heart-to-heart.

Although Loos was a very attractive woman, Lubitsch took care to see that the relationship stayed on the level of doting uncle and favorite niece, never diverging into the realm of the sexual. At the same time, he carefully chose gifts that would complement and please her. When she got her first important job, as a story editor for Hunt Stromberg, Lubitsch sent her a leather desk set from Tiffany's; for her birthday, it would be ruby and gold earrings.

Seeing their obviously intimate mutual understanding, friends occasionally thought that both people were missing an opportunity for happiness. Once, Loos and her best friend, Margo, later the wife of Eddie Albert, were at Lubitsch's house after having returned from a trip to Mexico. They were having a very good time, feeling cozy and at home, literally sitting at Ernst's feet, when he reached over and lovingly patted Loos's head. Later, the wife of Lewis Milestone took Loos aside.

"Why don't you marry him?" she asked.

"Kendall, we're not in love," replied Loos. "It's not that sort of thing. We're just good friends."

"Well," said Mrs. Milestone, "I've just been good friends with my husband for years!"

"If he'd ever asked me [to have a relationship] I'd have felt self-conscious," remembered Loos, gesturing. "He only came up to here on me."

Despite the attentiveness of his friends, there was a lost, wandering quality in Lubitsch at this time. Jeanette MacDonald would call Mary Loos and inquire "Do you want him for Thanksgiving or do you want him for Christmas?" For several years, the two women divided the responsibility for Lubitsch's holidays between them. Nobody wanted him to be sitting home alone.

Lubitsch finally reported back to the Fox lot on January 19, 1944. As his doctors had forbidden him to undergo the physical *sturm und drang* of directing, Zanuck agreed to keep him on the payroll as a producer for three films; if his health allowed, he could direct the last of the three. In April, Fox bid on the rights to Franz Werfel's hit play *Jacobowsky and the Colonel,* which Lubitsch would both star in and produce, but the studio was outbid by Columbia, who would wait thirteen years to make the picture, and with Danny Kaye in the role Lubitsch had wanted to play.

The first project under the new contract was to be a remake of Ernst's silent success *Forbidden Paradise,* to be retitled *A Royal Scandal.* Vincent Price went in to meet Lubitsch and be appraised for a part in the film. "He was enchanting," remembered Price, "and proved to me his genius by telling me the story in its entirety, as a great storyteller should, with the characters all completely realized, not as a movie but as a tale, dialogue at a minimum, character in every gesture. I was completely won over to a small part for a *big* director."

The director assigned to work under Lubitsch's supervision—probably with Lubitsch's approval—was Otto Preminger, who was also a new member of the Sunday afternoon social circle and a graduate of the Reinhardt apprenticeship program. Although Preminger would evolve into an egomaniac with an almost complete lack of directorial personality, he was shrewd and tough, and he could be a loyal friend to people like David Raksin, who, after a rocky start, scored *Laura* for him.

"He protected me from the politics at Fox, which were Byzantine," remembered Raksin, "although they weren't worse than they were at

MGM. MGM had a system in which they exhausted all the creative people to make sure they were not in danger of doing anything worth doing. They wore you out fighting the system."

"[Preminger] was not an outstanding director," remembered actor Leon Askin, who saw both his stage and film productions, "but what I call a 'window dresser.' Despite his successes as an actor, he was no actor. He was, however, a great showman and a fine producer."

Most people who worked with Preminger disliked him, and not without reason—he had a capacity for rage that astonished people who witnessed it. He specialized in humiliating then breaking actors or crew members who failed to meet standards he couldn't—or wouldn't—articulate. On the other hand, he was careful about who he screamed at. "Otto wouldn't scream at anybody who would scream right back," said Philip Dunne.

Socially, Preminger could be enormously charming, and there was a side to his character that he preferred to keep hidden. He was, for instance, financially generous to actors he respected who had fallen on hard times.

With Lubitsch peering anxiously over his shoulder, Preminger managed to restrain whatever "creative" impulses he might have had by taking Lubitsch's completed script and shooting it more or less verbatim. "Whatever changes I made were very small," he said nearly thirty years later.

But, as Vincent Price observed, "Otto had the sense of humor of a guillotine. [Lubitsch] had to sit on the soundstage every day to watch a humorless Otto Preminger murder the comedy. He made it very pedestrian. When Lubitsch had told me the story I was hysterical. Tallulah [Bankhead] was good, but she should have been better."

Lubitsch would sit on the set radiating impatience, regularly springing from his chair to confer with Preminger or the actors; the frustration must have been considerable, and probably resulted in far more aggravation and stress than if he had actually directed the picture. He had cut back on his smoking; on the set of *A Royal Scandal,* he usually had a cigar stuck in his mouth, but it was rarely lit.

Despite Preminger's later claims of intimate friendship, according to Vincent Price and others, Lubitsch merely "tolerated" the younger director. If Ernst had overtly negative feelings about Preminger, he managed to keep them largely concealed, or else Preminger was simply oblivious. He would later recall that he and Lubitsch regularly looked at rushes together and would discuss them. "He was very easy, actually; he was the only producer with whom I had no conflict. He was also a man who really knew, unlike, say Milton Sperling or Sam Goldwyn."

Yet, subtly, there were vast differences between the two men, and not just in the level of their talent. "Lubitsch had a wonderful gift for taking a situation and making it funny," said Preminger, "but—and this is where our main difference lay—he did it by distorting character. In *A Royal Scandal* he had scenes where the empress of Russia didn't act like an empress. Now, even in a comedy, an empress should stay an empress." Seldom has anybody missed the essence of the joke—any joke—with such complete certitude.

(Interestingly, George Cukor revealed himself to be every bit as much a hidebound realist. In Cukor's opinion, Lubitsch cast obviously mid-American actors like George Barbier as European kings because of an essential insensitivity to English, and would never have countenanced an equivalent casting in Germany, where he was more sensitive to nuances of dialect. But, as Sam Raphaelson would say, "We just laughed our heads off at kings. Neither Lubitsch nor I ever met a king. We were just having fun.")

The film is billed as "Ernst Lubitsch's *A Royal Scandal,*" and, although there is no question of the genuinely amusing shape of its witty script, Lubitsch's lack of direct control is evident. The film features more obvious editing than other Lubitsch movies of this period, with extraneous reaction shots that serve no function other than to disguise a cut between two competing medium shots. The performances tend to lack Lubitsch's sense of precise ensemble, as well as of size and gesture. Although Lubitsch works in lines that refer to such displays of skill in the saddle as "riding three days and three nights," neither the actors nor the directors seem able to summon the expertise needed to properly arch an eyebrow to accompany a punch line.

The story, while yet another rehash of the Catherine the Great legend, offers possibilities. For one thing, it reverses the usual Lubitsch formula; in most of Ernst's movies the leading characters are in on the joke; they're cheerfully amoral, know it, enjoy it, and never apologize for it. As written, *A Royal Scandal* is the story of the corruption of a priggish naif.

Preminger paces the dialogue very fast, á la Howard Hawks, which is not necessarily a bad idea, but it does tend to emphasize the artificiality of the material. For all the verbal speed of the dialogue, Preminger's timing is a sometime thing and the scenes tend to drag. Because the film is a throwback to the Lubitsch of the silent days, without human beings to really be involved with, and lacks charismatic performances on the part of either the actors or director, one is left to idly scan the sets and wonder why the film wasn't made in Technicolor.

The only serious problem that might be laid at the feet of Lubitsch rather than Preminger is that of the leading man, the uncharismatic—and noticeably short—William Eythe. Beautiful, sexy women jockeying to win a dreary, idealistic reformer like Eythe's Alexei isn't funny so much as it is incomprehensible. He's ardent but dull. When Alexei is emboldened by his sexual conquest of Catherine, believing that this gives him free rein to mold a new Russian empire, he says "There's going to be a pig in every family." He's promptly shot down by a grumpy drunk who mutters, "That's nothing new; there always is." He doesn't get it, of course.

Lubitsch had originally offered the part to Charles Boyer, which would have entailed some kind of rewrite, for Boyer was too old and too knowing an actor to convincingly play the part. For the jokes to be truly effective, Alexei needs to be gorgeous *and* dim, the equivalent of a dumb blonde. Tyrone Power could have acted it; Cornel Wilde could have been it. Scanning the always-thin list of Fox contract actors, even Glenn Langan might have played it.

A Royal Scandal is an authentic Lubitsch movie, but one for which deductions totalling about 15 percent have to be made; the essential misalliance between the director and the material muffles the movie, turning what could have been something delightful into something mediocre. The box office response was suitably tepid, a domestic gross of about $1.5 million against a cost of $1.7 million, a modest flop that put an end to Tallulah Bankhead's always uneasy movie stardom.

A few months later, the pattern was to be repeated on *Dragonwyck*. According to the recollections of Joseph L. Mankiewicz, the Anya Seton novel was purchased expressly for Ernst to produce, "and he asked me to write the screenplay and direct it." Mankiewicz had long wanted to become a director—that was the main reason he left a lucrative producer's job at MGM to work at Fox—so the chance to make his debut under the aegis of the man who had been his "friend, guide, and preceptor" since the Paramount days was eagerly seized by Mankiewicz. "I'd do the Santa Monica phone book if he asked me to," Mankiewicz remembered in 1991.

But Mankiewicz found that Lubitsch's illness had made him "stubborn and touchy." His mood wasn't helped by Darryl Zanuck's suggestions, which were far more subtly invasive than they ever would be on the pictures Lubitsch directed. In April 1944, Zanuck was planning *Dragonwyck* to star Gene Tierney, Gregory Peck, and John Hodiak. To the picture's loss, Peck and Hodiak would be replaced by the obvious villainy of Vincent Price and the stiffness of Glenn Langan.

In line with the prospective casting of Peck, which would have added a romantic element missing from the finished film, Zanuck heavily hinted to Ernst in April that "Every woman I have talked to who has read the book regrets that somehow Miranda did not end up with Nicholas . . . If you are still speaking to me, I will be available."

By December, with the script approaching its final stages, Zanuck had some serious qualms about the climax, which involved a large-scale fire, feeling it was too similar to the finishes of such recent pictures as *The Phantom of the Opera* and Fox's own *Hangover Square*. A month later, on January 2, 1945, Zanuck was still worried: "The audience [should] *sense* rather than be told something . . . a certain B-picture flavor has crept in . . . entirely over-written and over-emphasized."

Zanuck's suggestion that Lubitsch's efforts were worthy of a B movie must have infuriated the proud man. On top of that, his relationship with Joseph Mankiewicz was also souring, and would get worse once the picture reached the production stage. "We differed about some of the direction," Mankiewicz remembered, "mostly about where I put the camera.

"Lubitsch . . . felt that door handles were important. If you want to show some interesting body language for a character, don't have the door handle where it would normally be. Have it higher or lower, that way we can see what is going through their minds as they try to open a door. If the character [knows] that a handsome man is waiting for her on the other side, we'll see by the way she turns the handle. It's all in the imagination."

Standing on the set one day watching Mankiewicz work, Lubitsch turned to Gene Tierney and said, "What have I done? How could I give our picture to this novice? He knows nothing." While Mankiewicz's visual sense would never be more than nominal, it seems unlikely, as Tierney believed, that Lubitsch was afraid of Mankiewicz succeeding. Rather, Ernst's illness, his frustration over his body's inability to heal itself after two years, was affecting him so strongly that he couldn't see that Mankiewicz in fact had the makings of a very fine director.

Vincent Price recalls one example of the differing sensibilities and sensitivities of the two men. One day Lubitsch and Price were watching the rushes of a scene in which Price, as Nicholas, the evil master of the house, takes Gene Tierney into his bedroom to berate her. Suddenly, Lubitsch threw up his arms and said, "It will have to be reshot!"

"Was it something I did, Ernst?" inquired Price.

Lubitsch explained that when a gentleman is upbraiding his wife in their bedroom, he would close the door so the servants wouldn't hear. Mankiewicz had left the door open. Lubitsch proceeded to write a scathing memo to Mankiewicz, who acknowledged the essential correctness of his point.

Toward the end of the picture, communication broke down completely, although it was carefully kept behind closed doors. Then Zanuck added to Lubitsch's frustration by cutting his favorite scene out of the picture, one in which the evil Vincent Price explains his philosophy of life standing by a beautiful but deadly oleander plant. Lubitsch was so angered by Zanuck's insensitivity that he had his name removed from the film, thoroughly mystifying its director. The film's one-sheets had already been printed, so brown stickers were pasted over Lubitsch's name.

"Lubitsch was right," remembered Vincent Price. "[The] picture missed its promised perfection somewhat because of this stupid cut. But Joe Mankiewicz was a better student of Lubitsch than Preminger."

Aptly summarized by Robert Carringer as "An American Jane Eyre but with Rochester as a real villain," *Dragonwyck* lumbers toward its preordained conclusion. Gene Tierney is the obviously innocent heroine, Vincent Price is the obviously evil heavy, and Glenn Langan, the nominal male lead, is too weak to balance either. The fact that Lubitsch was involving himself with such trite material betrays his desperation to work.

Although, at a budget of $1.9 million, *Dragonwyck* was expensive for a black-and-white picture, it grossed $2.57 million domestically, slightly out-earning Ernst's own *Heaven Can Wait,* which must have galled him even further.

338

As if the course of his life and work since September 1, 1943, wasn't irritation enough, as *Dragonwyck* was in production in the early part of 1945, Ernst's sister Elsa moved out of her daughter Evie's apartment. The two women had never been on particularly good terms, and Evie and her husband were both working very hard to start up an insurance business, which left little time to entertain Elsa. Ernst took the news as a sign that Evie and her husband wanted to get rid of Elsa, which was not the case. Nevertheless, relations between Evie and her uncle would remain strained.

Then, in April, Elsa died suddenly of heart failure. Whatever his feelings, Ernst kept them private. His own heart condition forbade him making the cross-country trip to New York to attend the funeral. His niece noticed that he never even asked where his sister had been buried. "It was over for him," remembered his niece. "Not in a bad sense; he just thought that when a person died, that was that. That's how he was."

Lubitsch had produced the first two films of his three-picture deal; the last, which was to mark his return to direction, awaited his doctor's permission. While he waited, Ernst set to work preparing a script for *Cluny Brown*, a successful novel by Margery Sharp published in 1944. The Fox story department had spotted the book while it was still in galley form, and Darryl Zanuck thought it would be a good vehicle for Lubitsch's return to direction.

In addition to the requisite quota of social satire, the book must have appealed to Lubitsch because its title character and he shared an epiphany; at the end of the novel, Cluny Brown says farewell to her native England and all the people in it, the better to "[open] her heart to the United States"—just as Ernst had done more than twenty years before.

James Hilton *(Lost Horizon, Random Harvest)* prepared three treatments and a shooting script by December 1944, but Lubitsch threw most of Hilton's work out, bringing the central characters together more quickly and severely downplaying Hilton's farcical treatment of the climax.

While he was working on the script with Sam Hoffenstein and Elizabeth Reinhardt, Lubitsch asked to see the recently completed but unreleased *Anna and the King of Siam*. He came out calling it a "beautiful, wonderful" film, although, unbeknownst to him, the projectionist had accidentally skipped a reel. A few days later, Lubitsch was passing by when he overheard a conversation about the scene in which Linda Darnell dies.

A clearly concerned Lubitsch said "I have never gone to sleep in a movie in my life, and that scene was not there. The picture I saw was perfect as it was." Ray Klune, production manager for Fox studios, made some inquiries and found out what had happened. The more he thought about Lubitsch's reaction, the more he wondered if Darnell really had to die. As it turned out, the reel that Lubitsch had never missed was seriously shortened, but the death scene was retained; late in life, Klune believed the studio erred by not following Lubitsch's lead and deleting the entire reel.

Lubitsch had a first-draft script for *Cluny Brown* ready by May, and Zanuck's reaction was highly favorable. His invariably specific, often multitudinous suggestions were here kept to less than half a dozen: one line change, suggestions for the names of hotels featured in the script, and a minor suggestion for the playing of an initial embrace.

Finally, in November 1945, Ernst's doctors gave him the go-ahead to direct. A month later, he began production on *Cluny Brown*. Zanuck was now paying Lubitsch $12,500 a month, or $150,000 a year. It was slightly more than Zanuck was paying John Ford ($141,000) but not a lot compared to the $31,000 a month (or $375,000 a year) that Zanuck would pay Preston Sturges beginning in March 1947.

The first days of production seem to have been slightly edgy. Jennifer Jones reported to Fox having just finished David O. Selznick's operatically overwrought *Duel in the Sun,* which, due to reshoots and the tinkering of censors, wouldn't be released until six months after *Cluny Brown* was already in the theaters. Although Jones had made *The Song of Bernadette* at Fox a few years before, Zanuck had been away at war at the time and the studio had been run by William Goetz. Since Goetz was no longer at the studio, the nervous Jones had announced she would communicate with the Fox front office solely through production manager Ray Klune, who had ramrodded *Gone With the Wind,* among others, for her lover David Selznick.

One day, when Klune arrived on the set for a conference with Jones, Lubitsch said, "If the star wants to talk to you and it deals with story or direction, would you tell me?" The remark, humorous but with an underlying point, was vintage Lubitsch. For his part, Ernst was also nervous. "I feel," he said, "like a dancer who broke a leg and wondered if he'd ever dance again—until he finds out that he can."

Art directors Lyle Wheeler and J. Russell Spencer beautifully redressed the French town built for *The Song of Bernadette* to look English. Each day Lubitsch worked was carefully monitored. On February 11, 1946, he collapsed on the soundstage, but after two days of bed rest was back on the set. The picture was completed after sixty days of production. Except for that one spell, Lubitsch completed the picture without any problems, and he and Charles Boyer got along famously.

Boyer and his wife, Pat, attended the preview in Westwood, which was a roaring success. But, as Boyer would later observe, that was about the only time the picture played to a full house. It was not that *Cluny Brown* was a rank failure when it was released in June 1946—it ended up returning $1.64 million, almost exactly what it cost—it was just that Boyer's box-office appeal was waning, and Jennifer Jones's had not yet ascended. Without some particularly combustible quality in the picture itself, *Cluny Brown* struck audiences as mild, satisfactory entertainment but no more.

After the credits, which end with a caricature of Lubitsch holding a megaphone, we are introduced to England in the year 1938, characterized as a land of blithe snobs and inbred fools. Mostly, the English are impervious, not through stalwart will, but innate stupidity. Take the case of Adam Belinski, a Czech author in flight from the Nazis. A poet, a philosopher, Belinski, exclaims an ardent admirer, is "fighting for a better world." "What for?" replies Sir Henry Carmel (Reginald Owen), the Bertie Woosterish lord of the manor.

Belinski is the sort of bemused, courtly man who gazes at a stopped-up sink and murmurs, "an analog of human frustration." But the sink isn't stopped up for long, because of Cluny Brown, a plumber's niece.

Belinski and Cluny both find themselves at Sir Henry's country home, Belinski as a guest, Brown as a maid: a woman who doesn't know her place and a man who doesn't have one. The castaways commiserate about their fates and their inability to do what it is they really enjoy. "I wish I could roll up my sleeves," says Cluny "and roll down my stockings and unloosen the joint. Bang! Bang! Bang!"

The flamboyant double entendre gives way to the giggly caricature, as Cluny becomes enamoured of Mr. Wilson, the village chemist, played by Richard Haydn in all his quince-faced, glottal-voiced splendor. Mr. Wilson lives with his mother, who never speaks, just clears her throat incessantly but indicatively. Wilson is a brilliant comic caricature, but he is nobody's idea of a good catch. Cluny's attraction is not to him but to the idea of a home, of domesticity . . . even an enervated, aberrant domesticity.

Belinski is a benign, graceful creature of the air, a philosopher, a prince, able to coast through any situation. He is, however, no do-gooder; his achievements—which we have to take on faith—seem incidental to the simple sybaritic pleasure he takes in his own company, his own accomplishments. And, while he loves walks in the country, there is a limit; the nightingale outside his window, for instance, is slowly driving him insane.

Fortunately for Belinski, Cluny's engagement to Wilson is submarined when the plumbing in his house gets stopped up. She makes the mistake of interrupting a dinner party to clear the blockage by her favored method of vigorously banging on the joint. It is an unforgivable breach of decorum. Soon thereafter, Cluny leaves with Belinski. As the train pulls out, he tells her that he was going to write a tract entitled "Morality vs. Expediency," but has now decided to write a best-seller, to make enough money for both of them to live comfortably.

And what if there are three of us? Cluny inquires. Lubitsch dissolves to a coda, played without dialogue. The camera dollies up to a Fifth Avenue bookstore, where a window showcases Belinski's novel, *The Nightingale Murders.* Belinski and Cluny, looking the very essence of chic, pass by and are admiring the display, when she suddenly grows faint. Dissolve to the same window with another book display: *The Nightingale Strikes Again.* It's a snappy finish, ending the picture in fine style.

Structured as a gentle comedy of mores rather than manners, *Cluny Brown* is slightly lacking in energy, not in the direction or acting, but in the script; the obliviousness of the English is never really germane to the story; neither is Adam's anti-Nazi past. In fact, there is nothing driving any of the characters except the desire to be themselves. All this accounts for a certain air of being amiably becalmed, and there is a slight but perceptible sense that Lubitsch is harboring his energies; the film's location shots are limited to the back lot, and even then, process backgrounds are relied upon far more than usual.

Yet *Cluny Brown* is clearly the work of a serene, centered man. In its lack of a driving narrative engine, in its quiet charm, it's the most European, Renoiresque, of Lubitsch's American movies. Charles Boyer offers the polish and charm that never failed him, while Jennifer Jones's undertones of neurotic sexuality lend the character a needed subtext. Wisely, she doesn't attempt an accent and is quite winning, although she lacks sufficient technique to completely obliterate the stylized mechanics needed for a Lubitsch performance. As always, Jones is better at conveying fear, worry, and hurt than she is simple high spirits.

Lubitsch's style, once very busy and given to self-conscious, sprightly comments, is now simplicity itself, watching the characters in the frame with an accomplished ease. Visual metaphor, the basis of the Lubitsch Touch, has disappeared, because the director's attitudes are now so fully embodied in the characters that no camera embellishments are necessary.

Adam Belinski is one of Lubitsch's most endearing characters. He may be one of Hitler's worst enemies, a great liberal, but he is not averse to enjoying life's pleasures on someone else's tab. A taste for luxury, Lubitsch well knew, is not the worst thing in the world. Like Lubitsch,

Belinski has an instinctive feel for a person's weaknesses; his habit of opening the door to Wilson's drug store so that the bell rings, then quickly walking away, is perfectly calculated to drive an anal-retentive crazy.

But it is Belinski's courtliness, his spiritual freedom, that seems most moving, most liberating. He's a close cousin to Gaston Monescu, who rights what wrongs he can en route to his own definition of happiness. As always, Lubitsch's answer to the problems of a homicidal world lies in personal fulfillment—not on the world's terms, but those of the individual.

In America, the critics responded to *Cluny Brown* as they usually did with Lubitsch. *The New York Times* said that "Ernst Lubitsch has come up with a delectable and sprightly lampoon . . . among the year's most delightful comedies," while the *Herald-Tribune* said that the film was "first-rate," and the pleasurably vulgar *Variety* called it "Whammo entertainment."

The English, however, were not amused. The *Sunday Express* bellowed that the gentle little satire was like "kippers fried in cream, an anchovy laid across a strawberry ice . . . complete and awful wrongheadedness . . . Cars are too big, riding clothes too unridden-in; even when a quiet dinner party by candlelight is attempted, the ancestral dining hall is still flooded with the flat glare of a score of studio arc lights."

The *New Statesman* went considerably further and made perceptible anti-German (if not anti-Semitic) inferences that the mere names of writers Hoffenstein and Reinhardt were sufficient to convey its lack of authentic Englishness.

For the old guard of Hollywood's English colony, who read the *Times* every day and thus took these things very seriously, all this was mortifying. C. Aubrey Smith was sufficiently cowed to issue a formal apology for having appeared in the film and suggested that J. Arthur Rank might take a calculated revenge by "making an inaccurate film set in America," although that rather begged the question of why Rank was needed when the Messrs. Warner, Mayer et al had already made literally hundreds of inaccurate pictures about America.

Despite his pretense of a successful recovery, Ernst's condition had not really stabilized. Around the time of *Cluny Brown,* there was yet another heart seizure, this time at a party for an official of the Nuremberg trials that was being held at Otto Preminger's house at 333 Bel Air Road.

As the jurist was discussing the case for the rapt audience, Lubitsch beckoned Walter Reisch to his chair. Reisch immediately saw that Lubitsch was in physical distress, and quietly told him he'd meet him by the kitchen entrance. Reisch went out to the front yard where he grabbed the first car he found that had the keys in it and drove it around to the back, where he found Lubitsch doubled over, both hands pressing against his chest.

Reisch slowly drove the block to Lubitsch's house, but going up the driveway seemed to aggravate the pain. Reisch and the housekeeper (Otto had the night off) managed to get him inside where he lay on an antique wooden bench. While the housekeeper called Dr. Nathanson, Reisch untied Lubitsch's shoes and loosened his collar, but couldn't manage to get him upright to pull off a wool sweater. Lubitsch lay there muttering *"Es ist aus mit mir, es ist aus mit mir"* ("I'm done for").

In fact, after Dr. Nathanson arrived and examined his patient, Ernst's condition had improved to the point where he didn't even need to be hospitalized. If only, Nathanson told Reisch, the *patient* Lubitsch would stop being the *director* Lubitsch.

One Sunday afternoon at the Reischs, Lubitsch, sitting with Nicola, announced that he had invited "the man who had saved my life." When a slim, medium-sized man came walking into the house, Lupita Tovar Kohner responded with a cheery "My goodness, Max, how are you?"

Dr. Maximilian Edel was born in 1906 in Vienna, and began the practice of medicine there. But when his wife died despite his best professional efforts, Edel turned his back on medicine and became a sculptor. When he and his second wife, also an artist, came to California as refugees, the actor Alexander Granach introduced him to the Kohners. Impressed with his work, Paul Kohner persuaded his client Walter Huston to commission a bust from Edel. The bust turned out so well that it was used at Huston's memorial service after his sudden death in 1950.

Once his new home helped restore his emotional equilibrium, Edel returned to his first love, medicine, which alienated his second wife, who prided herself on being the wife of an artist.

In the late summer of 1946, as *Cluny Brown* was making its way around the theaters of America, Lubitsch's condition had become complicated to such an extent that Morris Nathanson, who had developed a heart condition of his own, could not give his patient the necessary care. He called in Edel, even though Edel had no interest in cardiology. "I didn't want to experience all that sadness, so many deaths," is the way Edel would put it.

Lubitsch's friends always assumed that the phrase "the man that saved my life" referred to Edel's ministrations to the director's heart. But the truth was considerably darker than that. Shortly after the completion of *Cluny Brown,* probably just after the coronary episode at Preminger's house, Lubitsch had become a drug addict.

The increasing attacks of angina had stoked Lubitsch's anxiety, which was now lurching over into a crippling fear. Demerol alleviated much of Ernst's sensitivity to the primary symptom of his failing heart, as well as his reaction to it. The angina attacks and Lubitsch's increasing drug dependency had been successfully kept from Darryl Zanuck. "Nathanson explained the situation to me," recalled Maximilian Edel. "Lubitsch had bribed his nurse to give him extra Demerol shots for the angina."

Soon, the Demerol began to affect Lubitsch's emotional equilibrium. He had mentioned to Mary Loos that he needed help finding a nurse for Nicola, whereupon Loos volunteered to locate one through her father's clinic. The next time Loos went to visit him, she found him eating lunch upstairs at a card table. Without warning, he turned on her. "You're trying to take my daughter away from me," he charged. "Everybody is trying to run things. I don't like the fact that you've interfered with my life."

Loos, aghast at the sudden change in him, left the house and went some months without seeing him. In talking with other mutual friends, it turned out that virtually all of them had also been verbally attacked. When Loos decided to marry the writer Richard Sale, she sent an announcement to Lubitsch, who sent a beautiful floral arrangement. She stopped by his house to thank him and realized that on account of the Demerol-induced outbursts, he had become isolated, a virtual anchorite in his house.

"What you have to do is live with him," Dr. Nathanson told Edel. "Work during the daytime, then go to his house for thirty nights."

Which is what Edel did. For thirty nights he stayed at 268 Bel Air Road, talking to the desperate, distraught man, occasionally holding him while he sobbed in the night. "He would wake up and cry. I didn't really have to restrain him. Well, almost. I held him lovingly, not restrainingly. He would cry, beg, sob. 'I go through so much pain. Please.' I was inspired by him. It was a big challenge."

Over and over Edel would explain the importance of Lubitsch not allowing his existence to be dependent on something illegal, illicit. Edel did not bother telling his patient that he would not have survived long with a Demerol addiction (the drug invites liver toxicity), because the hazy, enveloping warmth the drug provides obliterates any conventional fear of consequences.

During those long nights, Lubitsch opened up to Edel as much as he ever did with anybody. He told Edel about his brother Richard's death and confessed that he was terrified of dying the same way. "He was very sexual," said Edel. "The fear was not so much the condition he had; the fear was this image of his brother dying [during sex]. It was a great trauma for him. And it came true."

Through the thirty-day period, Lubitsch's condition improved, his thirst for the Demerol lessened; when the angina would flare up, Lubitsch would take nitroglycerin. But the fact of the matter was that there was little the medicine of that day could do but treat Lubitsch's symptoms.

For Lubitsch had progressive coronary artery disease. "Today, we probably would have done a bypass after the first heart attack," said Max Edel, "and maybe a second one after the second heart attack. But in those days it was impossible to diagnose which arteries were clogged. We didn't have the angiograms, the arteriography, the tools that visualize the condition. He was on borrowed time."

Nor did Edel ever consider prescribing an enforced retirement for his patient, for even the most cursory acquaintance could tell that such an order would have been pointless. "If he had retired, what would he have done with himself?" asked Mary Loos. "He certainly wouldn't have traveled. He could always have dictated something, but he couldn't really write in the sense of sitting down and doing a book. Film was his life."

"If I had said to him 'You could live longer if you retire,' I am sure he would have said 'Forget it,' " said Max Edel. "I had the same experience with Bruno Walter, who couldn't get from a parking lot to an office without suffering angina.

"Instead of thinking, 'Making a movie would kill Lubitsch,' or 'Conducting will kill Walter,' I think it was the other way around. The [filmmaking] kept him alive. Had Lubitsch retired after his first heart attack, he might not have lasted as long as he did."

So it was that Lubitsch became close friends with the man that saved his life. The older man demonstrated enormous generosity to Edel, occasionally offering fatherly advice. "Max, don't tell people that you're a sculptor," he said one day. "They'll think that you have more interest in sculpture than in medicine."

"He was interested that I should be successful," remembered Edel, "that I should not lose patients. And he was right." What struck Edel most strongly about his patient was his enthusiasm, the intensity that flamed from his black eyes, the way he carried his head slightly ahead of his body, not out of aggression, but out of avid curiosity as to what might be discovered around the next corner.

"He was a fiery man. When he described his feelings about visiting Russia, and going through the customs difficulty on the way out, the description was such that I wanted to stop him because he was as excited as he had been at the moment. He reproduced the situation exactly, including his reactions. In every situation he talked about, he relived its intensity."

One day Lubitsch phoned Edel with a dinner invitation for the coming Friday. Since Edel had a date lined up ("She was a violinist. I had a vision of a Nude with Violin") he declined, whereupon Lubitsch said, "Oh, that's too bad. Thomas Mann and his daughter are coming." Edel canceled his date.

"I was the only one there besides Ernst, Thomas and Erika Mann. Of course it was fascinating. Mann had just finished *Doctor Faustus* and told us all about it."

At Lubitsch's Christmas party in 1946, Lubitsch sat Edel next to Sinclair Lewis because of Edel's admiration for *Arrowsmith*. "To be able to talk to Sinclair Lewis," beamed Edel nearly fifty years later. "That to me was great generosity."

Through the Sunday afternoon gatherings at the Reischs, Edel was introduced to the elite of the European émigrés; in time he became the personal physician for Igor Stravinsky and Bruno Walter, among many others. Lubitsch's addiction, and Edel's part in banishing it, remained well-kept secrets. Even so, occasionally Edel would be approached by people like Oscar Levant and Ben Hecht, members of Hollywood's addict community, for prescriptions for illegal drugs, primarily morphine.

And the prospective Nude with Violin? "I never saw the girl again."

347

Early in January 1947, as word began to circulate through the inner circle that Lubitsch was himself again, Mary Loos got the idea of throwing a surprise birthday party for him. She, Richard Sale, and Talli Wyler rented out the smaller party room at the Bel-Air Hotel and invited Ernst, accompanied by Max Edel, to come to the hotel for a drink. When he arrived, he saw all of his old friends—the Reischs, the Wylers—and some of his new ones, including Rex Harrison. The birthday cake sported an enormous cigar made out of icing. The evening was a complete success; a few days later, Lubitsch sent Loos a set of fine crystal with a note: "Thank you for giving me back my friends."

It seemed that he had turned a corner. Fox announced that they had signed him to an unprecedented fifteen-year contract, although, given the reality of his physical condition, it was more a gesture of respect than anything else. Shortly thereafter, as was already something of a custom for major talents who had either been scandalously overlooked or were about to die, the Academy of Motion Picture Arts and Sciences voted Lubitsch a special Oscar. At the presentation ceremony, Mervyn LeRoy spoke of "a dark stranger with a rather stern face, a big black cigar, and the merriest pair of eyes under the sun.

"He had an adult mind and a hatred of saying things the obvious way. Because of these qualities and a God-given genius, he advanced the technique of screen comedy as no one else has ever done.

"Suddenly, the pratfall and the double take were left behind and the sources of deep inner laughter were tapped. The housebroken camera learned to stop at a closed door instead of peeping gawkily through the keyhole.

"A master of innuendo had arrived."

The severe episode of pulmonary edema that followed the Oscar ceremony was another sharp warning, but Lubitsch chose to pretend it had never happened. Again, the studio was not informed, for Lubitsch was about to make another movie, and he still could not bring himself to feel entirely comfortable at Fox for what were almost certainly highly subjective reasons.

"Ernst's life had been so bound up in Paramount," remembered Philip Dunne. "That's where he was at home and well known. Lubitsch was the heart and soul of Paramount, the leader of the people who really cared about good movies. Sure, they had DeMille, but that was soft porn masquerading as religion."

Lubitsch began to take part in one of the Fox social customs. Every afternoon at 4:30, a group gathered in the office of producer Fred Kohlmar, who had the office next to Ernst's. Kohlmar, Philip Dunne, Mary Loos, and her husband, Richard Sale, would all gather around Lubitsch for what Dunne remembered as "tea and mutual sympathy . . . Ernst was the center of our little group . . . we all admired him, and—what to me was more important—grew personally fond of him.

"Nobody sat at his feet. Far from it. He was just one of the group. The English secretary who made the tea was also part of the group. So many of the directors were pompous. John Stahl would always talk about his 'genius' and [Michael] Curtiz was the worst of all. But Ernst's humor had sparkle. He had a wonderful gift—the same one Don Stewart and Bob Benchley had. They could make you think you were as funny as they were. It was so spontaneous and infectious that you began to get into the spirit of it. Ernst had the capacity of elevating any conversation so it charmed."

One day in the Fox executive dining room, Lubitsch was having lunch with Ray Klune, Nunnally Johnson, and a few others. Since there was an unwritten rule forbidding the discussion of your own movies, the conversation usually slid over to politics and sports. A comparison of Babe Ruth with a current slugger was under way when someone mentioned that Ruth was slow and never could run.

"What did you say?" Lubitsch asked. "I thought that was why Ruth was great."

Not at all, it was explained. Ruth could simply hit the ball so far that he didn't really have to run at all, just trot around the bases.

Lubitsch, now thoroughly confused, said, "But doesn't 'home run' mean he's *got* to run?" Despite the best attempts of the men at the table, the intricacies of baseball stubbornly refused to be comprehensible. "This game is much more difficult than motion pictures!" Lubitsch said by way of ending the conversation.

He was trying so hard to stay alive that he was down to two cigars a day.

In the spring of 1947 Ernst was invited to attend a showing of *Trouble in Paradise* being presented by the Great Films Society at Rexford School in Beverly Hills. He brought Creighton Hale along with him, and introduced him as "one of my favorite actors."

After the screening he and Larry Swindell, one of the members of the society, went to a restaurant on the corner of Sunset and LaBrea for a cup of coffee. He began expounding on his films and career to Swindell, whose precociousness astounded him. Perhaps because of the context of the evening, he talked more about his older films. He was buoyed by the enthusiastic audience response to *Trouble in Paradise,* but not exuberant; Lubitsch knew that it was a consensus classic and he felt no need to defend it.

On the other hand, *Design for Living* had, he felt, gotten an undeserved bad press because Ben Hecht had rewritten Noël Coward's dialogue, and

Gary Cooper and Fredric March weren't Coward and Alfred Lunt. He told Swindell that he had only been interested in the basic premise of the story. He believed that Cooper and March were both excellent and that Edward Everett Horton was the greatest comic actor in movies.

His two favorite actresses, he said, were Carole Lombard and Miriam Hopkins. Hopkins, he admitted, was an excessive actress, which he liked because it was much easier to bring an excessive talent down than bring a recessive talent up. He confessed that he didn't particularly like to direct actors, that his method of working with them was to have them do what they wanted to do, then make them do less.

He told Swindell that he thought Gene Tierney's career had been terribly mishandled, and that he had wanted to direct Joseph L. Mankiewicz's beautiful film *The Ghost and Mrs. Muir,* which he had just seen at a studio screening prior to general release. (Internal Fox memos indicate Lubitsch had never been considered for the film, but that John Stahl had been. Zanuck had originally wanted to star either Norma Shearer, because he thought she still had one good picture in her, or Claudette Colbert.)

"You couldn't have guessed he was about to die," remembered Swindell, who would go on to write a fine series of star biographies, including one about Carole Lombard. "He was very outgoing and inclined to talk that night. A one-minute question would get a five-minute answer. I noticed that he had a cigar all the time but it was never lit."

With his friends, Lubitsch began discussing a variation of the comic idea he had hit upon in *Heaven Can Wait,* that of a couple who hate each other so much they can communicate only through an intermediary. It would, he told friends, be very funny if the intermediary was a dog.

Billy Wilder invited Ernst to see a rough cut of *The Emperor Waltz,* which, although shot between June and September of 1946, wouldn't be released until the summer of 1948. Lubitsch seemed to be enjoying the picture until Wilder began using a pair of dogs as metaphors for the lovers played by Bing Crosby (a democratic terrier) and Joan Fontaine (an overbred standard poodle).

The premise was very Lubitschean, but Wilder, in an atypically non-astringent mood, let the film decline into the flatfooted orthodoxy of a Crosby vehicle with mediocre songs. All Ernst could see was Wilder's close variation on his comic idea. Furious, he leaned over to Mary Loos and started whispering "That's my story, that's my story! The son of a bitch has taken my story!!"

Mostly though, he was preoccupied by plans for the future. That night after the screening of *Trouble in Paradise,* Lubitsch had let Swindell in on his plans. He had, he said in a joking way, accepted a challenge from Darryl Zanuck. The challenge would be to see if he could make Betty Grable into an actress.

This Is the Moment, to be retitled *That Lady in Ermine,* dated from a 1919 German operetta that had been adapted by Frederick Lonsdale and Cyrus Wood and opened on Broadway in October 1922. Lubitsch had been mulling over a film version since early 1943, initially as a vehicle for Irene Dunne and Charles Boyer. By 1944, Jeanette MacDonald had replaced Dunne as the star of the movie in his mind, but age and changing audience taste had conspired to render her rather obviously on the downhill slide, and a doubtful commercial proposition.

For Zanuck, who felt that it would be a good idea to try to broaden Betty Grable's audience before she wore out her welcome, it seemed an obvious idea to pair her with one of the premier talents of his directorial staff. Zanuck promoted her to Lubitsch and, in addition, dangled the prospect of a return to musicals. Ernst seems to have been doubtful, but the thought of making his first musical since *The Merry Widow* appealed to him, as did the possibility of smoothing over the pallid response to *Cluny Brown.*

There is a surviving continuity by Ladislas Fodor that is undated, and possibly derives from the Irene Dunne phase of the project. What is certain is that on February 18, 1947, Lubitsch handed in his treatment for the film, ten pages of straight narrative with no indication of musical numbers. Zanuck was immediately enthralled, penciling a note on the inside front cover: "Phone—tell Ernst great—will see him Tuesday."

At the meeting, Zanuck asked for explanations of the flashbacks, and wanted more of a sense of how the film would open. "In *Heaven Can Wait* you managed to combine farce and a tear," Zanuck noted. "Is it possible here with [the] love story?" As always, the producer's notes tended toward psychological realism, and he asked Lubitsch to keep in mind that the story needed a firmer foundation and had to play as at least half-honest.

Still, Zanuck thought the material was promising enough to proceed to a full screenplay. One last time, Lubitsch called on Sam Raphaelson, who was not enthusiastic about the material or the star. Besides that, Raphaelson was at his farm in Pennsylvania, working on a play.

Dorshka Raphaelson thought a reasonable compromise might be to invite Lubitsch to the farm to work on the project, and Lubitsch thought it was a good idea. But when Max Edel learned that Ernst would have to climb up and down steps, he forbade the trip.

Again, Lubitsch asked Raphaelson to head west, this time dangling a salary of $5,000 a week. Raphaelson relented. Raphaelson and his wife arrived in Hollywood on a Sunday morning and were at 268 Bel Air Road by the same afternoon. They shook hands—Lubitsch was not physically effusive and did not hug men—and Raphaelson and Dorshka stayed for dinner.

Unlike the writing of *Heaven Can Wait,* the script for *That Lady in Ermine,* was written in Lubitsch's office on the Fox lot, "to impress Zanuck," according to Raphaelson. It was a huge, airy, square room with light green walls, black-and-white paintings in wood frames, a grand piano in a corner, and deep leather furniture.

As the two men began work, Zanuck began to have second thoughts. *That Lady in Ermine* was obviously going to be an expensive picture, and a physically arduous one as well, if only because musicals entail long shooting schedules. Maybe, he reasoned, it would be safer and less stressful for Lubitsch if he did something else instead.

Zanuck pressured Sol Siegel, who had been assigned to produce a story then entitled *A Letter to Four Wives,* to offer the story to Lubitsch. Ernst, who had perused the material once before, still wasn't interested and went back to working on *That Lady in Ermine,* while Siegel elected to hire Joe Mankiewicz as the writer/director for *A Letter to Four Wives.* (Later, the prolix screenplay was reduced by the simple expedient of cutting out one of the wives, resulting in the minor classic *A Letter to Three Wives.*)

The script for *That Lady in Ermine* was written in March, April, and May of 1947. Ernst confided to Raphaelson that he had had two seizures in the past year. "And you can see, Sam, I'm taking good care of myself. I'm in great shape, I didn't smoke this morning—I chewed on that cigar. Did you notice?" Raphaelson had noticed. He had also noticed that Ernst's lusty appetite had been gelded to the point where a Lubitsch lunch consisted of little more than consommé and boiled chicken. He resolved not to give his old friend a hard time, even though, for the first time, "[Lubitsch] was repeating his mannerisms. The whole concept was an imitation of former Lubitsch pictures."

Because of his friend's physical condition, Raphaelson felt constrained. "I couldn't fight with him over scenes, characters, and dialogue in the healthy, vigorous way we had developed as the years brought us to closer understanding. I felt, 'Oh, the hell with it—I'll take the money. He'll make a picture; it'll be all right. The studio will like it. I won't be ashamed of it, and that's that.'' But Raphaelson could not avoid acknowledging Lubitsch's loss of vitality. The day began later, the breaks for lunch were longer. Lubitsch was gentling himself.

The special Academy Award on March 13 naturally provided opportunities for a few retrospective interviews. In *American Cinematographer,* Lubitsch again stressed his appreciation for the classical style of camerawork. ''The camera, to my mind, has been greatly misused in regard to moving shots. The moving shot is only good if you are not conscious of mechanical movement, just as a comedian is funny only when he doesn't convey the idea that he is trying to be funny.'' He also bewailed the fact that ''too many directors know all too little'' about just what a camera can do.

The *Los Angeles Times'* Philip Scheuer also visited. When he was asked why he was planning a musical after so many years, Lubitsch shrugged. ''One gets tired, one changes. When one has a personal style it is like one's handwriting—he can't get away from it. I had done so many musicals . . . that I felt the need of a different approach. But I had none. So . . . I returned to an earlier metier, comedy of the sophisticated sort.''

Now, in one of the last interviews he would ever give, Lubitsch told Scheuer his favorite pictures were (drama) *The Patriot,* (musical) *The Love Parade,* (comedy) *Trouble in Paradise,* (satire) *Ninotchka,* and *The Shop Around the Corner,* which he called ''the best picture I ever made in my life.''

Again, he returned to the old canard about trivial material that had first been spread by Jim Tully more than twenty years before, and a certain defensiveness crept in. Form, he declared, is more important than content. Most people's judgments of content are ''adolescent.''

''As soon as someone tackles a big theme with a message we take him seriously and call it art. We appreciate a painting of the crucifixion . . . whereas a simple Cézanne depiction of a vase and an apple may be far more enduring as art.

''I believe—and I am not comparing myself to Cézanne—in taking a lesser theme and then treating it without compromise. Leaving my own pictures out of it, there hasn't been a better picture of Americana than Preston Sturges's *Miracle of Morgan's Creek.* It had no pretensions, yet, despite the fact that people went around kicking each other's posteriors, it was truer artistically than most pictures made in America."

The retrospective mood was amplified a few months later when, on July 10, Lubitsch sent a long letter to the critic and enthusiast Herman G. Weinberg as an addendum to an index to his films prepared by Theodore Huff. Of the historical period, Lubitsch expressed a fondness for *Carmen, Madame DuBarry,* and *Anne Boleyn;* of the American silents, his favorites were *The Marriage Circle, Lady Windermere's Fan, The Patriot,* and *Kiss Me Again.*

"As to pure style I think I have done nothing better or as good as *Trouble in Paradise* . . . as to satire, I believe I probably was never sharper than in *Ninotchka* . . . as for human comedy I think I never was as good as in *Shop Around the Corner.* Never did I make a picture in which the atmosphere and the characters were truer than in this picture."

In closing, he responded to Theodore Huff's gentle ascribings of occasional mediocrity by saying, "I agree . . . wholeheartedly that I made sometimes pictures which were not up to my standard, but then it can only be said about a mediocrity that all his works live up to his standard."

The wisdom was inarguable, but what was also inarguable was the fact that in the photograph that accompanied the *Los Angeles Times* article, Lubitsch looked haggard and greatly aged. The delicacy of his physical condition was appallingly apparent, but Lubitsch pretended that everything was fine. After all, he had a picture to make.

The first-draft script for *The Lady in Ermine* was completed on June 3, and Zanuck's fertile mind immediately began riffling through the casting possibilities. If the picture was to go into production soon, Zanuck wanted Betty Grable and Cornel Wilde; if it could be held off till February, the alternatives were Rex Harrison and Gene Tierney. Either way, Zanuck wanted the movie to be in Technicolor.

Clearly, Tierney would have been preferable, even though her singing would have had to have been dubbed, and Harrison would have been ideal, but between Lubitsch's horror at the prospect of sitting around for eight months, and Zanuck's wanting to chart some new ground for a star whose musical-comedy welcome was about to wear out, production was scheduled for the latter part of 1947.

That meant Betty Grable, an idea greeted with ironically raised eyebrows throughout Hollywood. Even Nicola was appalled. "Not Betty Grable!" she exclaimed to her father, who responded by complaining to

Vivian that "I cannot work if your daughter contradicts me!" Mary Loos, who was a friend of Zanuck's as well as of Lubitsch's, says that Zanuck's patience during Lubitsch's long siege of ill health and the relative failure of *Cluny Brown* made Lubitsch feel that he had no choice but to acquiesce to Grable's casting. "He made the picture because she was good box office," said Loos.

To turn the cheerfully vulgar, slightly cheap (she always seemed to be chewing gum even when she wasn't) charm of Grable into a Lubitsch heroine was not going to be easy, but he managed to salvage something out of the casting process when he dodged the glassy, pallid, uncharming Cornel Wilde, persuading Zanuck to hire the free-lancing Douglas Fairbanks, Jr., instead.

"He asked me to have lunch with him and collaborate on the production," recalled Fairbanks. "I stuttered with pleasure."

Although Fairbanks had been cast in *Design for Living* before contracting pneumonia, he hadn't known Lubitsch that well. Quickly, however, they came to a relaxed friendship. "He was full of future plans; we discussed doing something later on. He would occasionally joke about my stepmother [Mary Pickford], to the effect that she looked so dainty but was really so tough." Fairbanks asked him to look over the script of the actor's next picture, *The Fighting O'Flynn,* which Fairbanks was also producing, and Lubitsch made some helpful and appropriate suggestions.

Beneath the surface geniality and high spirits, Ernst clearly knew that his heart was failing, for he confided to Fairbanks that "This will be my best epitaph." As it turned out, neither *That Lady in Ermine* nor *The Fighting O'Flynn* were to be remotely worthy of his efforts.

With the script and cast for the new picture both set, Lubitsch filled the days and nights before the start of production socializing with his friends. In September, along with Billy Wilder, Walter Reisch, Mary Loos, and Max Edel, he attended a screening of Vittorio De Sica's harshly realistic *Shoeshine.* After the film, he sat frozen, too deeply moved to take part in the voluble conversation that followed. He vowed to write De Sica to tell him of how deeply his movie had affected him as soon as he could find an Italian translator.

Ernst began his attempt to turn Betty Grable into an actress on October 20, 1947, with the largest budget he had ever had: $2.4 million. For the first several weeks of the production, everything went well. "You had to be ready for anything," Walter Abel recalled in 1979. "His improving on the set was, oh, magnificent improvisation." During rehearsals, Lubitsch took particular joy in acting Abel's part, until the slightly irritated actor inquired, "Mr. Lubitsch, I am going to play this part, am I not?" Douglas Fairbanks remembered that Lubitsch had "such vitality; he was tripping over himself with ideas. During rehearsal he'd laugh with pleasure and sometimes he'd even ruin his own takes. And yes, he loved acting all the parts; he was very good, actually."

Lubitsch's buoyance was at least partially attributable to a new relationship with the actress Natalie Schafer. The tart, intelligent Schafer impressed Ernst's friends as a good, solid match for him. Schafer had been married to Louis Calhern, until she became fed up with Calhern's alcoholism. When Calhern married Ilka Chase, Schafer sent her some dresses with a note: "Ilka Dear: Use these quickly." In addition to her wit, she was an unusual choice for Lubitsch in that she was older (she was born in Red Bank, New Jersey, in 1900) than most of his women.

During the first several weeks of filming, members of the crew would take the ever-hovering Steffie Trondle aside and tell her she was worrying too much, that Lubitsch was in better health than he had been during *Cluny Brown*. And, so long as they were working on the soundstage, that seemed to be the case. But as soon as the production moved to the back lot, for exteriors by a riverbed, Lubitsch began to get tired. One day he became chilled and Trondle insisted on taking him home at 4 P.M. Lubitsch was so exhausted that he even mentioned to Trondle the possibility of Otto Preminger finishing the scene for him, but the next morning he had thought better of it.

Still, he felt well enough to spend several nights at the restaurant L'Aiglon, listening to the Hungarian violins that he loved so much. In addition to Schafer, there was a new, more casual relationship in his life. Although he didn't take it seriously, it perked him up sufficiently so that he went to the tailor's for a new suit.

On Saturday, November 29, Lubitsch was photographing the long shots for a scene in which Cesar Romero, disguised as a gypsy fiddler, plays for Douglas Fairbanks, Jr. Both Fairbanks and Romero thought that Lubitsch seemed in good spirits and good health. Max Edel dropped by the set and was introduced to Betty Grable. Lubitsch invited him to dinner, but Edel had other plans and begged off.

Since Edel was busy, and Natalie Schafer was in New York, Lubitsch decided to go out on a date with his latest casual amour. She was neither an actress nor a prostitute, but typically attractive to Lubitsch in that she was blonde and full of fun; he thought enough of her to wear his new suit.

Ever the personal romantic, he told Otto that just touching her gave him an electric thrill.

He told Steffie Trondle to begin Christmas shopping on Monday, and had her ask Foster's, in Westwood, to stay open late one night the following week so he could come in and personally pick out a few gifts. On Sunday, he arose earlier than usual and briskly made plans for the day. That afternoon, he had a date to be at the Wyler's house to attend a screening of *Le Diable au Corps;* Marlene Dietrich had told him that its star, Gérard Philipe, would make a perfect Octavian for the film of *Der Rosenkavalier* he someday aspired to make. The Wylers had invited the A list: Preminger, Wilder, Edmund Goulding, and Dietrich, among others. Lubitsch jokingly said that he would attend on the condition that he would not have to look at Marlene's Presidential Medal of Freedom, which he was tired of seeing displayed.

Walter Reisch called. Lubitsch was in fine fettle, pleased with his actors, pleased with Zanuck's reaction to the rushes, pleased even with his health. Reisch closed by telling him that Marlene and he would come fetch him personally. Just before noon, Lubitsch called Natalie Schafer in New York, and told her that as soon as the picture was finished he would be traveling east to visit her.

After lunch, he welcomed the woman he had had dinner with the night before. Shortly after two o'clock in the afternoon, Lubitsch retired to his den with her. They made love. A few minutes later, he felt the familiar tightness in his chest. The constricting pain began to encircle him, possess him. He excused himself and went into the bathroom, probably to get to his angina medicine. Then, a sudden, tearing explosion inside his chest overwhelmed and obliterated all that was Ernst Lubitsch.

Otto, summoned by the terrified woman, picked Lubitsch up and placed him on the couch fifteen feet away, beside his bookshelves. Otto first called Max Edel, telling him that "Lubitsch is very bad." Edel instructed him to call an ambulance and told him he was on the way. Otto then dialed Mary Loos, but by this time he could tell that there was nothing any ambulance squad would be able to do.

"The old boy just died," he told her. "I think you better come." She stuttered out something about coming over right away. Otto replied that he would have to "take the lady out of the house" but he would be right back. Mary immediately called her father, Dr. Clifford Loos. They arrived about ten minutes later to find Steffie Trondle in the driveway having hysterics, refusing to go in and see Lubitsch.

Loos and her father found that they had been beaten by the Beverly

Hills Pulmotor Squad, who had unsuccessfully tried to revive Lubitsch. He was lying where Otto had put him, on the sofa in the library, covered with one of the fake leopard throws that were common in Hollywood at that time. Loos looked around the room, taking it all in. She noticed that Ernst's Academy Award was serving as a jewelry tree: his watch was hanging on the Oscar. Then she looked down at Lubitsch's body; there was a slight, comfortable smile on his face.

There was nothing for Dr. Loos to do but officially declare Ernst Lubitsch dead as of 2:45 P.M., November 30, 1947.

At 3:15, Walter Reisch and Marlene Dietrich arrived at the house to pick up Lubitsch for the party. A stunned Dietrich stood by Lubitsch's body, trying to assimilate what had happened. Max Edel finally arrived, and assured everybody that Ernst had almost no time to know what was happening.

Beyond his personal grief, Edel's professional reaction was one of frustration and disappointment. He called Morris Nathanson to inform him of the situation and asked him if he wanted to come over. "What's the use?" asked Nathanson. Edel was struck by his mentor's detachment. Talking to Mary Loos and Otto Werner, he realized what had happened. A full stomach slightly lowers the heart's capacity, and, in Lubitsch's case, there wasn't any to spare. Add the exertion of lovemaking and, in Edel's words, "He overdid."

Reisch and Dietrich went back to Reisch's house. Reisch made plans to cancel the afternoon party, but Dietrich wouldn't hear of it. "Let everybody come and remember him," she said, and that was what happened. That Sunday, about fifty people arrived at the Reischs' to mourn their friend, "the biggest party we ever had," according to Lisl Reisch.

The hearse arrived at 4:30 to transport the body to the Delmer Smith Mortuary on Washington Boulevard. For the last time, Ernst Lubitsch left the house at 268 Bel Air Road that he had built and loved so much. It was certified that Lubitsch had died of a coronary thrombosis lasting one hour, due to coronary sclerosis lasting four years. There was no autopsy.

That night, Lubitsch's friends walked from Reisch's house down the block to the house at 268 Bel Air; the news began filtering out to Lubitsch's friends and coworkers. Back in New York, Dorshka Raphaelson was stunned. "I never thought of him dying," she would say. "I just thought he'd live forever with a heart problem."

"There was an enormous sense of loss," remembered Talli Wyler.

"There just wasn't anybody else like him; you felt that something irreplaceable was gone. At the time, we all thought he was so old. Now, I think, 'My God, how young!'"

During the informal wake at Lubitsch's house, Mary Loos and Talli Wyler were sitting by the door to the study when they were appalled to hear Otto Preminger on the phone to Darryl Zanuck. Lubitsch, Preminger was saying, had told him that if anything happened to him, he wanted Preminger to take the picture over.

Both women knew Preminger had to be lying; for one thing, Lubitsch never discussed the possibility of dying with anybody but Morris Nathanson and Max Edel. For another, his disappointment with the results of A Royal Scandal would hardly impel him to give Preminger a second chance at failing with a Lubitsch production. But Preminger was an avid careerist and he saw That Lady in Ermine as an opportunity. "He was an opportunist when it made sense to him to be so," said David Raksin. "Otto believed that in a dog-eat-dog world, you better get the first bite."

On Monday, December 1, Daily Variety's banner headline was hilariously blunt but indisputably accurate: LUBITSCH DROPS DEAD. The funeral arrangements were made jointly by Walter Reisch, Mary Loos, Steffie Trondle, and Talli Wyler. Services were the following Thursday at Forest Lawn's Church of the Recessional. That day the trade papers prominently displayed full-page ads paying tribute to Ernst from, among others, the Directors Guild.

At Forest Lawn, Ernst was laid out in the new suit he had worn to dinner the previous Saturday night. Mary Loos attended with Eva Gabor and Margo. Neither of her friends had ever seen a dead body before, let alone that of someone they loved. They were frankly terrified. Loos suggested that they just walk by the open casket and not look. Even so, she kept a firm hold on both their elbows just in case. Also inconspicuously attending were Leni Lubitsch Lewis and her son Eddie. Looking at her ex-husband for the last time, Leni broke down and cried. She did not introduce herself to Vivian or Nicola.

Honorary pallbearers were Rex Cole, Max Edel, Douglas Fairbanks, Jr., William Goetz, Frederick Hollander, Arthur Hornblow, Sam Katz, Al Kaufman, Fred Kohlmar, Paul Kohner, Henry Koster, Sol Lesser, Ernest Lindley, Leo McCarey, Rouben Mamoulian, Thomas Mann, Gene Markey, Rudolph Marx, Edward Mayer, Louis B. Mayer, Lothar Mendes, Lewis Milestone, William Perlberg, Otto Preminger, Joe Schenck, Lew

Schreiber, Charles Schwartz, Mendel Silberberg, Ben Thau, Charles Vidor, Walter Wanger, Franz Waxman, William Wyler, and Darryl F. Zanuck.

Among the flower arrangements was a small heart of red carnations sent by Nicola. Officiating was the powerful Los Angeles rabbi Edgar Magnin (whom Lubitsch had not cared for). Lubitsch, he said, "gave something to the world that will not perish. He brought beauty, interest, color, and romance to many, many people. He had the seed of genius in him. May God take him under his wings and give him perfect peace."

Jeanette MacDonald sang "Beyond the Blue Horizon" and "Waltz in A-Major," one of the songs Ernst had composed for Nicola. Mary Loos thought she sang beautifully, although she was sure that if he could have heard it, Lubitsch's response would have been "Why didn't she sing that well in the picture?"

Charles Brackett delivered the eulogy, saying that "with his artistic touch, Ernst Lubitsch helped bring a raw, gawky stumbling medium and taught it how to carry itself as becomes a personage of the world, how to wear it like a boutonniere, and how to imply droll, wonderful things without saying them at all.

"Every picture he made bore his imprint—male, deft, and unsentimental and joyous. He was no wild, impractical poet clashing with the businessmen who make picture history, but he was an unmitigated artist, blessedly incapable of meeting a standard of taste which wasn't his own."

Finally, Brackett tried to put an upbeat spin on the grim occasion by picturing Lubitsch approaching the gates of heaven and pausing reluctantly to toss away his cigar before entering. "Now," he said, "there will be some delightful Trouble in Paradise."

Mary Loos felt that the entire affair was a nightmare; all that pulled her through it was the thought of Lubitsch listening, eyes flashing as if to say, "Are they kidding?"

After the ceremony, Henry Blanke, Mervyn LeRoy, Gene Raymond, Gottfried Reinhardt, Richard Sale, Walter Reisch, Billy Wilder, and Otto Werner carried Lubitsch to the hearse. The proceedings nearly took a Mack Sennett turn when the pallbearers, unused to heavy lifting, almost dropped the coffin on their way out of the church. The situation was saved by Richard Sale, who wedged his knee underneath the casket until the mortuary attendants came to the rescue.

After the graveside ceremony, Billy Wilder and William Wyler walked down the slope to the waiting cars in a deep silence. "Well, no more Lubitsch," sighed Wilder. "Worse than that," replied Wyler. "No more Lubitsch movies."

The grave of Ernst Lubitsch is on a steep, wooded hillside, and is marked by a simple stone. Beneath his name and dates of birth and death is one phrase: "Beloved Daddy."

e p i l o g u e

Lubitsch's will was filed for probate the day after he was buried. Dated March 13, 1945, the will left Vivian fifteen percent of his net estate and $10,000 each to Richard Lubitsch's widow, Regina, and to Ruth Hall. Steffie Trondle, who had been with him since the last days in Germany, and Otto Werner, who had been with him twenty-two years, also were bequeathed $10,000 apiece. Since neither Regina Lubitsch nor Hans, her son, could be located, the money was provisionally remanded into the general estate account. (Unbeknownst to Lubitsch, Regina had been deported to the Sobibor concentration camp on July 20, 1943, and executed three days later. No trace of Hans Lubitsch was ever found.)

The remainder of the money went into a trust for Nicola, who was to receive portions when she was twenty-one, twenty-five, and thirty, with the remainder of the estate coming to her at the age of thirty-five, with the proviso that "in the event that my daughter . . . shall be adopted by any person or shall legally or in any other manner other than by marriage, change her surname to any other name but *'Lubitsch'* . . . my trustees shall pay no income to or for the support of my said daughter . . . until [she] shall reach the age of 21 years." In the event that Lubitsch's heirs did not survive him, the estate was to be divided one-third to the United Jewish

363

eyman

scott

Welfare Fund of Los Angeles and two-thirds to Regina or Hans Lubitsch, and Ruth Hall.

Although Lubitsch had died with only $20.87 in his pockets, the estate inventory showed cash savings slightly in excess of $112,000, bonds worth more than $300,000, not to mention stocks (including 100 shares of Allied Chemical, 100 shares of Du Pont, 67 shares of the Hollywood Turf Club, and 6 shares of Paramount Pictures) worth slightly less than $80,000. There was also a life insurance policy for $133,762. After the usual bills were paid—$3,085 to Forest Lawn, $175 to one Marjorie Corso for "white net dress ordered and completed at the request of decedent as a Christmas present for his daughter, Nicola Lubitsch"—it was determined that Simon and Anna Lubitsch's younger son had left an estate valued at $857,212, the rough equivalent of $3 million in 1993 currency.

The day before the funeral, Fox announced that, instead of Preston Sturges or the far more appropriate Edmund Goulding, both of whom had offered to complete the picture, Otto Preminger would direct the rest of *That Lady in Ermine*. Preminger finished the picture, all right, and in more ways than one.

"I think Zanuck replaced Lubitsch with Preminger because he had the same accent," Douglas Fairbanks, Jr., remembered ruefully. The difference between the authoritarian Preminger and the charming, bubbling Lubitsch was implicit in their on-set demeanor. In place of Ernst's cajoling enthusiasm, Preminger would stand by the camera idly playing with a solid gold yo-yo. Soon after he took the picture over, Preminger set off on one of his infamous tirades, this time at an electrician. Appalled at the behavior and the language, Fairbanks stalked off the set, followed closely by Preminger.

"Otto, you can't talk to people like that," said Fairbanks. "You must apologize."

"Don't be foolish," snapped Preminger.

"Then I'm going home."

Fairbanks got in his car but was stopped at the studio gate and informed that the matter was being taken care of. He returned to the set and found that Preminger had indeed apologized. It might have been better if Fairbanks had kept on driving.

"When Preminger came in he changed everything," said Walter Abel, who had a good-sized supporting part in the picture. Fairbanks and Abel were deeply concerned, for Lubitsch had rehearsed the entire picture with them and they knew that Preminger's slant would render parts of the script unplayable, not to mention incoherent. Finally, they approached him with what Abel recalled as "nothing but kindness and delicacy in our minds" and tried to explain exactly what Lubitsch's intentions and plans had been.

"Mr. Lubitsch is dead," he told them. "*I* am the director of this picture."

"So," remembered Walter Abel, "there was no more fun in Hollywood, not with that man."

In addition to shooting the rest of the picture, Preminger reshot some Lubitsch footage, "because it was too subtle," according to Fairbanks. The first thirteen pages of the script, which Lubitsch had already shot, were cut, as was the ending, effectively deleting a running gag revolving around just what the lady was wearing under her ermine coat.

Even more regrettably, Preminger cut two musical numbers that Lubitsch had already shot, one of which, "It's Always a Beautiful Day," had words by Leo Robin and music by Lubitsch himself. The overall effect was to make what might very well have been delightedly witty and lyrical (Raphaelson's original script, despite his doubts, has some rather nice repartee) severely less so.

One can always sense, and occasionally actually see, what Lubitsch had in mind: in the prominent play given to the gypsy violins Lubitsch loved; in the waggish production number "Ooh, What I'll Do to That Wild Hungarian"; in the sweeping romanticism of the lyrical "This Is the Moment"; in grace notes like a supposedly brutal conqueror disturbed by the composition of a painting; and, finally, in a woman who leaves her husband because "He didn't believe in dreams."

But it is like looking through smudged glass at a conceptually lovely watercolor that has been badly framed. The colors are distorted, and cheap materials have been used.

True, some of the fudging is Lubitsch's; Colonel Teglash's bellowing of "Horvath!" is a steal from Concentration Camp Ehrhardt's screams for "Schultz!" in *To Be or Not to Be*. Other moments, notably a series of fast-motion shots—the sun slamming into the sky, a series of screens rapidly unfolding in front of an orchestra so they won't be able to observe the dancers—are welcome bits of rambunctious cartoon humor that lend astringency to the wedding cake material, in addition to constituting a return to the self-conscious little pieces of camera trickery with which Ernst had made his reputation in other, better times.

But the plot is garbled, the result of the recutting and reshooting, and the ending is truncated, lumpy, and painfully abrupt. The lilt, the assured, sprightly Lubitsch rhythm, is absent.

Under the title *That Lady in Ermine*, the film was finally released in August 1948, at a brief running time of eighty-nine minutes: Lubitsch was the only director credited. The stuffy Bosley Crowther of *The New York Times* actually liked the picture, but *Variety* was much closer to the mark when it said that "[the Lubitsch touch] is not sufficiently sustained to generate topnotch comedy . . . the story is lacking in movement." The film earned $1.4 million, a million less than it cost.

After the usual slogging through probate, the bequests Lubitsch had provided for in his will were finally paid out on December 1, 1950. In July 1951, the house at 268 Bel Air Road was sold for $67,100. For an extra $256, the drapes were included. There were still some lingering debts; Salka Viertel owed Lubitsch $250, but the estate determined that as of November 1, 1951, she was insolvent, so the debt was canceled.

By this time, Nicola was receiving $1,250 a month from the trust, with the estate hovering around the half-million-dollar mark (the trust would not be depleted until 1983).

A public auction of Lubitsch's effects was held on June 8, 1952. Billy Wilder bought a porcelain ashtray and a Mexican cigarette box for $75. Then came the art collection. Charles Vidor bought a Diego Rivera painting for $1,200; Mrs. Laurence Rockefeller bought a Utrillo and a Grandma Moses for $2,950. A Chagall, a Dufy, a Rivera, and three framed movie posters sold for $1,800. There were seven Renoirs, and they, a Boudin and a Grant Wood, among others, went for equally incredible (by contemporary standards) prices. With the exception of Wilder, most of Lubitsch's friends stayed away from the auction out of residual fondness for his memory and the belongings that had once enveloped them all in an affectionate cocoon.

The death of an inherently convivial man like Lubitsch left a vast chasm in the lives of all his friends. Mary Loos tried to pull a couple of particularly distraught friends through their grief by telling them that they should keep him alive by trying to think like he had thought whenever they needed support.

Despite his promise to Nicola that he would never remarry, Lubitsch had spoken to Natalie Schafer about their "being together"; when Schafer arrived back in Hollywood she confided to Mary Loos that she thought they might have gotten married.

The Sunday afternoon parties at the Reischs continued for some years until people began to move away (Otto Preminger, Joe Mankiewicz) or got divorced and brought younger girlfriends and wives (virtually everybody else). Toward the end, more alcohol seemed to be consumed than coffee. It just wasn't the same.

"It got to the point," remembered Lisl Reisch, "where hardly anybody was around, you know?" Occasionally, Lisl would whip up a batch of *Lubitschkoch;* before serving it, she would always say "Poor Ernst, wherever you are, this is for you." Mary Loos's career would encompass many successful movies and novels, and she would come to believe that Lubitsch "helped me, left an indelible training that he didn't know. You couldn't be around him a lot without absorbing something of him. That's why he'll never die in the minds of his friends."

Otto Werner went to work as a gardener for Loos; whenever he would come to mow the lawn, they would reminisce about Lubitsch. Steffie Trondle became private secretary to Jean Negulesco, but her health soon began to deteriorate. "I had always known what a wonderful friend I had in Mr. Lubitsch," she wrote to Sam Raphaelson, "but I had never realized how closely my life had become linked with his, especially during the last few years, and when he was gone I felt completely lost."

Steffie died in October 1950. In death, as in life, she stayed close to Lubitsch; she was buried just a few feet away from him. In December 1965, Nicola married Robert G. Goodpaster and bore him two daughters. The marriage ended in divorce, and she resumed using her maiden name.

No one kept the flame of Lubitsch's sensibility so alive as Billy Wilder, albeit tinged with a sardonic edge that was alien to the older man. Over the years, Wilder would make an occasional romantic comedy in explicit homage to his friend and mentor, but films like *Love in the Afternoon* and *Avanti,* despite their many excellences, tended to elude the public.

When Sam and Dorshka Raphaelson went to see *Love in the Afternoon,* they watched a scene wherein a water truck, dousing the early morning streets of Paris, soaks a pair of young lovers who fail to notice. Raphaelson leaned over to Dorshka and said, "What a mistake! Now, if I were doing that scene with Lubitsch, we would have first shown the truck spraying water moving toward the young lovers. But when the truck gets to them, the water shuts off. After it passes them, then the water starts up again. Now, *that's* the Lubitsch Touch!"

In the summer of 1975, Billy Wilder looked wistfully out of a window. "You know," he said, "if one could *write* Lubitsch touches, they would still exist, but he took that secret with him to his grave. It's like Chinese glass-blowing; no such thing exists anymore. Occasionally, I look for an elegant twist and I say to myself, 'How would Lubitsch have done it?' And I will come up with something and it will be *like* Lubitsch, but it won't *be* Lubitsch. It's just not there anymore."

For Wilder, Lubitsch remained the touchstone; in 1987, when it was announced that Wilder would receive The American Film Institute's Life Achievement Award, he reacted with brooding suspicion. "I'm getting it," he told a friend, "because Lubitsch is dead."

There were places where Lubitsch continued to be loved outside the memories and imaginations of the people that knew him. There were tributes at the Cinemathèque Francais (*The Shop Around the Corner* ran for sixty-six weeks in Paris in 1986 and 1987, making it the most successful reissue ever in France), and full-scale American tributes were mounted at the Museum of Modern Art in 1968, the Los Angeles County Museum in 1978, the Academy of Motion Picture Arts and Sciences in 1982, the Pacific Film Archive in 1983, and the Museum of the Moving Image in 1987, while the Berlin Film Festivals of 1968 and 1984 featured major retrospectives.

Of all the retrospective commentators, it was Andrew Sarris who wrote most elegantly about Lubitsch. In 1978, he wrote that Lubitsch "suggests the art of a lilting waltz or bubbling champagne but there is something more as well . . . In Lubitsch's late films, particularly, a sense of sadness infiltrates the gaiety. Lubitsch himself is getting older, of course, but there is something more than that. The implications of a style grounded in wit and discretion become more explicit. It is as if Lubitsch were mourning the ever imminent demise of a world of manners, and of a cinema in which doors closed decorously."

For Sarris, Lubitsch would always be the bridge "between humor and horror, a jovial little man with twinkling eyes and a big cigar [who] transcended the times in which he lived to become an artist for the ages. He had begun his career by making jokes. By the time he ended it he had traced the configurations of a vanishing civilization in which people played by the rules to the very edge of eternity. And the neatly clipped style that once seemed so sly and wicked now seems infinitely merciful and loving."

The centennial of Ernst's birth in 1992 sparked yet another series of retrospectives around the world, including the Cannes Film Festival. Invited to Berlin to celebrate her father's one-hundredth birthday, Nicola placed a plaque on the house on Lothringer Strasse where he was born. She and her Aunt Evie made a pilgrimage to the Weissensee Cemetery, the burial site of Simon and Anna Lubitsch. The chains that used to set the graves apart from the surrounding tombs had vanished, and the years had eroded the surface of the tombstones so that the inscriptions were barely legible.

With the passing years, it became increasingly clear that Ernst Lubitsch had accomplished something only vouchsafed the greatest artists: he had created a self-contained universe with a sensibility so singular, behavioral beauties so intense, that it forever altered the world view of those lucky enough to experience it. He believed in his dreams so strongly that millions of others came to believe in them as well, and the fact that the values and style of Lubitsch's work constituted the finest examples of the discarded heritage of elegant screen comedy made his everlasting, gentle brilliance even more poignant.

About a week after Lubitsch was buried, Mary Loos wrote to Sam Raphaelson about the funeral, and urged him to write about the man that had made such a difference in their lives, "so people will know a wonderful person."

It took a while—thirty-four years to be exact—but Sam Raphaelson finally got around to it. He called his memoir "Freundschaft," German for "friendship," and, when it was published in *The New Yorker* of May 11, 1981, it proved to be worth the wait; simultaneously an acute character analysis, a hail and farewell, and Raphaelson's own acknowledgment of and accommodation to the ironic reality of his career. "To think," he once said, "that I should be remembered for the bloody movies! It's simply absurd!"

A few years earlier, in 1973, Raphaelson had sat down with the historian Robert Carringer to discuss his work with Lubitsch. Summing up, he said, "I don't have any sentimental illusions about him. He was a very complex person, but I do love him and I would love it if he were alive. And I would love it to do at least one thing with him every two years until we are both dead. It would have been a very great pleasure. I have never met anybody like him since. And I've never had a relationship like that since; and it's been a lonely spot in my life that I haven't."

Then, speaking for all of Lubitsch's friends, and all of Lubitsch's audiences, Samson Raphaelson said, "What an emptiness it might have been if I hadn't met him."

a c k n o w l e d g m e n t s

This book exists because of Kevin Brownlow. At the beginning of 1990, having recently completed a biography of a life more tormented than most, I was mulling over future plans. I decided I wanted to write about a director and ran several possibilities, including Ernst Lubitsch, past Kevin.

"Do Lubitsch," he shot back with no hesitation at all. "Lubitsch would be *fun.*"

He was right, one of his more irritating traits. Writing the life of Ernst Lubitsch has been the most gratifying endeavor of my professional life, partially because of the joy with which he lived, but also because of the fact that he was what a psychiatrist might call an integrated personality. With most creative people, the positive energies go into the work and one has to make continual allowances for the squalor of their emotional lives—or, given the current trend toward what Joyce Carol Oates calls "pathography," wallow in that squalor.

But Lubitsch lived a life that, the more I studied it, seemed to me largely admirable and fulfilled, full of vivacity and intellectual power; an indomitable generational and cultural life force first revealed to me some twenty years ago in long lunches with Fritz Lang at the Swiss Cafe in Beverly Hills.

Writing this book enabled me to meet some remarkable people: Talli Wyler, serenely dangling a grandchild on her knee at her Malibu beach house; Mary Loos, radiating the beauty and brio that had entranced Lubitsch all those years ago; Dr. Max Edel, still practicing medicine at the age of eighty-two, still creating strong and vigorous sculptures to decorate his office on North Bedford Drive.

Put simply, you couldn't ask for a better man—and better people—to spend more than three years of your life with.

To them, and to all the following, my thanks and my gratitude.

Jeff Heise, a trusted friend of nearly fifteen years' (!) standing, a film historian in his own right, was magically transformed into a research assistant because I needed him to be one. Not only did Jeff run down leads and create many of his own, he graciously put up with my carefully crafted imitation of Sheridan Whiteside when I was his houseguest in Los Angeles during my extended time in that city. Thanks, pal; I couldn't have done it without you.

The list of friends both new and old goes on: Howard Green, who, all by himself justifies the existence of the Disney studio; Ted Hallas, Joe Savage, Dale Kuntz, Leonard Maltin, David Pierce, Gene Stavis, David Stenn, and Tom Toth.

Russell Merritt not only held my hand, he introduced me to Le Giornate del Cinema Muto in Pordenone, Italy, for which I will always be in his debt. Never has research been so much exhilarating fun, never have silent films flourished in such an enlightened, enthusiastic atmosphere. Thus, my gratitude to Paolo Cherchi Usai, Lorenzo Codelli, Livio Jacob, and Piera Patat.

Speaking of hand-holding, Dennis Doros and Amy Heller-Doros, better known as Milestone Films, have been the stoutest of friends, continually funneling moral support and research material to me for the entire duration of this project.

372

Old friends Lou Giannetti, Sheldon Wigod, Charlie Haddad, and Keith Joseph read parts of the manuscript and helped keep me pointed in the right direction, while James Drake interviewed Irving Caesar for me.

Robert Carringer, Tim Murphy, Michael Frank, Jef Abraham, and Liza Wilkie helped with sources, as did Marc Wanamaker, Rosanna Maule, Randy Skretvedt, James Harvey, and David Shepard, one of film history's best friends. At American Movie Classics, Jim Weiss and Dave Sehring helped immeasurably. Bruce Long contributed some fascinating material, and Joe Yranski and Peter Hanson contributed the cream of their fine still collections. Steve Weissman and Carol Horn, M.D., supplied valuable insights of both a psychological and medical nature, while Selise Eiseman of the Directors Guild cleared up a few nagging gray areas.

Ingrid Scheib-Rothbart of Goethe House was always there, and Nancy Barnes at the Museum of Modern Art was unfailingly generous. Edna McCown expertly and quickly translated the German material for me, while Mike Bodle did the same for the French material. Fred Zipp threw himself into the translating fray at the eleventh hour and calmly made an enormous difference, helping far more than he knew.

My friends in the Fourth Estate never failed me: Pat Wilks Battle at the *New York Post,* Michael Connelly at the *Los Angeles Times,* Tom Blackburn of the *Palm Beach Post,* Joseph McBride and Larry Cohn at *Variety,* and Richard Leiby of *The Washington Post.*

The keepers of the archives did their jobs with unfailing dispatch. In particular, I thank the Louis B. Mayer Library at The American Film Institute (Ruth Spencer), the University of Illinois Library (Maynard Brichford, Robert Dunkelberger), the University of Wisconsin (Harold Miller), the National Center for Jewish Film at Brandeis University (Richard Pontius), Southern Methodist University (Ronald L. Davis, Tanya Jimenez), Brigham Young University (James V. D'Arc), University of Wyoming (D. Claudia Thompson), the Hampden-Booth Theatre Library (Raymond Wemmlinger), the Cinema Library of the University of Southern California (Steve Hanson and Ned Comstock), and a deep bow to Leith Adams, director of the Warner Bros. Archives at that college.

In addition, the Theater Arts Library at UCLA (Brigitte Kueppers) and, for the Jeanette MacDonald papers, David Zeidberg. Sam Gill and Michael Freund of the Academy of Motion Picture Arts and Sciences were invaluable. The Federal Bureau of Investigation files on Lubitsch were obtained under the Freedom of Information Act, and thanks go to Emil Moschella, chief of the Records Management Division.

At the George Eastman House, Jan-Christopher Horak supplied me with a copy of his thesis on Lubitsch, and Paolo Cherchi Usai arranged screenings.

The following far-flung correspondents and historians were invaluable in making my research reliable and my travels enjoyable:

In Los Angeles: Kenneth Anger, Rudy Behlmer, David Chierichetti, Miles Kreuger, the late Herbert Luft, Erik Stogo, and, of course, "Raffles."

In Washington, D.C.: Peggy Parsons, Rob Bamberger, and Tom Vandervoort.

In Munich: Enno Patalas and Eva Weniger.

In Berlin: Michael Hanisch, Wolfgang Jacobsen.

In Moscow: Yuri Tsivian, Nikolai Izvolov.

In British Columbia: Tom Saunders.

And, of course, I owe an enormous, unpayable debt to the friends, relatives, and associates of Ernst Lubitsch: Don Ameche, Leon Askin, Jack Barry, Joan Benny, Evie Bettelheim-Bentley, Sonia Blanke, David Brown, Norma Churchill Pagano, J. J. Cohn, Patsy Ruth Miller Deans, the late Philip Dunne, the late Dr. Maximilian Edel, Douglas Fairbanks, Jr., Rudi Fehr, Harold Grieve, Ruth Hall, Bob Hope, Artie Jacobson, the late Hans Koenekamp, Lupita Tovar Kohner, Walter Laemmle, Hedy Lamarr, Dorothy Lamour, Paul Lazarus, Jr., Paul Lazarus III, Julian (Bud) Lesser, Edmund and Betty Lewis, Mary Loos, the late Sam Marx, Burgess Meredith, Dick Moore, Joan Marsh Morrill, John Pommer, Vincent Price, David Raksin, the glorious Dorshka Raphaelson, Gottfried Reinhardt, Lisl Reisch, Maria Riva, Cesar Romero, Helen Vreeland Smith, Robert Stack, Meri von Sternberg, George Stevens, Jr., Jack Warner, Jr., the late Talli Wyler, and Joe Youngerman.

Eddie Sears, Tom O'Hara, and especially Jan Tuckwood of the *Palm Beach Post* have been unfailingly supportive and encouraging; they make you believe in journalism all over again.

My agent, Fran Collin, has stood steadfast and true; her belief in my talent and instincts have helped override my own doubts. As he has before, Jim Hensel helped get me over the highest hurdles of all.

At Simon & Schuster, Chuck Adams believed in this book. He edited the manuscript with an amazing attention to detail, an unswerving concentration on narrative, and the friendliest persuasion imaginable. Virginia Clark's copy-editing defined and refined the book even further.

And, of course, there is my wife, Lynn: my best editor, my gentlest critic, Negri and MacDonald and Dietrich and Tierney all rolled into one. I love you.

Scott Eyman
January 1990–April 1993

Los Angeles, New York, Pordenone, Munich, Venice, Paris, Washington, D.C., Rochester, Fort Lauderdale

F i l m o g r a p h y

Compiled by Jeff Heise.

Films are listed in order of release.

This filmography is based on the following books: *Ernst Lubitsch: A Guide to References and Resources* by Robert Carringer and Barry Sabath, and *Lubitsch,* by Hans Helmut Prinzler and Enno Patalas.

THE GERMAN FILMS

Unless otherwise listed, all films are directed by Lubitsch, and all of the German films were made for Projektion-A.G. Union, in Berlin.

The Ideal Wife (1913)

Deutsche Bioscop GmbH, Berlin. Director unknown. Scenario by Hanns Heinz Ewers and Marc Henry. 2 reels. Released July 7. *Cast:* Lyda Salmonova, Grete Berger, Lubitsch.

Meyer on the Lam (1913)

Union Film. Director, length, release date unknown. *Cast:* Lubitsch, Sophie Pagay.

The Firm Marries (1914)

Directed by Carl Wilhelm. Scenario by Walter Turszinsky and Jacques Burg. 4 reels. Released January 23. *Cast:* Lubitsch, Victor Arnold, Resl Orla, Hans Kräly.

Condition–No Dependents (1914)

Deutsche Bioscop GmbH, Berlin. Directed by Stellan Rye. Scenario by Luise Heilborn-Körbitz. 3 reels. Released March 11. *Cast:* Hans Wassmann, Albert Paulig, Emil Albes, Lubitsch.

The Pride of the Firm (1915)

Directed by Carl Wilhelm. Scenario by Walter Turszinsky and Jacques Burg. 4 reels. Released January 9. *Cast:* Lubitsch, Martha Kriwitz, Victor Arnold.

Miss Piccolo (1915)

Luna-Film GmbH, Berlin. Written and directed by Franz Hofer. 3 reels. Release date unknown. *Cast:* Dorrit Weixler, Franz Schwaiger, Alice Hechy, Lubitsch.

Poor Marie (1915)

Directed by Willy Zeyn. Scenario by Robert Wiene and Walter Turszinsky. Length unknown. Released May 12. *Cast:* Hanni Weisse, Lubitsch, Felix Basch.

A Trip on the Ice (1915)

Malu-Film, Berlin. Scenario by Hans Kräly. Length unknown. Released in late May. *Cast:* Albert Paulig, Lubitsch.

Blind Man's Bluff (1915)

1 reel. Released May 28. *Cast:* Lubitsch, Resl Orla.

Sugar and Spice (1915)

Malu-Film, Berlin. Directed by Ernst Mátray and Lubitsch. Scenario by Mátray, Lubitsch, and Greta Schröder-Mátray. 2 reels. Released May 28. *Cast:* Ernst Mátray, Lubitsch, Helene Voss.

Miss Soapsuds (1915)

1 reel. Released June 25. *Cast:* Lubitsch.

The next four films were one reel in length and released sometime in 1915.

Soldier Meyer

Union Film. Director unknown.

His Only Patient

The Bully

The Last Uniform (The Last Suit)

Robert and Bertram (1915)

Directed by Max Mack. 3 reels. Release date unknown. *Cast:* Eugen Berg, Ferdinand Bonn, Wilhelm Diegelmann, Lubitsch.

How I Was Murdered (1915)

Deutsche Bioscop GmbH, Berlin. Directed by Louis Ralph. Length and release date unknown. *Cast:* Lubitsch.

Where Is My Treasure? (1916)

Union Film. Length unknown. Released February 25. *Cast:* Lubitsch.

Do the Dead Exist? (1916)

3 reels. Released February 25. *Cast:* Lubitsch.

Doctor Satansohn (1916)

Written and directed by Edmund Edel. 3 reels. Released March 17. *Cast:* Lubitsch, Hans Felix, Yo Larte.

Shoe Salon Pinkus (1916)

Scenario by Hans Kräly and Erich Schönfelder. 4 reels. Released in May. *Cast:* Guido Herzfeld, Else Kenter, Lubitsch, Ossi Oswalda, Hans Kräly.

Black Moritz (1916)

Unknown production company and director. Written by Louis Taufstein and Eugen Berg. Length unknown. Released on June 2. *Cast:* Lubitsch, Erna Albert, Margarete Kupfer.

The Mixed Ladies Chorus (1916)

2 reels. Released June 9. *Cast:* Lubitsch.

The Most Beautiful Girl (1916)

1 reel. Released November 24. *Cast:* Lubitsch.

The Tenor, Inc. (1916)

4 reels. Released December 22. *Cast:* Lubitsch, Ossi Oswalda, Victor Janson.

Lieutenant by Command (1916)

1 reel. Release date unknown. *Cast:* Lubitsch.

His New Nose (1917)

Length and release date unknown. *Cast:* Lubitsch.

Ossi's Diary (1917)

Scenario by Erich Schönfelder. 3 reels. Released October 5. *Cast:* Ossi Oswalda, Hermann Thimig.

The Blouse King (1917)

Scenario by Lubitsch and Erich Schönfelder. Set design by Paul Leni. 3 reels. Released November 2. *Cast:* Lubitsch, Käthe Dorsch, Guido Herzfeld.

Hans Trutz in a Fool's Paradise (1917)

Written and directed by Paul Wegener. Designed by Rochus Gliese. 4 reels. Released November 4. *Cast:* Paul Wegener, Lyda Salmonova, Lubitsch.

When Four Do the Same (1917)

Scenario by Ernst Lubitsch and Erich Schönfelder. 4 reels. Released November 16. *Cast:* Emil Jannings, Ossi Oswalda, Margarete Kupfer.

The Merry Jail (1917)

Scenario by Lubitsch and Hans Kräly, based on the operetta *Die Fledermaus* by C. Haffner and Richard Genée. 5 reels. Released November 30. *Cast:* Harry Liedtke, Kitty Dewell, Agda Nilsson, Erich Schönfelder, Emil Jannings.

Prince Sami (1918)

Scenario by Lubitsch and Danny Kaden. 4 reels. Released in January. *Cast:* Lubitsch, Ossi Oswalda, Wilhelm Diegelmann.

The Toboggan Cavalier (1918)

Scenario by Lubitsch and Erich Schönfelder. 5 reels. Released March 1. *Cast:* Lubitsch, Ferry Sikla, Ossi Oswalda.

The Rosentopf Case (1918)

Scenario by Lubitsch and Hans Kräly. 4 reels. Released September 20. *Cast:* Lubitsch, Trude Hesterberg.

The Eyes of the Mummy Ma (1918)

Scenario by Hans Kräly and Emil Rameau. 5 reels. Released October 3. *Cast:* Pola Negri, Emil Jannings, Harry Liedtke.

I Wouldn't Want to Be a Man (1918)

Scenario by Lubitsch and Hans Kräly. 4 reels. Released in October. *Cast:* Ferry Sikla, Ossi Oswalda, Margarete Kupfer, Kurt Götz.

The Ballet Girl (1918)

Scenario by Hans Kräly. 3 reels. Released December 6. *Cast:* Ossi Oswalda, Margarete Kupfer, Ferry Sikla, Harry Liedtke.

378 *Carmen* (1918)

Scenario by Hans Kräly, based on the novel *Carmen* by Prosper Mérimée. Photographed by Alfred Hansen. Costumes by Ali Hubert. 6 reels. Released December 17. *Cast:* Pola Negri, Harry Liedtke, Leopold von Ledebour, Grete Diercks. *First National released the film in the U.S. on May 8, 1921, under the title* Gypsy Blood, *with subtitles by Myron Stearn.*

Meyer from Berlin (1919)

Scenario by Hans Kräly and Erich Schönfelder. 4 reels. Released January 17. *Cast:* Lubitsch, Ethel Orff, Heinz Landsmann, Trude Troll.

My Wife, the Movie Star (1919)

Scenario by Lubitsch and Hans Kräly. 5 reels. Released January 24. *Cast:* Victor Janson, Ossi Oswalda, Hans Kräly, Paul Biensfeldt.

The Dutch Cheese King (1919)

Scenario by Lubitsch and Erich Schönfelder. 2 reels. Released in March. *Cast:* Lubitsch.

The Oyster Princess (1919)

Scenario by Hans Kräly and Lubitsch. 4 reels. Released June 25. *Cast:* Victor Janson, Ossi Oswalda, Harry Liedtke, Curt Bois, Julius Falkenstein.

Intoxication (1919)

Argus-Film GmbH, Berlin. Scenario by Hans Kräly, based on the play *There Are Crimes and Crimes* by August Strindberg. Photographed by Karl Freund. Set design by Rochus Gliese. 6 reels. Released on October 1. *Cast:* Asta Nielsen, Alfred Abel, Carl Meinhard, Grete Diercks.

Madame DuBarry (Passion) (1919)

Scenario by Fred Orbing (Norbert Falk) and Hans Kräly. Costumes by Ali Hubert. Technical advisor: Kurt Waschneck. 8 reels. Released September 18. *Cast:* Pola Negri, Emil Jennings, Reinhold Schünzel, Harry Liedtke.
The film was retitled by First National, the U.S. distributor, with new titles by Katherine Hilliker. It premiered in New York on December 12, 1920, and returned for a second engagement on June 24, 1923, at the same theater, the Capitol.

The Merry Husband (1919)

Directed by Leo Lasko. Scenario by Lubitsch, from an idea by Richard Wilde. 3 reels. Released in October.

The Doll (1919)

Scenario by Lubitsch and Hans Kräly, inspired by the themes of E. T. A. Hoffmann and their operatic adaptations by A. M. Willner. 5 reels. Released December 5. *Cast:* Ossi Oswalda, Hermann Thimig, Victor Janson.
The Doll was shown in a few select U.S. locations by its distributor, The 55th St. Playhouse Group, in 1928.

The Housing Shortage (1920)

No director credit. Scenario by Lubitsch and Hans Kräly. 2 reels. Released January 30. *Cast:* Ossi Oswalda, Marga Köhler.

Kohlhiesel's Daughter (1920)

Messter-Film GmbH, Berlin. Scenario by Lubitsch and Hans Kräly. 4 reels. Released March 9. *Cast:* Henry Porten, Emil Jannings, Gustav von Wangenheim.

Romeo and Juliet in the Snow (1920)

Maxim-Film-Ges. Ebner & Co., Berlin. Scenario by Hans Kräly and Lubitsch. 4 reels. Released March 28. *Cast:* Jacob Tiedtke, Marga Köhler, Lotte Neumann.

Sumurun (One Arabian Night) (1920)

Scenario by Hans Kräly and Lubitsch, based on writings by Friedrich Freska. 8 reels. Released September 1. *Cast:* Pola Negri, Jenny Hasselquist, Margarete Kupfer, Paul Wegener, Lubitsch.
Distributed in the U.S. by First National. The English titles were by Lesley Mason, and the film opened on October 2, 1921.

Anne Boleyn (Deception) (1920)

Scenario by Fred Orbing (Norbert Falk) and Hans Kräly. 10 reels. Released December 14. *Cast:* Emil Jannings, Hedwig Pauli, Hilde Müller, Henny Porten.
Paramount released this in the U.S. on April 17, 1921.

The Mountain Cat/The Wild Cat (1921)

Scenario by Hans Kräly and Lubitsch. Sets and costumes by Ernst Stern. 6 reels. Released April 14. *Cast:* Pola Negri, Victor Janson, Marga Köhler, Edith Meller.

The Loves of Pharaoh (1922)

Ernst Lubitsch Productions, in association with Europäischen Filmalliance GmbH (EFA), Berlin. Scenario by Norbert Falk and Hans Kräly. Photographed by Theodor Sparkuhl, Alfred Hansen, and numerous others. 8 reels. Released March 14. *Cast:* Emil Jannings, Harry Liedtke, Dagny Servaes, Paul Wegener, Lyda Salmonova.
In an unusual move, Paramount, the U.S. distributor, opened the film in New York on February 21, three weeks before the German premiere. The English titles were by Julian Johnson and Randolph Bartlett.

The Flame (1923)

Ernst Lubitsch-Film GmbH, Berlin, for EFA. Scenario by Hans Kräly and Rudolph Kurtz, based on the play *Die Flamme* by Hans Müller. 9 reels. Released September 11. *Cast:* Pola Negri, Hilde Wörner, Alfred Abel.

Lubitsch's last German film did not reach the U.S. until mid-1924, after Paramount had done some editing (two reels). Hector Turnbull wrote new titles, and the title was changed to Montmartre.

UNREALIZED GERMAN PROJECTS:

1919
The Man in the Glove
The Boudoir
The Golden Calf

1921
Macbeth
The Robber
The Merry Wives of Windsor

1920
Medea
Mephistopheles
Minna von Barnhelm
Manon Lescaut
Salomé

1922
Waltzdream

The following films are sometimes listed in Lubitsch's filmography:

The Miracle (1913)

Directed by Max Reinhardt.
Even though Lubitsch is rumored to have appeared in or to have had some creative input into this film, Ernst Mátray strongly denied it in a 1969 article.

Lieutenant in Command (1916)

Written and directed by Danny Kaden.
No real documentation about Lubitsch's alleged participation exists for this film.

Mania (1918)

Lubitsch is thought to have directed this Pola Negri film, with sets by Paul Leni. But research points to Eugen Illès as the true director.

The Girl from Swabia (1919)

Generally considered a Lubitsch film mostly because of the casting of Ossi Oswalda, and a director credit to an "Ernst Jacoby." There was a director named George Jacoby at the time, but nothing more is known.

THE AMERICAN FILMS

Unless noted, all of the American films were produced by Lubitsch.

381

scott eyman

Rosita (1923)

Mary Pickford Productions, released through United Artists. Adaptation and scenario by Edward Knoblock. Photographed by Charles Rosher. 9 reels. Released September 3. *Cast:* Mary Pickford, Holbrook Blinn, Irene Rich, George Walsh.

The Marriage Circle (1924)

Warner Bros. Adapted by Paul Bern, from the play *Only a Dream* by Lothar Schmidt. Photographed by Charles J. Van Enger. 9 reels. Released February 16. *Cast:* Adolphe Menjou, Marie Prevost, Monte Blue, Florence Vidor, Creighton Hale.

Three Women (1924)

Warner Bros. Adapted by Lubitsch and Hans Kräly, from the novel *Lilli's Marriage* by Iolanthe Marees. Photographed by Charles J. Van Enger and John Mescall (uncredited). 9 reels. Released October 5. *Cast:* May McAvoy, Pauline Frederick, Marie Prevost, Lew Cody.

Forbidden Paradise (1924)

Famous Players–Lasky/Paramount. Adapted by Hans Kräly and Agnes Christine Johnson, from the play *The Czarina* by Lajos Biró and Melchior Lengyel. Photographed by Charles J. Van Enger. 8 reels. Released October 27. *Cast:* Pola Negri, Rod La Rocque, Adolphe Menjou, Pauline Starke.

Kiss Me Again (1925)

Warner Bros. Adapted by Hans Kräly, from the play *Let's Get a Divorce* by Victorien Sardou and Emile de Najac. Photographed by Charles J. Van Enger. 7 reels. Released August 1. *Cast:* Marie Prevost, Monte Blue, John Roche, Clara Bow.

Lady Windermere's Fan (1925)

Warner Bros. Adapted by Julien Josephson, from the play by Oscar Wilde. Photographed by Charles J. Van Enger. 8 reels. Released December 26. *Cast:* Ronald Colman, Irene Rich, May McAvoy, Bert Lytell.

So This Is Paris (1926)

Warner Bros. Adapted by Hans Kräly, from the play *Réveillon* by Henri Meilhac and Ludovic Halévy. Photographed by John Mescall. 7 reels. Released July 31. *Cast:* Monte Blue, Patsy Ruth Miller, André Beranger, Lilyan Tashman, Myrna Loy.

The Student Prince in Old Heidelberg (1927)

Metro-Goldwyn-Mayer. Adapted by Hans Kräly, from the story *Karl Heinrich* by Wilhelm Meyer-Förster, its play version *Alt Heidelberg,* and the operetta *The Student Prince* by Dorothy Donnelly and Sigmund Romberg. Photographed by John Mescall. 10 reels. Released September 21. *Cast:* Ramon Novarro, Norma Shearer, Jean Hersholt.

The Patriot (1928)

Famous Players–Lasky/Paramount. Adapted by Hans Kräly, from the play by Alfred Neumann. Photographed by Bert Glennon. 10,172 feet (silent version); 9,819 feet (music, sound effects, talking sequences). Released August 17. *Cast:* Emil Jannings, Lewis Stone, Florence Vidor.

Eternal Love (1929)

United Artists. Adapted by Hans Kräly, from the play *Der König der Bernina* by Jacob Christoph Heer. Photographed by Oliver Marsh. 6,498 feet (silent version); 6,515 feet (music & sound effects). Released May 11. *Cast:* John Barrymore, Camilla Horn, Victor Varconi.

The Love Parade (1929)

Famous Players–Lasky/Paramount. Screenplay by Ernest Vajda; libretto by Guy Bolton, based on the play *The Prince Consort* by Léon Xanrof and Jules Chancel. Music by Victor Schertzinger. Lyrics by Clifford Grey. Photographed by Victor Milner. 8 reels (silent version); 110 minutes (sound version). Released November 19. *Cast:* Maurice Chevalier, Jeanette MacDonald, Lupino Lane, Lillian Roth.

Paramount on Parade (1930)

Famous Players–Lasky/Paramount. Lubitsch directed three sequences: "Origin of the Apache" (no author credit); "A Park in Paris," song: "All I Want Is Just One Girl" by Richard A. Whiting and Leo Robin; "The Rainbow Revels" (photo-graphed in Technicolor), song: "Sweeping the Clouds Away" by Sam Coslow. Photographed by Harry Fishbeck and Victor Milner. 128 minutes, edited to 102 minutes. Released April 19. *Cast:* Maurice Chevalier, Evelyn Brent (1st sequence). 383

Monte Carlo (1930)

Famous Players–Lasky/Paramount. Screenplay by Ernest Vajda, based on the play *The Love Coast* by Hans Müller, and episodes from the operetta *Monsieur Beaucaire* by Booth Tarkington and Evelyn Greenleaf Sutherland, adapted from Tarking-ton's novel. Additional dialogue by Vincent Lawrence. Music by Richard A. Whiting and W. Franke Harling. Lyrics by Leo Robin. Photographed by Victor Milner. 90 minutes (also released in a silent version). Released August 4. *Cast:* Jack Buchanan, Jeanette MacDonald, Claud Allister, ZaSu Pitts.

The Smiling Lieutenant (1931)

Famous Players–Lasky/Paramount. Screenplay by Ernest Vajda and Samson Raphaelson, based on the operetta *A Waltz Dream* by Leopold Jacobson and Felix Doermann, and the book by Hans Müller. Music by Oscar Straus. Lyrics by Clifford Grey. Photographed by George Folsey. 95 minutes. Released May 22. *Cast:* Maurice Chevalier, Claudette Colbert, Miriam Hopkins, Charlie Ruggles.

The Man I Killed (1932)

Paramount Publix. Screenplay by Samson Raphaelson and Ernest Vajda, based on the play *L'Homme que j'ai tué* by Maurice Rostand, and the American adaptation by Reginald Berkeley. Photographed by Victor Milner. 94 minutes, edited down to 77 minutes and retitled *Broken Lullaby*. Released February 26. (The New York premiere on January 19 had the original title and the longer running time.) *Cast:* Lionel Barrymore, Nancy Carroll, Phillips Holmes.

One Hour With You (1932)

Paramount Publix. Screenplay by Samson Raphaelson, based on the play *Only a Dream* by Lothar Schmidt. Assistant: George Cukor. Music by Oscar Straus. Lyrics by Leo Robin. Photographed by Victor Milner. 80 minutes. Released March 25. *Cast:* Maurice Chevalier, Jeanette MacDonald, Genevieve Tobin, Charlie Ruggles, Roland Young.

Trouble in Paradise (1932)

Paramount Publix. Screenplay by Samson Raphaelson, based on the play *The Honest Finder* by Aladar Laszlo. Adapted by Grover Jones. Song: "Trouble in Paradise": music by W. Franke Harling, lyrics by Leo Robin. Photographed by Victor Milner. 83 minutes. Released November 8. *Cast:* Miriam Hopkins, Kay Francis, Herbert Marshall, Edward Everett Horton, C. Aubrey Smith.

If I Had a Million (1932)

Paramount Publix. Sequence: "The Clerk," written and directed by Lubitsch. Based on the novel *Windfall* by Robert D. Andrews. No photography credit. 88 minutes. Released December 2. *Cast:* Charles Laughton.

Design for Living (1933)

Paramount. Screenplay by Ben Hecht, based on the play by Noël Coward. Photographed by Victor Milner. 90 minutes. Released November 22. *Cast:* Fredric March, Gary Cooper, Miriam Hopkins, Edward Everett Horton.

The Merry Widow (1934)

Metro-Goldwyn-Mayer. Produced by Irving Thalberg. Screenplay by Ernest Vajda and Samson Raphaelson, based on the operetta by Franz Lehár. Libretto and lyrics by Victor Leon and Leo Stein. Additional music by Richard Rodgers. Additional lyrics by Lorenz Hart and Gus Kahn. Photographed by Oliver T. Marsh. 99 minutes. Released October 11. *Cast:* Maurice Chevalier, Jeanette MacDonald, Edward Everett Horton, Una Merkel.

Angel (1937)

Paramount. Screenplay by Samson Raphaelson, based on the play by Melchior Lengyel and its English adaptation by Guy Bolton and Russell Medcraft. Photographed by Charles Lang. 89 minutes. Released October 29. *Cast:* Marlene Dietrich, Herbert Marshall, Melvyn Douglas, Edward Everett Horton.

Bluebeard's Eighth Wife (1938)

Paramount. Screenplay by Charles Brackett and Billy Wilder, based on the play by Alfred Savoir and the American adaptation by Charlton Andrews. Photographed by Leo Tover. 80 minutes. Released March 23. *Cast:* Claudette Colbert, Gary Cooper, Edward Everett Horton, David Niven.

Ninotchka (1939)

Metro-Goldwyn-Mayer. Screenplay by Charles Brackett, Billy Wilder, and Walter Reisch, based on an original story by Melchior Lengyel. Photographed by William Daniels. 110 minutes. Released October 6. *Cast:* Greta Garbo, Melvyn Douglas, Ina Claire, Bela Lugosi, Sig Rumann, Felix Bressart, George Tobias.

The Shop Around the Corner (1940)

Metro-Goldwyn-Mayer. Screenplay by Samson Raphaelson, based on the play *Parfumerie* by Nikolaus Laszlo. Photographed by William Daniels. 97 minutes. Released January 12. *Cast:* Margaret Sullavan, James Stewart, Frank Morgan, Joseph Schildkraut.

That Uncertain Feeling (1941)

Co-production with Sol Lesser, released through United Artists. Screenplay by Donald Ogden Stewart, based on the adaptation by Walter Reisch of the play *Let's Get a Divorce* by Victorien Sardou and Emile de Najac. Photographed by George Barnes. 84 minutes. Released April 20. *Cast:* Merle Oberon, Melvyn Douglas, Burgess Meredith, Alan Mowbray.

To Be or Not to Be (1942)

Produced in association with Alexander Korda, released through United Artists. Screenplay by Edwin Justus Mayer, based on an original story by Melchior Lengyel and Lubitsch. Photographed by Rudolph Maté. 99 minutes. Released March 6. *Cast:* Carole Lombard, Jack Benny, Robert Stack, Felix Bressart, Lionel Atwill, Sig Rumann.

Heaven Can Wait (1943)

20th Century-Fox. Screenplay by Samson Raphaelson, based on the play *Birthday* by Laszlo Bus-Feketé. Photographed by Edward Cronjager (Technicolor). 112 minutes. Released August 11. *Cast:* Gene Tierney, Don Ameche, Charles Coburn, Marjorie Main, Laird Cregar, Spring Byington, Eugene Pallette.

Cluny Brown (1946)

20th Century-Fox. Screenplay by Samuel Hoffenstein and Elizabeth Reinhardt, based on the novel by Margery Sharp. Photographed by Joseph La Shelle. 100 minutes. Released June 1. *Cast:* Charles Boyer, Jennifer Jones, Peter Lawford, Helen Walker, Reginald Gardiner, C. Aubrey Smith, Richard Haydn.

That Lady in Ermine (1948)

20th Century-Fox. Co-directed by Otto Preminger (uncredited). Screenplay by Samson Raphaelson, based on the operetta by Rudolf Schanzer and Ernst Welisch, and its English-language translations. Lyrics and music by Leo Robin and Frederick Hollander. Photographed by Leon Shamroy (Technicolor). 89 minutes. Released August 24. *Cast:* Betty Grable, Douglas Fairbanks, Jr., Cesar Romero.

LUBITSCH AS PRODUCER

On the following films, Lubitsch served only as producer.

Desire (1936)

Paramount. Directed by Frank Borzage. Screenplay by Edwin Justus Mayer, Waldemar Young, and Samuel Hoffenstein, based on the play *Die schönenn Tage von Aranjuez* by Hans Székely and Robert Adolf Stemmle. Photographed by Charles Lang. 89 minutes. Released April 11. *Cast:* Marlene Dietrich, Gary Cooper, John Halliday.

A Royal Scandal (1945)

20th Century-Fox. Directed by Otto Preminger. Screenplay by Edwin Justus Mayer, adapted by Bruno Frank from the play *The Czarina* by Lajos Biró and Melchior Lengyel. Photographed by Arthur Miller. 94 minutes. Released April 11. *Cast:* Tallulah Bankhead, Charles Coburn, Anne Baxter, Vincent Price.

Dragonwyck (1946)

20th Century-Fox. Directed by Joseph L. Mankiewicz. Screenplay by Mankiewicz, based on the novel by Anya Seton. Photographed by Arthur Miller. 103 minutes. Released April 10. *Cast:* Gene Tierney, Walter Huston, Vincent Price.

ADDITIONAL FILMS:

The Last Command (1928)

Famous Players–Lasky/Paramount. Directed by Josef von Sternberg. Scenario by John F. Goodrich, based on a story by Lajos Biró. Photographed by Bert Glennon. 9 reels. *Cast:* Emil Jannings, Evelyn Brent, William Powell.
Lubitsch supplied the original idea for this film.

Mr. Broadway (1933)

Directed by Johnny Walker.
Lubitsch makes a cameo appearance in this feature-length travelogue, as a patron of the Central Park Casino.

Know Your Enemy: Germany (1942)

20th Century–Fox. Army training film.
Lubitsch completed this film, but it was never released.

The Meanest Man in the World (1943)

20th Century–Fox. Directed by Sidney Lanfield. *Cast:* Jack Benny, Priscilla Lane. Retakes on this film were done by Lubitsch when director Lanfield was unavailable.

b i b l i o g r a p h y

Adamson, Joe. *Byron Haskin*. Metuchen, N.J.: Directors Guild of America and Scarecrow Press, 1984.

Agee, James. *Agee on Film*. New York: Grosset and Dunlap, 1958.

Alpert, Hollis. *The Life and Times of Porgy and Bess*. New York: Alfred A. Knopf, 1990.

Askin, Leon, with Davidson, C. Melvin. *Quietude and Quest*. Riverside, CA: Ariadne Press, 1989.

Balio, Tino. *United Artists: The Company Built by the Stars*. Madison: The University of Wisconsin Press, 1976.

Barsacq, Leon. *Caligari's Cabinet and Other Grand Illusions*. Revised and edited by Elliot Stein. Boston: New York Graphic Society, 1976.

Baum, Vicki. *It Was All Quite Different*. New York: Funk and Wagnalls, 1964.

Beaton, Cecil. *Memoirs of the '40s*. New York: McGraw-Hill Book Company, 1972.

Behrman, S. N. *People in a Diary: A Memoir*. Boston: Little, Brown, 1972.

Benny, Mary Livingston, and Marks, Hilliard, with Borie, Marcia. *Jack Benny*. Garden City: Doubleday, 1978.

Bergman, Andrew. *We're in the Money*. New York: New York University Press, 1971.

Bodeen, DeWitt. *More from Hollywood*. South Brunswick, N.J.: A. S. Barnes and Co., 1977.

Broman, Sven. *Conversations with Greta Garbo.* New York: Viking, 1992.

Brownlow, Kevin. *The Parade's Gone By.* New York: Alfred A. Knopf, 1968.

Carringer, Robert L., ed. *The Jazz Singer.* Madison: The University of Wisconsin Press, 1979.

Carringer, Robert, and Sabath, Barry. *Ernst Lubitsch: A Guide to References and Resources.* Boston: G. K. Hall and Co., 1978.

Castanza, Philip. *The Films of Jeanette MacDonald and Nelson Eddy.* Secaucus, N.J.: Citadel Press, 1976.

Casty, Alan. *Development of the Film.* New York: Harcourt Brace Jovanovich, Inc., 1973.

Ceplair, Larry, and Englund, Steven. *The Inquisition in Hollywood.* Berkeley: University of California Press, 1983.

Chevalier, Maurice as told to Eileen and Robert Mason Pollock. *With Love.* Boston: Little, Brown and Co., 1960.

Colman, Juliet Benita. *Ronald Colman: A Very Private Person.* New York: William Morrow and Co., 1975.

Connell, Brian. *Knight Errant: A Biography of Douglas Fairbanks, Jr.* New York: Doubleday, 1955.

Corliss, Richard. *Talking Pictures.* Woodstock, N.Y.: The Overlook Press, 1974.

Coursodon, Jean-Pierre, with Sauvage, Pierre. *American Directors.* New York: McGraw-Hill, 1983.

Cronyn, Hume. *A Terrible Liar.* New York: William Morrow and Co., 1991.

Crowther, Bosley. *Hollywood Rajah.* New York: Henry Holt and Co., 1960.

Curtis, James. *Between Flops.* New York: Harcourt Brace Jovanovich, 1982.

d'Acosta, Mercedes. *Here Lies the Heart.* London: André Deutsch, Ltd., 1960.

d'Antonio, Joanne. *Andrew Marton.* Metuchen, N.J.: Directors Guild of America and Scarecrow Press, 1991.

Dardis, Tom. *Harold Lloyd: The Man on the Clock.* New York: Viking, 1983.

Daum, Raymond. *Walking with Garbo.* New York: HarperCollins, 1991.

de Mille, Agnes. *Martha: The Life and Work of Martha Graham.* New York: Random House, 1991.

DeMille, Cecil B. *Autobiography.* Englewood Cliffs, N.J.: Prentice-Hall, 1959.

Deutsch, Armand. *Me and Bogie.* New York: G. P. Putnam's Sons, 1991.

Dickens, Homer. *The Films of Gary Cooper.* New York: Citadel Press, 1970.

Dietrich, Marlene. *Marlene Dietrich's ABC.* New York: Frederick Ungar Publishing Corp., 1984.

Dill, Jr., Marshall. *Germany: A Modern History.* Ann Arbor: University of Michigan Press, 1961.

Drew, William M. *Speaking of Silents.* Vestal, N.Y.: Vestal Press, 1989.

Dunne, Philip. *Take Two: A Life in Movies and Politics.* New York: McGraw-Hill, 1980.

Durgnat, Raymond, and Simmon, Scott. *King Vidor, American.* Berkeley: University of California Press, 1988.

Ecksteins, Modris. *Rites of Spring.* New York: Anchor Books, 1990.

Eisner, Lotte. *The Haunted Screen.* Berkeley: University of California Press, 1973.

Ephron, Henry. *We Thought We Could Do Anything.* New York: W. W. Norton and Co., 1977.

Everett, Suzanne. *Lost Berlin.* New York: Gallery Books, 1979.

Eyman, Scott. *Five American Cinematographers.* Metuchen, N.J., and London: Scarecrow Press, 1987.

——. *Mary Pickford: America's Sweetheart.* New York: Donald I. Fine, 1990.

Finch, Christopher, and Rosenkrantz, Linda. *Gone Hollywood.* Garden City: Doubleday, 1979.

Forslund, Bengt. *Victor Sjöström: His Life and Work.* New York: Zoetrope, 1988.

Fowler, Gene. *Good Night, Sweet Prince.* New York: Viking, 1944.

Freedland, Michael. *The Warner Brothers.* New York: St. Martin's Press, 1983.

Friedrich, Otto. *Before the Deluge.* New York: Fromm International Publishing Corp., 1986.

Friedrich, Otto. *City of Nets.* New York: Harper and Row, 1986.

Fromm, Bella. *Blood and Banquets: A Berlin Diary 1930-38.* New York: Simon & Schuster, 1992.

Gabler, Neal. *An Empire of Their Own.* New York: Crown Publishers, 1988.

Gardner, Gerald. *The Censorship Papers.* New York: Dodd, Mead, 1987.

Geist, Kenneth L. *Pictures Will Talk.* New York: Charles Scribners and Sons, 1978.

Gilbert, Martin. *The Atlas of Jewish History.* New York: William Morrow, 1993.

Gomery, Douglas. *The Hollywood Studio System.* New York: St. Martin's Press, 1986.

Goodman, Ezra. *The Fifty-Year Decline and Fall of Hollywood.* New York: Simon and Schuster, 1961.

Hake, Sabine. *Passions and Deceptions: The Early Films of Ernst Lubitsch.* Princeton: Princeton University Press, 1992.

Hambley, John, and Downing, Patrick. *The Art of Hollywood.* London: Thames Television, 1979.

Hanisch, Michael. *Auf den Spüren der Filmgeschichte.* Berlin: Henschel Verlag, 1991.

Harris, Marlys J. *The Zanucks of Hollywood.* New York: Crown Publishers, 1989.

Harvey, James. *Romantic Comedy in Hollywood.* New York: Alfred A. Knopf, 1987.

Heisner, Beverly. *Hollywood Art.* Jefferson, N.C.: McFarland and Company, Inc., 1990.

Henderson, Brian, ed. *Five Screenplays by Preston Sturges.* Berkeley: University of California Press, 1985.

Higham, Charles. *Cecil B. DeMille.* New York: Charles Scribners Sons, 1973.

——. *Marlene: The Life of Marlene Dietrich.* New York: W. W. Norton and Co., 1977.

Hirschhorn, Clive. *The Warner Brothers Story.* New York: Crown Publishers, 1979.

Horn, Camilla. *Verliebt in die Liebe.* Munich: Herbig, 1989.

Jacobs, Jack, and Braun, Myron. *The Films of Norma Shearer.* South Brunswick, N.J. and New York: A. S. Barnes and Co., 1976.

Jannings, Emil. *Theater, Film—das Leben und Ich.* Berchtesgaden: Verlag Zimmer and Herzog, 1951.

Josefsberg, Milt. *The Jack Benny Show.* New Rochelle, N.Y.: Arlington House, 1977.

Kazan, Elia. *A Life.* New York: Alfred A. Knopf, 1988.

Kendall, Elizabeth. *The Runaway Bride.* New York: Alfred A. Knopf, 1990.

——. *Gotta Sing Gotta Dance.* New York: Exeter Books, 1983.

Kobal, John. *People Will Talk.* New York: Alfred A. Knopf, 1985.

Kobler, John. *Damned in Paradise: The Life of John Barrymore.* New York: Atheneum, 1977.

Koszarski, Richard. *Hollywood Directors 1914-1940.* New York: Oxford University Press, 1976.

Kotsilibas-Davis, James. *The Barrymores: The Royal Family in Hollywood.* New York: Crown Publishers, 1981.

Kotsilibas-Davis, James, and Loy, Myrna. *Myrna Loy: Being and Becoming.* New York: Donald I. Fine, Inc., 1988.

Kracauer, Siegfried. *From Caligari to Hitler.* Princeton: Princeton University Press, 1947.

Kulik, Karol. *Alexander Korda: The Man Who Could Work Miracles.* New Rochelle, N.Y.: Arlington House, 1975.

Lambert, Gavin. *Norma Shearer.* New York: Alfred A. Knopf, 1990.

——. *On Cukor.* New York: Capricorn Books, 1973.

Lasky, Jr., Jesse L. *Whatever Happened to Hollywood?* New York: Funk and Wagnalls, 1975.

Lawrence, Jerome. *Actor: The Life and Times of Paul Muni.* New York: Putnam, 1974.

Leamer, Laurence. *As Time Goes By: The Life of Ingrid Bergman.* New York: Harper and Row, 1986.

Lloyd, Norman, interviewed by Parker, Francine. *Stages.* Metuchen, N.J. and London: Directors Guild of America and Scarecrow Press, 1990.

laughter

in paradise

Loos, Anita. *Cast of Characters.* New York: Grosset and Dunlap, 1977.

——. *A Girl Like I.* New York: Viking Press, 1966.

Loos, Mary. *The Beggars Are Coming.* New York: Bantam Books, 1974.

Madsen, Axel. *Billy Wilder.* Bloomington: Indiana University Press, 1969.

Madsen, Axel. *William Wyler.* New York: Thomas Y. Crowell Co., 1973.

Maltin, Leonard, ed. *Hollywood: The Movie Factory.* New York: Popular Library, 1976.

Mandelbaum, Howard, and Myers, Eric. *Screen Deco.* New York: St. Martin's Press, 1985.

Mank, Gregory William. *Karloff and Lugosi.* Jefferson, NC: McFarland and Co., 1990

Mankiewicz, Joseph L., with Carey, Gary. *More About All About Eve.* New York: Random House, 1972.

Manvell, Roger, and Fraenkel, Heinrich. *The German Cinema.* New York: Praeger Publishers, 1971.

Martin, Jeffrey Brown. *Ben Hecht, Hollywood Screenwriter.* Ann Arbor: UMI Research Press, 1985.

Marx, Groucho. *The Groucho Phile.* Indianapolis: Bobbs-Merrill, 1976.

Marx, Groucho, and Anobile, Richard. *The Marx Brothers Scrapbook.* New York: Darien House, 1973.

Marx, Samuel. *Mayer and Thalberg.* New York: Random House, 1975.

Mast, Gerald. *The Comic Mind.* 2nd ed. Chicago: University of Chicago Press, 1979.

McBride, Joseph. *Frank Capra: The Catastrophe of Success.* New York: Simon & Schuster, 1992.

McDonald, Gerald; McGregor, Dion; and Ricci, Mark. *The Films of Greta Garbo.* New York: Citadel Press, 1968.

McGilligan, Pat, ed. *Backstory.* Berkeley: University of California Press, 1986.

Menjou, Adolphe, with Musselman, M. M. *It Took Nine Tailors.* New York: Whittlesey House, 1948.

Meryman, Richard. *Mank: The Wit, World and Life of Herman Mankiewicz.* New York: William Morrow and Company, 1978.

Mills, Robert William. "The American Films of Ernst Lubitsch." Ph.D. diss., University of Michigan, Ann Arbor, 1976.

Milne, Peter. *Motion Picture Directing.* New York: Falk Publishing Co., 1922.

Mordden, Ethan. *The Hollywood Musical.* New York: St. Martin's Press, 1981.

Morley, Sheridan. *Tales from the Hollywood Raj.* New York: The Viking Press, 1984.

Moshier, W. Franklyn. *The Films of Jennifer Jones.* San Francisco: Moshier, 1978.

Murray, Bruce. *Film and the German Left in the Weimar Republic.* Austin: University of Texas Press, 1990.

Nacache, Jacqueline. *Lubitsch*. Paris: Edilig, 1987.

Negri, Pola. *Memoirs of a Star*. Garden City, N.Y.: Doubleday, 1970.

Negulesco, Jean. *Things I Did . . . and Things I Think I Did*. New York: Linden Press/Simon & Schuster, 1984.

Niven, David. *The Moon's a Balloon*. New York: G. P. Putnam's Sons, 1972.

Odets, Clifford. *The Time Is Ripe*. New York: Grove Press, 1988.

O'Leary, Liam. *Rex Ingram: Master of the Silent Cinema*. Dublin: The Academy Press, 1980.

Ott, Frederick. *The Films of Fritz Lang*. Secaucus, N.J.: Citadel Press, 1979.

——. *The Great German Films*. Secaucus, N.J.: Citadel Press, 1986.

Palmer, Christopher. *The Composer in Hollywood*. London and New York: Marion Boyars, 1990.

Patterson, Frances Taylor, ed. *Motion Picture Continuities: A Kiss for Cinderella, The Scarlet Letter, The Last Command*. New York: Columbia University Press, 1929.

Paul, William. *Ernst Lubitsch's American Comedy*. New York: Columbia University Press, 1983.

Peary, Danny. *Close-Ups*. New York: Workman Publishing, 1978.

Pensel, Hans. *Seastrom and Stiller in Hollywood*. New York: Vantage Press, 1969.

Peters, Margot. *The House of Barrymore*. New York: Alfred A. Knopf, 1990.

Petley, Julian. *Capital and Culture: German Cinema 1933-45*. London: British Film Institute, 1979.

Petrie, Graham. *Hollywood Destinies*. London: Routledge & Kegan Paul, 1985.

Poague, Leland A. *The Cinema of Ernst Lubitsch*. South Brunswick, N.J. and New York: A. S. Barnes and Company, 1978.

Pratley, Gerald. *The Cinema of Otto Preminger*. New York: Castle Books, 1971.

Pratt, George C. *Spellbound in Darkness*. Greenwich, CT: New York Graphic Society Ltd., 1973.

Preminger, Otto. *Preminger: An Autobiography*. New York: Doubleday and Company, 1977.

Prinzler, Hans Helmut, and Patalas, Enno. *Lubitsch*. Munich: Bücher, 1984.

Raphaelson, Samson. *The Human Nature of Playwriting*. New York: The Macmillan Company, 1949.

Reiners, Ludwig. *The Lamps Went Out in Europe*. Cleveland and New York: World Publishing Company, 1966.

Reinhardt, Gottfried. *The Genius*. New York: Alfred A. Knopf, 1979.

Ringgold, Gene, and Bodeen, Dewitt. *The Films of Cecil B. DeMille*. New York: Citadel Press, 1969.

——. *Chevalier*. Secaucus, N.J.: The Citadel Press, 1973.

Riva, Maria. *Marlene Dietrich*. New York: Alfred A. Knopf, 1993.

Rivkin, Allan, and Kerr, Laura. *Hello, Hollywood.* Garden City, N.Y.: Doubleday, 1962.

Robinson, David. *Chaplin: His Life and Art.* New York: McGraw-Hill, 1985.

Rosenberg, Bernard, and Silverstein, Harry. *The Real Tinsel.* New York: Macmillan, 1970.

Rosenberg, Deanna. *Fascinating Rhythm.* New York: Dutton, 1991.

Rowan, Bonnie G. *Scholars Guide to Washington, D.C., Film and Video Collections.* Washington: Smithsonian Institution Press, 1980.

Rozsa, Miklos. *Double Life.* New York: Hippocrene Books, 1982.

Sabath, Barry. "Ernst Lubitsch and Samson Raphaelson: A Study in Collaboration." Ph.D. diss., New York University, 1979.

Schatz, Thomas. *The Genius of the System.* New York: Pantheon Books, 1988.

Schwartz, Nancy Lynn. *The Hollywood Writers' War.* New York: Alfred A. Knopf, 1982.

Server, Lee. *Screenwriter: Words Become Pictures.* Pittstown: The Main Street Press, 1987.

Seton, Marie. *Sergei M. Eisenstein.* New York: A. A. Wyn, Inc., 1952.

Sikov, Ed. *Screwball: Hollywood's Madcap Romantic Comedies.* New York: Crown Publishers, 1989.

Silke, James R. *Here's Looking at You, Kid.* Boston: Little, Brown and Co., 1976.

Spears, Jack. *Hollywood: The Golden Era.* New York: Castle Books, 1971.

Starr, Kevin. *Material Dreams: Southern California Through the 1920s.* New York: Oxford University Press, 1990.

Stenn, David. *Clara Bow: Runnin' Wild.* New York: Doubleday, 1988.

Stern, Ernst. *My Life, My Stage.* Translated by Edward Fitzgerald. London: Victor Gollancz, 1951.

Swindell, Larry. *Charles Boyer: The Reluctant Lover.* New York: Doubleday, 1983.

——. *The Last Hero: A Biography of Gary Cooper.* Garden City, N.Y.: Doubleday and Co., 1980.

——. *Screwball: The Life of Carole Lombard.* New York: William Morrow and Company, 1975.

Taylor, John Russell. *Strangers in Paradise.* New York: Holt, Rinehart and Winston, 1983.

Tierney, Gene, with Herskowitz, Mickey. *Self-Portrait.* New York: Wyden Books, 1979.

Tiomkin, Dimitri, with Buranelli, Prosper. *Please Don't Hate Me.* Garden City, N.Y.: Doubleday, 1959.

Todd, Jr., Michael, and Todd, Susan McCarthy. *A Valuable Property.* New York: Arbor House, 1983.

Toller, Ernst. *I Was a German*. 1933. Reprint. New York: Paragon House, 1991.

Turk, Edward Baron. *Child of Paradise*. Cambridge: Harvard University Press, 1989.

Usai, Paolo Cherchi, and Codelli, Lorenzo, eds. *Before Caligari: German Cinema 1895-1920*. Pordenone: Edizione Biblioteca dell'Imagine, 1990.

Vidor, King. *A Tree Is a Tree*. New York: Harcourt, Brace and Company, 1953.

Viertel, Salka. *The Kindness of Strangers*. New York: Holt, Rinehart and Winston, 1969.

von Sternberg, Josef. *Fun in a Chinese Laundry*. New York: Macmillan Co., 1965.

Walker, Alexander. *Garbo*. New York: Macmillan Publishing Co., Inc., 1980.

Wallis, Hal, with Higham, Charles. *Starmaker*. New York: Macmillan, 1980.

Webb, Michael, ed. *Hollywood: Legend and Reality*. Boston: Little, Brown and Co./New York Graphic Society, 1986.

Weinberg, Herman G. *The Lubitsch Touch*. 3rd ed. New York: Dover Publications, 1977.

Wolfe, Charles. *Frank Capra: A Guide to References and Resources*. Boston: G. K. Hall and Co., 1987.

Wollenberg, H. H. *Fifty Years of German Film*. London: The Falcon Press, 1948.

Zolotow, Maurice. *Billy Wilder in Hollywood*. New York: G. P. Putnam, 1977.

laughter

in   paradise

index

laughter

in paradise

411

eyman

scott

412

413

laughter

in paradise

PHOTO CREDITS

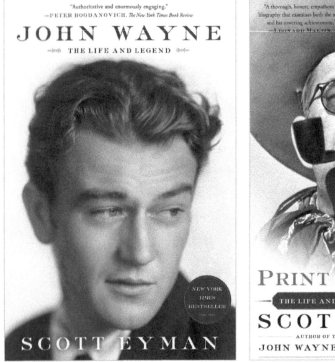